MW00358833

"Written with a sure-handed command of Heidegger's corpus and the historical context of his thinking, *Heidegger's Shadow* makes a powerful case for its persisting transcendental character. . . . Tightly and lucidly argued, this book is scholarship at its finest, a major contribution to understanding the promise of Heidegger's later writings."
—Daniel O. Dahlstrom, Boston University, USA, author of *Heidegger's Concept of Truth*

"Chad Engelland's provocative and carefully researched book is the most sustained treatment to date of the role that transcendental philosophy plays throughout Heidegger's path of thinking."
—Steven Crowell, Rice University, USA, author of *Normativity and Phenomenology in Husserl and Heidegger*

"Engelland tells an insightful story about the continuity of Heidegger's thought while shedding light on many of its essential impulses."
—Richard Polt, Xavier University, USA, author of *The Emergency of Being: On Heidegger's 'Contributions to Philosophy'*

"With *Heidegger's Shadow* Chad Engelland has given us the best book in any language on the transcendental in Heidegger."
—Thomas Sheehan, Stanford University, USA, author of *Making Sense of Heidegger: A Paradigm Shift*

"*Heidegger's Shadow* not only makes a powerful case for the continuing significance of the transcendental (and so also of Kant as well as Husserl) throughout Heidegger's thinking, but also shows why the transcendental, even if it is not all that philosophy is, nevertheless remains an essential part of it."
—Jeff Malpas, University of Tasmania, Australia, author of *Heidegger's Topology: Being, Place, World*

Heidegger's Shadow

Heidegger's Shadow is an important contribution to the understanding of Heidegger's ambivalent relation to transcendental philosophy. Its contention is that Heidegger recognizes the importance of transcendental philosophy as the necessary point of entry to his thought, but he nonetheless comes to regard it as something that he must strive to overcome even though he knows such an attempt can never succeed. Engelland thoroughly engages with major texts such as *Kant and the Problem of Metaphysics*, *Being and Time*, and *Contributions* and traces the progression of Heidegger's readings of Kant and Husserl to show that Heidegger cannot abandon his own earlier breakthrough work in transcendental philosophy. This book will be of interest to those working on phenomenology, continental philosophy, and transcendental philosophy.

Chad Engelland is Assistant Professor of Philosophy at the University Dallas in Irving, Texas. He is the author of *Ostension: Word Learning and the Embodied Mind* and *The Way of Philosophy: An Introduction*.

Routledge Studies in Twentieth Century Philosophy

For a full list of titles in this series, please visit www.routledge.com

Heidegger's Shadow

Kant, Husserl, and the Transcendental Turn

Chad Engelland

Routledge
Taylor & Francis Group

LONDON AND NEW YORK

First published 2017 by Routledge

2 Park Square, Milton Park, Abingdon, Oxfordshire OX14 4RN
52 Vanderbilt Avenue, New York, NY 10017

*Routledge is an imprint of the Taylor & Francis Group,
an informa business*

First issued in paperback 2019

Copyright © 2017 Taylor & Francis

The right of Chad Engelland to be identified as author of this
work has been asserted by him in accordance with sections 77
and 78 of the Copyright, Designs and Patents Act 1988.

All rights reserved. No part of this book may be reprinted or
reproduced or utilised in any form or by any electronic, mechanical,
or other means, now known or hereafter invented, including
photocopying and recording, or in any information storage or
retrieval system, without permission in writing from the publishers.

Notice:
Product or corporate names may be trademarks or registered
trademarks, and are used only for identification and explanation
without intent to infringe.

Library of Congress Cataloging-in-Publication Data
Names: Engelland, Chad, author.
Title: Heidegger's shadow : Kant, Husserl, and the transcendental
    turn / by Chad Engelland.
Description: 1 [edition]. | New York : Routledge, 2017. |
    Series: Routledge studies in twentieth-century philosophy;
    40 | Includes bibliographical references and index.
Identifiers: LCCN 2016047699 | ISBN 9781138181878
    (hardback : alk. paper)
Subjects: LCSH: Heidegger, Martin, 1889–1976. | Kant,
    Immanuel, 1724–1804. | Husserl, Edmund, 1859–1938. |
    Transcendentalism—History.
Classification: LCC B3279.H49 E54 2017 | DDC 193—dc23
LC record available at https://lccn.loc.gov/2016047699

ISBN: 978-1-138-18187-8 (hbk)
ISBN: 978-0-367-25836-8 (pbk)

Typeset in Sabon
by Apex CoVantage, LLC

To my parents,
who gave their children
life and love

Such a task exceeds even the capacity of a great thinker. It demands nothing less than to leap over one's shadow. No one can do this. . . . Nevertheless, every philosopher *must* want to do this. This "must" is his vocation.
—Heidegger on Kant in 1935,
on the eve of writing his *Contributions*

Contents

Tables

Conventions

Citations

All citations of Heidegger first list the pagination of the German edition followed by the pagination of an English translation, should one be available (G/E). For editions used, please consult the bibliography.

I cite texts by listing the volume number in Heidegger's collected works, *Gesamtausgabe* (GA), or by providing complete bibliographical information. As an exception to this rule, I have abbreviated Heidegger's major work as follows:

SZ   *Sein und Zeit*

I refer to Kant's major work as follows:

KRV   *Kritik der reinen Vernunft*

Terms

I have modified English translations without comment in order to render a consistent and readable technical vocabulary.

appropriation	*Ereignis*
fundamental disposition	*Grundstimmung*
leap	*Sprung*
being	*Sein*
be-ing	*Seyn*
entities	*Seiendes*
handiness	*Zuhandenheit*
on-handness	*Vorhandenheit*
temporality	*Temporalität*
timeliness	*Zeitlichkeit*
bringing forth	*Zeitigung*

Previous Publications

Part of Chapter 1 appeared as "Disentangling Heidegger's Transcendental Questions," *Continental Philosophy Review* 45 (2012): 77–100, © Springer Science+Business Media B.V. 2011, and is reprinted here with kind permission from Springer Science+Business Media.

Part of Chapter 2 appeared as "Heidegger's Distinction between Scientific and Philosophical Judgments," *Philosophy Today* 51 Supplement (2007): 33–41.

Part of Chapter 2 appeared as "The Phenomenological Kant: Heidegger's Interest in Transcendental Philosophy," *Journal of the British Society for Phenomenology* 41 (2010): 150–69. For journal information, visit http://www.tandfonline.com/.

Part of Chapters 3 and 4 appeared as "Heidegger on Overcoming Rationalism through Transcendental Philosophy," *Continental Philosophy Review* 41 (2008): 17–41, © Springer Science+Business Media B.V. 2007, and is reprinted here with kind permission from Springer Science+Business Media.

Part of Chapter 4 appeared as "The Wonder of Questioning: Heidegger and the Essence of Philosophy," *Philosophy Today* 49 Supplement (2005): 185–92.

Acknowledgments

During the week of Thanksgiving in 2005, relieved from teaching duties, I delved into the fourth and final chapter of my dissertation, and in doing so I finally glimpsed what was at stake in Heidegger's reading of Kant. Dimly then did I realize that this discovery in fact called for an entirely new book. Two other monographs intervened, and now, after a decade, I am finally able to bring to light the insight that dawned during that week of unaccustomed leisure.

I am thankful to several philosophers who opened up Heidegger's world to me. Among those, I would mention four in particular. Richard Velkley showed me how to interpret Heidegger productively, Robert Sokolowski made phenomenology compelling, John C. McCarthy read my earlier work with meticulous care, and Riccardo Pozzo modeled the scholarly art.

Parts of this book were given as presentations to audiences at the American Philosophical Association, the Society for Phenomenology and Existential Philosophy, the Catholic University of America, and the Franciscan University of Steubenville. I am thankful to the stimulation those venues afforded, and I am grateful to Brad Stone, Gretchen Gusich, Theodore Kisiel, Molly Flynn, and Jonathan J. Sanford for comments on those occasions.

Routledge delivered to me invaluable suggestions for revisions thanks to a team of anonymous reviewers, and the book would not have the focused form it does if it were not for their contribution.

Since 2014, I have had the good fortune of calling the University of Dallas my intellectual home. A healthy attitude toward Heidegger permeates students and faculty, for they neither dismiss him out of hand nor are they enthusiasts; Heidegger is one important thinker among many. My remarks in the final chapter were shaped in the context of the conversation I have been fortunate enough to have here, both in and out of the classroom. I am thankful to my colleague, Robert E. Wood, for remarks on the manuscript, and to my colleague and neighbor, Ivan Eidt, for help on the finer points of the German idiom, *über den eigenen Schatten springen*.

For some time, my oldest child, now nine, has been eagerly asking me to tell him more about "Heidegger's shadow." This book, conceived before my children were, now is as nothing compared to their presence, which fills my wife and me with such joy. As Heidegger expressed it in a peculiarly lucid moment, "Another possibility of such manifestation [of beings as a whole] is concealed in our joy in the presence of the Dasein—and not simply of the person—of a human being whom we love" ("What Is Metaphysics?" *Pathmarks*, p. 87). Clearly, I have much to be thankful for.

Introduction
The Problem of Motivation

He who wants to learn to philosophize must . . . regard all systems of philosophy only as the *history of the use of reason* and as objects for exercising his philosophical talent.

—Immanuel Kant[1]

Can I understand the phenomenological reduction of another without performing it myself or at the very least falling into a motivation in which it forces me?

—Edmund Husserl[2]

We have to look around in factical life experience in order to obtain a motive for its turning around.

—Martin Heidegger[3]

On the verge of writing his magnum opus, Heidegger abruptly abandons the plan of his 1925–26 lecture course on Aristotle to spend weeks avidly interpreting Kant. When he writes *Being and Time* several months later, he freely adopts a transcendental vocabulary. His interest in Kant becomes even more pronounced later in the decade, and he offers the 1929 *Kant and the Problem of Metaphysics* as an historical introduction to the problematic broached in *Being and Time*. A decade after the dramatic conversion to Kant, Heidegger gives the 1935–36 lecture course as a correction to the "overinterpretation" of Kant accomplished in the 1929 book.[4] In this second major interpretation, he makes the observation that no philosopher can leap over his shadow but that every philosopher must try. By shadow, he means the finitude of the human being (*die Endlichkeit des Menschen*), the fact that he or she emerges out of a particular situation, a particular problematic, and remains bound to it as his or her point of departure.[5] A philosopher's major work both expresses this limit and presses the limit in such a way that through the work a new horizon of inquiry can be glimpsed, however obscurely. Having written the *Critique of Pure Reason* in which thinking is systematically related to intuition, Kant should have rethought logic on different grounds, but this he was not able to do. The philosopher's inability is not a psychological one; it rather reflects the inherent finitude of thought at work in human beings. While teaching the course, Heidegger embarks on an ambitious effort to attempt the impossible and leap over the shadow of his earlier, expressly transcendental work. Several years later, he completes *Contributions to Philosophy*, but it would not see the light of day until 1989. In that work, Heidegger attempts to subvert *Being and Time* by rooting language more originally in affectivity and history.

What is Heidegger's own shadow? His shadow, I argue, is principally transcendental thinking, which he engages especially in its Kantian form. Heidegger knows that transcendental thinking finally falsifies his path, but he also knows that it alone initially affords the path. He cannot disavow transcendence without undermining the initial motivation to his path of thinking. The later Heidegger always offers *Being and Time* as the right entrance to his topic, even as he deploys historical and affective strategies to complement its transcendental approach; and he likewise continues to recommend Kant as the antidote to contemporary scientific positivism and as the gateway to philosophy. His quandary, then, takes the following form: *affirm* transcendental philosophy and thereby distort his terminus or *deny* transcendental philosophy and thereby obscure his beginning. Hence he displays a marked ambivalence to transcendental philosophy in general and Kant in particular. This book exposes this ambivalence and its cause in the nature of philosophy itself.

When Heidegger talks about something such as a hammer or a jug, he reconnects it to a context of movement, a play of presence and absence that lets it be understood as the sort of thing it is. The hammer comes into its own by hammering, and when we hammer, our attention goes beyond the hammer, beyond the nail, beyond the home improvement project, and beyond that to care for ourselves and our loved ones. By contrast, when the hammer is unavailable or broken, it becomes conspicuous, the object of our thematic concern; we come back from the horizons of experience to focus on this present thing. At the heart of Heidegger's thought is the quest to experience the dynamic movement of experience: "Phenomenological intuition," he tells us in 1919, "is the experience of experience."[6] His concern for the movement of experience is threefold: concern for the *going beyond* that enables us to encounter things, concern for the *opening up of the domain* in which the encountering takes place, and concern for how experiencing the going beyond and opening up might be *motivated*. The movement of experience cannot be accounted for in terms of the push and pull of physical forces; the play of presence and absence is not a matter of undergoing physical changes but of having things made available in their intelligibility. Consequently, it requires one for whom presence and absence happens; it requires the human qua Dasein rather than the human qua object of the natural sciences.[7] It is here with the inability of the natural sciences to grapple with this sort of fundamental movement that Heidegger feels the allure of the transcendental tradition. For the dynamic "stepping-beyond" inscribed in all varieties of transcendentalism—ancient, medieval, and modern—expresses a movement native to the life lived by the sorts of entities we are. The Heidegger of the late 1920s expresses this *a priori* movement in terms of the bringing forth accomplished by timeliness, and he finds this dynamic expressed with particular clarity in the halcyon depths of Kant's *Critique of Pure Reason*. This sort of movement is discovered through the authenticity of the transcendental researcher, who initiates the transcendence of transcending experience and thereby achieves insight into the real definition or inner structure of transcendence. The Heidegger of the mid 1930s and later underscores the reciprocity of the movement, a reciprocity obscured by the unilaterality of transcendence and its mode of access to the essence through authentic research, and he accordingly looks for another motivation. Heidegger says that the transcendental turn is in fact a *return* enabled not by authentically carrying out the ground-laying of the essence but by the need felt in the historical play of fundamental dispositions, and again he sees a hint of this reciprocity at work in Kant's *Critique*. It is not that Heidegger later disavows the unilateral movement of transcendence; it is rather that he retains its native "stepping-beyond" dynamic within a more comprehensive, bilateral movement that constitutes the domain of experience and motivates us to think about it. He thereby continues to recommend transcendental philosophy as the way to enter into his later thinking.

In working out his conception of the transcendental, Heidegger finds a collaborator in Kant, a Kant understood—Heidegger explicitly acknowledges—through the fundamental categories of Husserlian transcendental phenomenology. To appreciate the strangeness of Heidegger's reading, it is helpful to recall J. N. Mohanty's lucid distinction between two versions of transcendental philosophy: the Kantian and the phenomenological. The former *constructs* experience through argument and principles, *prinzipien-theoretisch*, while the latter *reflects* on the field of givenness, *evidenz-theoretisch*.[8] Heidegger makes the same distinction in *Being and Time*: "But to disclose the *a priori* is not to make an 'a-prioristic' construction. Through Edmund Husserl, we have learned not only to understand once more the sense of every genuine philosophical 'empiricism' but also to handle the necessary tools for it."[9] The power of Heidegger's interpretations of Kant lies in his paradoxical quest to assimilate, as far as possible, Kant's philosophy to phenomenological transcendental philosophy. Heidegger's Kant, after the fashion of both Husserl and Heidegger, attempts to disclose rather than construct the *a priori* condition for the possibility of experience. Kant traces thought back to legitimating sources of intuition, and Heidegger finds in this general program the expression of a basically phenomenological outlook.

Kant's continued relevance, reads Heidegger, is based on the transcendental attitude that neither analyzes articulated objects themselves (as in science and everyday experience) nor the form of articulations or judgments considered apart from the objects (as in logic) but thinks the prior, primordial unity of the two. Kant thereby retains some measure of the *logos-phenomena* of the ancient Greeks and of phenomenology. In the late 1920s and especially in *Being and Time*, Heidegger is taken by the thought that what unites language and the givenness of things is time, an insight he thinks Kant suggests in the form of the schematism. In the late 1930s, he thinks the union of language and thing happens within the pre-subjective and pre-objective open "between" (*Zwischen*), and again he thinks Kant's transcendental thinking discloses this domain, albeit obliquely. Heidegger thus reads Kant as attempting to overcome his basis in principles toward greater givenness, an attempt that we may yet bring to completion today and in doing so, find ourselves working as transcendental phenomenologists in the Heideggerian tradition.

Now, this careful reading of Heidegger's Kant is available only to those interpreters of Heidegger who take Husserl seriously, for it is all too common to dismiss Husserl out of hand as somehow superseded by Heideggerian fundamental ontology. Hubert Dreyfus, for instance, thinks that Heidegger makes " 'phenomenology' mean exactly the opposite of Husserl's proposed method."[10] On this view, Husserl remains mired in Brentano's mental contents and Descartes's virtual solipsism. But the Heidegger of *Being and Time* does not make *this* criticism of Husserl; as I will show in the first chapter, he regards being-in-the-world as the organic development of Husserlian intentionality rather than its inversion; his criticisms of Husserl lie elsewhere. And as will become clear in the second chapter, Heidegger explicitly credits his reading of Kant to Husserl, and he takes up Kant in order to defend phenomenology from the neo-Kantian attack. Heidegger, then, agrees with Robert Sokolowski and the "East Coast" reading of Husserl in which the founder of phenomenology has already broken out of the Cartesian egocentric predicament.[11] As such, Heidegger's conception of the transcendental, worked out in dialogue with the Kant he could embrace only thanks to Husserl, constitutes a development of, rather than a departure from, his Husserlian heritage.

1 Making Sense of Heidegger by Making Sense of Transcendence

The new century has witnessed the emergence of two new trends in Heidegger scholarship, trends that converge in the project of this book. The first of these trends is the explosion of interest in Heidegger's transcendentalism despite the fact that the term and the tradition enjoy little following in the larger philosophical community.[12] Before I turn to the second trend, the interest in the transcendental merits extended discussion. Eminent scholars such as Steve Crowell, Jeff Malpas, Daniel Dahlstrom, William Blattner, Taylor Carman, Tristan Moyle, and Lee Braver have given much attention to the positive place of the transcendental in Heidegger's path of thinking.[13] While their work is dogged by Heidegger's later criticisms of transcendental thinking, several points are worth highlighting. First, *Being and Time*, in which species of transcendental thinking proliferate, figures prominently as their point of departure; for these scholars, it is a work of continued relevance. Second, Heidegger's transcendental thinking engages other philosophical traditions; for them, he still has something to say within the conversation that is philosophy, because he does not simply reject its history or abandon its conceptuality. Third, the seminal insight of Heidegger's transcendental approach is the "space," "disclosedness," or "topos" of meaning and being. Some want to see the persistence of the transcendental motif in his later thinking, despite his apparent protests. For the transcendental focus, Kant naturally suggests himself as the nodal point for the inquiry.

These scholars of the transcendental rightly keep to the domain disclosed in *Being and Time*, but they do not explain how its transcendental approach, which becomes the subject of Heidegger's criticism, is related to his later thinking. For example, in the introduction to *Transcendental Heidegger*, Crowell and Malpas observe that "while the idea of the transcendental is explicitly disavowed in Heidegger's later thought, there still seems to be an important sense (though one that remains in need of clarification) in which that thinking retains a broadly 'transcendental' character."[14] Many of the contributors to that volume identify remnants of the transcendental that persist in the later Heidegger; Crowell for one identifies the commitment to thinking about the space of reasons and Dahlstrom the interplay of Dasein and being.[15] Malpas's suggestion calls for particular attention. He distinguishes two senses of transcendence: the movement of Dasein into the world and the place of understanding; the later Heidegger suppresses the former while retaining the latter. Malpas writes, "Heidegger's abandonment of the transcendental is thus an abandonment of the preoccupation with transcendence, not an abandonment of the topology that is itself a crucial element in the idea of the transcendental and that is even present, I would suggest, in Kant."[16] Despite these insights, Malpas does not follow the framework of *Being and Time*, which distinguishes a preparatory question, focused on transcendence, from a fundamental question, focused on the topology of being. As a consequence, the telegraphed shift from one question to the other, built into the very plan of *Being and Time*, appears as the abandonment of transcendence rather than its completion. From this perspective, the topological residue of the transcendental seems unrelated to the issue of transcendence and the problematic of the published portions of *Being and Time*.

The work of these scholars makes much-needed progress, but unless Heidegger's transcendental questions are disentangled, transcendental philosophy will wrongly appear to be little more than a momentary phase in his thinking. The focus on Heidegger's interpretation of Kant allows me to answer two puzzles still found in these scholars: the precise relation of Heidegger's later thought to transcendental philosophy and the historical roots of Heidegger's transcendental inquiries. I argue, contrary to the main trend of the above scholars, that Heidegger's later thought remains inextricably bound to the historical roots of his transcendental inquiries in the figures of Kant and Husserl, and it does so in a way that Heidegger himself realizes.

The recent interest in the transcendental overlaps with the focus of some of the classic interpretations of Heidegger's Kant. Henri Declève and Frank Schalow treat the corpus as a whole and offer a kind of synoptic view or commentary on the various passages.[17] Books with a thematic focus, such as those by Charles Sherover or Martin Weatherspoon, handle only the interpretation from the late 1920s.[18] The uniqueness of the present study is that it treats both major interpretations of Kant and shows that the enduring theme is Heidegger's attempt to come to terms with the limits of his own thinking. Heidegger cannot abandon Kant and Husserl, and he cannot reject his own earlier breakthrough work in transcendental phenomenology. Though he can and must attempt to move farther into the domain opened up in that way, he can never replace the beginning of his path of thinking. It led him into the domain, and it alone affords the opportunity for his contemporaries to enter the path of thinking. This is the first book to interrelate Heidegger's interpretations of Kant and Heidegger's understanding of his own transcendental history.

Besides the renewed interest in the transcendental, the new century has nourished a second surprising movement in Heidegger studies. Despite ninety years of interest in Heidegger, there is a lack of consensus in the scholarly community concerning what Heidegger was after through the one hundred volumes of notes, publications, and idle musings that constitute his collected works. It seems that anything one might want to find (or might not want to find) can be found somewhere in those volumes. The question of what we are supposed to make of it all naturally arises. For this reason, Thomas Sheehan and Richard Capobianco have independently undertaken the momentous task of *clarification*, of making sense of the unity of Heidegger's program by making sense of his lasting topic, the *Seinsfrage*. In doing so, they come to opposing conclusions: for Sheehan, the lasting topic is the finitude of human existence as that which makes meaning possible;[19] for Capobianco, the lasting topic is the manifestation of being.[20] For support, Sheehan turns to Heidegger's Aristotle, and Capobianco to Heidegger's pre-Socratics. Sheehan emphasizes the phenomenological perspective of the givenness of meaning to institute a new paradigm for Heidegger studies that is geared to the matter itself.

Aristotle's understanding of *psyche* as "a *paschein ti*, a transcendental openness-to-receive" provides the inspiration for this approach.[21] Sheehan applies what he calls "Heidegger's razor" to the *Contributions* and indeed Heidegger's thinking as a whole. The razor says, with Heidegger, that the multiplication of names does not undermine the simplicity of the matter or its questioning. Hence, Sheehan attempts to "demystify" Heidegger by tracing back the "apocalyptic language" of the esoteric writings to the demystified topic, namely, "the openness opened up by our essential finitude."[22] Sheehan formulates Heidegger's fundamental question as follows: "What is responsible for the *correlation* between an entity's givenness and the dative of that givenness?"[23] The published investigations of *Being and Time*, then, are preparatory. They display on the one hand the phenomenological interpretation of being as givenness and on the other the dative of that givenness as the open comportment called Dasein.[24] Heidegger's fundamental question concerns the reciprocal relation of the two: "Heidegger moves beyond transcendentalism to the a priori fact of the clearing."[25] Capobianco thinks the prominence of subjectivity in Sheehan's clarification of Heidegger's path crucially misses Heidegger's program: "It was this decisive turn in modern philosophy to the human *logos*—and to the preoccupation with 'meaning'—that he sought to counter by a decisive *return* to the question of *Being*."[26] Even accepting Capobianco's criticism, there is still the question concerning how the modern turn and Heidegger's return interface with one another.

Sheehan is correct that the ontological and poetic language of the later Heidegger cloaks the Heideggerian program in obscurity; Capobianco, for his part, is correct that Heidegger invokes such language precisely to unsettle subjectivity and that such unsettling is understated in Sheehan's presentation of Heidegger. Is there a way to clarify Heidegger's vocabulary while minding the movement away from subjectivity? Yes, I think so, for that is precisely what Heidegger saw in the various strands of transcendentalism: Kant, Husserl, *Being and Time* and more distantly, Aquinas, Aristotle, and the pre-Socratics. Charting the movement through *Being and Time* to the later thinking is the task necessary for clarifying Heidegger's path of thinking. In this way, we will be able to see that transcendentalism provides the essential motive for its own immanent transformation; Sheehan's choice of the Heideggerian Aristotle and Capobianco's choice of the Heideggerian pre-Socratics obscure just this dynamic; for right there in modern thought Heidegger finds the seeds for its own overcoming. Focusing on the Heideggerian Husserl and Kant will enable us to see beyond the opposition of the two efforts of clarification. For what Capobianco rejects in Sheehan is his "transcendental-phenomenological" reduction of being to meaning, which misses Heidegger's deepest theme, namely, "*Sein qua manifestation* . . . in relation to Dasein."[27] However, the idea of *relation* here is clearly bound up with Heidegger's transformed sense of the transcendental in a manner

Capobianco does not clarify: "Thus, Being *qua* manifestation is structurally prior to, and the ontological condition of, meaning."[28] Moreover, Capobianco underscores the central role of experience in Heidegger's program, but for Heidegger, the commitment to experience is transcendental in origin. Sheehan, for his part, thinks Capobianco's fidelity to the Heideggerian vocabulary obscures the Heideggerian program, and he offers his own approach as a kind of transcendental reading of Heidegger, under a question I might formulate as "What is the condition for the possibility of Heidegger's making sense?"[29] Central to this task is to identify the movement, intrinsic to *Being and Time*, that leads beyond the horizon of that work; this is the movement that can make sense of Heidegger's twisted path of thinking. The Sheehan-Capobianco impasse suggests that the condition for the possibility of clarifying Heidegger's path of thinking is to clarify Heidegger's multifaceted and dynamic transcendentalism.

To make sense of Heidegger by making sense of his transcendentalism, I focus on Heidegger's corpus, offering a reading of major texts such as *Kant and the Problem of Metaphysics*, its 1935 revision, *Being and Time*, and *Contributions* in the context of the surrounding lecture courses. The goal is to understand Heidegger the thinker as he understood himself when he was most self-aware and self-critical. With the exception of some introductory considerations in the various chapters, I do not focus on biographical details and external historical events but instead develop a careful synthetic reading of the collected works.[30]

The first part, "The Shadow Is Cast," identifies the transcendental infrastructure of Heidegger's thought. Chapter one examines *Being and Time* and surrounding lecture courses to identify the transcendental character of its questioning and the role transcendental philosophy plays in its account of the history of philosophy. *Being and Time*'s two transcendental questions emerge in the dialogue with Husserl and Kant, and Heidegger aims to leap over their respective shadows. Heidegger, captivated by phenomenology and gripped by the problem of motivating the transcendental turn, nonetheless regards the neglect of the being of the transcendental ego as Husserl's greatest omission. Heidegger's method of formal indication and his critique of the ancient focus on isolated judgment and the modern *mathesis universalis* emerge in the radicalization of a distinction native to Husserl between generalization and formalization. Heidegger's subsequent turn to the historicity of fundamental dispositions unfolds in the space first afforded by formal indication and transcendental philosophy. Heidegger moves beyond transcendentalism by means of furthering the movement constitutive of transcendentalism. The second chapter shows how Heidegger constantly reads and rereads Kant in light of Husserl's program and in light of Husserl's own interpretations of Kant. The highpoint of this reading is his attempt to provide a historical introduction to the transcendental questions by deploying a book-length phenomenological reading of Kant on the structure of transcendence. Heidegger, however, does chastise Kant for being in effect inauthentic; in the second edition of the work, Kant retreats from his discovery and downplays the pre-judicative ground of reason.

The second part, "The Attempt to Leap over the Shadow," follows Heidegger's self-conscious efforts to accomplish the impossible and break with his transcendental origins. It begins in the third chapter by considering the revision of his Kant book undertaken in the 1935–36 lecture course. Heidegger still lauds Kant's phenomenological advance that uncovers the pre-judicative "between," but he no longer thinks Kant thought about the constitution of this "between." He asks only the preliminary transcendental question of *Being and Time*, not the fundamental one. Kant's failure to turn to the between explicitly was not a failure of authenticity; Heidegger no longer accuses him of "shrinking back." Rather, it is simply the limitation of his own task of philosophy not to have been able to start over again with the discovery achieved by his thought. Nonetheless, Heidegger recommends that in our contemporary situation we reenact Kant's transcendental turn to divest ourselves of our scientism and be prepared to enter into the domain of philosophy. The fourth chapter shows how in the contemporary lecture courses as well as in the *Contributions*, largely written in 1936, Heidegger develops a new presentation of his philosophy couched specifically in the historical progression of fundamental dispositions; despite this different emphasis, Heidegger continually affirms the necessity of the transcendental, especially that of *Being and Time*, but also that of Kant, in granting access to the problematic that he is fine tuning. Heidegger's attitude is marked by a deep ambivalence: "The *transcendental* way (but another 'transcendence') only provisionally, in order to prepare the reversing-momentum and leaping-into."[31] The ambivalence toward transcendental philosophy, jointly affirming both its necessity and its insufficiency, dogs every discussion of it throughout the rest of Heidegger's career. Kant and in some sense Husserl occupy an ambivalent place in Heidegger's history of being. Their phenomenology of judgment's context reconnects with the end of the Greek beginning in Plato and Aristotle, allowing Heidegger to delve into the context as such, which was obliquely named by the pre-Socratic thinkers. The genealogy of Heidegger's own thinking requires the recovery of the Greek sense of being, a recovery afforded by phenomenology and its transcendental pairing of thought and intuition. Heidegger therefore cannot shake the transcendental path, since it provides the historical motivations to his own thinking. The concluding fifth chapter briefly examines Heidegger's late (and occasional) discussions of transcendental thinking before discussing the finitude of philosophy and critically evaluating Heidegger's efforts to leap over his own shadow.

2 The Transcendental Problem of Introduction

In 1772, Immanuel Kant wrote to Marcus Herz that he had discovered "the key to the whole secret of metaphysics, hitherto still hidden from itself."[32] Nine years later, Kant finally published his magnum opus, the *Critique of Pure Reason*, which in his judgment posed and answered a question no one had previously asked: "How are *a priori* synthetic judgments possible?"[33] The scope and byzantine complexity of the work obscured its central claim, and Kant was dissatisfied with its reception. In a desire to make its contents accessible to his contemporaries, he issued in 1783 an introduction to this work, *The Prolegomena to Any Future Metaphysics That Will Be Able to Come Forward as a Science*. The *Critique* took a synthetic approach and began with the elements of cognition before examining how they might come together to achieve cognition. The *Prolegomena* works backward, beginning with mathematics, physics, and metaphysics, and inquiring into their ultimate cognitive foundations. In 1787, Kant issued a major revision of the *Critique of Pure Reason*, that shifted emphasis from the imagination to understanding as the ultimate agent of cognition.

In 1900 and 1901, Edmund Husserl published the *Logical Investigations*, which refuted psychologism and yet nonetheless rooted truth in the dynamics of experience. Several years later, Husserl realized that to make sense of the phenomenological breakthrough of the *Logical Investigations* it was necessary to make the transcendental turn. Accordingly, in *Ideas I* in 1913, he emphasized the transcendental character of phenomenology. At the same time, Husserl remained deeply troubled by the difficulty he experienced in making transcendental phenomenology intelligible to others: "Anyone who misconstrues the sense and performance of transcendental-phenomenological reduction is still entangled in psychologism."[34] Every work he brought to print sought to introduce phenomenology, and he chastises his students, and in particular Heidegger, for not understanding the transcendental turn.

In 1919, Martin Heidegger happened upon his lasting topic, the pretheoretical world of experience. After nearly a decade of experimentation, operating under pressure to publish or perish, in 1927 Heidegger produced his magnum opus, *Being and Time*, which focused on the central question, "What is the meaning of being?" by means of analyzing the questioner of being. Desiring to make this difficult work more intelligible to his contemporaries, he brought forth an introduction called *Kant and the Problem of Metaphysics* in 1929. While the published *Being and Time* took a systematic approach, the "Kant book" adopted a historical mode of exposition and translated Heidegger's central problematic into Kant's systematic analytic. At the time, Heidegger thought Kant was the only one in the entire history of philosophy who could serve in this capacity; the *Critique*'s central question broke into the domain operative in Heidegger's question. In 1936, Heidegger undertook a new work, *Contributions to Philosophy*, that amounted to a revised approach to the question targeted by *Being and Time*. In the ambit of this revised approach, he conceived a revision to the Kant book, the 1935–36 lecture course. In this revision, he retracts the claim that Kant directly asked his fundamental question. Instead, Kant leads in an indirect fashion to the site of Heidegger's question.

A central problem with the transcendental turn concerns the problem of introducing it, of making it intelligible to those who have not made it and of motivating them to make it. Of course, the problem of introduction is a perennial one in philosophy. Consider, for example, a central question of Plato's *Republic*: How can a philosopher come about? The interests of the everyday seem all consuming, and to be a philosopher the soul must be turned around. The allegory of the cave appeals to an odd grace, the unlocking of the first prisoner, who is then strangely entrusted with the responsibility of liberating others. The perennial philosophical problem of introduction is particularly difficult for transcendental philosophy insofar as it emphasizes a turning around of one's attention from mundane ends to transcendental considerations concerning the conditions of knowledge, experience, or intelligibility: How can one make intelligible beforehand what can be understood only through the performance of a radical reorientation? How can one be motivated to undertake this reorientation when the necessity and possibility of doing so cannot be understood beforehand? The problem of introduction is a central problem in transcendental philosophy, which Heidegger inherits from Husserl and Kant. Heidegger's *Kant and the Problem of Metaphysics* takes its place alongside Kant's *Prolegomena* and Husserl's later publications. Though Heidegger's shift to history seems to amount to a rejection of transcendental thought, it is really an attempt to come to terms with the difficulty of adequately motivating the transcendental turn, a difficulty keenly felt by anyone who wishes to make such a turn accessible to others.

3 Husserl and the Problem of Motivation

To set the stage for Heidegger, it is worthwhile to consider Husserl's attempts to introduce others to transcendental phenomenology by generating a historical motivation. Central to transcendental phenomenology is the transcendental reduction, which shifts from the usual engagement with items in the world to contemplation of the various ways those items can be intended, constituted, or given to experience. The related epoché sets aside the usual theories we employ for making sense of the world; it brackets the push and pull of causality that can be identified through empirical methods in order to be receptive to the intelligibility that is intrinsic to the transcendental domain. For Husserl, understanding and performing the reduction (which go hand in hand) are absolutely

essential for the comprehension of phenomenological inquiry and its disclosed spiritual domain.[35] But understanding and performing the reduction are difficult tasks; the reduction effects a complete "break" with
the world in a reorientation that enables phenomenological reflection by
granting a new domain of inquiry, a domain that includes but exceeds the
pregiven world. Because this reorientation is completely discontinuous,
leading others into the reduction and consequently into phenomenology
proves to be a daunting task. The first problem of transcendental phenomenology, then, is the problem of *introduction*, of *leading others into
the reduction* and thus into phenomenology. Husserl was well aware of
this problem, which is why most of the writings he brought to print were
"introductions" to phenomenology.[36] How can one caught up in the natural attitude be moved to perform the epoché and reduction and thereby
break free from all natural ends and motivations? Rather than the action
of an autonomous will, Husserl came to see a prior passive displacement,
opened in history, as the more satisfactory account of motivation and
thus introduction.

Even though Husserl appropriates the epoché from the Cartesian
method of doubting, he is careful to extract only a single aspect of doubt,
an aspect that he can articulate only with such metaphors as "bracketing" or "putting out of play" or "setting aside" [*Ausschaltung*].[37]
Unlike Descartes's doubting, which Husserl equates with a negation of
the world, the phenomenological epoché leaves the world be and gives
the phenomenologist a perch above the play, above the modalities and
objects, opening the world and its constitution as a new field of analysis.
Thus Husserl can assert, "I am *not negating* this 'world' as though I were
a sophist; I am *not doubting its factual being* as though I were a skep-
tic."[38] The epoché is a certain refraining from belief, but a refraining that
is compatible with naturally maintaining the surest convictions rooted in
evident truth.[39] The convictions remain, but in order to open them up to
analysis as acts of consciousness regarding constituted objects, the phenomenologist achieves a new kind of distance toward them. Thus, even
though all interest in the modalities of the world are "put out of play"
and the world itself is "bracketed,"[40] the philosopher does not for that
relegate himself to the role of an apathetic recluse, but rather still lives
through the natural life,[41] although he has achieved a newfound spiritual
freedom of reflection:

> All natural interests are put out of play. But the world, exactly as it
> was for me earlier and still is, as my world, our world, humanity's
> world, having validity in its various subjective ways, has not disap-
> peared; it is just that, during the consistently carried-out epoché, it is
> under our gaze purely as the correlate of the subjectivity which gives
> it ontic meaning, through whose validities the world "is" at all.[42]

That is to say, the world of objects and ends, of interaction and interests has lost nothing because of the new phenomenological attitude, an attitude that reduces or traces back all phenomena to the correlated constituting activity of the transcendental ego: ". . . the being of the objective world in the natural attitude, and this attitude itself, have lost nothing through the fact that they are, so to speak, 'understood back into' [*zurückverstanden*] the absolute sphere of being in which they ultimately and truly are."[43] In this tracing back, the epoché and the reduction open up an infinite, unexplored field of transcendental being, of structures and manners of constituting givenness.[44]

The transcendental turn of phenomenology takes the world as given and inquire into the *how* of the giving, the manner of its givenness, the *how* of its acquisition of meaning.[45] There is a twofold need for the reduction and a corresponding twofold character of the reduction. False theories[46] and misleading prejudices[47] bar access to the truth and so must be sloughed off by a purgative reduction, and natural naïveté conceals the transcendental domain and so must be put out of play in the reduction, thereby granting access to a new domain of inquiry. The reduction, then, both purges prejudices and grants access to a new domain. This new domain of the transcendental ego requires a new science to articulate its field of constitution, whether it be of self, others, or objects. The transcendental reduction is "the gate of entry to genuine knowledge of self and of the world"[48] wherein a vast new spiritual world[49] opens up with a new way a life and a vantage point *above* the world and its interests.[50] With the purgation, then, nothing but error is lost and in truth everything is gained.

The question of motivation involves the difficult issue of prompting, within the natural attitude, the transcendental turn. Husserl thinks the total change of interest is "founded on a particular resolve of the will,"[51] but this opens up the problem of a mundane act having a transcendental end, a problem Eugen Fink amplifies and clarifies when he observes that "no *mundane* motivation is adequate to the transgressing of the world that takes place in the transcendental reduction."[52] This difficulty prompts Thomas Prufer to ask what "chance, violence, or grace" could move us into the epoché or effect the turn from mundane living to reflection on egological world-constitution.[53] Outside the reduction, asks John Drummond, how can the necessity of the reduction be felt and its achievement be effected?[54] As William Jon Lenkowski remarks, "From a transcendental standpoint, the *primary* question seems not to be: How does it come about that one comes to have a 'world'?—but rather: How does it *become possible to ask* how this comes about?"[55] Now, we might want to see some inkling of the transcendental attitude in the natural one—some transcendental clues nestled in the mundane—that could capture the philosopher's attention and motivate him to move into the transcendental attitude. In my concluding chapter, I will make my own proposals in this regard. But as Fink, Prufer, and Lenkowski observe, for Husserl the shift to the transcendental standpoint is in no way a mundane possibility but only a transcendental one. Moreover, not only does the matter itself raise the question of motivation, but Husserl himself makes it an issue. With Zahavi, we can say that the question of motivation cannot be ignored "because of Husserl's own occasional insistence upon the radical distinction between the natural attitude and the transcendental attitude."[56]

Husserl addresses the question of motivation by developing two motivated ways to the reduction.[57] The Cartesian way, developed first, is motivated by an appeal to philosophical virility and authenticity: every philosopher to be a philosopher must at some time in his life subject all his convictions to a radical purgation so that he may rebuild them on solid, apodictic ground. In the *Crisis*, Husserl briefly refers to the motivation of the Cartesian way: ". . . it is thought of as being attained merely by reflectively engrossing oneself in the Cartesian epoché of the *Meditations* while critically purifying it of Descartes's prejudices and confusions."[58] The difficulty, however, is put back a level: What motivated Descartes's epoché? Why should one undertake to do what Descartes did? While the Cartesian way is a motivated way, it is not clear that its motivation is something that naturally occurs to one engrossed in the world; in short, it is not clear how it could be what I call an *adequate* motivation. In the *Crisis*, Husserl's final attempt to introduce the new phenomenology, Husserl exhibits a new way to the reduction. The so-called ontological way, nestled within the historical reflection of the *Crisis*, gradually leads to the reduction by first making the achievements of modern science questionable and then by making the pregiven lifeworld itself questionable. Husserl comes to realize that the transcendental turn is not fully intelligible as the projection of an autonomous will; instead, it becomes fully intelligible as a passively experienced motivating pull that can become a goal of the will only in hindsight.

Husserl's own way into the reduction provides essential illumination to the question of introduction. At first glance, his way seems to be by chance, and his remarks in the *Crisis* characterize this way as a response to a particular historical situation.[59] The *Logical Investigations* was a "breakthrough" work that first disclosed for him the *a priori* correlation of objects and manners of givenness, a correlation that he says never evoked philosophical wonder prior to his work on the *Logical Investigations*.[60] In his deep struggles to refute psychologism and clarify the basic concepts of logic, Husserl had stumbled upon something truly wondrous: the pure figure of givenness and the correlation of experienced objects and their modes of givenness. This insight would fundamentally affect Husserl the rest of his life.[61] Though this insight occurred in 1898, it was not until 1904/5 that Husserl could realize that his analyses had been naïvely carried out within the reduction, that his fidelity to the task of his work had drawn him into this realm without his realizing it as such:

> Of course, the epoché, as an explicit methodical basic requirement, could be a matter of the subsequent reflection only of one who, with a certain naïveté and through a historical situation, was already pulled into [*hineinziehen*] the epoché, so to speak, who had already taken possession of a piece of this new "internal world," in a certain sense a proximal field within it, with an obscurely prefigured distant horizon. Thus it was not until four years after concluding the *Logical Investigations* that he arrived at an explicit but even then imperfect self-consciousness of its method. But along with this also arose the extraordinarily difficult problems connected with the method itself, with the epoché and the reduction and their own phenomenological understanding and their extraordinary philosophical significance.[62]

It was some time after already moving, albeit clumsily, within the transcendental sphere that the methodological requirements of phenomenology began to become clear to him, the demands that necessitate the reduction and epoché. He had to be within the reduction before he could understand the reduction. If this was the case for Husserl, it is presumably the case for others as well. Any introduction to the reduction presupposes that one has already unknowingly been displaced—confusedly to be sure—but displaced nonetheless, into the transcendental sphere. An introduction would thus be no more than a "phenomenology of the phenomenological reduction" that would make explicit what was already implicit.[63]

Husserl turns to history in order to elevate his chance discovery into something necessary and indeed normative for others. In the *Crisis*, he develops the theme of historical realization of the implicit *telos* of all philosophy, as the "historically motivated path" or ontological way to the reduction.[64] In the Vienna Lecture, delivered six months before the Prague lectures upon which the *Crisis* was based, he articulates this *telos*:

> The spiritual *telos* of European humanity, in which the particular *telos* of particular nations and of individual men is contained, lies in the infinite, is an infinite idea toward which, in concealment, the whole spiritual becoming aims, so to speak. As soon as it becomes consciously recognized in the development as *telos*, it necessarily also becomes practical as a goal of the will; and thereby a new, higher stage of development is introduced which is under the guidance of norms, normative ideas.[65]

What secretly draws Husserl into the reduction, then, seems to be the necessary *telos* of European humanity, the destiny, in fact, of the whole world. European history, then, seems to have the peculiarity of having an end that transcends the world. Husserl will take up this question of this *telos* as the theme of the whole of the *Crisis*, asking whether the *telos* of Europe, the *telos* of Greek philosophy, is delusion or destiny—"whether this *telos* . . . is merely a factual, historical delusion, the accidental acquisition of merely one among many other civilizations and histories, or whether Greek humanity was not rather the first breakthrough to what is *essential to humanity as such*, its *entelechy*."[66] This question can be decided only by bringing reason to see its own possibilities for universality. Husserl proceeds to show that the inner orientation of philosophy has been toward this new apodictic philosophy, resting on apodictic ground.[67] Transcendental phenomenology is the fulfillment of what the origin of philosophy emptily intended in its first beginnings: "We attempted thereby to awaken the full insight that only such a philosophy, through such a regressive inquiry back to the last conceivable ground in the transcendental ego, can fulfill the meaning which is inborn in philosophy from its primal establishment."[68] Thus, in the historical exposition Husserl can obliquely refer to the current silently drawing in the would-be transcendental philosopher by mentioning "the pathway we allowed ourselves to be drawn into, along which we allowed ourselves to be propelled."[69] Husserl here moves away from talk of a wholly active stance in which the will effects the reduction to one that emphasizes the active passivity or receptivity involved in *allowing* oneself to be *drawn* along. The move to the reduction is less a self-enclosed command and more an issue of philosophical desire.[70]

History itself prepares the way for the realization of the necessity of the transcendental attitude and motivates its performance: ". . . the whole long history of philosophy and its sciences was needed before the consciousness of the necessity for this radical reorientation, and the resolve to observe it with conscious consistency, could be motivated."[71] Transcendental phenomenology, then, reveals itself as a task "put to us by history"[72]—and not by nature. In this way, Husserl's own happening upon the transcendental domain was a response to something that was felt even among the pre-Socratics:

> The correlation between world (the world of which we always speak) and its subjective manners of givenness never evoked philosophical wonder (that is, prior to the first breakthrough of "transcendental phenomenology" in the *Logical Investigations*), in spite of the fact that it had made itself felt even in pre-Socratic philosophy and among the Sophists—though here only as a motive for skeptical argumentation. This correlation never aroused a philosophical interest of its own which could have made it the object of an appropriate scientific attitude.[73]

Husserl's being pulled into this domain by the pathos of philosophical wonder can now be seen as the movement of history, the *telos* of Europe realized. Husserl's project here has obvious affinities with Hegel's, but Husserl appeals to his doctrine of empty and filled intentions and not a dialectic to explain the unfolding of history. In this he exhibits remarkable similarities with Aristotle, who turns to a history of the development of the sciences and a history of philosophy to show the culmination of these two in his project of a first philosophy considering four causes.[74] Kant, too, concludes the *Critique of Pure Reason* with a chapter entitled, "The History of Pure Reason." His aim, in that chapter, is to motivate the critical philosophy by showing that it is the inevitable result of previous philosophical impasses: "The *critical* path alone is still open."[75] For Husserl as for Kant, the problem of introduction, of leading others into the transcendental turn, naturally becomes historical.

4 Squaring Transcendence and History

Heidegger's 1913 dissertation and his 1915 habilitation already signal his concern with the phenomenological breakthrough concerning judgment. The dissertation, *The Doctrine of Judgment in Psychologism: A Critical-Positive Contribution to Logic*, follows Husserl in criticizing the reduction of judgment's logical content to the psychical act of judging. The habilitation, *Categories and Theory of Meaning in Duns Scotus*, approaches a medieval theory of meaning (in this case that of the Scotist Thomas of Erfurt) in terms of Husserl's doctrine of categorial intuition and Emil Lask's attempt to integrate Aristotle and Kant on the proper "place" of logic.[76] The 1916 conclusion of that work, the last thing he published before *Being and Time* in 1927, lays out three tasks for a theory of categories: (1) to distinguish objects into "categorially irreducible" domains; (2) to understand categories "within the problems of judgment and the subject"; and (3) to work out "the *cosmos* of categories" by including "history and the teleological interpretation of culture."[77] In *Being and Time*, Heidegger retains and transforms these three tasks: (1) the categories are worked out according to the irreducible domains of the handy, on-hand, and being-in-the-world; (2) judgment is understood on the basis of the disclosedness of Dasein; and (3) "the *cosmos* of categories" is not so much history but the historical disclosedness of timeliness. In the habilitation, Heidegger says the decisive thing is to turn from judgment to its context: "We cannot at all see logic and its problems in their true light if the context *from* which they are interpreted is not a translogical one."[78] How might this turn come about?

The problem of introduction is a problem that Heidegger inherits from Husserl and seeks to answer similarly, first by appealing to authenticity and subsequently to history. As early as 1920, Heidegger sees the crucial issue of motivation arising principally from experience and secondarily from history. Everyday life is engrossed in the object-pole of experience; to shift experience toward the quality of experiencing requires a counter-movement, a turning around, that must be motivated:

> The falling tendency of factical life experience, constantly tending toward the significant connections of the factically experienced world, its gravity, as it were, conditions a tendency of factically lived life toward the attitudinal determination and regulation of objects. . . . We have to look around in factical life experience in order to obtain a motive for its turning around [*ein Motiv für ihre Umwendung*].[79]

Heidegger regards the identification of this motive as a most difficult venture. He therefore proposes to his students an alternate way to inspire this "turning around" through the history of philosophy:

> It is, to be sure, possible to find this motive, but is very difficult. For this reason, we will choose a more convenient route [*einen beque-meren Weg*], since we possess knowledge of past and contemporary philosophy. The factical existence of the history of philosophy is, in itself, certainly no motivation to philosophize. Nevertheless, as a cultural possession, one can take it as a starting point and, with its help, clarify for oneself motivations to philosophize.

Six years later, Heidegger still sees these two ways to motivate philosophy existing, as it were, side by side. In *Being and Time*, part one, he appeals to authenticity and the call of conscience. In *Being and Time*, part two, which was never published, he had anticipated working out an historical motivation. In 1929, he instead publishes a work on Kant as a historical introduction/motivation.

Thereafter Heidegger shifts his manner of motivation. In the mid-1930s, he suppresses the way through authenticity and instead develops a way through the historical play of fundamental dispositions; while doing so, he distances himself from Kant though he still recommends him as the gateway to the domain of thought. In this new approach to motivation, Heidegger does not move *from* the transcendental turn *to* history. Transcendental philosophy naturally raises the question of introduction, and Heidegger is not the first to realize that such an introduction and its corresponding motivation cannot be handled through ahistorical appeals to Cartesian-style authenticity. Dasein cannot generate its own motive to do philosophy. Transcendental philosophy needs affectivity to provide the momentum to its own performance. Heidegger stops seeking a precursor in a philosopher and instead locates a momentum intrinsic to the philo-sophical enterprise that will effect the transition to another beginning. Heidegger's turn to history aims to remedy the problem of motivation by rereading the tradition in terms of its privations or that which remains unthought. The absence can effect a normative force in us: what has for good reason not been thought becomes, for us, experienced as that which should be thought. Heidegger's "history" is really his attempt to give affectivity its due in the philosophical life. As Kant traces all thought to intuition, so Heidegger returns the transcendental turn to the givenness of fundamental dispositions. What causes these dispositions to stir in us is the thoughtful critique of what has been thought, a critique that brings out what is essential and brings with it a momentum over to what still needs to be thought. Encountering the limits of others compels us to think, to make a purified transcendental turn that considers the condition for the possibility of the transcendental turn.

In the 1919–1920 lecture course, Heidegger writes, "In its actual driving forces, every genuine philosophy is a struggle for method, indeed in such a way that every method that is nearest to it (and the modes of cognition and the ideals of cognition) must always be overcome anew."[80] Heidegger's repeated attempts to overcome the transcendental tradition demonstrate its nearness to his lasting project. At no point after 1925 does Heidegger criticize the transcendental turn *per se*. Instead he identifies various insufficiencies in the turn that his own philosophy aims to remedy. In the late 1920s, he points to the neglect of the mode of being of the transcendental subject and remedies it with Dasein. In the mid-1930s, he criticizes the neglect of the historical in transcendental thinking and remedies it with his account of fundamental dispositions. The transcendental domain is not only the condition for the possibility of judgments; in the historical play of fundamental dispositions it is the condition for the possibility of being Dasein. He continues to recommend Kant as the antidote to the modern mathematical mode of thinking that makes us unfree in our experience of things. Heidegger's turn to history is an attempt to make manifest the affectivity that lies at the heart of the transcendental turn.

The first two chapters recount Heidegger's embrace of the transcendental tradition in the late 1920s. This period constitutes, as it were, the casting of his shadow. In the first chapter, I detail Heidegger's attempt in *Being and Time* to radicalize Husserl's transcendental turn by thinking about the transcendental domain and our relation to it. This radicalization serves to render the problem of motivation even more troublesome. Heidegger thinks it is the confrontation with philosophical error that motivates analysis—the transcendental refutation of modern rationalism has the effect of disclosing the domain that disrupts the classical focus on judgment as the locus of truth. In the second chapter I examine Heidegger's efforts in *Kant and the Problem of Metaphysics* to find in Kant a critical forerunner to his program and thereby motivate for his contemporaries his own unique brand of transcendental thinking. These two books firmly plant Heidegger within the transcendental tradition.

In the late 1930s, Heidegger then undertakes the impossible: to leap over the limitations of his own transcendental program as expressed in these two books. The third chapter attends to the revision of the Kant book he makes on the eve of writing his *Contributions*. In the 1935–36 lecture course, he adjusts his assessment of Kant's transcendental philosophy. Kant is not his choice phenomenological collaborator in inquiring into the domain. Rather, like Husserl, he is a distant, although crucial forerunner to Heidegger's project. Heidegger begins where Kant leaves off, with the domain in which mind and world meet and judgments are possible. Kant did not see into the new vistas his work opened up; he remained bound by the horizon of the work he produced. In the *Contributions*, subject of the fourth chapter, Heidegger aims to confront his own finitude and to push forward the inquiry made possible by *Being and Time*, the inquiry that enlarges the horizon of that work. He underscores that the transcendental domain is available thanks to affectivity; it is not the result of a turn accomplished by the philosopher but a result of something that happens to the thinker. In the context of attempting the impossible, of surpassing his shadow, he displays a marked ambivalence: at times he rebukes Kant and at other times he recommends him as the path to his later thinking. He clearly distinguishes his own earlier project from Kant's while simultaneously seeing Kant naturally lead to his own earlier project just as his own earlier project naturally leads to his later program. In view of the shortcomings of the transcendental tradition, Heidegger tries to extricate himself from its grip. In view of the vistas opened by transcendental thinking, Heidegger cannot deny its validity in affording a first approach to the domain to be thought. The transcendental illusion of a horizon opposite the subject remains a necessary illusion for breaking into the domain in which such illusions will turn out to be nothing more than an error in perspective, for the domain was already open before the would-be philosopher began to philosophize for the first time. Heidegger cannot leap over his shadow, but he was obliged to try. Transcendental philosophy remains the necessary motivating path to his lasting topic.

In the concluding chapter, I explore the implications of this study for our understanding of Heidegger. I briefly indicate the persistence of the ambiguous relation to transcendental thought in later texts. Then I argue that my study calls for a positive conception of Heidegger's relation to Husserl, and I make the case that Heidegger's contribution is a "post-subjective, affective transcendentalism." I identify Heidegger's three ways to the transcendental turn, the heroic, the poetic, and the Kantian-Husserlian analysis of judgment. Finally, I argue that in several respects Heidegger failed to recognize the shadow of his thinking, and I urge us, his readers, to recognize this shadow and surmount it in our own thought.

Heidegger, as I read him, had only one topic, namely the task of bringing experience to experience in all its native richness. At first, he construed this task non-historically as bringing to experience *the a priori* condition for the possibility of experience; later he became convinced that the condition for the possibility of experience necessarily comes to be experienced differently in different eras. As far as I can tell, he is right to think he is the first thinker to give sustained attention to the topic. Yet it is also true that he never could have happened upon the topic or given it any thought except by means of following closely the work of his philosophical predecessors, and it is also the case that there is no chance of his making himself intelligible to others except by means of a creative reading of the philosophical tradition. So the paradox: his topic is both novel and inherited. Heidegger found himself entangled with a tradition that enabled him to be Heidegger but also obscured his originality. So, to read Heidegger is to be confronted with a bewildering array of counterclaims: Husserl and Kant are alternatively given the highest praise or dismissed with strident rebukes. Here I propose reading Heidegger's engagement with the unthought in his work as he grapples with the unthought in his philosophical forbearers, particularly Husserl and Kant.

Notes

1 *Logic*, trans. Robert S. Hartman and Wolfgang Schwarz (Indianapolis: The Library of Liberal Arts, 1974), 30.
2 Husserliana XV, *Zur Phänomenologie der Intersubjektivität*, Texte aus dem Nachlass, Dritter Teil, 1929–35, ed. Iso Kern (The Hague, Netherlands: Martinus Nijhoff, 1973), 537.
3 GA 60, 18/13.
4 GA 3, xiv/xviii.
5 GA 41, 153/150 and GA 94, 219.
6 GA 56/57, 219/187.
7 For a defense of these claims, carried out in reference to Husserl and Heidegger, see Chad Engelland, *Ostension: Word Learning and the Embodied Mind* (Cambridge, MA: MIT Press, 2014), 193–214; and "Heidegger and the Human Difference," *Journal of the American Philosophical Association* 1 (2015): 175–93.
8 *The Possibility of Transcendental Philosophy* (Dordrecht: Martinus Nijhoff Publishers, 1985), 214–16. To be sure, Mohanty defends phenomenological transcendental philosophy from what he sees as Heidegger's rejection of it. Ibid., 217–19 and 234–40. Crowell, however, underscores the importance of transcendental phenomenology for Heidegger as well; the difference is that for Husserl it has epistemological and for Heidegger ontological implications. *Husserl, Heidegger, and the Space of Meaning* (Evanston, IL: Northwestern University Press, 2001), 168–9.
9 SZ 50/490.
10 *Being-in-the-World: A Commentary on Heidegger's 'Being and Time,' Division I* (Cambridge, MA: MIT Press, 1991), 30.
11 See Robert Sokolowski, *Introduction to Phenomenology* (Cambridge: Cambridge University Press, 2000); John Drummond, *Husserlian Intentionality and Non-Foundational Realism: Noema and Object* (Dordrecht: Kluwer, 1990); and Dan Zahavi, *Husserl's Phenomenology* (Stanford, CA: Stanford University Press, 2003), 53–68.

12 Several recent edited volumes indicate that this following may nevertheless be growing, both inside and outside the phenomenological movement. See *From Kant to Davidson: Philosophy and the Idea of the Transcendental*, ed. Jeff Malpas (New York: Routledge, 2003); *Transcendental Philosophy and Naturalism*, ed. Peter Sullivan and Joel Smith (Oxford: Oxford University Press, 2011); *Phenomenology and the Transcendental*, ed. Sara Heinämaa, Mirja Hartimo, and Timo Miettinen (New York: Routledge, 2014); and *The Transcendental Turn*, ed. Sebastian Gardner and Matthew Grist (New York: Oxford University Press, 2015).

13 Crowell, *The Space of Meaning*; Crowell, *Normativity and Phenomenology in Husserl and Heidegger* (Cambridge: Cambridge University Press, 2013); Crowell and Malpas, *Transcendental Heidegger* (Stanford, CA: Stanford University Press, 2007); Malpas, *Heidegger's Topology: Being, Place, World* (Cambridge, MA: The MIT Press, 2006); Dahlstrom, *Heidegger's Concept of Truth* (Cambridge: Cambridge University Press, 2001); Dahlstrom, "Heidegger's Transcendentalism," *Research in Phenomenology* 35 (2005): 29–54; William Blattner, *Heidegger's Temporal Idealism* (Cambridge: Cambridge University Press, 1999); Taylor Carman, *Heidegger's Analytic: Interpretation, Discourse, and Authenticity in 'Being and Time'* (Cambridge: Cambridge University Press, 2003); Tristan Moyle, *Heidegger's Transcendental Aesthetic: An Interpretation of the 'Ereignis'* (Aldershot: Ashgate Publishing, 2005); and Lee Braver, *A Thing of This World: A History of Continental Anti-Realism* (Evanston, IL: Northwestern University Press, 2007). A more historical approach to these themes can be found in *Heidegger, German Idealism, and Neo-Kantianism*, ed. Tom Rockmore (Amherst, NY: Humanity Books, 2000).

14 "Introduction," in *Transcendental Heidegger*, 1.

15 Crowell, *Space of Meaning*, 9–10 and 222–43; Dahlstrom, "Transcendental Truth," in *Transcendental Heidegger*, 69; Dahlstrom expands his list of transcendental "vestiges" in "Heidegger's Transcendentalism," *Research in Phenomenology* 35 (2005): 45–51.

16 "Heidegger's Topology of Being," in *Transcendental Heidegger*, 130.

17 Declève, *Heidegger et Kant* (The Hague: Nijhoff, 1970), and Schalow's two books: *The Renewal of the Heidegger-Kant Dialogue* (Albany, NY: SUNY Press, 1992) and *Departures: At the Crossroads between Heidegger and Kant* (Berlin: Walter de Gruyter, 2013).

18 Sherover, *Heidegger, Kant, and Time* (Bloomington, IN: Indiana University Press, 1971), and Weatherspoon, *Heidegger's Interpretation of Kant: Categories, Imagination and Temporality* (New York: Palgrave Macmillan, 2003).

19 "*Kehre* and *Ereignis*: A Prolegomenon to *Introduction to Metaphysics*," in *A Companion to Heidegger's 'Introduction to Metaphysics'*, ed. Polt and Gregory Fried, 3–16 (New Haven: Yale University Press, 2001); Sheehan, "A Paradigm Shift in Heidegger Research," *Continental Philosophy Review* 34 (2001): 183–202; "Astonishing! Things Make Sense," in Daniel Dahlstrom, ed. *Gatherings: The Heidegger Circle Annual* 1 (2011): 1–25; Sheehan, *Making Sense of Heidegger: A Paradigm Shift* (London: Rowman and Littlefield, 2015).

20 *Engaging Heidegger* (Toronto: University of Toronto Press, 2010), and *Heidegger's Way of Being*. (Toronto: University of Toronto Press, 2014).

21 "*Kehre* and *Ereignis*," 8. See Aristotle, *De Anima*, 424a1 and 429c24–25.

22 "A Paradigm Shift in Heidegger Research," 200.

23 "*Kehre*," 7.

24 "*Kehre*," 9.

25 *Making Sense of Heidegger*, 222.

26 *Heidegger's Way of Being*, 4.

27 *Heidegger's Way of Being*, 100 and 8.

28 *Heidegger's Way of Being*, 4–5.

29 Sheehan says Capobianco's "questions about 'being' (summer 2003) woke [him] up from a long dogmatic slumber." See his "Dasein," in *A Companion to Heidegger*, ed. Hubert L. Dreyfus and Mark A. Wrathall (Malden, MA: Blackwell Publishing, 2005), 207. I am thankful to Jamie Despres for this reference.

30 The most significant event would be the Davos disputation between Ernst Cassirer and Martin Heidegger. For details, see Michael Friedman, *A Parting of the Ways: Carnap, Cassirer, and Heidegger* (Chicago: Open Court, 2000) and Peter E. Gordon, *Continental Divide: Heidegger, Cassirer, Davos* (Cambridge, MA: Harvard University Press, 2010). I think Friedman and Gordon are right to see the debate as significant for twentieth century intellectual history, but the debate sheds little light on the topic of this book, namely Heidegger's efforts to come to terms with his own transcendental history by revising his interpretation of Kant.

31 GA 65, 305/215.

32 *Correspondence*, trans. and ed. Arnulf Zweig (Cambridge: Cambridge University Press, 1999), 133.

33 KRV B 19.

34 *Cartesian Meditations: An Introduction to Phenomenology*, trans. Dorion Cairns (The Hague: Martinus Nijhoff, 1977), 86.

35 See Dan Zahavi, *Husserl and Transcendental Intersubjectivity: A Response to the Linguistic-Pragmatic Critique*, trans. Elizabeth A. Behnke (Athens, Ohio: Ohio University Press, 2001), 4.

36 Husserl called three of his later publications "Introductions": *Ideas Pertaining to a Pure Phenomenology and to a Phenomenological Philosophy. First Book. General Introduction to a Pure Phenomenology, The Cartesian Meditations: An Introduction to Phenomenology*, and *The Crisis of European Sciences and Transcendental Phenomenology: An Introduction to Phenomenological Philosophy*.

37 *Ideas Pertaining to a Pure Phenomenology and to a Phenomenological Philosophy, Vol. I*, trans. F. Kersten (The Hague: Martinus Nijhoff, 1982), 59. Kersten translates this latter term as "excluding," but I think that has a far too negative connotation and misses the neutrality that Husserl is trying to express.

38 *Ideas I*, 61.

39 *Ideas I*, 60.

40 Husserl notes that the metaphor of "bracketing" lends itself better to the sphere of objects and the phrase "putting out of play" seems more appropriate for the sphere of acts or consciousness. *Ideas I*, 60.

41 *The Crisis of European Sciences and Transcendental Phenomenology*, trans. David Carr (Evanston, Illinois: Northwestern University Press, 1970), 176.

42 *Crisis*, 152.

43 *Crisis*, 189.

44 Husserl does not employ the same sense for the terms *reduction* and *epoché* in all their uses. Sometimes he uses the terms to denote an abstractive process, an "abstractive epoché" with a reduction that corresponds to it, as he does when he speaks of the move to the sphere of ownness that is carried out within the transcendental reduction, *Meditations*, 95, 97. This methodic move, which one commentator calls a *reductio ad absurdum*, serves to show that—contrary to Descartes—even within my ownmost, the other remains, and there is thus no final *solus ipse*. See Mitchell P. Jones, "Transcendental Intersubjectivity and the Objects of the Human Sciences," *Symposium* 4 (2000): 213–16.

45 *Crisis*, 144ff. In contrast, Descartes failed by immediately inquiring into the *quidditas* of the ego, rather than its *how* or manner of givenness. See *Crisis*, 79.

46 Physicalism, for example. *Crisis*, 265.

47 *Meditations*, 53. Also: "habits of thought of a centuries-old tradition are not so easy to overcome," *Crisis*, 245.

48 *Crisis*, 263.

49 *Crisis*, 249, *Meditations*, 149.

50 *Crisis*, 150.

51 *Crisis*, 145.

52 In conversation recorded by Dorion Cairns, *Conversations with Husserl and Fink* (The Hague: Marinus Nijhoff, 1976), 93. Husserl indicates this problem in the Vienna Lecture when he says that "*special* motives are required when one who is gripped in this world-life reorients himself and somehow comes to make the world itself thematic, to take up a lasting interest in it." In *Crisis*, 281. Emphasis mine.

53 *Recapitulations: Essays in Philosophy* (Washington, DC: The Catholic University of America Press), 57. See also his earlier "Reduction and Constitution," in *Ancients and Moderns*, ed. John K. Ryan (Washington, DC: The Catholic University of America Press, 1970), where chance had yet disclosed itself as a possibility: "for the worldly and human *cogito*, reduction breaks in as an anonymous and unmotivated act, a violence or a grace," 343.

54 "Since phenomenology's transcendental attitude can be clearly understood only when we have departed the natural attitude and assumed the transcendental attitude, mere recitation of the differing characteristics of these two attitudes is not sufficient to explain to one who remains in the natural attitude why he should abandon it when doing philosophy. Husserl, therefore, must provide a further account of how we are *motivated* to perform this reduction." John. J. Drummond, "Husserl on the Ways to the Performance of the Reduction," *Man and World* 8 (1975): 47.

55 "What is Husserl's *Epoche*?" *Man and World* 11 (1978): 321.

56 Zahavi, 2n2.

57 The number of ways to the reduction has been the subject of several important studies. Iso Kern argues that there are in essence three ways, viz. the Cartesian way, the way through psychology, and the ontological way, and thereby corrects such "eminent interpreters" as Rudolf Boehm and Eugen Fink who thought there were four, because they saw a way through the critique of the positive sciences. Kern sees the critique of the positive sciences and the ontological way to be ultimately the same path. John Drummond criticizes Kern's view, arguing that there are in the end but two *motivated* ways to the reduction, because the way through intentional psychology is unmotivated. See Kern, "The Three Ways to the Transcendental Phenomenological Reduction in the Philosophy of Edmund Husserl," in *Husserl: Expositions and Appraisals*, ed. Frederick A. Elliston and Peter McCormick (Notre Dame, Indiana: University of Notre Dame Press, 1977), 126–49, and Drummond, "Husserl on the Ways to the Performance of the Reduction," *Man and World* 8 (1975): 47–69.

58 *Crisis*, 155.

59 Though see Husserl's remarks in *Erste Philosophie II*: "*Niemand kann in die Philosophie hineingeraten.*" Rather, the philosopher must resolve to be radically self-grounded. Quoted in Lenkowski, "Husserl's *Epoche*," 304.

60 *Crisis*, 165.

61 "The first breakthrough of this universal a priori of correlation between experienced object and manners of givenness (which occurred during work

on my *Logical Investigations* around 1898) affected me so deeply that my whole subsequent life-work has been dominated by the task of systematically elaborating on this a priori of correlation. The further course of the reflections in this text will show how, when human subjectivity was brought into the problems of correlation, a radical transformation of the meaning of these problems became necessary which finally led to the phenomenological reduction to absolute, transcendental subjectivity." *Crisis*, 166.

62 *Crisis*, 243.

63 *Crisis*, 247.

64 *Crisis*, 147.

65 "The Vienna Lecture," in *Crisis*, 275.

66 *Crisis*, 15. Emphasis mine. Because the Greek *telos* leads to *what is essential to humanity as such*, Husserl is not advocating a simple *Eurocentrism*; rather, European philosophy is motivated by a *telos* that does not belong to it because it belongs to the whole of humankind. On the limits of the appeal to history, see the final section of my concluding chapter.

67 *Crisis*, 16. Note that Husserl's understanding of the history of philosophy leads to a very positive appraisal of Descartes.

68 *Crisis*, 192. See Prufer, *Recapitulations*, 50.

69 *Crisis*, 182.

70 Cf. Sokolowski's criticism of Husserl's "puritanical way" to start philosophy by emphasizing autonomy and responsibility: "Husserl takes the beginning of philosophy as he does because he conceives the will as the imperative faculty, instead of accepting it as rational desire." *Husserlian Meditations: How Words Present Things* (Evanston, Il: Northwestern University Press, 1974), 179. Later texts show that Husserl moves away from the position Sokolowski criticizes and toward the one he commends.

71 *Crisis*, 240. Husserl also includes in this historical motivation the way through descriptive psychology.

72 *Crisis*, 265.

73 *Crisis*, 165.

74 *Metaphysics*, 981b13–982a2, 993a11–23. Aristotle's account of the formation of the *polis* as the *telos* of earlier forms of community (family and village) is an end which is natural but in some sense historical (*Politics*, 1252b9–35).

75 KRV A 856, B 884.

76 See Theodore Kisiel, *The Genesis of Heidegger's "Being and Time"* (Berkeley: The University of California Press, 1993), 25–38; Crowell, *Space of Meaning*, 76–92; Dahlstrom, *Concept*, 5–8; Sean J. McGrath, "Heidegger and Duns Scotus on Truth and Language," *Review of Metaphysics* 57 (2003): 339–58; and John van Buren, *The Young Heidegger: Rumor of a Hidden King* (Bloomington: Indiana University Press, 1994), 70–112.

77 GA 1c, 400–1/63 and 408/67. On these three tasks, see Crowell, *Space of Meaning*, 93–111, and van Buren, *The Young Heidegger*, 95–110.

78 GA 1c, 405/65.

79 GA 60, 17–18/12–13.

80 GA 58, 135/104.

Part I
The Shadow Is Cast

1 *Being and Time* (1927)

In the confusion and lack of discipline in today's "thinking," one needs an almost scholastic formulation of its ways in the shape of characterized "questions."

—Martin Heidegger, 1936[1]

Heidegger captured the attention of many through the power of his questioning. But just what, at bottom, was he questioning? In the *Contributions*, he says he has only one question, which he calls "the question of all questions."[2] As readers of *Being and Time* know, this is "the question of the meaning of being" or what in the *Contributions* is called "the question of the truth of be-ing." Yet, the careful reader of *Being and Time* should find herself puzzled, for the sprawling work that proposes to work out the meaning of being does nothing of the sort. Instead there are analyses concentrated on the *questioner* of the meaning of being, the one who transcends entities. There is no posing of the question concerning the meaning of being in general let alone an answer to the question. There are indeed clues as to how he would handle the question but there is no systematic treatment as promised. What is the source of the confusion? The introductory matter of *Being and Time* (SZ) introduces a two-part work with three divisions each, and yet the work that follows includes but two divisions of the first part (SZ I.1–2, not I.3 or II.1–3). From the first, systematic part, only two out of the three divisions appear, and these divisions first pose (SZ I.1) and then answer (SZ I.2) the preparatory question about the questioner of being, whom he calls "Dasein." The third, unpublished division (SZ I.3) was to have posed and answered the fundamental question about the meaning of being. The introduction accentuates but one question, the fundamental question about being's meaning; emphasis is placed on Dasein as the means to formulate the fundamental question, but the specific question about Dasein itself is left without formulation. Hence, the published *Being and Time* has a question about the meaning of being with no answer and an answer about Dasein with no question; the work appears to have only one question, which it never gets around to asking. Commentators mishandle the problematic in various ways; they fail to distinguish and relate the preliminary question about Dasein and the fundamental question about the meaning of being.[3] The analytic becomes misunderstood as but a philosophical anthropology, and his question about the meaning of being in general becomes either subjective or purely aporetic.

The Heidegger of both the *Contributions* and *Being and Time* targets one fundamental question, but he thinks he can do so only by means of a preparatory question. From the moment his pen touched the paper to write the first line of *Being and Time*, he knew the preparatory question was inadequate. After all, that is why he called it preparatory. But he also knew it was essential, which is why he began with it. The published *Being and Time* (SZ I.1–2) was intended to be transitional to the question and answer of the unpublished section (SZ I.3) and *Contributions*.

What then is the difference between the Heidegger of *Being and Time* and the Heidegger of *Contributions*? When he wrote *Being and Time* he thought both questions, the preparatory and the fundamental question, were broadly transcendental in nature. The main difference between Heidegger early and late is the realization that the fundamental question, while targeted by the preliminary transcendental question, is not itself adequately stated in transcendental terms. So, here is the correct way to view the situation: Heidegger had but one fundamental question that could be arrived at only via a transitional question that he always knew was transitional. The published portion of *Being and Time* worked out the transitional question in dialogue with the transcendental tradition in order to target the domain of the fundamental question. Heidegger came to realize that the transcendental approach distorted the domain of the fundamental question *even as it led into it*. Hence, Heidegger comes to criticize the form of the transitional-transcendental question while simultaneously recommending it as the only path into the domain of his later thinking. Disentangling Heidegger's two transcendental questions is the key to making sense of Heidegger.

While writing *Being and Time*, Heidegger has two transcendental questions, a preparatory one about the timely openness of Dasein, and a fundamental one about the temporal reciprocity of that openness and being. Once he was within the transcendental domain, thanks to the success of the preparatory question, he can see the inadequacy of its terms for formulating the fundamental question. He thereafter must sustain this ambiguity: to recommend the preparatory question and its transcendental character in order to grant entry to its domain and yet to deny the adequacy of the transcendental for formulating the fundamental question. This joint affirmation and denial of transcendental philosophy makes sense only in light of a distinction between his two questions. The importance of the transcendental questions in Heidegger's clarified path of thinking will then come to the fore.

To this end, I must introduce an array of distinctions. In the ambit of *Being and Time*, Heidegger employs three senses of transcendence.[4] The first is the "*transcendence of Dasein's being*," the subjectivity of the subject as that entity open to entities within the world. This sense recalls and surpasses Kant but also Aristotle and Augustine.[5] The second is the *transcendence of being*, which Heidegger calls the "transcendens pure and simple." This sense recalls and surpasses the Aristotelian tradition. Finally, the "*transcendental horizon*" *of time* is that in terms of which the particular transcendence of Dasein and the universal transcendence of being are related. It is the horizon for the questioner who is Dasein and the questioned that is being; it specifies the site, field, domain, or openness of philosophy. This sense was only obscurely, if at all, glimpsed by Kant. The first is the target of his preliminary or preparatory question; the second is the target of the traditional question of being; the third is the target of his fundamental question, the *toward-which* or *horizon* of being. The first sense corresponds to divisions one and two of the published *Being and Time* (SZ I.1–2); the second sense is subordinated to the third, and both correspond to the unpublished third division (SZ I.3). The three senses of transcendence are deeply entwined with the division of questions and the very structure of *Being and Time*.

Along with the three senses of transcendence and the two principal transcendental questions, another distinction is necessary. The insufficiency of the preparatory question, an insufficiency indicated in its very "preparatory" character, differs in kind from the insufficiency of the transcendental formulation of the fundamental question. While writing *Being and Time*, Heidegger already knew the preparatory question was only a way, but he did not yet realize that the fundamental question was finally more than could be said in transcendental terms. The failure to keep these two insufficiencies distinct leads to misunderstandings about the genuine difference between Heidegger, early and late, a difference in terminology but not of domain to be thought. The way to the domain of thought, early and late, is transcendental (SZ I.1–2), but late and not early, the transcendental is incapable of naming all that shows up within that domain (SZ I.3).

By relating Heidegger's two principal questions, this chapter shows that his fascination with the transcendental turn was substantive and permanent. By remedying the shortcomings of Husserl and Kant, he developed a transformed transcendental program that, despite some later adjustment, would continue to determine the trajectory of his path of thinking until the end. In the third and fourth chapters, I will turn to the attempt to leap over that shadow. In this chapter, I distinguish and relate Heidegger's two principal questions in order to demonstrate his enduring transcendental commitments. First, I identify his two questions as they emerge in dialogue with Husserl and as they are formulated more clearly in the book on Kant. Then I examine *Being and Time* and his efforts to formulate the preparatory question in division one (SZ I.1), his efforts to give a preliminary answer in division two (SZ I.2), and finally his efforts, which belong to the unpublished third division (SZ I.3), to reverse the preparatory question into the fundamental question. I reconsider the transcendental question in view of his later criticisms of it. A key part of my strategy is to respect the divisions of *Being and Time* even while reading his other works; this amounts to a kind of *topography* of Heidegger's questions. In the second part of the chapter, I turn to the question of history (SZ II) and show that the reading of history at work in *Being and Time* in fact is a function of an early engagement with Husserlian method. Heidegger's critique of historical prejudice was the fruit of his reading of Husserl and his appropriation of the transcendental turn.

1 Husserl's Shadow and Heidegger's Two Tasks

Against the backdrop of Husserl's philosophy, Heidegger clearly distinguishes the preparatory and the fundamental questions in the summer semester 1925 lecture course. He thinks that transcendental phenomenology recovers the possibility of ancient ontology, but it does so by neglecting the being of the transcendental ego. In contrast to the Neo-Kantian epistemologists, Husserl and Scheler are noteworthy in their concern for ontology, but neither gives a satisfactory account of the being of the human being as the dative of manifestation. Heidegger would very much like to pose again the ancient question about being, but he must first appropriate phenomenology in such a way that he clarifies the being of the dative of manifestation, the transcendental ego. The necessity for asking the preliminary question is to remedy a lack in phenomenology itself, which reveals an even greater lack in the modern epistemological tradition.

Husserl's transcendental phenomenological reduction uncovers a "veritable abyss" between the absolute being of consciousness and the adumbrated being of reality.[6] What the phenomenological reduction reveals is a radical distinction in being. Husserl writes and Heidegger quotes, "The system of categories most emphatically must start from this most radical of all distinctions of being—being *as consciousness* and being as 'transcendent' being '*manifesting*' itself in consciousness."[7] For Husserl, this distinction is founded on the fundamental difference in givenness: consciousness is given without adumbration and transcendent entities are given with adumbration. Heidegger appropriates this phenomenological difference while transforming its terms. Specifically, he agrees that the human being is the dative of manifestation, but he is bothered by the paradoxical fact that the dative of manifestation for the being of entities is also an entity. In his terms, the human being, Dasein, is both ontological and ontic. This peculiar conjunction becomes his focus, and he purifies the Husserlian distinction with the following question about the unity of the human being:

> How is it at all possible that this sphere of absolute position, pure consciousness, which is supposed to be separated from every transcendence by an absolute gulf, is at the same time united with reality in the unity of a real human being, who himself occurs as a real object in the world?[8]

He takes as his task thinking through this paradoxical conjunction, and it is this problematic that provides the immediate context for appreciating his formulation of the transcendental question: How must this entity, Dasein, be, in order to be open to all entities? Husserl did not realize that intentionality "must revolutionize the whole concept of the human being," as Heidegger would say in 1928.[9] We are not one natural kind among many, for we are as *opened* to things.[10]

Heidegger does not just want to remedy this lack of philosophical anthropology in Husserl. He also wants to continue on the path, which Husserl and Scheler have already blazed, and work out the "system of categories" or the question of being itself. Such a question concerns, among other things, basic distinctions in being. The dialogue with Husserl, then, yields two neglected questions: "*Two fundamental neglects pertaining to the question of being can be identified. On the one hand, the question of the being of this specific entity, of the acts, is neglected; on the other, we have the neglect of the question of the meaning of being itself.*"[11] In Heidegger's own terms, there is a question about Dasein and a question about the horizon of being as such, though their inter-relationship in this text is somewhat unclear. On the one hand, they are two expressions of one fundamental question;[12] on the other, they are independent of each other.[13]

The preparatory question about Dasein fulfills a need Heidegger expressed in 1924 to pose the question about the meaning of being in a concrete and not merely formal way. To do so, he realized that he needed to enter into the right domain by means of specific preparation: "Rather the task is to understand that this putting of the question concerning the meaning of being itself requires an elaboration, an elaboration of the ground [*Boden*] upon which the interrogation of entities as to their being is at all possible. We need to uncover and elaborate the *milieu* in which ontological research can and has to move in general."[14] The emphasis on domain was undoubtedly suggested to him by Husserl, who says in *Ideas I* that the reduction achieves "the free vista of 'transcendentally' purified phenomena and, therewith, the field of phenomenology in our peculiar sense."[15] Husserl thinks Kant was the first to correctly see this field.[16] In 1929, Heidegger says that Husserl's phenomenology "created an entirely new space for philosophical questioning, a space with new claims, transformed assessments, and a fresh regard for the hidden powers of the great tradition of Western philosophy."[17] On the final page of the published portion of *Being and Time*, Heidegger will recall the need to secure the domain or horizon of question and answer.[18] This is the "field" for posing the cardinal question.[19] The function of the preparatory question is necessary for a first approach to the domain occupied by the fundamental question. Indeed, in the 1925 lecture course, what will become SZ I.1 bears the title, "Preparatory Description of the Field in Which the Phenomenon of Time Becomes Visible."[20] Openness, target of both the transcendental and demystifying approaches to Heidegger scholarship, first emerges out of the preparatory question about Dasein.

Shortly after the 1927 publication of *Being and Time*, Heidegger had occasion to clarify his relationship to Husserl in the failed attempt to collaborate on the *Encyclopedia Britannica* article. Heidegger again agrees with Husserl that the dative of manifestation differs in being from manifested entities, but again he pushes further than Husserl to grasp the unity of the human as both the dative and an entity. Now he can state that this is *Being and Time*'s central problem, targeted by the preliminary question about Dasein:

> *What is the mode of being of the entity in which "world" is constituted?* That is *Being and Time*'s central problem—namely, a fundamental ontology of Dasein. It has to be shown that the mode of being of human Dasein is totally different from that of all other entities and that, as the mode of being that it is, it harbors right within itself the possibility of transcendental constitution.[21]

He also puts the priority of Dasein in Husserlian terms. "Accordingly, the problem of being is related—all-inclusively—to what constitutes and to what gets constituted."[22] Dasein is peculiar in being the entity that constitutes other entities (i.e., allows them to show themselves from themselves).

Two years later, Heidegger brought to print an " 'historical' introduction" that aimed to "clarify the problematic" of the published portion of that text.[23] As Kant's *Prolegomena* stands to his *Critique of Pure Reason*, so Heidegger's *Kant and the Problem of Metaphysics* stands to his *Being and Time*. Heidegger will come to reassess the book's worth as an interpretation of Kant but not as a presentation of his own questioning.[24] In this book, Heidegger formulates his preparatory or preliminary question of SZ I.1–2 in its clearest terms: "How must the finite entity that we call 'human' be according to its innermost essence so that it can be at all open to an entity that it itself is not and that therefore must be able to show itself from itself?"[25] He formulates his fundamental, cardinal, or lasting question of SZ I.3 as follows: "From whence are we at all to comprehend the like of being, with the entire wealth of articulations and references which are included in it?"[26] While the preparatory question traverses entities toward being, the cardinal question traverses being toward time. It is not the metaphysical question about entities, for these have been transcended, but it is also not the ontological-transcendental question about being. Rather, the question concerns that which engenders the meanings of being. The answer is that time or more specifically the horizon of Dasein's timeliness, temporality, is that out of which we understand being. Heidegger becomes increasingly critical of the language he employs, but as I will show, the critique relies on the initial success of the transcendental program.

The dialogue with Husserl comes to expression in this encounter with Kant. We can rekindle the question of being only if we pay heed to the being of the questioner of being. Husserl's wonder before the distinction between the dative and given entities is presupposed in the preparatory question, which targets the specific being of the dative as that entity who is the dative. Having now identified the preparatory and fundamental questions, let us see how they illumine the structure of *Being and Time*.

2 The Preparatory Question (SZ I.1–2)

At the outset of the first division (SZ I.1, §§12–13), Heidegger severely criticizes epistemology and the traditional inquiry into the subject-object relation with its difficulties of explaining how consciousness moves outside of itself to an object. More fundamental than the epistemological subject is Dasein's being-in-the-world or transcendence: Dasein's "primary kind of being is such that it is always 'outside' near entities which it encounters and which belongs to a world already discovered."[27] The essence of Dasein *enables* us to be such that we encounter or access entities that are independent of us. That is, any actual intentional relation to entities is founded on a prior power to dwell among them, expressed variously as being-in-the-world, transcendence, or openness.[28] He identifies the Aristotelian enabling power of essence and the Kantian condition for the possibility of cognition. He says that Kant's concern for the "condition for the possibility" is "the transcendental concept of essence."[29] We are open as dis-closed, thrown open in our disposed understanding. At the heart of Heidegger's preparatory question is wonder about our essential openness to otherness.

In §§ 41–44 Heidegger points to the understanding-of-being and transcendence as the preliminary answer to the preparatory question about our ability to receive entities: ". . . only if the understanding of being *is*, do entities as entities become accessible."[30] The understanding of being comes about because Dasein projects possibilities for itself on the basis of its being thrown into the world, and only thereby is it able to encounter other entities. Accordingly, he defines "care," the *being* of Dasein, as "ahead-of-itself-being-already-in-(the-world) as being-near (entities encountered within-the-world)."[31] In 1928, he clarifies the meaning of transcendence, the subjectivity of the subject, or being-in-the-world. Our understanding of being steps beyond the entity and enables us to receive it in its otherness:

> Because the step beyond [*der Überschritt*] exists with Dasein, and because with it entities, which Dasein is not, are stepped beyond, such entities become manifest as such, i.e., in themselves. Nothing else but transcendence, which has in advance surpassed [*übersprungen*] entities, first makes it possible for these, previously surpassed *as entities*, ontically to *stand opposite* [gegenübersteht] and as opposite to be apprehended in themselves.[32]

We can encounter entities because we tend out beyond them and thereby meet with their otherness. In *Being and Time*, Heidegger follows Augustine in terming this phenomenon, "care," but he also finds points of contact with Aristotle's "for-the-sake-of-which" and Kant's concern for *a priori* synthetic judgments.

Transcendence enables us to encounter entities, but what enables transcendence? The unfolding of the preliminary question about Dasein finds itself confronted with "temporality as the metaphysical essence of Dasein."[33] In SZ I.2, Heidegger does not leave the problem of transcendence behind, but keeps it in mind throughout, explicitly dealing with it in § 69.[34] Indeed, the clearest formulation of the transcendental question is to be found in that section, although it is conflated with the possibility of science: "What makes it ontologically possible for entities to be encountered within-the-world and objectified as so encountered?"[35] He says the answer is transcendence and its timely constitution: "This can be answered by recourse to the transcendence of the world—a transcendence with an ecstatic-horizonal foundation." Transcendence is itself made possible by timeliness. Showing why and how this is the case is his principal task in SZ I.2.

Now, Heidegger's discussion of the connection between ecstasis and horizon is sketchy at best. We can make some progress in understanding what he had in mind by attending to the job he thinks it must do to account for the condition for the possibility of transcendence. Timeliness must account for the dual aspect of transcendence. First, it must account for the origination of the transcending movement. Second, it must account for the determinate direction of the transcending movement, whether to one's own possibilities in projection or in making something present. Dasein, to encounter others, not only transcends, but it transcends in specific ways. Timeliness has two essential characteristics that account for the tendencies of Dasein as well at its determinacy. As ecstatic, timeliness originates the tendencies, and as horizonal, it originates the determinacy of the tendencies. Timeliness, because it ecstatically tends and tends horizonally, provides the matrix of possible relations in which Dasein transcends toward itself beyond others. Let us take each of these characteristics in turn.

Timeliness is ecstatic (§ 65). To secure the overthrow of the subject-object paradigm, Heidegger must show the ground for both the dative and the manifesting entities. Timeliness is a unity of three ecstases: the future, the having been, and the present. The threefold unity corresponds to the threefold unity of care as projecting in understanding, thrown in dispositions, and falling in making present. Timeliness, then, unites and also specifies the matrix of relations of transcendence.

> Future, having-been, and present, show the phenomenal characteristics of "towards-itself," the "back-to," and "letting-be-encountered-by." . . . *Timeliness is the originary "outside- itself" in and for itself.* . . . Timeliness is not, prior to this, an entity which first emerges from *itself*; its essence is to bring forth in the unity of the *ecstases*.[36]

Timeliness, as ecstatic, accounts for the transcendental openness of Dasein. It stands Dasein out of itself in determinate directions toward its authentic self, its world, or entities in the world.

Timeliness is horizonal (§ 69). Timeliness is not ecstatic and as an addition horizonal. Rather, as ecstatic it is horizonal. "Ecstases are not simply raptures in which one gets carried away. Rather, there belongs to each ecstasis a 'whereto' of getting carried away. This 'whereto' of the ecstasis we call the 'horizonal schema.'"[37] Heidegger himself will regret using the word *horizon*, and many commentators follow suit, but he uses it to name something essential to ecstatic timeliness. The word is dispensable, but the determinacy of the ecstases that the word designates is not. He needs it in some form to account for the determinate domain of intentionality. He uses the language of horizon to articulate how the ecstatical unity of timeliness accomplishes the opening up of the place, the world, the "Da," which belongs to Da-sein and in which other entities can be encountered.[38] Ecstases alone do not grant the wherein of world.

> The horizon of timeliness as a whole determines that *toward-which* factically existing entities are essentially *disclosed*. With one's factical being-here [Da-sein], a potentiality-for-being is in each case projected in the horizon of the future, one's "being-already" is disclosed in the horizon of having been, and that with which one concerns oneself is discovered in the horizon of the present. . . . [O]n the basis of the horizonal constitution of the ecstatical unity of timeliness, there belongs to that entity which is in each case its own "here," [Da] something like a world that has been disclosed.[39]

With the horizon of timeliness, the answer to the question, "What nourishes the toward-which of the understanding of being?" is achieved. Timeliness itself, in its ecstatic-horizonal constitution, enables and nourishes the toward-which of the understanding of being. By delimiting the ecstases, the horizon provides the "enclosure" (*der Umschluß*) for understanding and thereby enables transcendence.[40] "Horizon" expresses the *finis* of finitude.

The finite entity that we call "human" must be according to its innermost essence *timely as ecstatic-horizonal* so that it can be open to an entity that it itself is not and that therefore must be able to show itself from itself. To receive what is, we must be ecstatically opened and horizonally related. "Timeliness brings itself forth" (*Zeitlichkeit sich zeitigt*), and this process is the "primal event" (*das Urereignis*) of world-entry in which Dasein can meet with entities.[41] In bringing itself forth, timeliness always already draws Dasein beyond entities toward Dasein's futural possibilities, and this surpassing enables entities to be present in their otherness. Heidegger writes, "Being-in-the-world, transcending toward world, brings itself forth as timeliness and is only possible in this way. This implies that world-entry only happens if timeliness brings itself forth. And only if this happens can entities manifest themselves as entities."[42] To access an entity, then, is not to have an idea of it or for it to produce causally a representation in us; rather, to access is to draw something near and allow it to show itself as it is itself. Timeliness, then, enables Dasein to transcend in the peculiar sense of being other than the epistemological dyad immanent-transcendent. In transcending entities, Dasein is always already intimate with them.[43]

In the final pages of *Being and Time*'s published text, Heidegger looks back at the preparatory question and forward to the cardinal question. He warns that however "illuminating" the answer to the preparatory question may be, with its distinction between the being of Dasein and the being of other entities, philosophy cannot rest content with it.[44] Instead, it must press forward within the space it has won and inquire into the cardinal question. "[O]ur way of exhibiting the constitution of Dasein's being remains only *a way*. Our *aim* is to work out the question of being in general."[45]

3 Reversing the Question (SZ I.3)

The clarification of the preparatory transcendental question makes it possible to understand its reversal and persistence in Heidegger's clarified itinerary. The original intent of SZ I.3 was to effect a shift from the question about Dasein and its preparatory attempt to clarify being, to the question about being as such in terms of its temporal horizon. This shift involves a reversal of perspectives. Instead of asking a particular question about the being of Dasein in terms of timeliness, Heidegger poses the universal question of being in terms of temporality. In making this shift, he does not leave the analysis of Dasein behind, but he takes it up as one of the questions of being. The title of SZ I leaves for SZ I.3 the task of explicating "time as the transcendental horizon of the question of being." In 1929 he writes,

> What has been published so far of the investigations on "Being and Time" has no other task than that of a concrete projection unveiling *transcendence* (Cf. §§ 12–83; especially § 69). This in turn occurs for the purpose of enabling the *sole* guiding intention, clearly indicated in the *title* of the *whole* of Part I, of attaining the "*transcendental* horizon of the *question* concerning being." All concrete interpretations, above all that of time, are to be evaluated *solely* in the perspective of *enabling* the *question* of being.[46]

SZ I.3, then, must shift from the transcendence of Dasein (SZ I.1–2) to the transcendental horizon for the question of being. The preparatory question about Dasein must yield to the cardinal question about the horizon of being's understandability. In 1927, he formulates the "beginning, final, and basic question of philosophy," topic of SZ I.3, in the following way: "Whence—that is, from which pre-given horizon—do we understand the like of being?"[47]

Now, SZ I.3 was initially held back because of publishing constraints, then because Heidegger was unsatisfied with its formulation, and finally because he was unsatisfied with any formulations possible within the horizon of the work.[48] My task here is to indicate how SZ I.3 was to shift from the preliminary question to the fundamental question, and then how the fundamental question is related to the genuine intention of SZ I.3. In section 5, I contend that his fundamental question belongs to SZ I.3, which is to say, it remains accessible by means of SZ I.1–2 and accomplishes the original intent of SZ I.3 to universalize the question about being. What is changed is the language about condition for the possibility and essence and hence the basic characterization of timeliness as that which enables Dasein to encounter entities.

From the Timeliness of Dasein to the Temporality of Dasein and Being

How, then, does the preparatory question about the transcendence of Dasein transform itself into the cardinal question about the temporal relation of Dasein's transcendence to the transcendence of being? Heidegger selected the question about Dasein as the way to the question about being, because entities with the character of Dasein have a special relation to the question of being. "In the question of the meaning of being there is no 'circular reasoning' but rather a remarkable 'relatedness backward or forward' which what we are asking about (being) bears to the inquiry itself as a mode of being of an entity."[49] SZ I.1–2 looks forward from Dasein to being; the task of SZ I.3 is, among other things, to look back from being to Dasein, to show the temporal origin of existence. SZ I.3 also needs to show the genesis of the other meanings of being, its modifications, and its derivatives. The question drives us beyond the question of "being as such" to the question of being's origin: "From whence are we at all to comprehend the like of being, with the entire wealth of articulations and references which are included in it?"[50]

The question "How must we be to receive what is?" is reversed into: "How does the ecstatic-horizonal unity of time engender the various meanings of being, including Dasein's existence as opened to that being?" In §§ 6 and 83, as he looks forward to SZ I.3, he says that since timeliness grounds Dasein, being must likewise arise in timeliness. "*Time* needs to be *explicated originarily as the horizon for the understanding of being, and in terms of timeliness as the being of Dasein, which understands being.*"[51] Heidegger characterizes this shift as the turn from the timeliness of Dasein to the temporality of being, the turn from *Zeitlichkeit* to *Temporalität*.

> Thus the way in which being and its modes and characteristics have their meaning determined originarily in terms of time, is what we shall call its "*temporal*" determinateness. Thus the fundamental ontological task of interpreting being as such includes working out the *temporality of being*. In the exposition of the problematic of temporality the question of the meaning of being will first be concretely answered.[52]

To justify the turn from timeliness to temporality, Heidegger needs to show why timeliness itself is the ultimate horizon and can thus serve as temporality, the "horizon for the understanding of being." Dreyfus, for one, says that Heidegger's own principles render such a turn impossible, for a deeper horizon could always become accessible. Indeed, Heidegger seems to admit as much in *Being and Time* itself.[53] Why then does Heidegger think there is reason to regard timeliness as ultimate? It is the deepest horizon, because it is productive and articulates itself ecstatically and horizonally. It thereby motivates the determinate trajectories of understanding and provides the context in which something like intentionality or understanding's toward-which is possible.

> Because the ecstatic-horizonal unity of timeliness is intrinsically self-projection pure and simple, because as ecstatic it makes possible all projecting upon . . . and represents, together with the horizon belonging to the ecstasis, the condition of possibility of a toward-which, an

out-toward-which in general, it can no longer be asked upon what the schemata can on their part be projected, and so on in infinitum.[54]

The ecstatic-horizonal unity of timeliness, as the origin of the possibilities of understanding, can serve as temporality and show the ways the various meanings of being originate. Timeliness is the ultimate originary context, that which enables all understanding, and for that reason, Heidegger takes it as the ultimate horizon. It is earlier than every possible earlier because it enables all possibilities. This is just another way of saying that timeliness is the ground for the *a priori*, for temporality, and only because of it are all possibilities *a priori* as well.[55] It must be said that Heidegger does not develop talk of the ecstatic-horizonal character of timeliness to his satisfaction, and he ultimately will find such language unhelpful for saying what must be said. The important thing to note is the role Heidegger thought timeliness had to play in the context of SZ I.3. As I will discuss below and in Chapter 4, he will come to find other language more appropriate for characterizing the phenomenon.

In light of time as the horizon for the understanding of being, SZ I.3 was to undertake two tasks. The first was to handle four sets of problems concerning being: (1) the ontological difference; (2) the basic articulation of being; (3) the possible modifications of being and the unity of its manifoldness; (4) and the truth-character of being.[56] The second was to work out the phenomenological method, including its "*a priori*" terms as well as the continued priority of Dasein even within the cardinal question. This last point calls for considerable amplification. In shifting from the particular question about the being of Dasein to the universal question of being, it turns out he does not leave behind the priority of Dasein but it obstinately announces itself in every aspect of the universalized question of being. Heidegger's new elaboration of SZ I.3 in the summer semester 1927 lecture course makes this especially clear. Whenever he clarifies the four systematically related problem-areas of being, Dasein comes to the center again and again. He seems uncertain regarding the phenomenological solution of these problems but not about the priority of Dasein. The priority of Dasein is especially apparent in the truth-character of being:

> It is precisely the analysis of the truth-character of being which shows that being also is, as it were, based in an entity, namely, in the Dasein. It gives being [*Sein gibt es*] only if the understanding of being, hence Dasein, exists. This entity accordingly lays claim to a distinctive priority in the problematic of ontology. It makes itself manifest in all discussions of the basic problems of ontology and above all in the fundamental question of the meaning of being in general.[57]

Dasein, the entity that is ontically distinctive in that it is ontological, thus introduces into the domain of ontology an ineluctably ontic foundation.

Husserl handled this entanglement by sharply distinguishing the transcendental attitude and the natural attitude. Only within the natural attitude are entities at issue; the transcendental attitude dispenses with entities and turns to their givenness alone. But Husserl's clarity on the issue involves the absurdity of an unbridgeable chasm between the transcendental ego and the mundane ego. Again, Heidegger regards this as a neglect of the specific being of Dasein, which can lose itself into the world inauthentically or gain itself authentically as that for whom the world is disclosed. Hence, Heidegger, in the crucial SZ I.3 speaks of "the ontic foundation of ontology."[58] In the *Cartesian Meditations*, Husserl rejects this as the absurd position of "transcendental realism" in which the dative of the world is also a "tag end of the world."[59] Now, Heidegger does not intend to "define entities as entities by tracing them back in their origin to some other entities, as if being had the character of some possible entity."[60] What he has in mind is not an ontic explanation, then, but an ontological one. Dasein, that entity that is ontological, is a necessary but not sufficient condition for the givenness of being. "It gives being [*Sein gibt es*] only if disclosedness is, that is to say, if truth is. But truth is only if an entity exists which opens up, which discloses, and indeed in such a way that disclosing belongs itself to the mode of being of this entity. We ourselves are such an entity."[61] Without the disclosive activity of such an entity, ontology is simply not possible: "Ontology cannot be established in a purely ontological manner. Its own possibility is referred back to an entity, that is, to something ontic—the Dasein."[62] In the domain of SZ I.3 it becomes necessary, then, to enact a third, even more radical interpretation of Dasein.[63] This is the analysis of Dasein qua transcendental ego, which is nonetheless necessarily always also an entity. To be given, being needs a dative, and to be a dative, one needs to be an entity. Heidegger will come to be somewhat troubled by this state of affairs, and I will return to the point below.

Just what does the temporal repetition of Dasein reveal? In 1928, referring to SZ I.3, Heidegger writes about how the play of timeliness enables the being of Dasein:

> Timely bringing forth [*Die Zeitigung*] is the free swinging of originary, whole timeliness; time swings itself and swings itself back. (And only because of swing is there throw, facticity, *thrownness;* and only because of swinging is there *projection.* Cf. the problem of time and being indicated in *Being and Time*.)[64]

The more radical interpretation of Dasein, then, shows not only the unity of Dasein as timeliness (SZ I.2) but the very emergence of the interplay of throw and project (*Wurf-Entwurf*) in the self-articulation of time (SZ I.3). As ecstatic and horizonal, time "brings itself forth, swinging as a worlding."[65] Time makes possible being-in-the-world, because it "is essentially a self-opening and releasing [*ein Sich-öffnen und Ent-spannen*] into a world."[66] Heidegger can then conclude that "time as pure self-affection forms the essential structure of subjectivity."[67] In Kantian terms, this swinging is the interplay of spontaneous receptivity and receptive spontaneity characteristic of the transcendental power of imagination.[68] Temporality, then, enables the interplay of thrownness and projection characteristic of that entity uniquely capable of understanding being.

Phenomenology as Temporal Science

At the heart of transcendental philosophy is the transcendental method, which involves a turn from the empirical to the transcendental standpoint. Husserl and Kant have a lot to say about such a turn, and yet Heidegger hardly ever speaks about it. In the introduction to *Being and Time*, he merely (and basically unhelpfully) rehearses the etymology of the word "phenomenology" and iterates three meanings of "transcendence" with a promise to return to the topic at greater length in SZ I.3. The later Heidegger identifies the summer semester 1927 lecture course, "The Basic Problems of Phenomenology," as "a new elaboration of division 3 of part 1 of *Being and Time*."[69] Though the third part of the course was to treat of methodology, Heidegger manages to make it only into the second projected part of the course. So we end up with a situation similar to that of *Being and Time* in that the relevant methodological section is left undeveloped. Nonetheless, the course does conclude with some important methodological indications on the heels of a protracted treatment of the timely origin of the ontological difference between being and entities. As we saw in *Being and Time*, timeliness provides the possibility of comporting ourselves to entities by enabling understanding's "toward-which," that is, being.[70] "The *distinction between being and entities is brought forth in the bringing forth of timeliness*."[71] Time is self-interpreting and articulates itself in accordance with horizonal ecstases, and therefore it serves as the end and source of projection.

> Because the ecstatic-horizonal unity of timeliness is intrinsically self-projection pure and simple, because as ecstatic it makes possible all projecting upon . . . and represents, together with the horizon belonging to the ecstasis, the condition of possibility of an toward-which, an out-toward-which in general, it can no longer be asked upon what the schemata can on their part be projected, and so on in infinitum. The series, mentioned earlier, of projections as it were inserted one before the other—understanding of entities, projection upon being, understanding of being, projection upon time—has its end at the horizon of ecstatic unity of timeliness. [. . .] But this end is nothing but the beginning and starting point for the possibility of all projecting.[72]

Phenomenology, as it were, listens to the self-articulating of timeliness and brings it to disclosure and articulation. Now, all projecting implicitly involves the distinction between being and entities so that Heidegger can even say that "existence means, as it were, 'to be in the performance of this distinction.'"[73] Since this *distinction* is always latent, there remains the possibility that it can become explicitly understood as a *difference* and thus be conceptually comprehended in *logos*.

The "bringing forth" (*Zeitigung*) of timeliness and the constitution of Dasein provides two basic possibilities for objectification and thus two basic possibilities for science and discourse. "Objectification" (*Vergegenständlichung*) here means understanding what is given as such.[74] On the one hand, *entities* can be objectified in the manner of positive science and its apophantic discourse. On the other hand, *being* can be objectified in the manner of phenomenological science and its timely discourse. Timeliness makes these two directions both possible and necessary: "*timeliness is the root* and the *ground for* both *the possibility* and, properly understood, the *factical necessity of the objectification of the given entities and the given being.*"[75] Positive science moves in the everyday direction toward entities, and phenomenological science moves in the counter tendency toward the projection of being in terms of timeliness. The "basic act" of phenomenological science is the objectification of being—that is to say, the "projection of being upon the horizon of understandability." But it is this horizon of understandability that the philosophical tradition has not methodologically secured: "The history of philosophy bears witness that all ontological interpretations, with regard to the horizon essentially necessary for them and to the assurance of that horizon, are more like a groping about than a definite methodical inquiry."[76] Why is it that this "basic act" is so overlooked? Why is it that it "is delivered up to uncertainty and stands continually in danger of being reversed"?[77] Because it "must necessarily move in a projective direction that runs counter to everyday comportment towards entities." The two directions of objectification, then, are rooted in the two directions of Dasein: either (1) falling inauthenticity and the on-hand in general or (2) resolute authenticity and the phenomenon of world. We can make ontic judgments about things and ontological judgments about the context in which we can meet with things.

Now the phenomenological science of being is both temporal and transcendental. It is *temporal*, because its objectification is made possible by temporal projection.[78] It is *transcendental*, because transcendence is what enables the understanding of being:

> Transcendence first of all makes possible existence in the sense of comporting oneself to oneself as an entity, to others as entities, and to entities in the sense of either the handy or the on-hand. Thus transcendence as such, in the sense of our interpretation, is the first

condition of possibility of the understanding of being, the first and nearest upon which an ontology has to project being. . . . The science of being thus constituted we call the science that inquires and interprets in the light of transcendence properly understood: *transcendental science.*[79]

As Heidegger has shown, though, both in the lecture course and in *Being and Time*, transcendence is rooted in the horizonal structure of timeliness and temporality: "*time is the primary horizon of transcendental science, of ontology,* or in short, it is the *transcendental horizon.*"[80] Consequently, the propositions of this science are themselves temporal: "All the propositions of ontology are *temporal propositions.* Their truths unveil structures and possibilities of being in the light of temporality. All ontological propositions have the character of *temporal truth, veritas temporalis.*"[81] And because such assertions about being are timely, they are *a priori* propositions and exhibit what makes experience possible.[82] The *logos* of phenomenology, then, because it is temporal, fulfills the original connection of truth and being and thereby exhibits authentic discourse.[83]

What Heidegger aimed to do was to bring method to the point in which it coincided with the subject matter. As Kisiel chronicles it, "The breakthrough to the topic [of *Being and Time*] is a double play of matter and method, What and How, drawn to a point where they are one and the same: a hermeneutics *of* facticity."[84] Crowell argues that the working out of this union leads "toward a hermeneutic transcendental phenomenology."[85] From what we have seen, we can say that ontology and phenomenology, being and truth, are hermeneutically brought to their primordial conceptualization in terms of the transcendence of temporality. "Every disclosure of being as the *transcendens* is transcendental knowledge. *Phenomenological truth (the disclosedness of being) is veritas transcendentalis.*" "Transcendental," then, designates the basic connection of truth and being. "Transcendental" equally names method and manner, phenomenology and ontology, and "temporality" the horizon for both.

4 The Motive for Transcendental Questioning in History (SZ II)

Being and Time not only elaborates Heidegger's systematic project, but it also offers the outline of a history of philosophy that tends toward his program. At the heart of this outline is the modern mathematical projection, which comes to undermine the ancient approach to being. That ancient approach, according to Heidegger, focused on the categories of judgment fitted to on-hand things. Dahlstrom has usefully termed this prejudice, "the logical prejudice."[86] The modern tendency, inaugurated by Descartes, takes the subject as the point of departure for a universal projection of objectivity. We can follow Heidegger in terming this "the mathematical prejudice." Heidegger's own program aims to dislodge both prejudices by means of unearthing pre-judicative but also pre-subjective disclosedness.

Heidegger hints at the toppling of the logical and mathematical prejudices in the rough indication of phenomenological method that he provides in § 7 of *Being and Time*. Crucially and pivotally, phenomenology recovers the unity of speech and experience: speech lets something be shown, and experience amounts to the self-showing of things. Against rationalist restrictions that posit a thought disconnected from experience, phenomenology proposes a thought intrinsic to experience; phenomenological thought is a *letting something be seen*.[87] Thought is subordinate to the self-showing of the phenomena. Hence, he interprets phenomenology as letting "that which shows itself be seen from itself in the very way in which it shows itself from itself."[88] The phenomena themselves constrain speech about them; phenomenology recovers the original sense of speech as subordinate to the self-showing of phenomena. In doing so, phenomenology puts us back into contact with the Greek sense of things. Now this return of thought to intuition occurs on two levels: judgment and its context. The secondary, or ontic, level is judgment; the primary, or ontological, level is the context in which we can meet with entities. Just as ordinary judgments must be rooted in experience, so articulations of the context must themselves be the fruit of experience. It is this context of experience that Heidegger says accords with the Kantian transcendental program of identifying space and time as the forms of intuition.[89] The analogy and yet difference of the two levels, judgment and context, is central to Heidegger's phenomenological transcendentalism. The logical prejudice ignores the context for judgment and the mathematical prejudice seeks to explain the context in terms of the projection of the modern subject. Heidegger's own program is to disclose the primary truth, the domain in which (among other things) judgments take place.

Heidegger has an original and developed method, which he calls "formal" or "hermeneutic indication" in the ambit of *Being and Time*. Heidegger's first and most detailed discussion of philosophical conceptuality occurs in the winter semester 1920–21 lecture course, "Introduction to the Phenomenology of Religion," although even this is incomplete. Apparently some of the non-majors complained to the dean about the difficulty of the topic, and an exasperated Heidegger reluctantly agreed to break off this crucial discussion of his method: "I will, without further consideration for the starting point and method, take a particular concrete phenomenon as the point of departure, however for me under the presupposition that you will misunderstand the entire study from beginning to end."[90] Those who would approach Heidegger and his account of history without keeping formal indication in mind are just as disadvantaged as those students. Formal indication, appropriated from Husserl, is the backbone of Heidegger's account of history. This section shows that

Heidegger's later approach to history flows from his earlier concern with formal indication, itself a development of Husserlian themes.

In the 1920–21 lecture course, Heidegger for the first time introduces his formally indicative conceptuality, and he does so as the furtherance of a distinction native to Husserl between generalization and formalization. Formal indication is still more formal than formalization because it resists the generalization still implicit in formalization. Heidegger's aim is to develop a philosophic conceptuality that includes the living relation of the self to things. Rather than a system of categories geared to things, he wants categories appropriate to our way of being open to things: "through the explication of factical Dasein, the entire traditional system of categories will be blown up—so radically new will the *categories of factical Dasein* be."[91] Before we attend to the distinction Heidegger aims to further, we need to consider the full sense of phenomenon and how it was missed by the traditional categories.

Heidegger thinks every phenomenon or experience has a threefold totality of sense. There is a content sense (a "what"), a relation-sense ("how" it is experienced), and the enactment-sense (*how* the relation-sense happens). It is this last sense that proves decisive, for it can be enacted either attitudinally or phenomenologically. If enacted attitudinally, the living relation ceases and the object comes to dominate. " 'Attitude' is a relation to objects in which the conduct [*verhalten*] is absorbed in the *material complex*. I direct myself only to the *matter*, I focus away from *myself* toward the *matter*. With this 'attitude' [*Einstellung*] the *living* relation to the object of knowledge has 'ceased' ['*eingestellt*']."[92] If enacted phenomenologically, the totality of sense is held open. " 'Phenomenology' is explication of this totality of sense; it gives the 'logos' of the phenomena, 'logos' in the sense of '*verbum internum*' (not in the sense of logicalization)."[93] Phenomenology is needed because of our natural tendency toward attitudinal enactment in which the content sense dominates.

Heidegger's phenomenological method of formal indication bears centrally on the "phenomenon of *differentiating*."[94] It provides the *how* of phenomenology itself. Curiously, Heidegger does not root his method in Husserl's specific reflections on method but rather on Husserl's distinction, both in the *Logical Investigations* and *Ideas I*, between formalization and generalization. Heidegger writes:

> Husserl first differentiated "formalization" from "generalization".... This difference had been known implicitly for a long time in mathematics (already since Leibniz), but Husserl first carried out its logical explication. He sees the meaning of the difference, above all, in terms of formal ontology and in the grounding of a pure logic of objects (*mathesis universalis*). We want to attempt to further this differentiation and, in this furtherance, explain the sense of formal indication.[95]

Heidegger follows Husserl in wielding the mathematical or formal against the logic of the general, but he goes further than Husserl in rejecting the residue of the general within the mathematical-formal itself. Husserl's program of a *mathesis universalis* is symptomatic of this persistent generalization.

Heidegger presents Husserl's distinction as follows. Generalization proceeds from species to genus, ascending an order determined by the material domain under consideration. So, for instance, generalizing "red" leads to the genus "color," which in turn leads to "sense quality." By contrast, in formalization there is no need to lead through an order of stages or consider the material domain. Rather I look past the "what-content" of the object and instead grasp the relational givenness of the object. Returning to the example, formalizing "sense quality" can lead to "essence," and anything can be formalized as "object." Formalization has no direct regard for the stratification of genus-species or for material-content.

Heidegger makes two criticisms of this articulation of formalization. The first is that it is mired in an "inauthentic theoretical attitude" that prejudices the phenomena. Both generalization and formalization follow from the theoretical attitude, but the former has its origin in the content sense and the latter in the relation-sense. The second criticism is that formalization has implicit regard for the material domain and thus likewise falls under the sense of "general." He illustrates the implicit role of the material in formalization by pointing to certain differences that emerge in formal analysis: while anything can be called an "object" not every object is an "essence." This difference indicates a certain regard for the material domain and thus an implicit application of the sense "general." The theory of the formal-ontological (*mathesis universalis*) is "indirectly" an ordering "insofar as it is *formed out* into a formal object-category to which a 'region' corresponds."[96]

Formal indication, by contrast, circumvents the dominance of generalization by having a different enactment-sense. On Heidegger's reading, philosophy is not an attitude, and it is not theoretical, but it is open to being determined by the things themselves. "'Formal indication' does not concern an order. In the formal indication one stays away from any classification; everything is precisely kept open. The formal indication has meaning only in relation to the phenomenological explication."[97] Just what this openness entails can be clarified by contrasting formal indication and its enactment-sense with the theoretical enactment-sense of formal-ontological investigation. The latter, because it is "indifferent" to its matter, "prescribes" the theoretical relational sense and hides the enactmental sense.

> Exactly because the formal determination is entirely indifferent as to content, it is fatal for the relational- and enactment-aspect of the

phenomenon—because it prescribes, or at least contributes to pre-
scribing, a theoretical relational sense. It hides the *enactment*-charac-
ter—which is possibly still more fatal—and turns one-sidedly to the
content.[98]

His answer is a formal indication in which the three senses of a phenomenon are kept open and defended against theoretical or scientific
prescription.

> A phenomenon must be so stipulated, such that its relational sense
> is held in abeyance. One must prevent oneself from taking it for
> granted that its relational sense is originally theoretical. The relation
> and enactment of the phenomenon is *not preliminarily determined*,
> but is held in abeyance. That is a stance which is opposed to science
> in the highest degree. There is no insertion into a material domain,
> but rather the opposite: the formal indication is a defense, a prelimi-
> nary *securing*, so that the enactment-character still remains free.[99]

The phenomenological task, then, is to "retrieve" and "explicate" the
phenomenon in the threefold "totality of sense." Formal indication
functions to retrieve the phenomenon from our tendency to theoretical objectification.[100] The "*logos*" can then explicate the phenomena
authentically.[101] Earlier in the course, Heidegger had characterized the
attitudinal relation as one in which the self is wholly "absorbed in the
material complex" and the "*living* relation to the object of knowledge
has 'ceased.'"[102] By implication, the phenomenological relation must be
one of authentic self-possession in which the living relation to what is
known is kept alive.

The distinction between generalization, which regards the content,
and formalization, which regards the relation and implicitly the content,
frames Heidegger's subsequent history of being. Formalization constitutes
an advance on generalization, but both are enacted attitudinally. Generalization explicitly entails an order and formalization does so implicitly.
Already in this early discussion he sees a mathematical tendency at work
in the history of philosophy.

> A glance at the history of philosophy shows that formal determina-
> tion of the objective entirely dominates philosophy. How can this
> prejudice, the pre-judgment, be prevented? This is just what the *for-
> mal indication* achieves.[103]

Such a philosophy turns about from ordering and any kind of projecting
to the very enactment of factical life experience.[104] A year later, Heidegger
names the phenomenological return "research": "Philosophy is a basic
mode of life itself, in such a way that it authentically 'brings back,' i.e.,

brings life back from its downward fall into decadence, and this 'bringing back' [or re-petition, 're-seeking'], as radical re-search, is life itself."[105]

In *Being and Time*, the three senses of the phenomenon from 1920–21 are transposed into the familiar terminology of the ontological investigation. He distinguishes three irreducible modes of being: (1) "on-handness" (*Vorhandenheit*) in which entities are thematically regarded as worldless; (2) "handiness" (*Zuhandenheit*) in which entities are unthematically involved in the nexus of relations constitutive of world; and (3) "being-in-the-world" (*In-der-Welt-sein*) in which the world is disclosed. Judgments and the traditional categories relate to on-hand entities alone, so wholly pass over the mode of handiness and the phenomenon of worldliness, which in part constitutes Dasein. In SZ 1.1, he led to the existential of worldliness by distinguishing on-handness from handiness and leading handiness back to the full phenomenon of worldliness and the openness of Dasein. The relation-sense and content sense are traced back to being-in-the-world and the timely disclosedness of care. The enactment-sense becomes the differentiation between authentic and inauthentic manners of Dasein, such that inauthentic being falls to an on-hand consideration of entities and authentic being allows the disclosedness of care to show itself from itself. *Being and Time* ever struggles against the leveling of ontological distinctions to the merely on-hand and in so doing labors to trace philosophical concepts back to their givenness in the enactment of individual Dasein. Formal indication points to the task of grasping the matrix of conceptuality in its original unity as existing Dasein.

In SZ II, Heidegger had planned to provide a targeted critique of three key figures from the philosophical tradition: Kant, Descartes, and Aristotle. But the first half of the work itself deals explicitly with inadequate "presuppositions and prejudices"[106] and shows their questionable character. Presuppositions are "basically undiscussed ontological 'foundations.' "[107] He concerns himself with presuppositions and prejudices, because Dasein is primordially in both truth and untruth. He thus adopts a Kantian motif by demonstrating that semblance necessarily arises because of the very constitution of Dasein.[108] It becomes necessary, then, to take over the tradition and trace semblance back to its primordial givenness.

> It is therefore essential that Dasein should explicitly appropriate what has already been uncovered, defend it *against* semblance and disguise, and assure itself of its uncoveredness again and again. The uncovering of anything new is never done on the basis of having something completely hidden, but takes its departure rather from uncoveredness in the mode of semblance.[109]

Engagement with the tradition and its prejudices, then, has the "positive"[110] aim of providing a phenomenological opportunity to return to the obscured primordial phenomenon. This is especially clear concerning what we have termed the logical and mathematical prejudices. I will take each one in turn.

The Logical Prejudice

Heidegger defines the logical prejudice in § 44 as the position that truth occurs in the judgment and that the essence of truth consists in the agreement of the subject's judgment and the object in question. Holders of this view typically ascribe it to Aristotle.[111] To lead to the more original sense of truth, Heidegger aims to make the traditional determination of truth as agreement questionable. He can then exhibit the original phenomenon of truth and show that agreement is a derivative phenomenon. Agreement, classically formulated as *adaequatio intellectus et rei*, is possible only on the basis of a wider "context of being" (*Seinszusammenhang*).[112] Not only is the basis of agreement questionable, but the being of the relation is itself questionable. He thinks that the attempt to explain such a relation as a coordination of the ideal and the real is problematic. Here, one distinguishes between the ideal content of the judgment on the one hand and the real psychic act or the real object on the other. But such a connection does not clarify the kind of being of the *adaequatio*.

Assertions are directed toward entities that they disclose. Assertions, though, also communicate by preserving what is disclosed. Consequently, they can be taken over by others so that others too are directed toward the disclosed entities. Such expressions are handy and are in-the-world. The phenomenon of agreement arises when an assertion is submitted for confirmation so that its direction toward entities might be demonstrated. But this is to make the relation of the judgment to its entities thematic: "Now to demonstrate that it is something which uncovers means to demonstrate how the assertion by which the uncoveredness is preserved is related *to* these entities."[113] Since an assertion is always "an uncoveredness *of* something," this relation to entities is taken invariably to be itself something on-hand between on-hand entities. Then truth switches over to a relation between two on-hand things, the judgment and the object. "The uncoveredness of something becomes the on-hand conformity of one thing which is on-hand—the assertion expressed—*to* something else which is on-hand—the entity under discussion."[114] This conformity is the phenomenon of agreement. "Truth as disclosedness and as a being-towards uncovered entities—a being which itself uncovers—has become truth as agreement between things which are on-hand within-the-world."[115] This understanding covers over the phenomenon of truth by reducing it to on-hand relations. He has thus shown the derivative nature of the second thesis of the traditional concept of truth, namely that the essence of truth is agreement.

Uncoveredness is itself founded on a more primordial sense of truth, being-in-the-world. The disclosedness of Dasein is the primary sense of truth, because it is only "*with* and *through*" it that the uncoveredness of entities occurs.[116] Dasein's disclosedness, and not the assertion, is the locus of truth.

> Assertion is not the primary "place" of truth. *On the contrary*, whether as a mode in which uncoveredness is appropriated or as a way of being-in-the-world, assertion is grounded in Dasein's uncovering, or rather in its *disclosedness*. The most primordial "truth" is the "place" of assertion; it is the ontological condition for the possibility that assertions can be either true or false—that they may uncover or cover things up.[117]

Heidegger thereby transforms the first thesis of the traditional concept of truth in accordance with the phenomena. This transformation has methodological implications. As disclosedness, Dasein is "in the truth." But because Dasein is also falling, it is equiprimordially in "untruth." Consequently, entities both reveal and conceal, showing themselves only "in the mode of semblance." The task of phenomenology, then, is to "wrest" truth from semblance.[118]

Heidegger cites some passages to illustrate that the third thesis is false, namely that Aristotle himself held that assertion is the place of truth and agreement is the essence of truth. In § 33, he observed that passing over the hermeneutical "as" is what reduces Aristotle's phenomenology of the *logos* to a "superficial 'theory of judgment,'" in which judgment becomes the binding or separating of representations and concepts."[119] Aristotle is missed because Aristotle is not read phenomenologically.[120]

In §§ 33 and 34, Heidegger also provided some further criticisms of the traditional concept of truth. In § 34, he criticizes the tradition for taking assertion as the standard for all discourse, since discourse is much broader than assertion. Judgment in turn becomes interpreted in a derivative way that becomes decisive for ancient ontology.[121] "Grammar sought its foundations in the 'logic' of this *logos*. But this logic was based upon the ontology of the on-hand."[122] Rather than taking its orientation from assertion, the tradition would have done better to begin with an analysis of Dasein. As he writes in § 33: "By demonstrating that assertion is derived from interpretation and understanding, we have made it plain that the 'logic' of the λόγος is rooted in the existential analytic of Dasein."[123] The disclosedness of Dasein and not the truth of assertion is the primary sense of truth. How does this primary context of being become manifest historically? By way of the mathematical prejudice.

The Mathematical Prejudice

In §§ 19–21, Heidegger tells us that Descartes initiates the change from ancient ontology to "modern mathematical physics and its transcendental foundations."[124] This entails a shift from gaining access to entities through perceptual beholding to gaining access through an *a priori* projection of entities as on-hand.[125] Descartes rigorously enforces an understanding of entities as on-hand, and he enacts a basic distinction between two kinds of finite substances, *res cogitans* and *res extensa*. What substance is in general, though, is left unclarified, and the term confusedly carries both ontic and ontological meanings.[126]

Descartes "prescribes" that entities be understood as constant on-handness rather than allow entities to present their manner of being. His esteem for mathematics *follows* from this basic orientation to being as constant on-handness and is not constitutive for it. "Thus his ontology of the world is not primarily determined by his leaning towards mathematics, a science which he chances to esteem very highly, but rather by his ontological orientation in principle towards being as constant on-handness, which mathematical knowledge is exceptionally well suited to grasp."[127] Since Descartes interprets entities within-the-world as on-hand or worldless, the being of *res corporea* is *extensio*, that which remains constant.[128] Moreover, he likewise construes the being of Dasein substantially. The fact that intentionality is grounded in being-in-the-world is thus missed.[129]

In § 69, Heidegger has occasion to amplify his analyses of the mathematical project and its basis in being-in-the-world, while discussing the genesis of scientific, theoretical behavior and its correlate, on-hand entities. Modern physics views its objects under the projection of constant on-handness. He identifies three features of this projection: "the articulation of the understanding of being," "the delimitation of an area of subject-matter," and "the sketching-out of the way of conceiving which is appropriate to such entities."[130] Taken together, these three constitute what he terms "thematizing." In thematization, entities within-the-world are freed so that they can be encountered as *objects*, entities "thrown against" discovering. "Thematizing objectifies. It does not first 'posit' the entities, but frees them so that one can interrogate them and determine their character 'objectively.'"[131] What makes the thematizing of the on-hand possible is being-in-the-world, which Heidegger now terms "transcendence." "If the thematizing of the on-hand—the scientific projection of nature—is to become possible, *Dasein must transcend* the entities thematized. Transcendence does not consist in objectifying, but is presupposed by it."[132] This transcendence is nothing other than the horizonal-unity of ecstatic timeliness. The modern mathematical project or thematization leads back to timeliness as its possibility.[133]

Unfolding the mathematical prejudice leads to a curious consequence in the overcoming of the logical prejudice. The Cartesian mathematical projection entailed the discovery of the *a priori* and introduced a crucial philosophical theme. "When Descartes was so radical as to set up the *extensio* as the *praesuppositum* for every definite characteristic of the *res corporea*, he prepared the way for the understanding of something *a priori* whose content Kant was to establish with greater precision."[134] Husserl's phenomenological method gave a way to conduct concrete research into the Kantian *a priori*. Heidegger shows that this *a priori* is the timely disclosure of care or more simply *truth*. Truth is the *a priori* which makes all presupposing possible; it is the presupposition of every presupposition.[135]

> *Why must we presuppose that there is truth?* . . . "We" presuppose truth because "we," being in the kind of being which Dasein possesses, *are* "in the truth." It is not we who presuppose "truth"; but it is "*truth*" that makes it at all possible ontologically for us to be able to *be* such that we "presuppose" anything at all. Truth is what first *makes possible* anything like presupposing.[136]

To presuppose is "to understand something as the ground for the being of some other entity."[137] But the ground for all understanding is the disclosedness of Dasein. The analysis of the mathematical prejudice, in leading to the discovering of the *a priori*, leads to the discovery of the "presupposition" of presuppositions, ontological truth. The mathematical prejudice, then, leads to the overcoming of the logical prejudice, and thus the remote ground of itself. Truth, as the disclosed ground of presuppositions, is not properly speaking a presupposition, if presuppositions are undiscussed ontological foundations. Truth is the ground, what he calls the *veritas transcendentalis*.

Phenomenology primarily specifies a *how* of research and only secondarily a subject matter of research. Its how is to trace semblance back to the self-showing of phenomena,[138] and its subject matter is intentionality construed broadly to include its ground in timely transcendence.[139] Heidegger names this subject matter "fundamental ontology." What phenomenology provides is the method for "genuine philosophical 'empiricism,'" because it enables the disclosure of the *a priori* rather than its rationalistic construction. "But to disclose the *a priori* is not to make an '*a-prioristic*' construction. Through Edmund Husserl, we have learned not only to understand once more the sense of every genuine philosophical 'empiricism' but also to handle the necessary tools for it."[140] Modern rationalism attempts to construct the *a priori* or world on the basis of an on-hand interpretation of entities. By contrast, phenomenology rigorously enacted discloses the *a priori*, that is, the timely disclosedness of care. The Husserlian distinction between generalization and formalization now comes to frame the difference between the logical and the mathematical so as to set the stage for Heidegger's transcendental phenomenology. By way of the critique of the mathematical, the logical becomes transformed into the phenomenological, and the context of judgment is recovered. Heidegger reads the history of philosophy as the slow enactment of the transcendental turn.

5 From the Temporality of Dasein and Being to Appropriation (SZ I.3)

The second half of *Being and Time* never did appear. Instead, Heidegger undertook a new way of posing the question, most fully developed in the *Contributions*. Chapter 4 will examine this new approach, but what needs to be shown here is that the new approach sticks to the domain originally assigned to the unpublished portion of *Being and Time*. In this regard, it is important to realize that Heidegger's dissatisfaction with SZ I.3 had nothing to do with its original aim to turn from projection upon the ultimate context to show the origination of understanding from out of that context. The dissatisfaction, in other words, had nothing to do with the shift from the question about Dasein's timeliness to the question about the temporality of being as such. In 1937–38, he writes, "For the inadequacy of the withheld section of 'Time and Being' was not because of an uncertainty concerning the direction of the question and its domain, but because of an uncertainty that only concerned the appropriate elaboration."[141] The domain or site targeted by the preparatory question was not the problem. Just what were these grounds of dissatisfaction then? The "remarkable back and forth relatedness" of the thrown project, Dasein, to being was formulated inadequately.

The being of Dasein transcends entities and can therefore ask questions, and being is the *transcendens* pure and simple.[142] The root of these two transcendencies is temporality, which serves as the "transcendental horizon for the question of being."[143] The transcendence of the questioner's being and the transcendence of being as such belong together and are made possible in the bringing forth of timeliness. In "On the Essence of Ground," Heidegger says that Dasein's transcendence allows entities to be discovered. A marginal note expands this vision and introduces his later language:

> But Dasein and be-ing itself? Not yet thought, not until *Being and Time*, second half [i.e., I.3 of the unpublished "second half"]. Dasein belongs to be-ing itself as the simple onefold of entities and being; the essence of the "occurrence"—bringing forth of temporality [*Zeitigung der Temporalität*] as a preliminary name for the truth of be-ing.[144]

The interplay of Dasein and being is intended in the very structure of *Being and Time*. Heidegger comes to balk at transcendental language and instead opts for new language concerning the truth of be-ing. Transcendence comes to be renamed "event of appropriation" (*das Ereignis*) as the correlation of Dasein and be-ing: "transcendence as the ecstatical—timeliness—temporality" when approached "from the truth of be-ing" is "appropriation."[145]

Central to transcendence is the surpassing (*Übersprung*) of entities. The phenomenological researcher recovers such a movement by resolutely resisting the falling tendency of Dasein. "The question of being is nothing other than the radicalization of an essential tendency-of-being which belongs to Dasein itself—the pre-ontological understanding of being."[146] In this way, the *a priori* structure of transcendence, the schematism of temporality, is the correlate of the researcher's authenticity. The dynamic of research is squarely rooted in Dasein and its timeliness. On this view, then, the variety of viewpoints in the history of philosophy has to be explained in terms of the resoluteness of its philosophical researchers. The movement comes in transcending (*Schwung*) entities, not in reciprocally relating (*Gegenschwung*) to be-ing. Even though Dasein is thrown, research is projection, and it therefore cannot account for the historical horizons of being-interpretations. The philosophers all transcended entities but in terms of various meanings of being. Heidegger accordingly thematizes the originary affectivity of the philosopher, which he terms "need" (*Not*). The need arises in a disposition: "The need compels by disposing, and this disposing is a displacing [*Versetzung*] in such fashion that we find ourselves disposed (or not disposed) toward entities in a definite way."[147] Philosophy, then, arises from the origin of this affectivity: "Philosophy, if it is, does not exist because there are philosophers, nor are there philosophers because philosophy is taken up. On the contrary, philosophy and philosophers exist only when and how *the truth of be-ing itself appropriates itself* [die Wahrheit des Seyns selbst sich ereignet]."[148]

Another difficulty for Heidegger, besides the historically diverse meanings of being, is whether the metaphysical tradition can contribute to the inquiry into the reciprocity of be-ing and Dasein. Finding encouragement in his reading of Aristotle and Kant, he initially thinks that it can. But their language of essence and condition for the possibility, articulated in the ontological or transcendental perfect tense[149] in the end is rooted exclusively in what he comes to call the "mathematical." This means that it begins from an entity and therefrom projects being; consequently, it is ill-suited to name the reciprocity of Dasein and be-ing. In *Contributions*, he writes, "Therefore, the effort was needed to come free of the 'condition for the possibility' as going back into the merely 'mathematical' and to grasp the truth of be-ing from within its *own* essential sway (appropriation)."[150] Indeed, the language itself seems to make be-ing into an "object" opposite Dasein, but this was never his intention. Consequently, in *Being and Time* he intended something more than he could say in terms of its ontological-transcendental language. Thereafter, he dispenses with the mathematical tendency of research. The need for inquiry is no longer rooted in the falling of Dasein but instead the historical withdrawal of that which gives be-ing to Dasein. With a different disposition comes a different essence of Dasein. In this way, Dasein belongs to be-ing and its need. Temporal horizon, then, yields to appropriation, and transcendental research yields to a leap into the truth of be-ing.

With "truth of be-ing" Heidegger adopts and transforms language already part of his operative vocabulary in *Being and Time*. He speaks of *veritas transcendentalis*, disclosedness of being, and *veritas temporalis*.[151] Here the genitive is both subjective and objective; it expresses the reciprocity of disclosedness (Dasein) *and* being. He does not see this reciprocity as mechanical, a function of the methodological research activity of Dasein, but instead as historical. The transcendental pathway (SZ I.1–2) is retained but only to motivate its abandonment into the domain it discloses (SZ I.3). "Only provisionally the *transcendental* way . . . in order to prepare the swinging around and leaping into."[152] Not transcendence's "upswing" (*Schwung*) and "leaping beyond" (*Übersprungen*) entities, but instead the "swinging around" (*Umschwung*) and "leaping into" (*Einsprung*) the "reciprocity" (*Gegenschwung*) of Dasein and being. Be-ing *needs* Dasein and Dasein *belongs* to be-ing.[153] The terminus of the leap, then, is no longer adequately expressed with the language of transcendental philosophy and its metaphysical heritage. Condition for the possibility, the transcendental concept of essence, does not capture the affective emergence of that possibility. The essence of Dasein itself proves to be at stake in the truth of be-ing. Heidegger's anticipated repetition of the Dasein-analytic in SZ I.3 occurs now in terms of the reciprocity of Dasein and be-ing, named by the "truth of be-ing."[154] The shift is not from Dasein to be-ing but from Dasein *as the researcher into being* to Dasein *as the appropriated site or truth of be-ing.* Here, the question of the truth of be-ing is equally the question of the be-ing of truth.[155] Instead of asking about the horizon of reciprocity, he shifts to the affective happening of reciprocity and formulates his fundamental question as follows: "How does the truth of be-ing sway?"[156]

Conclusion

Heidegger sharply distinguishes his grounding question about the horizon of being from what he takes to be the guiding question in the history of metaphysical inquiry, "What is an entity?"[157] This question, he argues, interprets the being of entities as constant presence. The preliminary question about Dasein is his own path for crossing from the first to the other question, from the limited horizon of metaphysics to what he calls in *Contributions* "another beginning." As such it is properly placed, uncomfortably to be sure, between the guiding and the grounding questions. The preliminary question targets Dasein's ontic distinction of being ontological. It is an entity open to the being of entities. The grounding question then asks what is responsible for the correlation of Dasein and being, whether this be temporality or *Ereignis*. Neither the preliminary question nor the grounding question is couched in terms of the guiding question of metaphysics. But there is no way to approach the grounding question except by means of the preparatory question about Dasein. The preparatory question, then, is central in motivating the shift from the question about entity to the question about the reciprocity of Dasein and being.

Through the 1930s and later, Heidegger's thought remains concerned preliminarily with the "to be" of the dative for the givenness of entities and primarily the opening up of the domain in which we can be the dative of being. The preliminary question considers our openness to things and the primary question considers our openness as the site of being. The primary question is had only by means of the preliminary question, but the primary question shows that the preliminary question is inadequately put. Consequently, in *Contributions*, he can remark regarding the difference between the openness and entities, a difference that emerges only in the preparatory transcendental question: "For as necessary as this distinction is (to think in traditional terms), in order to provide at all a preliminary perspective for the question of be-ing, just as disastrous does this distinction continue to be."[158] The success of the preliminary question leads to its surpassing. He can cease to ask the preliminary question precisely because he moves deeper within the domain it opens. The evidence suggests, then, that the first transcendental question, though formulated in unfortunate metaphysical terms, does prove to be continually relevant, because it engages the history of philosophy in a productive way. In *Contributions*, he observes, "When coming from the horizon of metaphysics, there is at first no other way even to make the question of being conceivable as a task."[159] The destructive program of SZ II, then, receives its direction from the questioning belonging to SZ I.1–2, aiming as it does at the field of SZ I.3.

In the introduction, I identified two important threads among Heidegger scholars that have emerged in the last fifteen years: the transcendental motif and the clarification of his lasting question. While both make welcome headway in understanding Heidegger, both leave obscure the role of the transcendental in the "turn." Specifically, the transcendental program of *Being and Time* appears fundamentally mistaken, and this appearance conceals the essential motivating role transcendence plays in making a first approach to the space of the fundamental question. The key to clarifying this matter is disentangling his two questions and showing their interplay, especially in the troubled SZ I.3. The reconstruction of the preparatory question (SZ I.1–2) and its reversal (SZ I.3) reveals that Heidegger's later criticism of the (preparatory) transcendental question in fact relies on the success of the question. Transcendental terms become translated into the terms of *Ereignis* and its "reciprocity" (*Gegenschwung*). The intended "reversal" (*Umschwung*) is accomplished, in part, by means of the "upswing" (*Schwung*) of Dasein's transcendence. The "leap" (*Sprung*) is prepared for by the "leaping ahead" (*Übersprung*) of Dasein's transcendence. Transcendence, then, is taken up into a more comprehensive movement of reciprocity. It is not annulled but completed. In a certain sense, it is fitting to speak of Heidegger's cardinal question as a transcendental one, insofar as he realized transcendence was a "preliminary name" (*Vorname*) for *Ereignis*; the appropriate name for this phenomenon first showed itself only by means of the (finally inappropriate) transcendental approach.[160] In the end, he remains a "transcendental" thinker, in a sense peculiarly his own yet one undeniably indebted to the tradition that carries that name (Husserl, Kant, and more liberally Parmenides, Aristotle, et al.).

The project of this chapter shows the need to distinguish and relate the "transcendental" questions operative in Heidegger's path of thinking. This distinction justifies two conclusions. The transcendental motif continues to be important due to its essential role in his clarified itinerary. The demystification project, approached transcendentally, lays bare the structure of *Being and Time* as it reverses the first to the other transcendental question. How must we be to access entities? *Essentially opened up ecstatically and horizonally by timeliness.* What is responsible for the reciprocity of Dasein and being? *The event of appropriation.* The shift from timeliness to appropriation (initially by means of transcendental temporality) happens within the domain opened by timeliness, the domain that belongs "topographically" to the unpublished but still fruitful SZ I.3.

In the next chapter, I will identify four phases of Heidegger's interpretation of Kant. The third stage, culminating in the 1929 *Kant and the Problem of Metaphysics*, interprets Kant within the horizon of Heidegger's fundamental question. The fourth stage, represented by the 1935–1936 *What Is a Thing?* and the 1961 "Kant's Thesis about Being," scales back the interpretation by reading Kant according to the preparatory question about our openness to entities. While the promise of a collaborator in Kant fades, the insistence that his philosophy is the crucial modern forerunner does not. What Heidegger finds fascinating in Kant's critique of rationalism is something that first emerges in Heidegger's early reading of Husserl. The father of phenomenology gave to Heidegger a phenomenological Kant, and the phenomenological Kant gave Heidegger the means to engage the history of philosophy in a productive way.

In the 1930s, Heidegger distances himself from transcendental philosophy, not only in its Husserlian and Kantian forms, but also in Heidegger's own earlier program. His justification for doing so concerns principally the charge that transcendental philosophy neglects the historicity of thought in favor of the freedom of the transcendental researcher. From this charge, commentators routinely conclude that Heidegger disavows transcendental thought. In this chapter, I questioned such a disavowal by showing that it is the very logic of formal indication, developed in dialogue with Husserl and deployed in *Being and Time*, which provides the outline of Heidegger's history of being. I do not question that Heidegger saw the need for going beyond transcendental thought by means of embracing the historicity of fundamental dispositions. I simply maintain that such going beyond is a continuation of the going beyond contained in Heidegger's original formulation of formal indication. The movement of Heidegger's history of being first comes to him as he appropriates the thought of Husserl. Heidegger's turn to history is not a turn from transcendental philosophy. It is a turn within transcendental philosophy, which presupposes and does not renounce the transcendental turn, while attending to the fact that the transcendental turn happens not simply thanks to the authenticity of the transcendental researchers but principally thanks to the fundamental dispositions the philosopher experiences.

Notes

1 GA 65, 74/51–2.
2 GA 65, 11/8.
3 To take three important commentators as examples: Michael Gelven, citing a passage from the later Heidegger, does not distinguish the questions. Richard Polt registers the difference between SZ I.1–2 and SZ I.3, but he also suggests that a shortcoming of SZ I.1–2 is that it does not answer the question assigned to SZ I.3. Hubert Dreyfus distinguishes them but does not relate them; he counts as anathema to the hermeneutic of Dasein that it should disclose anything like *the* horizon for the question of being, and so he says there can be no reversal from the first to the second question. See Gelven, *A Commentary on Heidegger's 'Being and Time'*, rev. ed. (DeKalb, IL: Northern Illinois University Press, 1989), 18–19; Polt, *Heidegger: An Introduction* (Ithaca, NY: Cornell University Press, 1999), 36 and 25, respectively; and Dreyfus, *Being-in-the-World*, 12 and 38–9.
4 "Die Transzendenz des Seins des Daseins . . . ," "*Sein ist das transcendens schlechthin*," ". . . Zeit als des transzendentalen Horizontes der Frage nach dem Sein." SZ 38–9/62–3.
5 SZ 24/45. Though Heidegger in general strives to avoid the language of subjectivity, he says the "subjectivity of the subject" is the Kantian formulation of what he has in mind with Dasein. SZ 24/45.
6 *Ideas I*, 111, quoted by Heidegger, GA 20, 158n2/114n2.
7 *Ideas I*, 171, quoted by Heidegger, GA 20, 157/114. I have followed Kisiel's translation here.
8 GA 20, 139/101.
9 GA 26, 167/133. The preparatory question targets what Crowell recognizes as the decisive difference between Husserl and Heidegger. "Does the Husserl/Heidegger Feud Rest on a Mistake? An Essay on Psychological and Transcendental Phenomenology," *Husserl Studies* 18 (2002): 123–40.
10 See Chad Engelland, "Heidegger and the Human Difference," 175–93.
11 GA 20, 159/115.
12 Heidegger puts the "the fundamental question" as follows: "What is meant by being? What is the being of the intentional?" (GA 20, 191/140).
13 Because an entity can serve as our point of departure, "We do not need the specific entity of intentionality in order to awaken the question of the being of entities" (GA 20, 192/141).

14 GA 19, 448/310.
15 *Ideas I*, xix.
16 *Ideas I*, 142.
17 "For Edmund Husserl on his Seventieth Birthday, April 8, 1929," trans. Thomas Sheehan, in *Psychological and Transcendental Phenomenology and the Confrontation with Heidegger (1927–1931)*, ed. Thomas Sheehan and Richard Palmer (Dordrecht: Kluwer Academic Publishers, 1997), 476.
18 SZ 437/487.
19 SZ 27/49.
20 GA 20, 183/135.
21 Appendix to Heidegger's letter to Husserl from October 22, 1927, in *Becoming Heidegger: On the Trail of His Early Occasional Writings, 1910–1927*, ed. Kisiel and Sheehan (Evanston, IL: Northwestern University Press, 2007), 326. Emphasis mine.
22 Ibid., 327.
23 GA 3, XVI/xix.
24 In this way, Heidegger's 1973 preface to the text continues to recommend it as an introduction to "the horizon of the manner of questioning set forth in *Being and Time*" even though he now realizes "Kant's question is foreign to it" (GA 3, XIV/xviii). Nor is this horizon of questioning something that belongs to the past: "The Kant book remains an introduction, attempted by means of a questionable digression, to the further questionability which persists concerning the question of being set forth in *Being and Time*" (GA 3, XV/xviii).
25 GA 3, 43/30, and compare 38–39/27.
26 GA 3, 224/157. Heidegger italicizes this question.
27 SZ 62/89.
28 Cf. SZ 38/63 and GA 24, 438/308.
29 GA 65, 289/203.
30 SZ 212/255.
31 SZ 192/237.
32 GA 26, 212/166. See also GA 9b, 158–9/122–3.
33 GA 26, 214/167.
34 See GA 26, 170/135 and 214–15/168.
35 SZ 366/417–18. Earlier in the section, Heidegger puts the question more broadly: "how are 'independent' entities within-the-world 'connected' with the transcending world?" (SZ 351/402).
36 SZ 328–9/377.
37 SZ 365/416. See also GA 24, 429/302.
38 For Heidegger's own defense of the term, see GA 24, 438/308.
39 SZ 365/416–17.
40 GA 26, 269/208.
41 GA 26, 274/212.
42 GA 26, 274/211–12.
43 "Exactly that which is called immanence in theory of knowledge in a complete inversion of the phenomenal facts, the sphere of the subject, is intrinsically and primarily and alone the transcendent" (GA 24, 425/299).
44 SZ 436–7/487.
45 SZ 436/487. On this passage, see Crowell, *Space of Meaning*, 297.
46 GA 9b, 162n59/371.
47 GA 24, 19/15 and 21/16.
48 Kisiel has assembled much of the evidence regarding Heidegger's reticence. See "The Demise of *Being and Time*: 1927–1930," in *Heidegger's 'Being and Time': Critical Essays*, ed. Polt (Lanham: Rowman & Littlefield, 2005), 189–214. For speculations about the proposed content of this division, see

Division III of Heidegger's Being and Time: *The Unanswered Question of Being*, ed. Lee Braver (Cambridge, MA: The MIT Press, 2015).

49 SZ 8/28.
50 GA 3, 224/157. Heidegger italicizes the question in the text.
51 SZ 17/39.
52 SZ 19/40.
53 SZ 26/49. See Dreyfus, *Being-in-the-World*, 38–9.
54 GA 24, 437/307–8.
55 GA 24, 463/325.
56 See GA 24, 33/24, and GA 26, 193–4/153.
57 GA 24, 26/19.
58 GA 24, 33/24.
59 63/24. Crowell, despite his accurate diagnosis of the Husserl-Heidegger feud, yet sides with Husserl regarding the inappropriateness of the ontic within the ontological. See *Space of Meaning*, 235.
60 SZ 6/26.
61 GA 24, 25/18.
62 GA 24, 26/19.
63 GA 24, 319/224; GA 26, 215/168.
64 GA 26, 268/208.
65 GA 26, 270/208–9.
66 GA 26, 271/210.
67 GA 3, 189/132.
68 GA 3, 196/137.
69 GA 24, 1/1. Kisiel suggests that this identification was made by Heidegger only in 1975 when the lecture course came to print. See *Genesis*, 488. Now, why a "new" elaboration? As Heidegger tells us in 1941, conversations with Karl Jaspers during the printing of the first two divisions led him to think that "the elaboration of this all important division (I, 3) drafted up to that point had to be incomprehensible." Quoted in Kisiel, *Genesis*, 486.
70 "If transcendence makes possible the understanding of being and if transcendence is founded on the ecstatic-horizonal constitution of timeliness, then timeliness is the condition of the possibility of the understanding of being." GA 24, 429/302. He then proceeds to show how the understanding of handiness is made possible. A handy entity may turn up as unavailable; understanding this interplay of presence and absence is possible, because it is projected upon the timely horizon that Heidegger calls *praesens*. Heidegger uses Latin terms to designate timeliness when it serves as the condition for the possibility of the understanding of being. GA 24, 429–44/302–12. Likewise, time makes negation possible. GA 24, 443/311.
71 GA 24, 454/319.
72 GA 24, 437/307–8. The first ellipsis is Heidegger's, and the ellipsis in brackets is mine. The fact that "temporality as origin is richer and more pregnant than anything that may arise from it" explains Heidegger's controversial claim "that within the ontological sphere the possible is higher than everything actual," which he says "is relevant throughout the whole dimension of philosophy." GA 24, 438/308.
73 GA 24, 454/319.
74 What Heidegger has in mind with "objectification" is not what he will later criticize as the oblivion of being in the priority of method over matter. Rather, he offers a phenomenological understanding of science, whether positive or phenomenological-ontological, in which *logos* is subordinated to phenomena: "Science is a cognizing for the sake of unveiledness as such. . . . What is to be unveiled is the sole court of appeal of its determinability, of the concepts that are suitable for interpreting it." GA 24, 455/320. What is so "objectified"

must be given beforehand and so is in no way the product of construction. Nonetheless, it does involve projection: for positive science the "projection of the ontological constitution of a region of entities," and for ontology the "projection of being upon the horizon of its understandability," namely time. GA 24, 457–9/321–2. As we will see in chapter 4, Heidegger will later back away from projection as the adequate means for understanding being as such.

75 GA 24, 456/321.

76 GA 24, 459/322.

77 GA 24, 459/323.

78 "Because temporal projection makes possible an objectification of being and assures conceptualizability, and thereby constitutes ontology in general as a science, we call this science in distinction from the positive sciences the *temporal science*." GA 24, 459–60/323.

79 GA 24, 460/323.

80 GA 24, 460/323.

81 GA 24, 460/323. Perhaps an example from earlier in the course will help illumine what Heidegger has in mind here; in this case the understanding of the being of handy entities is articulated in terms of time: "The handiness of the handy, the being of this kind of entities, is understood as praesens, a praesens which, as non-conceptually understandable, is already unveiled in the self-projection of timeliness, by means of whose bringing forth anything like existent commerce with entities handy and on-hand becomes possible." GA 24, 438–9/309.

82 "*Time is earlier than any possible earlier* of whatever sort, because it is the basic condition for an earlier as such. And because time as the source of all enablings (possibilities) is the earliest, all possibilities as such in their possibility-making function have the character of the earlier. That is to say, they are a priori." GA 24, 463/325.

83 Kisiel very densely but ably sketches the differences between the language of this temporal science and the language of traditional ontology: "The very fact that *Being and Time* stresses, and even overstresses, prepositional schematisms must be understood in the larger context of a comprehensive grammatology bent upon a thorough review and revision of the formal grammars of our classical languages, where the focus shifts from substantives to middle-voiced infinitives, reflexives, double genitives, transitive-intransitive relations, and the exclamatory impersonals of happenings." This shows that Heidegger's formalization is not oriented toward entities but temporality: "Heidegger's sense of formality is derived, not from a formal mathesis of objects linked to the substantifying tradition of philosophy, but from a non-objective gramma(on)tology of time's tenses." "The Genetic Difference in Reading *Being and Time*," *American Catholic Philosophical Quarterly* 69 (1995): 182.

84 *Genesis*, 21.

85 *Space of Meaning*, 117–28.

86 See *Heidegger's Concept of Truth*, xvii. Cf. Heidegger's claim: "For this is one of the greatest prejudices of Western philosophy, namely, that thinking must be determined 'logically,' i.e., with respect to *assertion*." GA 65, 460–1/324.

87 SZ 32/56.

88 SZ 34/58.

89 SZ 31/54–55.

90 GA 60, 65/45. Kisiel observes that formal indication is one of the casualties of this "*cursus interruptus*" for Heidegger "will never again return to this subject in the deliberate and systematic way that he had begun here." Heidegger's continual deferrals in discussing method in the 1920s may have their origin in this unfortunate situation. See *Genesis*, 171–3. In this section

and the next as well as in chapter 4, I detail the transformation of the not-yet-historical transcendentalism of formal indication into the historical transcendentalism of his rhetoric of being.

91 GA 60, 54/36.
92 GA 60, 48/33.
93 GA 60, 63/43
94 GA 60, 55/38.
95 GA 60, 57/39. He refers his students to *Logical Investigations*, vol. I, trans. F. N. Findlay (Amherst, NY: Humanity Books, 2000), chapter 11, "The Idea of Pure Logic," and *Ideas I*, § 13, "Generalization and Formalization." For an account that emphasizes continuity with Husserl, see Crowell, *Space of Meaning*, 126ff and 141.
96 GA 60, 61–62/42.
97 GA 60, 64/44.
98 GA 60, 63/43.
99 GA 60, 63–64/44.
100 "The necessity of this precautionary measure arises from the falling tendency of factical life experience, which constantly threatens to slip into the objective, and out of which we must still retrieve the phenomena." GA 60, 64/44.
101 Or as Heidegger writes "in the sense of 'verbum internum' (not in the sense of logicalization)." GA 60, 63/43. Cf. GA 60, 85/59: "The language of the study of the material is not original. There is a more original conceptuality already in factical life experience, from out of which the material conceptuality that is common to us first derives. This reversal in conceptuality must be enacted, or else it is hopeless to ever grasp the situation."
102 GA 60, 48/33. Cf. GA 60, 82/57: "Object-historical understanding is determination according to the aspect of the relation, from out of this relation. So that the observer does not come into question. By contrast, phenomenological understanding is determined by the *enactment* of the observer."
103 GA 60, 63/43.
104 GA 60, 82/57 and 90/63.
105 GA 61, 80/62.
106 SZ 2/22.
107 SZ 89/122.
108 In the introduction, Heidegger puts forth as one of his tasks to show that "the specific kind of being of ontology hitherto, and the vicissitudes of its inquiries, its findings, and its failures, have been necessitated in the very character of Dasein." SZ 19/40. Later in the text, he can say that this takes place because of Dasein's *falling*. SZ 206/250. In the 1930s, Heidegger shifts from rooting the phenomenon of falling in the timely structure of care to rooting it in the historical unfolding of fundamental dispositions.
109 SZ 222/265.
110 SZ 23/44. In this regard, see the whole of § 6, "The Task of a Destruction of the History of Ontology," 19–27/41–9.
111 SZ 214/257.
112 SZ 216/259.
113 SZ 224/267.
114 SZ 224/267.
115 SZ 225/267–8.
116 SZ 220/263. Tugendhat agrees that disclosedness is the condition for the possibility of truth, but he thinks Heidegger is vacuously calling disclosedness the primary sense of truth; on his reading, Heidegger makes a kind of non sequitur by thinking that the condition for x should be called the

primary sense of x. As Dahlstrom points out, however, Heidegger does have reason to call disclosedness truth. In the first place, disclosedness provides the final horizon of existential-hermeneutic sense; it thus grounds both derivative senses, the existentiel-hermeneutic sense and the apophantic sense that underlies judgmental truth. In the second place, disclosedness shows itself as it is, that is, truly and without the possibility of error. See Tugendhat, "Heidegger's Idea of Truth," in *Martin Heidegger: Critical Assessments*, ed. Christopher Macann, vol. 3, *Language* (London: Routledge, 1992), 79–92, and *Der Wahrheitsbegriff bei Husserl und Heidegger*, 2d ed. (Berlin: de Gruyter, 1970), 259h, as well as Dahlstrom, *Concept*, 398–403.

117 SZ 226/269. Tugendhat makes a second, more trenchant critique of Heidegger than the one discussed in the previous note. He charges that Heidegger's doctrine of truth rests on an ambiguity between uncoveredness as a pointing out (irrespective of truth and falsity) and the specific uncoveredness of truth as opposed to the coveredness of falsity. Therefore, he thinks Heidegger is without a workable concept of falsity and its other, truth. While it is true that § 44 provides little guidance on the specific nature of falsity and only states that it is possible on the basis of the more primordial kind of truth, § 7 does provide some guidance. Falsity is such that it covers over by uncovering something as something other than it is. Truth, then, uncovers by uncovering something as it is. SZ 33/56–7. Tugendhat would be right to be troubled by an ambiguity between uncoveredness in general and uncoveredness in the sense of truth, but as I have indicated here, I think that Heidegger himself does not fail to distinguish between the two. See "Heidegger's Idea of Truth," 79–92, and Dahlstrom, *Concept*, 403–7.

118 SZ 222/265. And hence the method of formal indication is needed.

119 SZ 159/202.

120 For an insightful phenomenological exposition of Aristotle on these issues, see Thomas Sheehan, "*Hermeneia* and *Apophansis*: The Early Heidegger on Aristotle," in *Heidegger et l'idée de la phénoménologie*, ed. Franco Volpi et al (Dordrecht: Kluwer, 1988), 67–80.

121 In § 33, he says that ancient ontology takes *logos* as something on-hand about on-hand entities. SZ 203/160.

122 SZ 165/209.

123 SZ 160/203.

124 SZ 96/129.

125 In § 69, he broadens this characterization to modern physics. What enables modern science is "*the way in which Nature herself is mathematically projected.*" SZ 362/413–4.

126 SZ 94/127.

127 SZ 96/129.

128 SZ 91/125.

129 SZ 98/131.

130 SZ 363/414.

131 SZ 363/414.

132 SZ 363/415.

133 "The 'problem of transcendence' cannot be brought round to the question of how a subject comes out to an object, where the aggregate of objects is identified with the idea of the world. Rather we must ask: what makes it ontologically possible for entities to be encountered within-the-world and objectified as so encountered? This can be answered by recourse to the transcendence of the world—a transcendence with an ecstatico-horizonal foundation." SZ 366/417–8.

134 SZ 101/134.
135 See also § 69 in which Heidegger connects the disclosure of the *a priori*
     and understanding's projection of being: "In the mathematical projection
     of nature, . . . what is decisive is that this projection *discloses something
     that is a priori.* Thus the paradigmatic character of mathematical natural
     science . . . consists . . . in the fact that the entities which it takes as its theme
     are discovered in it in the only way in which entities can be discovered—by
     the prior projection of their state of being." SZ 362/414.
136 SZ 227–8/270.
137 SZ 228/270.
138 The "method" of phenomenology, then, is but the specification for the man-
     ner of access to the subject matter, which consists, in the words of Crowell,
     "in the entire spiraling movement from everyday being-in-the-world to the
     authentic temporalizing of anticipatory resoluteness." *Space of Meaning*,
     129.
139 GA 20, 185–6/137.
140 SZ 50/490.
141 GA 66, 414/367.
142 SZ 38/62. In his draft of the *Encyclopedia Britannica* article, Heidegger
     expresses these two transcendencies as follows: "Because the being of eve-
     rything that can be experienced by the subject in various ways—the trans-
     cendent in the broadest sense—is constituted in this pure subjectivity, pure
     subjectivity is called transcendental subjectivity" (*Becoming Heidegger*,
     307).
143 SZ 39/63.
144 GA 9b, 159/123.
145 Marginalia, SZ 440. See Sheehan, "*Kehre*," 15.
146 SZ 15/35.
147 GA 45, 161/140.
148 GA 45, 105/120.
149 Marginalia, SZ 441–2.
150 GA 65, 250/176.
151 SZ 38/62 and GA 24, 460/323.
152 GA 65, 305/215.
153 "This reciprocity of *needing* and *belonging* makes up be-ing as appropri-
     ation; and the first thing that is incumbent upon thinking is to raise the
     swinging of this reciprocity [*die Schwingung dieses Gegenschwunges*] into
     the simplicity of knowledge and to ground the reciprocity in its truth" (GA
     65, 251/177). Sheehan explains, "This reciprocity . . . between the fact that
     givenness needs its dative . . . and the dative's *belonging* to givenness . . .
     is what Heidegger means by *das Ereignis*, and it is the central topic of his
     thought" ("*Kehre*," 9).
154 GA 66, 414/367.
155 GA 65, 20/15.
156 GA 66, 422/373.
157 GA 3, 222–4/156–7; GA 65, 75/52; and GA 40, 15/21 and 25/35.
158 GA 65, 250/176–7.
159 GA 65, 450/317.
160 GA 9b, 159/123.

2 The Kant Book (1929)

Every philosophical thinker builds his own work, so to speak, on the ruins of another.

—Immanuel Kant[1]

Any appeal to Kant against phenomenology basically collapses already in the first sentence of the *Critique*.

—Martin Heidegger[2]

Heidegger's philosophical breakthrough, as Theodore Kisiel has so carefully demonstrated, occurs in the 1919 war emergency semester, when he happens upon his lasting topic: pre-theoretical inquiry into the "primal something" (*Ur-etwas*) that makes experience possible.[3] In subsequent lecture courses, Heidegger seeks illumination for this project in St. Paul and St. Augustine before turning in a sustained way to Aristotle. The Scholastic Aristotle becomes, in Heidegger's hands, an able phenomenological partner in this project. During this time, Kant's philosophy is kept at arm's length. In 1925, for example, Heidegger criticizes Kant's "old mythology of an intellect which glues and rigs together the world's matter with its own forms."[4] But during the 1925–26 lecture course, Heidegger's interest curiously shifts from Aristotle to Kant. Suddenly and seemingly inexplicably, Kant is Heidegger's precursor of choice. The Kantian influence on the 1927 *Being and Time* is noticeable, and Kant continues to occupy Heidegger's thoughts throughout the late 1920s, an occupation that culminates in the 1929 publication of Heidegger's only complete monograph, *Kant and the Problem of Metaphysics*.[5] Abruptly, however, his interest wanes. Heidegger later admits that Kant was "a refuge" and that he had greatly misread Kant.[6]

The turn to Kant is a curious and significant fact, occurring as it does at a crucial juncture of Heidegger's development, and it calls for explanation. Based on their masterful studies of Heidegger's earliest way of thinking, John van Buren and Kisiel understand the interest in Kant and the Kantian *Being and Time* as a "departure" (*Abweg*) from his early and later thought.[7] These commentators think that the turn to Kant and transcendental philosophy leads Heidegger to falsify his most original intentions. Under Kant's influence, *Being and Time* speaks of philosophy as scientific and construes the happening of world as the accomplishment of time and its horizonal schematisms. The later Heidegger will rejoin the youthful Heidegger in denying the scientific character of philosophy and the adequacy of the schematism. For these commentators, *Being and Time* is therefore an aberration in these fundamental respects.

Daniel Dahlstrom also subscribes to this "aberration" thesis, but he notes its fundamental problem, namely, it leaves "unexplained why Heidegger took the Kantian turn."[8] This is an excellent question, and its answer, I argue, undermines the aberration thesis itself. The interest in Kant, which culminates in *Kant and the Problem of Metaphysics*, follows from the deepest motivations of Heidegger's phenomenological method. The Neo-Kantian Kant becomes, in Heidegger's hands, an able phenomenological partner. His motive is to defend and safeguard Husserl's discovery of phenomenological givenness against Neo-Kantian objections to the immediate, and he wants to press further into the givenness of being in terms of time. Later, Heidegger admits that his own question of givenness of being is other than Kant's, and that Kant was therefore distorted in the exchange. This means that it was not Heidegger who was ensnared by Kant but Kant who was ensnared by Heidegger; and thus the Kant book remains a reliable testament to Heidegger's thinking rather than Kant's. Heidegger subsequently tries to correct the distorted horizon of questioning by reading Kant according to his native horizon of questioning. Surprisingly, though, the Kant that becomes visible in this rereading is still close to Heidegger's original and final phenomenological impulses; Kant still has a phenomenological understanding of knowledge though he is only obliquely concerned with the givenness of the ontological horizon as such. The elusive promise of the phenomenological Kant drives Heidegger's interest in Kant's transcendental philosophy.

In this chapter, I first identify the motive and phases of Heidegger's reading of Kant's transcendental program. Heidegger seeks to find the place of phenomenology in the history of philosophy and to defend phenomenology from contemporary criticisms coming from those who regard Kant as an authority. The distinctions of this section will allow us to dispel common misunderstandings of Heidegger's turn to Kant: The *aberration* thesis, according to which Heidegger abandons his early pre-theoretical insight into the happening of experience, the *alternative* thesis, according to which the Kant book follows a method other than phenomenology, and the *rejection* thesis, according to which Heidegger's later dissatisfaction with his transcendental program involves a rejection of the phenomenological Kant. The ground will then be cleared for a detailed reading of the two most significant phases of Heidegger's engagement with Kant represented, respectively, by the 1929 Kant book and the 1935–36 lecture course on Kant. In this chapter, the principal focus is *Kant and the Problem of Metaphysics*, which Heidegger offers as a historical motivation to the transcendental problematic of *Being and Time*. Then, in the next chapter, focus will shift to the 1935–36 course, which revises the horizon of questioning operative in the Kant book.

The unstated hermeneutical key to Heidegger's 1929 *Kant and the Problem of Metaphysics*, oddly enough, is Leibnizian in origin. I say "oddly enough," because Heidegger sees Kant's phenomenological leanings arise in reaction to rationalism, and Leibniz is generally regarded as a thoroughgoing rationalist. However, in the 1928 lecture course on Leibniz, Heidegger shores up his anti-Neo-Kantian reading of Kant by reenacting Leibniz's critique of Cartesian rationalism. Heidegger emphasizes the inadequacy of clear and distinct cognition and the priority of real definition for Leibniz. The requirements for real definition in Leibniz form the heart of Heidegger's Kant book, as he seeks to find in Kant the real essence of transcendence. He finds this, above all, in the successive stages of the analytic, culminating in the schematism and the highest principle of all synthetic judgments. At the same time, he reads Kant according to the phenomenological distinctions operative in *Being and Time*. Veritative and synthetic *a priori* judgments mirror *Being and Time*'s ontic and ontological judgments. Heidegger sees Kant return veritative judgments to intuitive givenness; he takes this as justification for finding in Kant's *Critique* the intuitive givenness of ontological judgments. Kant's transcendental method is essentially a phenomenological exhibition; Kant's analytic anticipates Heidegger's own analytic in *Being and Time*. Nonetheless, for Heidegger, Kant remains an ambiguous reference point. While he recommends Kant's transcendental philosophy, phenomenologically understood, as a great collaborator in his own project, he censures Kant for what he sees as an inauthentic "step back" from the discovery of a pre-judicative ground for reason.

1 The Four Phases of Kant-Interpretation

The four phases of Heidegger's interpretation of Kant can be outlined as follows. First, even before the beginning of his mature teaching career, Heidegger is interested in Kant, but Heidegger is bothered by Kant's non-phenomenological character. Second, in the 1925–26 course, "Logic," he turns to Kant with renewed interest in connection with the thesis regarding the centrality of time and finds in Kant a phenomenological forerunner. Third, soon after *Being and Time*, he develops an *even more phenomenological* interpretation of Kant in which the subjectivity of the subject discloses the finite and temporal ground of being; this reading bears fruit in *Kant and the Problem of Metaphysics*. Fourth, beginning in the 1930s Heidegger offers a more distanced but still broadly phenomenological interpretation of Kant as undermining the dominance of modern science by establishing the limits of its mathematical project.

Table 2.1 Phases of Heidegger's Reading of Kant

Phases	Dates	Major Publication	Description
1. Non-Phenomenological	1912–1925	N/A	A remote interest in Kant who falls short of Husserl's phenomenology
2. Precursor	1925–1927	*Being and Time*	Conversion to the quasi-phenomenological Kant who anticipates Husserl
3. Collaborator	1927–1929	*Kant and the Problem of Metaphysics*	An even more phenomenological Kant who surpasses Husserl
4. Precursor Again	1930 and later	*1935–36 Lecture Course on Kant*	Kant is still phenomenological but on par with Husserl

Each phase is carried out with explicit or implicit reference to Husserl's phenomenology. At first, Husserl surpasses Kant, then Kant surpasses Husserl to varying degrees, and finally, from the vantage of Heidegger's later thinking, both anticipate his own thought to the same degree.

Unless we understand and keep distinct the four phases of Heidegger's Kant, we will misunderstand what is at stake in Heidegger's relation to Kant. We might think Heidegger's Kant offers an alternative to phenomenology in general and Husserl's phenomenology in particular, we might think *Being and Time* betrays his pre-theoretical phenomenology, we might misunderstand the Kant book as the fulfillment of the announced destruction of Kant scheduled for the second half of *Being and Time*, or we might think that because the later Heidegger retracts the center of the Kant book, he rejects the phenomenological Kant. As this section demonstrates, not one of these commonplace views is correct. Heidegger does not see in Kant an alternative to his pre-theoretical phenomenology but an important forerunner and then collaborator; later, when he can no longer see Kant as a collaborator, he continues to read him as a phenomenological forerunner.

Non-Phenomenological (1912–1925): A Remote Interest in Kant Who Falls Short of Husserl's Phenomenology

The first phase of Heidegger's Kant-interpretation begins in Heidegger's student days, continues through his breakthrough lecture course, and remains through 1925. Heidegger sharply distinguishes phenomenology from the Neo-Kantian proclivities for construction. Kant himself is applauded for his interest in constitution, but only phenomenology has the means to disclose the structure of experience from experience, while Kant imposes such a structure onto experience. In this phase, Heidegger's phenomenology does not skip over Kant, but it advances his problematic in a wholly novel way.

The beginning of this phase can be dated confidently to 1912.[9] In the middle of 1912, Heidegger the scholastic still dismisses Kant as a phenomenalist.[10] But by the end of 1912, under the influence of the Neo-Kantian Heinrich Rickert, he comes to regard Kant much more sympathetically in a series of articles. First, he sides with the transcendental (and Neo-Kantian) interpretation of Kant against the psychological interpretation.[11] He regards this anti-psychologism as an important point of agreement between Neo-Kantianism and Husserl, but he thinks Husserl's *Logical Investigations* go farther than Neo-Kantianism, "for they have truly broken the psychological spell and brought the above-mentioned clarification of principles into play."[12] He also provides an appreciative though critical assessment of the centrality of judgment in Kant: "Kant's recourse to a table of judgments is today rejected as a mistake in a number of respects. But there is still a kernel of truth here, since it is in the judgment that Kant touched the very nerve of knowledge."[13] In a 1915 retrospective, he describes his changing relation to Neo-Kantianism in 1912–1913 as involving systematic and historical discoveries:

> In this new school I learned first and foremost to understand philosophical problems as problems, and I acquired insight into the essence of logic, the philosophical discipline that still interests me the most. *At the same time I acquired a correct understanding of modern philosophy from Kant onward*, a matter that I found sparsely and inadequately treated in the Scholastic literature.[14]

Nonetheless, this newfound Kantian sympathy does not yet undermine his fundamental scholastic orientation, and he adds, "My basic philosophical convictions remained those of Aristotelian-Scholastic philosophy." In 1912 Kant changes from being a caricature to being an interlocutor, but Kant does not yet occupy a privileged place in relation to Heidegger's developing philosophy. In the latter half of that decade, by jettisoning scholasticism and deepening his phenomenological understanding, Heidegger sets the stage for a more radical confrontation—first with Neo-Kantianism and then with Kant himself. Until 1925, the confrontation follows the same narrative: Kant (that is, the Kant of Neo-Kantianism) approaches but does not attain the phenomenological insight of Husserl.

In 1919, against Natorp's objection to the claimed immediacy of phenomenological intuition, Heidegger says that phenomenology does not theoretically construct experience by appeal to principles but discloses experience sympathetically. In this connection, Heidegger introduces a crucial distinction between the principle in Neo-Kantianism and in phenomenology. Discussing Husserl's "principle of principles," Heidegger writes:

> If by a principle one were to understand a theoretical proposition, this designation would not be fitting. However, that Husserl speaks of a *principle* of principles, thus of something that precedes all principles, in regard to which no theory can lead us astray, already shows (although Husserl does not explicitly say so) that it does not have a theoretical character. It is the primal intention of genuine life, the primal bearing of life experience and life as such, the absolute *sympathy with life* that is identical with life experience.[15]

As the fruit of a radical sympathy with life, phenomenology uncovers the "primal something" (*Ur-etwas*) of pre-theoretical life. Phenomenology experiences experience out of its motivation, thereby grasping its dynamic interplay. Consequently, phenomenological *logoi* "are at once preconceiving and reconceiving [*vorgreifend zugleich rückgreifend*], i.e. they express life in its motivated tendency or tending motivation."[16] Here Heidegger recapitulates Husserl's protentive and retentive analysis of time shorn of its theoretical flavor.[17] Formal indication is Heidegger's way to turn from latent theorizing and return to the experience of experience and its articulation. "A phenomenological criterion is just the understanding evidence and the evident understanding of experience, of life in and for itself in the *eidos*."[18] Heidegger calls phenomenology "primal science" (*Urwissenschaft*), not because he thinks it is "theoretical" in an ontic sense, but because it is the knowing saying of the *eidos*, which engenders the "primal something."

Heidegger writes in the summer semester 1919 lecture course, "Phenomenology and Transcendental Philosophy of Value," that phenomenology, which he takes to be identical with historical method, has as its aim the advancement of ways into genuine problems. The only philosophy that can foster such an advance is philosophy "which is also determined to advance the great traditions of Kant and German idealism in their enduring tendencies."[19] What Heidegger then criticizes in transcendental philosophy is its constructivist and non-phenomenological character. In the winter semester 1920–21 lecture course, "Introduction to the Phenomenology of Religion," Heidegger gives the most extended treatment of his method of formal indication as I noted in Chapter 1. In the context of introducing that discussion, he says that Husserlian phenomenology first enabled concrete research into the Kantian problem of constitution: "This problem [of constitution] was posed by Kant; but phenomenology (Husserl's) first had the means to carry out this study concretely."[20] Kant happens upon something worthy of inquiry, but he approaches it in a disappointingly non-phenomenological manner. Again, in the 1925 lecture course on time, Heidegger still regards Kant as an epistemologist whose *a priori* belongs to the subjective sphere. Phenomenology demonstrates, by contrast, that "the apriori is not limited to the subjectivity, indeed that in the first instance it has primarily nothing at all to do with subjectivity."[21] At this stage in the game, Heidegger has not yet caught sight of the phenomenological Kant.

Precursor (1925–1927): Conversion to the Quasi-Phenomenological Kant Who Anticipates Husserl

With the second phase, Heidegger now thinks Kant is not only on the right topic but also that he is a phenomenologist who anticipates and in part supersedes Husserl. The sudden advent of this phase is well documented. Toward the middle of the winter semester 1925–26 lecture course, "Logic," published as *Logic: The Question of Truth*, Heidegger abruptly abandons his planned outline and begins an in-depth exploration of the Kantian doctrine of schematism and time.[22] Two years later he alludes to his sudden interest in Kant: "Several years ago as I studied anew the *Critique of Pure Reason*, and read it as it were against the backdrop of Husserl's phenomenology, the scales fell from my eyes, and Kant became for me confirmation of the correctness of the way for which I was seeking."[23] Heidegger had discovered the phenomenological Kant.

Husserl was trained as a mathematician and is not known for his understanding of the history of philosophy. It makes it all the more surprising that he should have opened the door for Heidegger, renowned for the probity of his historical-philosophical investigations, to understand Kant. As presented in *Ideas I*, Husserl sees the history of modern philosophy develop toward phenomenology. "Phenomenology is, so to speak, the secret nostalgia of all modern philosophy."[24] Based on his own hard-won insight into the nature of phenomenology's province, Husserl can affirm that Kant happened upon it though he did not grasp as such.

> And then the first to correctly see it was Kant, whose greatest intuitions become wholly understandable to us only when we had obtained by hard work a fully clear awareness of the peculiarity of the province belonging to phenomenology. It then becomes evident to us that Kant's mental regard was resting on that field, although he was still unable to appropriate it or recognize it as a field of work pertaining to a strict eidetic science proper.[25]

Though Heidegger does not think the field involves a strict eidetic science, he does think nonetheless it needs to be brought to view and interpreted. So, in the first place, Husserl gave Heidegger a Kant trained on phenomenology's subject matter. But not only that. Husserl goes further in this passage and observes, "Thus, for example, the transcendental deduction in the first edition of the *Critique of Pure Reason* was actually operating inside the realm of phenomenology, but Kant misinterpreted that realm as psychological and therefore he himself abandoned it."[26] This is the key to the phenomenological Kant and the reason why Heidegger had no problem adopting the corresponding vocabulary of Kant and Husserl, namely transcendental horizon and schema, in order to explicate time as the sense of being.[27]

The 1925–26 lecture course worked out an immanent critique of phenomenology by appropriating Husserl's refutation of psychologism. Husserl refuted psychologism by proving that truth cannot be a real process, but he did so by introducing a distinction between the real and the ideal.[28] Heidegger finds this cleft between the ideal and the real troubling, and he wants to uncover the ground of the distinction and thus the possibility of their relation. As he would soon write in *Being and Time*, "How are we to take ontologically the relation between an ideal entity and something that is real and on-hand? . . . Is not psychologism correct in holding out against this separation, even if it neither clarifies ontologically the kind of being which belongs to the thinking that which is thought, nor is even so much as acquainted with it as a problem?"[29] To be sure, Heidegger does not take truth as a real process, but he handles truth in terms of the phenomenology of the *Sixth Logical Investigation*. Truth is not, as it is in the refutation of psychologism, the experienced identity of the ideal meaning and the real state of affairs, but the showing of an entity in its selfsameness across the interplay of presence and absence. This interplay, in turn, is made possible by being-in-the-world, which Heidegger terms truth in the most original sense, and this in turn is made possible by time.

Beyond the ideal-real divide, Husserl discovered the primacy of givenness, widening intuition over the categorial sphere. With this discovery, Heidegger thinks "Husserl has thought to the end the great tradition of Western philosophy."[30] Phenomenology is a recovery of this theme, which Heidegger immediately connects with a radically new Kant: "Kant was no Kantian."[31] Husserl's principles of all principles confirms what Kant himself maintained in the very first line of the *Critique* proper, that intuition is the essential ingredient in knowing.[32] Heidegger's real interest is in the possibility of such intuiting, and he senses in its very terms, "making present," a connection with time.[33] This is Heidegger's central insight, signaled in the very schematic title of his magnum opus, *Being* and *Time*, and so what caught Heidegger's eye and instigated the interest in Kant was the central role given time in the *Critique*'s analysis of the possibility of intuition. As a refrain, Heidegger formulates the claim that Kant was the first thinker to intimate the relation of being and time.[34] Specifically, Kant's doctrine of the schematism connects receptivity and spontaneity in terms of time. In this problematic Heidegger senses a collaborator in his project of formally indicating the primal something of experience.[35]

While Heidegger's enthusiasm for Kant is beyond question, he is still extremely critical of Kant and his epistemological point of departure.[36] Under the spell of Descartes and formal logic, Kant bungles "the critical phenomenological question concerning the relation of time and I" and conceives the self as an "empty I combine."[37] He can therefore not see that time is "the fundamental existential of Dasein."[38] The chief difficulty is Kant's inadequate doctrine of time:

> Aside from all dogmatic motives, the main obstacle for Kant seeing the time-character of the I think lies in the inadequate interpretation of time itself; although Kant made use of the more originary structure of the now in the schematism, he took the now and the now-series in the theory always in the sense of the traditional comprehension of time.[39]

Though Kant intimated the connection of being and time, he could not see that time was the structure of Dasein itself, because he lacked a phenomenology of time. Without such an understanding of time, Kant remains epistemological and negligent of the timely being of the subject.

Heidegger's discovery of the quasi-phenomenological Kant occurred just before the ultimate draft of *Being and Time*, largely written in March 1926, and the effect of the conversion on the latter is noticeable, though often over-stated.[40] The debate with Neo-Kantianism remains; Heidegger does not become a Kantian, but Kant becomes phenomenological. In *Being and Time*, Heidegger still distinguishes sharply between rationalistic construction and phenomenological experience. Again, he says that phenomenology provides the method for "genuine philosophical 'empiricism,'" because it enables the disclosure of the *a priori* rather than its rationalistic construction: "But to disclose the *a priori* is not to make an '*a-prioristic*' construction. Through Edmund Husserl, we have learned not only to understand once more the sense of every genuine philosophical 'empiricism' but also to handle the necessary tools for it."[41] The difference is that now Heidegger no longer reads Kant as a Neo-Kantian but instead as a quasi-phenomenologist or rather, in one respect, as the *proto*-phenomenologist: "The first and only person who has gone any stretch of the way towards investigating the dimension of temporality or has even let himself be drawn hither by the coercion of the phenomena themselves is Kant."[42] For Heidegger, Husserl has been superseded by the phenomenological Kant he made visible.

With Kant, Heidegger distinguishes two levels of phenomena, the ontic and the ontological. The two levels are analogous in that they call for the subordination of *logos* to phenomena, but they are different in that they call for fundamentally different inquiries and modes of investigations. Philosophy is phenomenological ontology, the exhibition of ontological phenomena. The ecstatic-horizonal bringing forth of timeliness engenders Dasein as thrown project as well as the other senses of being. Time, then, opens the context for philosophical investigation. Fundamental ontology uncovers the structure of that context in the schematic interrelation of time and being. The aim of this investigation is to grasp what is at work in the primal something, to return to the pre-theoretical basis of experience and elucidate it from out of itself. Heidegger employs "schema" not because he has abandoned his phenomenological project to return to the "old mythology of an intellect which glues and rigs together the world's matter with its own forms."[43] In fact it is precisely the schematic horizon of time that, in Heidegger's mind, justifies his claiming the opposite: "Thus the significance-relationships which determine the structure of the world are not a network of forms which a wordless subject has laid over some kind of material. What is rather the case is that factical Dasein, understanding itself and its world ecstatically in the unity of the 'there', comes back from these horizons to the entities encountered within them."[44] The schematic horizon of temporality names the *eidos* of time in and for itself. With temporality, Heidegger thinks he has discovered what Kant attempted to bring to expression: "Only when we have established the problematic of temporality, can we succeed in casting light on the obscurity of his doctrine of the schematism."[45]

The summer semester 1927 lecture course thrusts Kant to the fore, and clarifies the status of the Kant-interpretation just before the fully phenomenological Kant emerges in the following semester. Kant's transcendental method is not yet identified with phenomenology, but it needs to be transferred onto a properly phenomenal basis. The sticking point is the very place of convergence, the interpretation of being in terms of time, in which Kant shows himself to be in contact with the ancient Greek interpretation of being in terms of presence.

> But the reason why Kant calls being a logical predicate is connected with his ontological, that is, transcendental, mode of inquiry, and it leads us to a fundamental confrontation with this type of inquiry, which we shall discuss in the context of the interpretation of the *Critique of Pure Reason* next semester. With reference to the temporal interpretation of the being of the on-hand by means of praesens, in comparison with the Kantian interpretation of being as positing, it should have become clear how only a phenomenological interpretation affords the possibility of opening up a positive understanding of the Kantian problems and his solutions of them, which means putting the Kantian problem on a phenomenal basis.[46]

Thus, due to the peculiarity of Kant's methodology, "the phenomenologically decisive thing remains obscure."[47] In this second phase of the

Kant-interpretation, Heidegger unveils the proto-phenomenological Kant, a Kant who brings the *a priori* to givenness and who surely though obscurely was interested in the givenness of being in terms of time.

Collaborator (1927–1929): An Even More Phenomenological Kant Who Surpasses Husserl

In *Being and Time*, Heidegger writes that two things stood in the way of Kant's full insight into temporality: "In the first place, he altogether neglected the problem of being; and, in connection with this, he failed to provide an ontology with Dasein as its theme or (to put this in Kantian language) to give a preliminary ontological analytic of the subjectivity of the subject."[48] The 1929 *Kant and the Problem of Metaphysics* has as its central theses the opposite of these two assertions, though commentators typically neglect the difference between the two interpretations of Kant.[49] The 1929 preface to the Kant book, however, makes it clear that he there departs from the Kant interpretation of *Being and Time* in that he offers "by contrast, a progressive interpretation of the *Critique of Pure Reason*."[50] Rather than simply working out the destruction foreseen for SZ II, Heidegger writes a historical introduction to the manner of questioning operative in SZ I, and Kant alone can be the subject of such a study because he alone anticipated its horizon of questioning. The third phase takes Kant as a phenomenologist but in a still more robust sense, for Kant is no longer entangled in epistemology but is specifically interested in grounding metaphysics.

Heidegger provides the key to understanding this intensified interest in transcendental philosophy, which we can date to the 1927–28 lecture course.[51] He finds in Kant a *confirmation* for his approach. Just what is this approach that the backdrop of Husserlian phenomenology enabled him to see? In the first place, this is certainly the correctness of phenomenological method and its devotion to intuition as the foundation of knowledge, whether ontic or ontological.

> At the present time and independently of Kant, Husserl, the founder of phenomenological research, rediscovered this fundamental thrust of knowledge in general and of philosophical knowledge in particular. It is precisely this basic conception by phenomenology of the *intuitive character of knowledge* that contemporary philosophy resists. But any appeal to Kant against phenomenology basically collapses already in the first sentence of the *Critique*.[52]

Heidegger's professed reliance on Husserl in his interpretation of Kant challenges Schalow's claim that Heidegger's engagement with transcendental philosophy moves phenomenology "even further from its Husserlian beginnings."[53] Heidegger instead thinks his attempt to work out, alongside Kant, the peculiar givenness of the ontological holds on to what is essential in Husserl even as it moves deeper into the problematic he opens. Kant constitutes, moreover, a confirmation of the kind of intuition at work in philosophical, i.e., ontological knowledge: "If *knowledge as such* is primarily intuition . . . then ontological, i.e., philosophical, knowledge is also originally and ultimately intuition—but intuition in a sense which is precisely the central problem of the *Critique*."[54] Pure intuition cannot be intuited thematically as something on-hand but only "in an original, formative giving."[55] Kant confirms, then, both that thinking is in service to intuition and the peculiarity of the intuition at work in ontological knowledge.[56] What Heidegger found in Kant, then, was not a "new linguistic model" that had the effect of stilling the stream of factical life;[57] instead he found a partner in the *phenomenological* project of articulating the givenness of ontological truth.[58] In this he sees Kant more than Husserl as his predecessor. Heidegger's own method of formal indication now becomes expressed in terms of the *Critique of Pure Reason*'s "ground-laying" (*Grundlegung*) and architectonic.[59] The interest in Kant, then, is occasioned by the phenomenological interest that guides his thinking through the whole of the 1920s and beyond. His turn to Kant and transcendence *deepens* the phenomenological inquiry into the pre-theoretical *a priori* and its indifference to the distinction between subjective and objective.[60]

Heidegger offers a rereading of the nature of "principle" operative in Kant's highest principle of synthetic judgments. Rather than something on-hand that is posited for experience to be possible, the *Grundsatz* is a phenomenologically disclosed articulation of transcendence.

> The basic proposition [*Grundsatz*] is no principle [*Prinzip*] that is arrived at in the drawing of a conclusion that we must put forth as valid if experience is to hold true. Rather, it is the expression of the most original *phenomenological knowledge* of the innermost, unified structure of transcendence, laboriously extracted in the stages of the essential projection of ontological synthesis that have already been presented.[61]

As we have seen, the crucial distinction between a principle imposed on experience and an expression disclosed from experience is already present in Heidegger's first mature lecture course of 1919. Now, ten years later phenomenology and transcendence go hand in hand. Heidegger even interprets Kant's "analytic" as a phenomenological exposition, a *Sehenlassen*, of transcendence: "In Kant's own words, such an analytic is a bringing of 'itself to light through reason,' it is 'what reason brings forth entirely from out of itself.' (A xx). Analytic thus becomes a letting-be-seen [*Sehenlassen*] of the genesis of the essence of finite pure reason from its proper ground."[62] This identification helps clarify his characterization of *Being and Time* as an "analytic" of Dasein, that is, a phenomenology of transcendence. "Philosophizing happens as the explicit transcendence of Dasein."[63] Kant's transcendental philosophy, as interpreted by Heidegger, is no static theory that stills the stream of factical life; rather, it is a "happening" (*Geschehen*) that occurs in the ground-laying, a happening that is nothing other than Dasein itself.[64] Heidegger thus finds in Kant's transcendental philosophy an anticipation of his own phenomenological method of formal indication.

Retracting his 1926 criticism, he now thinks primordial time enables the "I think."[65] What the formally indicative ground-laying uncovers is human finitude as the site for experiencing something. This site is thrown open in our disposed understanding by means of the ecstatic-horizonal bringing forth of time. The Kant book points to transcendental imagination and its schematisms as enabling the interface at the heart of experience between receptive spontaneity and spontaneous receptivity. Heidegger thereby finds in Kant something of the interplay of factical life experience of his phenomenological project. Heidegger thinks the "primal something" is the target of Kant's question of the ontological synthesis. With this third phase, Kant is a phenomenological researcher into the happening whereby being is given.

Husserl, for his part, finds this phase of Heidegger's phenomenological Kant to be puzzling to say the least. In marginalia to his personal copy of the Kant book, he wonders about the extent of the primacy of intuition ("Is this Kant?"), pointing to the issue of the thing in itself.[66] Second, he affirms that he too is interested in "an essential unveiling of transcendence," thus indicating that he is by rights a phenomenological partner in Heidegger's program.[67] And yet, in the end, he wants to distance himself from the Kantian and Heideggerian discussion of finitude and anthropology, which, he thinks, indicates a failure to understand the transcendental reduction: "In this unclarity Heidegger joins Kant."[68]

Precursor Again (1930 and later): Kant Is Still Phenomenological But on Par with Husserl

As I will show in detail in the following chapter, in the 1930s, he distances himself from the interpretation of Kant developed in the 1929 book. As he would later write, "Kant's text became a refuge, as I sought in Kant an advocate for the question of being which I posed."[69] He needed such an advocate, because *Being and Time* was "susceptible to misinterpretation," and he came to think that Kant could become an ally in posing the question of being in terms of time. In this, he admits, he was mistaken:

> The refuge . . . determined in this way, led me to interpret the *Critique of Pure Reason* from within the horizon of the manner of questioning set forth in *Being and Time*. In truth, however, Kant's question was subordinated to a manner of questioning foreign to it, although conditioning it.[70]

Heidegger makes it clear that it is *Kant's* horizon of questioning that is overlooked, not his own. In the *Contributions* he accordingly denies that the horizon from which he interpreted Kant in the Kant book can be called Kantian: "But, if one contends—and rightfully so—that historically Kant here is distorted, then one must also avoid presenting as Kantianism the basic position from which and into which the distortion took place."[71] Heidegger wrote the Kant book to make his phenomenological inquiry more accessible, but the book missed Kant and made Heidegger out to be an updated Kantian. Is this the end of the phenomenological Kant?

In the late 1920s, Heidegger saw Kant as a formally indicating phenomenologist who illumines the schematic source of experience from out of itself. By the early 1930s, however, Heidegger had problems with formal indication and its targeted schematic essence. Schema is too infected with the theoretical and objectivating gaze to name the pre-theoretical context of experience. Heidegger keeps to the central insight of his phenomenology into the givenness of the pre-theoretical, but he employs more poetic tropes to evoke the requisite pathos. Accordingly, the happening occasioned by the transcendental horizon of time becomes named with the event of appropriation. The horizon is not the correlate of our research, but appropriation appropriates us via fundamental dispositions that we name in poetic terms. Phenomenological research is insufficiently phenomenological because it aims to uncover an *eidos*, but such an *eidos* is in fact a methodological imposition; formal indication remains infected with the objectification that it aims to overcome. The later critique does not simply rejoin the early phenomenological breakthrough. It leaves behind its concern for research and thus primal science, and it leaves behind the search for an *eidos* of experience, an *eidos* that Heidegger thought he found in the phenomenological Kant.

At the end of the 1929–30 lecture course, soon after the publication of the Kant book, Heidegger accordingly questions the science of ontology as adequate to his problematic: "Yet what are we then to put in place of ontology? Kant's transcendental philosophy, for instance? Here it is only the name and claims that have been changed, while the idea itself has been retained. Transcendental philosophy too must fall."[72] The following semester, Heidegger devotes his course to the examination of the relation of freedom and nature in Kant, arguing, in the end, that Kant failed to grasp freedom adequately.[73] Kant does not universalize the problem of being, but treats only on-hand entities.[74] "Also in the case of Kant the traditional guiding question of metaphysics—what are entities?—is not developed into the fundamental question bearing and leading this question: what is being? In it there lies simultaneously the question concerning the primordial possibility and necessity of the manifestness of being."[75] Along with this, Kant "lacked a metaphysics of Dasein" and "did not make the finitude of the human being into a sufficiently primordial problem" because he left the connection of time and "I think" unclarified.[76] Now Heidegger maintains that the time that comes to exposition in Kant is not the primordial time of *Being and Time*.[77] Heidegger also takes to referring to "phenomenology of consciousness" in a dismissive way, and now says that Kant's transcendental philosophy is "directed to what from the outset makes possible the cognition of objects as such."[78] The phenomenological partnership seems dissolved.

Heidegger's far more critical distance, however, is balanced by a new historical-motivational role that Heidegger finds for Kant, whose "new determination" of the essence of ontology is "on the whole a renewed solidification of the ancient approach to the question of being."[79] Heidegger unearths something wholly other within Kant's horizon of questioning. Heidegger reads Kant as seeking to grasp the objectivity of objects (and thus in a refracted way the being of entities) rather than the givenness of the subjectivity of the subject (Dasein). In this shift in interpretation Kant in fact comes somewhat closer to the emphases of the later Heidegger while remaining essentially phenomenological. In the face of modern subjectivity, Kant recovers something of the Greek experience of the phenomenological space more fundamental than subject and object.

In the 1920s, Heidegger sought to find the place of phenomenology within the history of philosophy. At first, he sought contact with religious thinkers, especially Augustine, before finding it in Aristotle and then, as we have seen, Kant. In the 1930s and later, Heidegger retains the identification of phenomenology and Kant and sees Kant as a recovery of Greek philosophy, which, in contrast to modern rationalism, is phenomenological in character. The significance of Kant for the later Heidegger is precisely this recovery of (Greek) phenomenological philosophy. In the lecture course of 1935–36, Heidegger does not connect his reading of Kant to the phenomenological breakthrough, but this is likely due to his reticence throughout the 1930s and 1940s to use the name "phenomenology."[80] Heidegger suppresses the name, but he does not suppress the idea, and he holds to the intuitive character of knowledge. Kant's transcendental thinking, which entails the subordination of thought to intuition, recovers the classical Greek theme of the subordination of *logos* to phenomenon, indicated in the title, phenomeno-logy.[81] The first sentence of the *Critique*, by prioritizing intuition in the definition of knowledge, offers the "first and completely decisive blow" against rationalism.[82] In phase three we saw that this passage demonstrated the basically phenomenological character of Kant's philosophy, and now that phenomenological character is set in opposition to rationalism. Neither intuition nor thought alone suffices for knowledge, and yet it is nonetheless the case that thought is directed toward intuition or, as Heidegger formulates it, thought "stands in the service of intuition."[83] The rest of Heidegger's analysis is dedicated to showing that Kant's exclusive concern is with rethinking thought on the basis of its essential relation to intuition. Consequently, with Kant's new "characterization of judgment, the primordial sense of *logos* as *gathering*, though dimmed, shines through."[84]

The transcendental attitude traces judgment and thing back to "something more primordial" (*etwas Ursprünglicheres*) out of which they can arise.[85] This more primordial something or between becomes opened up through the reciprocity of anticipating and encountering, a reciprocity named in the highest principle of synthetic judgment.[86] Kant is phenomenological in that he defines knowledge in general as essentially grounded in intuition, but he suffers from a number of phenomenological failures. The first is that he altogether neglects the familiar realm of everyday surrounding things and focuses exclusively on objectivity.[87] The second is that he approaches being as the objectivity of the object; he thinks rather than experiences the relation of thought and being.[88] Nonetheless, his exposition of the highest principle of synthetic judgment uncovers the pre-theoretical open between.

> The ground which [the principles] lay, the nature of experience, is not an on-hand thing, to which we return and upon which we then simply stand. Experience is a happening circling in itself through which what lies within the circle becomes opened up [*eröffnet*]. This open [*Offene*], however, is nothing other than the between [*Zwischen*]— between us and the thing.[89]

The principles articulate the interplay of thought and intuition, anticipation and encounter, by means of which entities are accessible in their intelligibility. Within this domain phenomenological experience is possible. In phenomenological fashion, transcendental philosophy considers an entity "in regard to how this object is an object *for us*, in which respect it is meant, that is, how our thought thinks it."[90] Kant uncovers the domain of experience, but he does not grasp it as such, nor does he situate it within the deeper happening of the domain's discovery, neglect, and recovery.

The Kant who emerges in the 1930s, in the ambit of the *Contributions*, and in contrast to the 1929 Kant book, is quasi-phenomenological. Such a reading continues, though in somewhat more critical form, through the last days of Heidegger's philosophical itinerary. Heidegger does criticize Kant severely, but only for being insufficiently phenomenological in Heidegger's own sense. Consider the famous letter to William Richardson, in which Heidegger recounts the phenomenological character of his own path, and sharply contrasts this phenomenology with that of Husserl and Kant: "Meanwhile 'phenomenology' in Husserl's sense was elaborated into a distinctive philosophical position according to a pattern set by Descartes, Kant and Fichte. The historicity of thought remained completely foreign to such a position."[91] To justify such a reading, Heidegger refers the reader to Husserl's 1910–11 essay, *Philosophy as a Rigorous Science*. We might be led to think, then, that Heidegger's *Being and Time*, as the aberration theory holds, momentarily fell prey to such a position, but Heidegger immediately corrects this view: "The question of being, unfolded in *Being and Time* parted company with this philosophical position, and that on the basis of what to this day I still consider a more faithful adherence to the principle of phenomenology."[92] But in the ambit of *Being and Time*, as we have seen, Heidegger prizes Kant and Husserl (though *not* Descartes and Fichte) precisely for their adherence to the principle of phenomenology. Just after *Being and Time*, with the advent of phase three, Heidegger did not become Kantian, but Kant became phenomenological in Heidegger's sense. By 1930, Heidegger saw that this was partially incorrect, because Kant's horizon of questioning was geared to the givenness of the thing and not the historical givenness of intelligibility. With the fourth phase, Heidegger continues to regard Kant as phenomenological but now in the Husserlian sense, not in the more pregnant sense as a partner in his own brand of phenomenology.

The fourth and final phase of his Kant-interpretation has Kant recover a phenomenology of judgment in the face of modern rationalism and thereby renew contact with Greek philosophy. As Husserl had independently and accidentally stumbled upon Kant's position, so Kant independently and accidentally stumbled upon Greek philosophy. "Frequently, without expressly knowing it, Kant comes with the certainty of a sleepwalker, or better, by virtue of genuine philosophical congeniality, back to the fundamental meaning of the primary philosophical concepts of the Greeks."[93] Heidegger has in mind, chiefly, the phenomenological subordination of thought to intuition: "Reason is the faculty—we can say—of anticipatory gathering—*logos, legein*." This comment attributes to Kant what Heidegger, eleven years earlier, had attributed to Husserl: "Without being explicitly conscious of it, phenomenology returns to the broad concept of truth whereby the Greeks (Aristotle) could call true even perception as such and the simple perception of something."[94] In this fourth phase, then, Heidegger translates Husserl's recovery of Kant into a Kantian recovery of Greek thinking. The phenomenological Kant thereby achieves a decisive significance in Heidegger's reading of the history of philosophy. Rather than a return to the first phase of relative disinterest, the fourth phase rejoins the second in finding a quasi-phenomenological Kant. Now, however, he is accorded decisive historical significance for the recovery of Greek thought.

2 The Phenomenological Kant

The motive for Heidegger's interest in Kant is phenomenological. He sought and found a phenomenological ally who shared the same goal of articulating the origination of sense. The interest in Kant, then, was not a detour but as Heidegger himself maintained, a confirmation of his earliest insights. If this was the motive for his interest in Kant, what was the motive for his later distancing? First, Heidegger grew dissatisfied with formally indicative research, and second, he came to realize that the interpretation of Kant said more about Heidegger than it did Kant. Heidegger retains the phenomenology in principle but cultivates within it an eye for history and the historical transformation of the phenomenologist. Even for the later Heidegger, Kant as well as Husserl remain critical forerunners to Heidegger's own historical reinterpretation of phenomenology.

The interest in Kant was at first a confirmation and later a distraction (or "refuge" as Heidegger termed it), but it was not an aberration. With *Being and Time*, penned in 1926, Heidegger is only tentative in his reading of the phenomenological Kant. Only the third phase, from 1927 till 1929, sees Kant as a phenomenological partner. The Kant book, belonging to the third phase, does not fulfill the projected plans of *Being and Time* for a destruction of Kant, but instead presents a "progressive," though still critical reading, which offers a new, collaborative interpretation of Kant. The reading of Kant from 1930 and later rejects the specifics of the progressive reading, and it thereby rejoins the quasi-phenomenological Kant first glimpsed in late 1925 and discernible in *Being and Time*. The aberration thesis cannot recognize the basic identity of the second and fourth phases, because it does not distinguish the second from the third phase. Heidegger's 1925 turn to Kant, phenomenological in motivation, was not an aberration, though the 1927–29 reading of Kant according to *Being and Time*'s horizon of questioning was undoubtedly a distraction.

The promise of the "phenomenological Kant" gave Heidegger entrance to a rich domain of investigation. As he sought to find the place of phenomenology in the history of philosophy, he found points of contact with Aristotle and then, through Husserl, Kant. Heidegger's phenomenological Kant became the means for him to surpass Husserl, and yet the phenomenological Kant at the same time signals Heidegger's continued indebtedness to Husserlian phenomenology. In four phases and with reference to Husserl, Heidegger interpreted Kant as first *falling short of* phenomenology, then *approaching* phenomenology, then *advancing* phenomenology, and finally *recovering* phenomenology. Heidegger's Kant is not an alternative to Husserl's phenomenology but its attempted advancement.

Registering the junctures of his reading allows us to get the history right. When we do the philosophical issues themselves can come to light. At no point in his life did Heidegger think his peculiar brand of phenomenological thinking sprang like Athena fully formed from the head of Zeus. Husserl, Kant, and certain Greek thinkers anticipated and prepared the way for the appropriation of the tradition undertaken by Heidegger. In the end, Heidegger took phenomenology and transcendental philosophy further in the direction he wanted to go than anyone had before, but he took them so far they ceased to be recognizable to others. Husserl, for one, came to realize he could "have nothing to do . . . with this brilliant, unscientific genius."[95] Nevertheless, the phenomenological

Kant remains one of the principal reference points for the variations of Heidegger's own peculiar "transcendental" and "phenomenological" thinking, whatever we (or Heidegger) might wish to call it.

3 The Leibnizian Key to the Kant Book

Now let us turn to the most intense phase of Heidegger's interpretation of Kant, which issues in the impressive *Kant and the Problem of Metaphysics*.[96] In the ambit of this interpretation, Heidegger sees in the Kantian concern for judgment a concern for the conditions for the possibility of ontology. Heidegger thereby seeks to undercut the dominant epistemological reading of the *Critique of Pure Reason*. Key to his entire project is a peculiar interpretation of Leibniz's doctrine of essence. In the 1928 summer lecture course, published as *The Metaphysical Foundations of Logic*, Heidegger builds the case that not only Kant but Leibniz too has a role to play in confirming the phenomenological path. Heidegger shows that both Leibniz and Kant found traditional accounts of judgment unsatisfying. By thinking through the concrete problem of judgment, they worked their way into the ambit of the phenomenological project of *Being and Time*. For both, judgment is found to be subordinate to the self-showing of entities, and the condition for the possibility of uncoveredness is the disclosedness of Dasein. Leibniz, though, is but a "preparation" for Kant's explicit distinction between the two levels of truth.[97] Leibniz readies for, but does not attain to Kant's transcendental account of experience.

Heidegger labors to dispel the epistemological reading of Kant, and he sees that even in Leibniz there is the recognition that knowledge is *founded* on being, and thus logic is founded on metaphysics. In particular, as we will see, Leibniz distinguishes between *cognitio distincta* and *cognitio adaequata*, between nominal and real definition. Heidegger says that Kant makes the same distinction, which, when overlooked, "misled the entire neo-Kantian interpretation of the *Critique of Pure Reason* into a misguided search for an epistemology in Kant."[98] Now, in these writings on Leibniz and Kant, he is not merely restating *Being and Time* in the terminology of his predecessors; rather he thinks he discovers in dialogue with them "a still more radical" interpretation of transcendence understood in terms of ontological freedom.[99]

Heidegger acknowledges that he understands Leibniz and Kant from the perspective of his own philosophizing.[100] That is, he reads them in terms of the phenomena they were trying to articulate rather than the judgments or formulations they made about those phenomena. Thus, Kant "must be read . . . for what he wanted to say."[101] In this way, he is clear that there is no Leibniz or Kant "in themselves," independent, that is, from the activity of philosophizing. "This historical Kant is always only the Kant that becomes manifest in an original possibility of philosophizing."[102] Heidegger is sure to note that this program apparently accords with Kant's own interpretative strategy. He quotes Kant:

> The *Critique of Pure Reason* can thus be seen as the genuine apology for Leibniz, even against his partisans whose eulogies scarcely do him any honor; just as it can be for many different past philosophers, to whom many historians of philosophy, with all their intended praise, only attribute mere nonsense. Such historians cannot comprehend the purpose of these philosophers because they neglect the key to the interpretation of all products of pure reason from mere concepts, the critique of reason itself (as the common source of all these concepts). They are thus incapable of recognizing beyond what the philosophers actually said, what they really meant to say.[103]

Thus, Kant himself did "violence" to the words of his predecessors. Insofar as the history of philosophy becomes accessible only through systematic investigation, Heidegger thinks the distinction between history and system becomes problematical. "Historical description is dead if it is not systematic, and systematic description is empty if it is not historical."[104] The way to systematic investigations is through the "critical dismantling" of the tradition in order to arrive at the phenomena themselves.[105] This accords with the general program of phenomenology, which traces semblance back to genuine phenomena or traces doctrine back to its presuppositions.[106] At the same time, Heidegger is not consistent on this point and sometimes reluctantly refers to his investigations of Leibniz and Kant as merely an "historical" introduction to the systematic investigations of *Being and Time*.[107]

The rationalists, such as Descartes and Spinoza, hold that thinking is the nearest, and therefore thinking determines being and logic determines ontology. Alternatively, some follow Aristotle in holding that being determines thinking and ontology determines logic. Where might Leibniz fit in this division? Are Bertrand Russell and Louis Couturat correct in thinking that Leibniz derives ontology from logic?[108] Heidegger thinks this choice trades on a problematic division into disciplines, a division that becomes questionable in Leibniz and is overcome in Kant: "The very possibility of such a question begins to vacillate precisely through Leibniz, and is first shattered in Kant."[109]

However, alongside the questioning of discipline-boundaries, Heidegger also sees a movement in Leibniz and Kant toward grounding logic in metaphysics. How are we to reconcile this with his claim that the distinction between disciplines is highly questionable? In this course, when Heidegger refers to metaphysics, he has in mind the project of fundamental ontology that he has already worked out to a great degree in *Being and Time*. The task now is to work out logic on the same fundamental level he had already given to "metaphysics."

Logic, says Heidegger, no longer has anything to do with philosophy. To again make logic philosophical, its *logos* needs to be returned to the phenomena: "Its contents ever so dead, it once arose from a living philosophy. The task now is to release it from petrification."[110] Consequently, the strategy of the course is to lead traditional logic back to its basic problems and then lead from the content of these problems to logic's presuppositions. By doing so, we gain "immediate access to philosophy itself" and thus disclose "the general horizon within which a philosophical logic must move."[111] Heidegger focuses on judgment, because it has been regarded as the basic phenomenon of logic since Aristotle. He inquires into its foundations in "basic principles" (*Grund-Sätze*). But how is the lawfulness of principles possible? That is, "how must that entity which is subject to such laws, Dasein itself, be constituted so as to be able to be thus governed by laws?"[112] The normativity of law points to freedom as its possibility: "Only what exists as a free entity could be at all bound by an obligatory lawfulness. Freedom alone can be the source of obligation. *A basic problem of logic, the law-governedness of thinking, reveals itself to be a problem of human existence in its ground, the problem of freedom.*"[113] Tracing judgment back to its possibility leads to the analysis of Dasein. This is the proper place to develop a philosophical logic or what amounts to the same, the metaphysical foundations of logic. Leibniz's doctrine of judgment leads to his monadology and thus shows that logic is rooted in the metaphysics of Dasein.

Heidegger focuses on the treatise, *Meditationes de Cognitione, Veritate et Ideis* (1684), in which Leibniz confronts Descartes.[114] Heidegger identifies the work as "an important stage on the way from Descartes to Kant regarding the problem of 'categories.'"[115] The confrontation with rationalism motivates transcendental thought. Leibniz demonstrates the inadequacy of the Cartesian criteria of truth by subjecting clarity and distinctness to further analysis. Knowledge can be (1) either obscure or clear; clear, in turn, can be (2) either confused or distinct; distinct, in turn, can be (3) either inadequate or adequate; adequate, in turn, can be (4) either symbolic or intuitive. The most perfect knowledge is not merely clear and distinct but also adequate and intuitive. In short, it is direct intuition. Let us take each of these levels in turn, since the unfolding of this analysis is the key to Heidegger's Kant-interpretation.

In the first place, knowledge can be either obscure or clear. If it is *obscure*, it is insufficient for recognition, and if it is *clear* then it suffices for recognition. In the case of obscurity, an animal or even a philosophical concept previously encountered may be conflated with another, and with clarity the animal or concept emerges with its given identity. In the second place, clear knowledge can itself be either confused or distinct. If it is *confused*, the distinguishing marks of what is known are not enumerated so flow together with the marks of other things, and if it is *distinct*, such attributes are enumerated and so distinguished. For instance, we may be able to clearly distinguish colors from odors through the evidence of our senses even though the distinguishing marks are confused, and so we are unable to explain the distinction to others. At this level are nominal definitions of composites and primitive notions that do not admit of analysis in terms of marks. In the third place, clear and distinct knowledge of composites can be either inadequate or adequate. If it is *inadequate*, the enumerated marks can nonetheless be confused, and if it is *adequate*, the analysis of the marks for a distinct concept is complete and no further clarification is possible. Leibniz says he is not sure fully adequate knowledge is possible for humans though mathematics approaches it.

In the fourth place, adequate knowledge can be either symbolic or intuitive. If it is *symbolic*, we do not have the totality of individual marks in view, and if it is *intuitive*, we have this totality in view. We may think of a chiliagon without at the same time thinking about all its constitutive notions (side, equality, the number one-thousand, etc.). Heidegger stresses that the difference between symbolic and intuitive knowledge is not a further level of analysis beyond adequate knowledge, for adequate knowledge itself is the completion of analysis. Rather the fourth distinction specifies the way in which knowledge is appropriated and possessed— either blindly or intuitively.

> Those mentioned earlier (*obscura—clara, confusa—distincta, inadaequata—adaequata*) each refers to a stage of analysis, a step in making explicit marks and moments of marks (*requisita*). With the last distinction, however, we are dealing with a possible double way of appropriating [*Aneignen*] and possessing the adequate, the completely analyzed as such.[116]

Leibniz indicates as much by saying that intuitive knowledge can be had of primitive notions even though they are fully analyzed with clarity and distinctness; they cannot be analyzed further, so the fourth distinction cannot be a still further level of analysis.[117]

Two things follow from the four distinctions found in the treatise. The first is that Leibniz is overcoming the Cartesian epistemological orientation, and the second is that Leibniz's idea of knowledge is oriented toward the self-showing of entities in their manifold identity. The departure from epistemology is evident in the difference between the second and third levels of analysis. Clear and distinct but inadequate cognition yields merely nominal definitions, but clear, distinct, and adequate cognition yields real definitions. The difference between these two is not a matter of "quantitatively more" clarity, but is a difference in principle. The enumeration accomplished in the second level of analysis does not grasp the "inner structure" of the marks but only lists them. This level of knowledge is not mere words but intends the thing itself; it "does not mean a simple verbal definition, but rather a knowledge of what is intended and named in the naming, and a knowledge sufficient for distinguishing the named from other things."[118] The third level of analysis, by contrast, grasps all the marks in their unity, and thus grasps the very possibility of the intended thing: "Adequate knowledge as knowledge of essence is a priori knowledge of what makes the known itself possible, for it is the clear grasp of thorough compatibility, *compatibilitas*."[119]

Heidegger underscores that Kant himself makes the same distinction between nominal and real definitions "almost verbatim" in § 106 of his "Logic" lecture.[120] Those who attempt to find an epistemology in Kant misunderstand this distinction. Kant endeavors to affirm the reality of the categories without making them empirical properties of objects; instead they are transcendental. Heidegger understands this distinction of Leibniz's, then, as a distinction between empirical properties and real determinations of objects; with his articulation of adequate knowledge, Leibniz is breaking upon the domain of the transcendental.

Leibniz, we can now see, deploys a fundamental critique of the Cartesian epistemological standpoint. Though he follows in the tradition by thinking ideas have a central place in an account of knowing being, he surpasses the Cartesian epistemological principle according to which clarity and distinctness are the measure of truth. Instead, knowledge occurs in the adequate intuition of essences. "Leibniz provides not only more rigorous concepts of clarity and obscurity, distinctness and confusion, but he shows there is an essentially higher stage above them, where we first attain knowledge of essence, since here the totality of the necessary marks of realities are first revealed."[121] Heidegger is sure to add that only with Kant does the critique of the epistemological standpoint become central; Kant "has a more radical grasp of the problem of the possibility of ontological knowledge of the intrinsic content of essence."[122] For him, intuition has a constitutive role, and the possibility of objects is the transcendental imagination. Heidegger adds that the phenomenological intuition of essences can be properly understood only by "radicalizing" this problematic.[123] Later in the text he notes that Husserl's method confusingly secures the *a priori* of essence *and* existence.[124] Heidegger continues to criticize eidetic intuition as "not even capable of seeing the phenomenon of transcendence."[125] He turns to real definition in Leibniz and Kant, not only to defend phenomenology from Neo-Kantian criticisms, but also to develop the phenomenological account of transcendence beyond the limits of the Husserlian program.

Heidegger relates this understanding of real definition to two well-known Leibnizian doctrines: judgment as inclusion and the metaphysics of the *Monadology*. Now, inclusion is founded on the ability to resolve to identity. How, then, do identity and being adequately perceived relate to one another? How do both of these name the same concept "truth"? Adequate perception intuits the harmony of identity: "What is known in adequate knowledge is the coherent connection of the thing's mutually compatible determinations. In fact, the thing, if adequately known, is known precisely with regard to the compatibility of its realities. Adequate knowledge is the total grasp of the harmony of multiplicity."[126] The unity of identity, then, is equivalent to the harmony of determinations, and thus truth as identity is the same as truth as adequately perceived. Identity is not an "empty uniformity stripped of difference" but the "entire richness of real determinations in their compatibility without conflict."[127] Heidegger does say that Leibniz ambiguously uses both the bare logical sense and the real sense of identity, but again this betrays his orientation to divine cognition in which all is simple. Kant, for his part, finds the unity of identity and truth in the synthesis of transcendental apperception.

After a creative review of Leibniz's monadology, Heidegger concludes that the Leibnizian doctrine of judgment is rooted in his metaphysics. The inclusion theory of judgment trades on a theory of truth as identity. Knowledge is obtained by tracing back judgment's determination of subject and predicate to harmonious unity in the subject. This harmony, in turn, must be determined in advance as unified, and this is the central task of his metaphysics. Heidegger can thus say that Leibniz's inclusion theory of judgment is founded in the dynamic unity of the monad:

> Reduction to identity, as a whole of mutually compatible and coherent determinations, is, as a mode of judging about entities, only possible metaphysically if the entity itself as entity is constituted through an original unity. Leibniz sees this unity in the monadic constitution of substance. Thus the monadic structure of entities is the metaphysical foundation for the theory of judgment and for the identity theory of truth. Our dismantling of Leibniz's doctrine of judgment down to basic metaphysical problems is hereby accomplished.[128]

Against the interpretations of Couturat and Russell, then, Leibniz does indeed prioritize metaphysics over logic.[129] With this interpretation of Leibniz, Heidegger is building his case against the epistemological orientation of Neo-Kantianism; the next step will be to argue that Leibniz's move to found logic on metaphysics is completed in Kant's transcendental philosophy. In Leibniz, then, Heidegger finds support for his developing interpretation of Kant and a transitional figure toward his own philosophy.

The monadology is a genuine metaphysics, meaning it seeks a concept of being general enough to apply to every entity and capable of specifying differences among entities. And yet such ontological knowledge is still obscure, since Leibniz does not clearly distinguish the ontic and the ontological: "The very nature of ontological knowledge, and its explicit development by Leibniz, is still, by and large, obscure and groping."[130] In this way, Heidegger can call Leibniz a preparation for Kant, who makes the distinction between metaphysical and non-metaphysical knowledge explicit: "Leibniz's thought is only a preparation for the eventual separation of metaphysical from non-metaphysical knowledge. The separation emerges with Kant, and then it is again completely buried."[131] Heidegger implicitly applies the stages of knowing—clear, distinct, and adequate— to three philosophical figures who think about the distinction between the ontic and the ontological: Leibniz, who is clear but obscure, Kant, who is clear and distinct but ultimately inadequate, and Heidegger, who is clear, distinct, and adequate, because he brings forth the inner structure that makes transcendence possible.

After tracing judgment back to the basic problems of metaphysics in the first half of the 1928 summer course on Leibniz, Heidegger seeks to clarify those problems themselves in the second half. He selects as his leitmotif Leibniz's principle of sufficient reason, *Nihil est sine ratione cur potius sit quam non sit*. Heidegger admits, though, that he must venture beyond Leibniz in order to elucidate it.[132] The central problem of this principles is to be found in the *potius quam*, the "rather than." Such a problem trades on the connection of possibility and actuality, namely that the "factual is the best realization of all that is possible."[133] The "rather than" opens "a connection of ground, *ratio*, and precedence, *potius*, of foundation and pre-ference, freedom of choice (ultimately, *propensio in bonum*), hence the connection of *ground and freedom*."[134] The principle, then, proves to be an articulation of Dasein's transcendence: "For this *potius* is only the expression of the surpassingness of world, of the upswing of freedom into possibility."[135] The central question for Heidegger, in the issue of real definition, concerns the proper expression of the movement of transcendence.

4 Kant as Phenomenological Collaborator

The key distinctions of *Being and Time* are operative in *Kant and the Problem of Metaphysics* in a manner more noticeable than in the Leibniz course. Heidegger again traces *logos* back to its ground in the givenness of phenomenon. And again, he distinguishes between two levels of truth, ontic and ontological. The difference is that these distinctions are now articulated in the vocabulary of Kant's transcendental philosophy. *Logos* is thought, and it is rooted in the givenness of intuition. The two levels of truth play out in terms of two kinds of judgment, because Kant, following the tradition, conceives of knowledge as judging.[136] Accordingly, ontic judgments are veritative syntheses that are derived from experience. Ontological judgments are synthetic *a priori* judgments which make evidential judgments possible: "This pure 'relation-to . . .' (synthesis) forms first and foremost the toward-which and the horizon within which the entity in itself becomes experienceable in the empirical synthesis."[137]

Kant's "Copernican Revolution," then, is the turn to that which makes ontic truth and thus correspondence possible, namely, ontological truth.[138] Kant proves to be an ally in overcoming the logical prejudice, because he provides an alternative locus of truth.[139]

What is at issue in the *Critique of Pure Reason*, however, is not onto-logical knowledge as the condition for the possibility of ontic knowl-edge; rather what is at issue is ontological knowledge itself. Heidegger and Kant's problem is the *possibility* of ontological synthesis, and such a problem concerns nothing other than the laying of the ground for meta-physics.[140] Consequently, Heidegger interprets Kant's designation of his work as "transcendental" knowledge to mean it is concerned with ontol-ogy.[141] He thinks Kant groped toward the bringing forth of timeliness as that which constitutes this domain.

Veritative Synthesis and the Primacy of Intuition

To exhibit the "field of origin" of the *Critique of Pure Reason*, Heidegger turns to the essence of knowledge. In the first lines of the first *Critique*, Kant underscores the subordination of thought to intuition: "In what-ever manner and by whatever means a mode of knowledge may relate to objects, *intuition* is that through which it is in immediate relation to them, and toward which [*worauf*] all thought as a means is directed."[142] For Kant, then, "knowing is primarily intuiting." Heidegger says that "this point must be hammered in" if we are to understand the project of the *Critique*.[143]

Thought is not something on-hand that is then related to intuiting, but it rather belongs to the nature of thought that it is related to intuiting. Both thinking and intuiting are manners of "presentation" (*repraesen-tatio*) brought together in objective perception, and neither of them is knowledge on its own.[144] But the finitude of human knowledge does not follow from the finitude of its thinking; rather, the human thinks only because his intuition is finite. By contrast, God has no need of thinking, because his intuition is not limited. "The finitude of human knowledge must first of all be sought in the finitude of its own intuition. That a finite, thinking creature must 'also' think is an essential consequence of the finitude of its own intuiting. Only in this way can the essentially subordinate place of 'all thinking' be seen in the correct light."[145] In this way, Heidegger says that calling knowledge "judging (thinking)" betrays "the decisive sense of the Kantian problem."[146] Thinking is subordinate to intuiting in the same way that *logos* is subordinate to phenomenon in *Being and Time*.

For intuition, the mark of finitude is receptivity. It allows "the object to be given," that is, intuition is "accepting" (*hinnehmend*).[147] Kant contin-ues after the first sentence of the *Critique*: "But intuition takes place only in so far as the object is given to us. This again is only possible, to man at least, in so far as the mind is affected in a certain way."[148] Kant then calls the capacity to receive "sensibility." Heidegger thinks that with this Kant "for the first time attains a concept of sensibility which is ontological rather than sensualistic."[149] Kant does not begin with sense organs and then reason to the finitude of intuition; rather he begins with the finitude of intuition, namely that it encounters entities it does not itself produce, and thereby reasons to sense organs as required for communicating the encounter.

Knowledge is primarily intuition, but it is secondarily and essentially also thinking.[150] Intuition grants immediate relation to objects, but thought grants mediate relation to the objects through concepts, which can apply to more than one object. Heidegger brings out the interrelation of intuition and thought: "Finite intuition, as something in need of determination, is dependent upon the understanding, which not only belongs to the finitude of intuition, but is itself still more finite in that it lacks the immediacy of finite intuiting."[151] The immediate presentation of an object, accomplished in intuition, is itself presented by the concept. Kant can thus define judgment as "the mediate knowledge of an object, that is, the presentation of a presentation of it."[152] Judgment, the conceptualization of the intuition's content, is an act of the understanding and makes the intuition understandable.[153] This determination of intuition through concepts, themselves drawn from the intuition, presents the intuitive presentation of the object and allows it to be known by others.

The unification of the two presentations, the one mediate and the other immediate, brings about the manifestation of the object. Heidegger can thus use phenomenological terms and call the synthesis of thinking and intuiting *truth*: "Accordingly, the synthesis of thinking and intuiting accomplishes the making manifest of the encountered entity as object. We will therefore call it the veritative synthesis, which makes true (manifest)."[154] The veritative synthesis itself comprehends two further syntheses: predicative synthesis, which unifies presentations into the unity of a predicate, and apophantic synthesis, which unifies a subject and a predicate.[155] The veritative synthesis unifies various presentations in the unity of the concept which it then unites to a subject; both syntheses are then joined in the presentation of an object through the synthesis of intuition and thought. The veritative synthesis shows, then, that finite knowing is "an accepting, determining intuition of the entity."[156] In the presentation of an entity, Heidegger downplays the difference between appearance and the thing-in-itself. Appearance simply is "the entity itself as object of finite knowledge."[157]

For Heidegger, the thing in itself is but the correlate to the divine creative intellect; appearance is the entity as the object of finite knowledge. "Accordingly, the 'mere' in the phrase 'mere appearance' is not a restricting and diminishing of the actuality of the thing, but is rather only the negation of [the assumption] that the entity can be infinitely known in human knowledge."[158] Consequently, the appearance is the entity: "Appearances [*Erscheinungen*] are not mere illusion [*Schein*], but are the entity itself."[159] Just what is the difference between the thing and its appearance? It is a subjective difference of respect; to illustrate this, Heidegger cites a passage from Kant's *Opus Postumum*: "The difference in the concept of a thing in itself and of the appearance is not objective, but merely subjective. The thing in itself is not another object [*Objekt*], rather another relation (*respectus*) of the presentation of *the same object* [Objekt]."[160]

Ontological Synthesis and the Principle of Reason

The veritative synthesis achieves the self-showing of an entity. The deeper question for Heidegger and Kant is the possibility of such a self-showing in the synthesis of intuition and thought. As Heidegger puts it, "How must the finite entity that we call 'man' be according to its innermost essence so that in general it can be open to an entity that it itself is not and that therefore must be able to show itself from itself?"[161] Heidegger thinks Kant roots such judicative truth in ontological synthesis or what Kant terms synthetic *a priori* judgment. Ontological synthesis enables Dasein to "pass beyond (transcend) the entity in advance" even though "this entity is not only something it did not create itself, but something at which it must be directed in order to exist as Dasein."[162] Ontological synthesis is the source of both intuition and thought and is thus the source of knowledge itself.[163] Because it is in some sense "creative," it can enable non-creative knowing by allowing the on-hand entity to show itself.[164]

Implicitly drawing on the notion of real definition developed in the Leibniz course, Heidegger thinks Kant unveils the structure of ontological synthesis in five stages. The first four stages enumerate the marks, and the fifth stage unveils the very possibility of this transcendence. Heidegger is not merely repeating the outer form of Kant's analysis; rather, his interpretation is a "retrieval" (*Wiederholung*) that seeks to grasp Kant's project in a more original way that is nonetheless in accord with Kant's deepest intention. Heidegger recognizes that the stages do not wholly correspond with Kant's "external architectonic," but maintains that the stages are in accord with the "inner course of the ground-laying."[165] The seeming priority of the Transcendental Logic in the architectonic, for instance, is made problematic by the course of the investigation itself, which returns thought to intuition and roots both in the transcendental imagination.[166] I will briefly trace the trajectory of the first four stages and then conclude with the fifth stage.[167]

The first stage of the ground-laying is the elucidation of "the essential elements of pure knowledge." To analyze the two elements of finite knowing, pure intuiting and pure thinking, Heidegger turns to the Transcendental Aesthetic and the first chapter of the Transcendental Analytic, the analytic of concepts. Space and time are pure intuitions. "What is presented in pure intuition is no entity (no object, i.e., no appearing entity), but at the same time it is not simply nothing."[168] Space and time constitute the "ontological αἴσθησις" that discloses the being of entities.

Space is not an entity alongside entities according to which they are relatable. Rather, space "must be presented as that 'within which' what is on-hand can first be encountered."[169] Though it applies to many, it is not a concept but a single unity given immediately and as a whole. While space is the condition for outer appearances, time is the condition for all appearances, whether inner or outer.[170] Time orders appearances according to succession. "What we look at in advance in the experience of these appearances, although nonobjective and unthematic, is pure succession."[171] We may think that with this doctrine of the primacy of time as the universal pure intuition Kant is a precursor of Heidegger's own project, but time as succession is the ordinary concept of time and not original timeliness. Heidegger's interpretation of Kant has the intention of showing, nevertheless, how time becomes more and more important in the course of the ground-laying and "reveals its own particular essence in a more original way than the provisional characterization in the Transcendental Aesthetic permits."[172]

The second element of finite knowing is pure thinking. Concepts are formed through reflection, which grasps a unity that applies to many. In empirical concepts, content comes from empirical intuiting. Pure concepts or notions make empirical unification possible by providing "the preliminary reference to a unity in light of which a unifying in general is possible."[173] The content of pure concepts is the act of reflecting itself. "Hence the pure concepts do not first arise by means of an act of reflection, they are not reflected concepts. Rather, they belong in advance to the essential structure of reflection, i.e., they are presentations which act in, with, and for reflection, i.e., reflecting concepts."[174] Because they make judging possible, pure concepts are ontological predicates or what the tradition calls "categories." Kant arranges them according to the Table of Judgments. Heidegger emphasizes, however, that at this stage of the problematic, when the elements of finite knowing are merely considered in isolation from one another, no clarification of the ontological importance of pure concepts is possible. Since thought is essentially in service to intuition, pure concepts "can only be determined as ontological predicates if they are understood as based on the *essential unity* of finite, pure knowledge."[175]

The second stage of the ground-laying, then, is the essential unity of pure knowledge. Heidegger calls the stage "the original union of pure, universal intuition (time) and pure thinking (the notions)" and focuses on the third section of the first chapter of the "Analytic of Concepts," which is entitled "The Pure Concepts of the Understanding, or Categories." He is clear about its importance for his interpretation: "Understanding these paragraphs is the key to understanding the *Critique of Pure Reason* as a laying of the ground for metaphysics."[176] The pure veritative synthesis or ontological synthesis joins the unified whole of intuiting, which Kant calls "synopsis," with the unity of reflecting concepts. In originally joining the elements, this synthesis forms both the "synopsis" and the unity of a concept. "Thus pure synthesis acts purely synoptically in pure intuition and at the same time purely reflectively in pure thinking."[177]

The power of imagination is the source of these two syntheses. Kant writes, "Synthesis in general, as we shall hereafter see, is the mere result of the power of imagination, a blind but indispensable function of the soul, without which we should have no knowledge whatsoever, but of which we are scarcely ever conscious."[178] Imagination, then, is the structural center of intuition and thought. As Heidegger writes, "In it, the pure synopsis and the pure, reflecting synthesis meet and join together."[179] Moreover, all the syntheses constitutive of the veritative synthesis, namely the apophantic and the predicative, derive their unity from this same function.[180] The central synthesis of imagination, Heidegger cautions, is not the unity of a formal principle, but that of a "multiform act" that can be clarified only "to the extent that it is itself followed in its leaping-forth [*Entspringen*]."[181] Here, where Kant says that "the matter itself is deeply veiled,"[182] the task must be to unveil the hidden source.

The third stage of the ground-laying, "the inner possibility of the essential unity of ontological synthesis," accomplishes the unveiling of this synthesis through an analysis of the "sense and task" of Kant's Transcendental Deduction of the Categories.[183] Heidegger focuses on the *Critique*'s first edition in which imagination is accorded an original role; in the second edition Kant instead prioritizes the understanding. The synthesis of imagination shows itself as the inner structure of transcendence. That is, it constitutes the "original turning-toward" which opens a "domain of movement" (*Spielraum*).[184] Within this opening "something like an entity can itself stand in opposition to a finite creature." Repeating language developed in the Leibniz course and made notorious by the 1929 lecture, "What Is Metaphysics?," Heidegger characterizes ontological knowledge as the "nothing" that allows something to show itself.[185] The letting-stand-against encounters "resistance" in the figure of the object, that which stands against.[186]

The sense of the deduction is "the analytical unveiling of the structural whole of pure synthesis."[187] It is thus not a "deduction" in the logical sense, which stands opposed to intuition.[188] To make this clear, Heidegger focuses on section three, "the relationship of the understanding to objects in general, and the possibility of knowing them a priori." The proof of the inner possibility of transcendence can move from understanding to intuition or from intuition to understanding.[189] But in these two ways, what is disclosed is the structural whole of transcendence as well as the central role of the imagination. "In this going back and forth between both endpoints, the unveiling of pure synthesis takes place."[190] Understanding is relative to imagination, which is relative to intuition.[191]

Though the deduction focuses on the connection between understanding or transcendental apperception and the synthesis of the imagination, Heidegger emphasizes that pure imagination itself is relative to time. Kant prefaces the deduction by mentioning the priority of time: "All our knowledge is thus finally subject to time, the formal condition of inner sense. In it they must all be ordered, connected, and brought into relation. This is a general observation which, throughout what follows, must be borne in mind as being quite fundamental."[192] Heidegger thinks the structure of pure apperception, pure power of imagination, and time shapes the "letting-stand-against of . . ." and thus the "horizon of objectivity in general."[193] He can consequently term this structure "ontological knowledge," since it is within it that Kant says "all relation of being or not being takes place."[194]

The fourth stage, "the ground for the inner possibility of ontological knowledge," explicitly relates imagination and understanding to time. Heidegger focuses on the section called "the Schematism of the Pure Concepts of Understanding" and takes it to be *the central core* of the whole voluminous work."[195] In order for an entity to be able to give itself, the horizon of its possible encountering must itself be given. Consequently, pure understanding's horizon is grounded in the givenness of pure intuition.[196] As the Transcendental Deduction showed, though, the pure power of imagination is the structural center of understanding and intuition. It thus plays the key role in making the horizon sensible by creatively forming the image of the horizon.[197] By constituting the horizon, pure making-sensible constitutes transcendence. This pure making-sensible is what Kant calls "schematism."[198]

Kant terms the presentation of a procedure for making a concept sensible its "schema."[199] Heidegger clarifies Kant's terminology by calling the image provided by the schema, the "schema-image," and he distinguishes it from two other senses of "image" that Kant also employs. It is not (1) the immediate look of an on-hand entity, that is, the "empirical intuiting of what shows itself," nor is it (2) a look that is a likeness, such as a photograph or a sketch, of something that was or could be on-hand. For, as Kant notes, neither of these are adequate to the empirical concept.[200] Rather the sense of "image" operative in the making-sensible of concepts is as Heidegger says "how something appears 'in general.'"[201] That is, the schema-image is "a possible exhibition" of "the rule of exhibition presented in the schema."[202] The schema and schema-image enable empirical knowing as a thinking intuiting.[203] Heidegger brings out the implications of the schema for undermining the dominance of thought in the logical prejudice: "Beyond the presentation of this regulative unity of the rule, the concept is nothing. What logic refers to as a concept is grounded in the schema. The concept 'always refers immediately to the schema' (A 141, B 180)."[204] The schema leads thought back to sensible givenness.

Kant contrasts the schema of the empirical concept with the schema of the pure concept or categories. The latter "can never be brought into any image whatsoever."[205] That is, it cannot be brought to the kind of schema-images applicable to empirical or mathematical concepts. It can, however, as Kant indicates, be brought to "the pure image" of time: "The pure image . . . of all objects of the senses in general is time."[206] Time, then, is the schema-image that relates to the schemata of pure concepts, and the schemata of the pure concepts determine time into determinate pure images.[207] Kant writes, "The schemata are thus nothing but *a priori* determinations of time in accordance with rules."[208] Kant says that time shows four basic determinations, which correspond to the four moments of the categories, namely quantity, quality, relation, and modality: "These rules relate in the order of the categories to the *time-series*, the *time-content*, the *time-order*, and lastly to the *scope of time*."[209] The transcendental determination of time mediates the categories to the appearances. It can bridge this heterogeneity, because it is both intellectual and sensible, while being "void of all empirical content."[210] Time is intelligible, yet nonetheless given.

Kant calls the schematism "transcendental," and Heidegger sees in it the ground for the possibility of ontological knowledge. The Transcendental Schematism, he says, "forms [*bildet*] that which stands against in the pure letting-stand-against in such a way that what is presented in pure thinking is necessarily given intuitively in the pure image [*Bilde*] of time."[211] Time, then, is the key to the fourth stage of the ground-laying, because it provides the givenness of the horizon of transcendence. It is the pure image that enables the empirical givenness of entities and makes possible the resistance of objectivity:

> As the unique, pure, universal image, it gives a preliminary enclosedness to the horizon of transcendence. This single and pure ontological horizon is the condition for the possibility that the entity given within it can have this or that particular, revealed, indeed ontic horizon. But time does not give just the preliminary, unified coherence to transcendence. Rather, as the pure self-giving it simply offers to it, in general, something like a restraint [*Einhalt*]. It makes perceivable to a finite creature the "contrariety" of objectivity, which belongs to the finitude of the transcending turning-toward.[212]

Time's self-givenness, then, enables the givenness of entities and the genuine otherness of the given entity. Having arrived at the self-givenness of time, the course of the ground-laying is now complete. The possibility of ontological synthesis, that is, transcendence, has been laid bare.

Heidegger interprets the section, "The highest principle of all Synthetic Judgments,"[213] as the fifth stage of the ground-laying. Since the possibility of ontological synthesis was already exhibited with transcendental schematism, the fifth stage is not a further level of analysis; rather it grasps the essence of transcendence unfolded in the previous stages. Kant begins this section by contrasting formal and transcendental logics. Though the possibility of synthetic judgments is of no consequence in formal logic, it is the central question for transcendental logic. Heidegger sees this remark as a critique of "traditional metaphysics" which would try to know an entity on the basis of thought alone.[214] Here thought is but the joining of subject and predicate in an analytic judgment. Rather than constituting knowledge, mere thinking is but a constitutive element of finite knowledge.

Analytic judgments are bound by the principle of non-contradiction alone. By contrast, in the synthetic judgment thinking opens beyond itself to something "wholly other," namely the entity itself. Kant writes, "But in synthetic judgment I have to advance beyond the given concept, viewing as in relation with the concept something *wholly other* from what was thought in it."[215] Heidegger identifies this relation, a relation that "brings near," as the veritative synthesis.[216] Kant says that such a going beyond to what is wholly other requires a "medium" in which this is possible. Summarizing the triad of elements that Heidegger outlined in the previous stages, Kant identifies this medium as follows: "It is but one whole in which all our presentations are contained, namely, inner sense and its *a priori* form, time. The synthesis of presentations rests on imagination; and their synthetic unity, which is required for judgment, on the unity of apperception."[217] Kant's medium, what Heidegger calls transcendence, is now displayed according to its inner articulation.

Heidegger again refers to the distinction between logical possibility and real possibility that emerged in Leibniz and was sounded in Kant's *Logic* lectures.[218] The fifth stage goes beyond the mere enumeration of the elements of transcendence and grasps it in its inner structure. That is, it manifests the *possibilitas, essentia,* or *realitas* of traditional metaphysics. Consequently, Kant defines the essence of finite knowledge as the "possibility of experience." "The *possibility of experience* is, then, what gives objective reality to all our *a priori* modes of knowledge."[219] Heidegger identifies in Kant two conditions for the possibility of experience. The condition for the possibility of *experiencing* is turning one's attention-toward, which lets the entity give itself. Such *a priori* devotion echoes the role of care in *Being and Time* and serves as the very ground of intentional experience. Here, though, it is articulated in a manner closer to Kant's terminology.

"That an object is given" means that it "is presented immediately in intuition" (A 156, B 195). But what does this mean? Kant answers:

"to relate the presentation [of the object] to experience (be it actual or still possible)." This relating, however, wants to suggest: in order for an object to be able to give itself, there must in advance already be a turning-towards such an occurrence, which is capable of being "summoned." This preliminary turning one's-attention-toward . . . occurs, as the Transcendental Deduction shows and as the Transcendental Schematism clarifies, in the ontological synthesis.[220]

The second condition, the condition for the possibility of the experienced object, is the horizon of its being able to stand against in a possible accordance. Truth is a characteristic of all knowledge, and Kant defines truth as "agreement with the object."[221] That which enables truth is the horizon in which an "object" (*Gegen-stand*) can stand against.

Kant brings these two conditions together in the following formulation, which Heidegger interprets as the full articulation of transcendence: "The conditions for the *possibility of experience* in general are at the same time conditions for the *possibility of the objects of experience*."[222] Not surprisingly, Heidegger focuses on the seemingly incidental phrase in the formulation, "at the same time." This expresses the intimate relation between the two conditions: "the letting-stand-against which turns itself toward as such forms the horizon of objectivity in general."[223] Because transcendence is ecstatical, it is horizonal. "The going-out-to . . ., which was previously and at all times necessary in finite knowing, is hence a constant standing-out-from . . . (*Ecstasis*). But this essential standing-out-from . . ., precisely in the standing, forms and therein holds before itself: a horizon. In itself, transcendence is ecstatic-horizonal."[224] Finite knowing can accept an entity it encounters, because in transcendence it is open to such an encountering in its very essence.

At the end of this section, Heidegger provides the following clarifying note, which connects the exposition of the Kant book to that of the Leibniz course: "The above interpretation of the highest synthetic principle shows the extent to which it determines the essence of synthetic judgments a priori and, at the same time, the extent to which it can be claimed as the properly understood, metaphysical principle of sufficient reason."[225] The structure of the note mirrors Kant's formulation of what Heidegger takes to be the full articulation of transcendence, brought together by the expression "at the same time." The reading of Leibniz's principle of reason leads to Kant's ontological project, expressed in the possibility of synthetic *a priori* judgments. We are thus led to recognize with Kant that empirical truth is founded on transcendental truth: "All our knowledge falls within the bounds of possible experience, and just in this universal relation to possible experience consists the transcendental truth which precedes all empirical truth and makes it possible."[226]

Kant's Retreat from the Transcendental Power of Imagination

The transcendental imagination constitutes transcendence. It is not a special power of the soul to be treated by an ontic science such as anthropology or psychology. Rather it is a matter for ontological investigation.[227] Kant uncovers the transcendental imagination as the root of sensibility and understanding. On Heidegger's reading, though, Kant shrinks back before "the abyss" in the second edition of the *Critique*, and instead grounds ontological synthesis in the understanding alone. Kant, whose doctrine of the transcendental power of imagination was the first attempt to liberate metaphysics from logic, thus in the end falls prey to the logical prejudice. Here I will first show how Heidegger's Kant derives the succession of time from the transcendental power of imagination and its implications for the doctrine of judgment. Then I will examine Heidegger's claim that Kant retreated from this monumental discovery.

Time as a succession of nows cannot be original, for if it were we would never be able to intuit more than the "current now."[228] Moreover, even intuiting this "current now" would be impossible since a present moment has "essentially continuous extension in its just now and right away." Prior to the succession of nows, then, is time in its primordiality. Heidegger thinks Kant identifies the transcendental power of imagination with this primordial time. To illustrate this, he turns to a preliminary remark found in a prefatory section for the Transcendental Deduction, called "The *A Priori* Grounds for the Possibility of Experience." The remark treats in turn three modes of synthesis, that of apprehension, reproduction, and recognition. Heidegger thinks each of these is a mode of the pure power of imagination.[229] Pure apprehension forms the "present" (*Gegenwart*), and pure reproduction forms "having-been-ness" (*Gewesenheit*). These are bound up with one another. As Kant writes, "But if I were always to drop out of thought the preceding presentations . . . and did not reproduce them while advancing to those that follow, a complete presentation would never be obtained. . . . The synthesis of apprehension is thus inseparably bound up with the synthesis of reproduction."[230] Heidegger has more difficulty interpreting the third synthesis in terms of original time, but again he takes his clue from a passage in which Kant grounds identity in the synthesis of recognition: "For this *one* consciousness [presenting this unity as conceptual presenting] is what combines the manifold, again and again intuited, and thereupon also reproduced, into one presentation."[231] In providing the possibility of identification, this synthesis explores the horizon for holding on to something. Heidegger thus characterizes it as futural: "As pure, its exploring is the original forming of this preliminary attaching, i.e., the future [*Zukunft*]."[232] These three modes of synthesis together constitute original time and give rise to the succession of everyday time.

Heidegger follows the Kantian analysis of time even further to disclose time as pure self-affection. Time can therefore constitute transcendence, the self-activity of subjectivity: "Pure self-affection gives the transcendental, primal structure of the finite self as such."[233] Heidegger's point of departure is Kant's claim that space and time "must . . . always affect" the concept of presented objects.[234] Time is the pure intuition that grounds all knowing, and as pure it means "becoming affected free of experience, i.e., self-affecting."[235] To substantiate this interpretation, Heidegger quotes Kant at length:

> Now that which, as presentation, can be antecedent to any and every act of thinking anything, is intuition; and if it contains nothing but relations, it is the form of intuition. Since this form does not present anything save insofar as something is posited in the mind, it can be nothing but the mode in which the mind is affected through its own activity (namely, this positing of their presentation), and so is affected by itself, i.e., according to an inner sense of its form.[236]

Time enables the mind to be a mind, and though Kant does not expressly say so, Heidegger thinks he identifies time and the "I think."[237] The suggestion, then, is that Kant returns the modern subject to the givenness characteristic of sensibility and thereby in principle overcomes the mathematical prejudice.

The three modes of pure synthesis, pure apprehension, pure reproduction, and pure recognition are "in themselves originally united" and therefore "constitute the bringing forth of time itself."[238] Time, as self-affection, enables the transcendental power of imagination to mediate between receptivity and spontaneity.

> Original time makes possible the transcendental power of imagination, which in itself is essentially spontaneous receptivity and receptive spontaneity. Only in this unity can pure sensibility as spontaneous receptivity and pure apperception as receptive spontaneity belong together and form the united essence of a finite, pure, sensible reason.[239]

Original time, then, in contradistinction to time as a pure succession of nows, proves to be the source of transcendence and the unity of the elements of knowledge. The pure power of imagination, which brings forth time, is the root of sensibility and understanding.

Now, the logical prejudice bases itself on understanding alone and takes its bearing from judgment. We have already seen that, along with tracing empirical truth back to transcendental truth, Kant returns judgment to the givenness of intuition. But in this return of judgment to intuition by means of imagination and time, judgment itself is transformed.

The Transcendental Deduction and the Doctrine of the Schematism demonstrate that judgments and notions are "artificially isolated elements" of the transcendental imagination.[240] While it is "appropriate" to say the essence of thinking is judging, it is only a "distant determination of its essence."[241] A better determination is that thinking is a "faculty of rules," since such a characterization indicates the connection of thinking with pure apperception.[242] The latter provides the anticipatory presentation of an enduring unity by which is formed the horizon of objectivity. Such a presentation draws the self out of itself toward something. Apperception is a basic act of the power of imagination and "is no thematic asserting of the unity, but is instead the unthematic bringing-itself-before of the presented."[243] Since judgment is traced back into the matrix of power of imagination it is better called pure imagining: "Now if Kant calls this pure, self-orienting, self-relating-to . . ., 'our thought', then 'thinking' this thought is no longer called judging, but is thinking in the sense of the free, forming, and projecting (although not arbitrary) 'conceiving' ['*Sichdenkens*'] of something. This original 'thinking' is pure imagining."[244]

Heidegger finds the freedom of thinking in the power of imagination. It is not an expression of pure spontaneity; rather the power of imagination "is the original unity of receptivity and spontaneity, and not a unity which was composite from the first."[245] Heidegger understands freedom with Kant to be "placing oneself under a self-given necessity."[246] Accordingly, the freedom of thinking is a receptive spontaneity: "Hence understanding and reason are not free because they have the character of spontaneity, but because this spontaneity is a receptive spontaneity, i.e., because it is the transcendental power of imagination."[247] Judgment, rooted in the power of imagination, is an expression of finite freedom.

Despite the radicalism of the discovery with its overcoming of the logical prejudice, nonetheless, "Kant shrank back from this unknown root."[248] In the shift from the first to the second editions of the *Critique of Pure Reason*, Kant carefully modifies the two most important passages that establish the primacy of the power of imagination.[249] While mention of the power remains alongside sensibility and understanding, the central synthesizing function shifts to the understanding. Why does this change take place? In the 1929 Kant book, Heidegger thinks Kant was motivated by fear of the unknown abyss and the influence of the tradition. The doctrine's repercussions were enormous:

> How is the baser faculty of sensibility also to be able to constitute the essence of reason? . . . What is to happen with the venerable tradition, according to which Ratio and Logos have claimed the central function in the history of metaphysics? Can the primacy of Logic fall? . . . Will not the *Critique of Pure Reason* have deprived itself of its own theme if pure reason reverts to the transcendental power of imagination? Does not this ground-laying lead us to an abyss?[250]

Kant retreated in the face of these questions and restored confidence in understanding. Five years earlier, Heidegger had made a similar claim about Husserl, namely, that he remained bound to the logical prejudice because of a certain fear of the unknown.[251] Although this does not constitute his final interpretation of Kant, as we will see in the next chapter, it does play an important role in Heidegger's late 1920's attempt to express transcendence in dialogue with modern thinkers. With German Idealism, the power of imagination becomes no longer an articulation of finitude. Mentioning Fichte, Schelling, and even Jacobi, Heidegger says his interpretation of Kant's power of imagination goes in the "opposite direction from that of German Idealism."[252] There, understanding, shorn of the finitude of intuition, takes center stage.[253] "All reinterpretation of the pure power of imagination as a function of pure thinking—a reinterpretation which 'German Idealism' even accentuated subsequent to the second edition of the *Critique of Pure Reason*—misunderstands its specific essence."[254] After Kant, the hegemony of the logical prejudice is unquestioned.

Conclusion

In the wake of *Being and Time*, Heidegger turns to Kant and finds in him an anticipation and a confirmation of his own project of unveiling transcendence. Kant emphasizes the priority of intuition in empirical knowledge and shows that this level of truth presupposes transcendental truth constituted by the self-givenness of time.[255] The Leibniz lecture course affords the key to understanding why Heidegger can find real definition at work in Kant's philosophy. Heidegger thinks Leibniz's understanding of the adequate knowledge of something is its real definition that grasps it in its possibility, and he thinks this understanding is explicitly developed in Kant's architectonic. The ground-laying of metaphysics is the full exposition of the essence of metaphysics, which is the same thing as unveiling its inner possibility and thus reality. Reality, here, does not mean actuality in the sense of modern epistemology but instead names the essential content: "As Kant himself aptly translates it, '*realitas*' means 'fact-ness' ['*Sachheit*'], and it alludes to the content [*Wasgehalt*] of the entity which comes to be delimited by means of the *essentia*."[256] This explains the central role accorded the inner rather than the external architectonic. The ground-laying is "the architectonic circumscription and delineation of the inner possibility of metaphysics, that is, the concrete determination of its essence."[257] This is nothing other than the disclosure of the possibility of ontological knowledge. Kant's *quaestio juris* really names an analytic or phenomenology of transcendence:

The problem of the "origin and the truth" (A 128) of the categories, however, is the question of the possible manifestness of being from entities in the essential unity of ontological knowledge. If this question is to be grasped concretely and taken hold of as a problem, however, then the *quaestio juris* cannot as such be taken as a question of validity. Instead, the *quaestio juris* is only the formula for the task of an analytic of transcendence, i.e., of a pure phenomenology of the subjectivity of the subject, namely, as a finite subject.[258]

Returning judgment to evidence and ontic truth to ontological knowledge or transcendence turns, then, on a methodological development, namely the emergence of phenomenology. Kant's method of universalization in which ontological knowledge is achieved thus approximates Heidegger's method of formal indication. "For the first time, the question of the ground-laying requires clarity concerning the manner of universalization and the character of the stepping-beyond which lies in the knowledge of the constitution of being."[259] Though Kant may not have brought "full clarification" to the problem, he at least "recognized its necessity" and "presented it."[260]

The identification of phenomenological and transcendental methodology is not widely admitted. Sherover's otherwise excellent study, for instance, sees *Kant and the Problem of Metaphysics* as offering "an alternate approach to his doctrine" which represents a non-phenomenological introduction to the issues of *Being and Time*.[261] Sherover writes, "His implicit claim here is that the method [of *Being and Time*] . . . is not crucial." Sherover concludes that Heidegger's close identification with Kant's "theory of knowledge" "places Heidegger into the heart of the modern philosophic tradition." Bringing out the centrality of phenomenology, however, suggests a different topology. The book on Kant offers a phenomenological reading of Kant; its result is not to place Heidegger into the heart of the modern tradition but rather to find within the modern tradition tendencies to exceed the limits of modern epistemology and thereby achieve Heidegger's unique brand of transcendental phenomenology.[262] By following the thread of this development from Leibniz through Kant to Heidegger, we are led to see that returning judgment to givenness motivates the real disclosure of the transcendental ground that makes judgment possible. Kant glimpsed that intentionality can happen thanks to the transcendence engendered by the ecstatic-horizonal bringing forth of timeliness. And what he glimpsed we may yet make the focus of concerted investigation today.

Notes

1 *Logic*, 29.
2 GA 25, 83/87.
3 *Genesis*, 21. He adds, "The importance of this groundbreaking course, in all its vital rawness and freshness pointing the way to all of Heidegger, in my view cannot be overestimated" (*Genesis*, 16).

4 GA 20, 96/70.
5 *Being and Time* is unfinished, and Heidegger's other publications consist of essays, lectures, lecture courses, and notebooks.
6 GA 3, xiv/xvii.
7 See, for instance, van Buren, *The Young Heidegger*, 366–7; Kisiel, *Genesis*, 451 and 458.
8 *Heidegger's Concept of Truth*, 435n64.
9 See Judith Wolfe, *Heidegger's Eschatology: Theological Horizons in Martin Heidegger's Early Work* (Oxford: Oxford University Press, 2013), 28.
10 GA 1a, 1–15/20–29.
11 GA 1b, 19/32 and 22/34.
12 GA 1b, 19/33.
13 GA 1b, 30/40.
14 GA 16a, 38/8, emphasis mine.
15 GA 56/57, 109–10/92. For Husserl's discussion of the "principle of principles," namely that intuition is the ultimate cognitive authority, see *Ideas I*, § 24.
16 GA 56/57, 117/99.
17 See *Ideas I*, §§ 81–2, and *On the Phenomenology of the Consciousness of Internal Time (1893–1917)*, trans. John Barnett Brough (Dordrecht: Kluwer, 1991). Kisiel observes, "The Husserlian vocabulary of 'primal impression,' 'primal apprehension' . . ., in describing the primal source (*Urquell*) of experience, clearly suggest Heidegger's 'primal something,' which even in its most hermeneutical moments of articulation here still trades off from Husserl's retentional and protentional scheme of temporality" (*Genesis*, 57). On Heidegger's unacknowledged appropriation of Husserl's analysis of time, see Prufer, *Recapitulations*, 74–7.
18 GA 56/57, 126/107. This passage is from the summer semester 1919 lecture course.
19 GA 56/57, 128/109. Nor can this simply be the result of the dominance of Neo-Kantianism as the philosophy of the day. Within the lecture course, Heidegger observes that Cohen "rediscovers" Kant's transcendental method as being a concern for neither knowledge's "physiologico-psychological process" nor the problem of the external world but instead the "logical and categorial conditions" of the possibility of "objectively given mathematical natural science" (142/120). Such a rediscovery brings transcendental philosophy into proximity with phenomenology's transcendental subject matter and the breakthrough of the *Logical Investigations*, although it remains foreign to the theme of the pre-theoretical.
20 GA 60, 57/39. The bracketed text is mine, but the parenthetical text is Heidegger's. Heidegger thinks that Husserl fails to capitalize fully on his method and therefore remains bound to the theoretical and general.
21 GA 20, 101/74.
22 The original outline, not carried out, had section C devoted to the topic of truth, not time and being in Kant. GA 21, 26.
23 GA 25, 431/292–3. Alongside the 1925–1926 lecture course, Heidegger was offering seminars on Kant's *Critique of Pure of Reason* and Hegel's *Logic*. On the Kant-conversion, see van Buren, *The Young Heidegger*, 363–7.
24 *Ideas I*, 142.
25 *Ideas I*, 142.
26 *Ideas I*, 142.
27 Cf. Otto Pöggeler, *Martin Heidegger's Path of Thinking*, trans. Daniel Magurshak and Sigmund Barber (Atlantic Highlands, NJ: Humanities Press International, 1987), 269. From Husserl, though, he perhaps also adopted the idea

of metontology or regional ontologies using the terminology of schema and
horizon. See, *Ideas I*, §§ 16–17 and § 149, among others.
28 See, in particular, *Logical Investigations*, § 51. Husserl's inquiry focuses on
the experience of their interplay: "One must clearly grasp what the ideal is,
both intrinsically and in its relation to the real, how this ideal stands to the
real, how it can be immanent in it and so come to knowledge" (193).
29 SZ 216–7/259–60.
30 GA 21, 114.
31 GA 21, 117.
32 GA 21, 114–18.
33 See the important footnote in *Being and Time* pointing to the temporal problem of the schematism (SZ 363/498).
34 GA 21, 194 and 200. This will recur in *Being and Time* as well (SZ 23/45).
35 Kisiel rightly makes the connection: "His fascination with Kant . . . came from
his own problem of formally indicating the phenomenological structures of
immediacy. It was thus Kant's way of getting on the inside of intuition, of sens-
ing the infrastructure of temporality operating at the interface of receptivity
and spontaneity . . ., in short, Kant's doctrine of the schematism of the productive imagination, that first caught Heidegger's critical fancy" (*Genesis*, 409).
36 GA 21, 407.
37 GA 21, 347 and 407–8, respectively.
38 GA 21, 403.
39 GA 21, 408.
40 Kisiel observes that in this draft he is "suddenly enthusiastic over Kant"
(*Genesis*, 489). Indeed, Kant is the philosopher most mentioned in *Being
and Time*, as Charles Sherover observes. See his "Heidegger's Use of Kant in
Being and Time," in *Kant and Phenomenology*, ed. Thomas Seebohm and
Joseph Kockelmans (Washington, DC: The Center for Advanced Research in
Phenomenology, Inc., 1984), 192. Frank Schalow offers an important qualification, given the repeated criticism of Kant in *Being and Time*: "But an
equally apt description might be Heidegger's nonuse of transcendental philosophy," *The Renewal of the Heidegger-Kant Dialogue*, 191.
41 SZ 50/490. Note that when he talks of the phenomenological method,
Heidegger is careful to use the terminology of the handy rather than the
theoretical.
42 SZ 23/45. Husserl, incredulous about this claim, writes in his own copy of
Being and Time, "Is that true?" *Psychological and Transcendental Phenomenology and the Confrontation with Heidegger*, 290.
43 GA 20, 96/70.
44 SZ 396/417.
45 SZ 23/45. Here, Heidegger seems to echo Husserl, whom we quoted above:
Kant's "greatest intuitions become wholly understandable to us only when
we had obtained by hard work a fully clear awareness of the peculiarity of
the province belonging to phenomenology." *Ideas I*, 118/142.
46 GA 24, 452/317–8.
47 GA 24, 451/317.
48 SZ 24/45.
49 Pöggeler, for instance, downplays any difference between *Being and Time* and
the book on Kant; he maintains that Heidegger continued to think that Kant's
subject was something merely on-hand. See *Path of Thinking*, 65.
50 GA 3, xvi/xix.
51 In the preface to the fourth edition (1973) of the Kant book, Heidegger dates
the book's interpretation of Kant to this lecture course (GA 3, xiv/xvii).

Stephan Käufer thinks Heidegger's memory here fails him; he should say the interpretation began in the 1925–26 lecture course. See his "Schemata, Hammers, and Time: Heidegger's Two Derivations of Judgment," *Topoi* 22 (2003): 86. However, Käufer fails to distinguish between the second and third phases of Heidegger's interpretation of Kant. Heidegger is not mistaken; the shift from the second to the third phase occurs in this course.

52 GA 25, 83/57. For an account of the Neo-Kantian background, see Dahlstrom, "Heidegger's Kant-Courses at Marburg," in *Reading Heidegger from the Start: Essays in His Earliest Thought*, ed. Theodore Kisiel and John van Buren (Albany, NY: State University of New York Press, 1994), 293–308.

53 *Heidegger-Kant Dialogue*, 150.

54 GA 25, 83/57.

55 GA 3, 144/101. cf. 155/108.

56 In the summer 1928 lecture course on Leibniz, Heidegger cites Kant in connection with the working out of these two problems: the problem of intentionality and its ground in transcendence. See GA 26, 163/130.

57 van Buren, *The Young Heidegger*, 365.

58 In the context of discussing the method of phenomenology at the conclusion of the 1927 and 1927–28 lecture courses, entitled "Basic Problems of Phenomenology" and "Phenomenological Interpretations of Kant's *Critique of Pure Reason*," respectively, Heidegger also praises Kant's discipline and scientific character.

59 Ground-laying is "the architectonic circumscription and delineation of the inner possibility of metaphysics, that is, the concrete determination of its essence. All determination of essence, however, is first achieved in the setting-free [*Freilegung*] of the essential ground." GA 3, 2/2.

60 GA 3, 170/119.

61 GA 3, 119/84. Emphasis mine.

62 GA 3, 56/29. Though this turn to the ontological *a priori* had been indicated to Kant by the method of the natural sciences, Heidegger says Kant's interest is not in grounding natural science so much as focusing on the problem of being itself (GA 3, 11/7).

63 GA 3, 242/170. cf. GA 26, 251/194: "World-entry happens when transcendence happens, i.e., when historical Dasein exists."

64 GA 3, 231/162.

65 "Kant brought both of them together in their original sameness—without, to be sure, expressly seeing this as such for himself" (GA 3, 192/134).

66 *Confrontation with Heidegger*, 442.

67 *Confrontation with Heidegger*, 447.

68 *Confrontation with Heidegger*, 453.

69 Preface to the fourth edition (1973) of the Kant book (GA 3, xiv/xvii).

70 Ibid.

71 GA 65, 253/179.

72 GA 29/30, 522/359.

73 Heidegger praises Kant as the first thinker who brought freedom into connection with problems of metaphysics even though he understands freedom in terms of ontic causality (GA 31, 21/15 and 246/167, respectively).

74 GA 31, 192/134 and 213/147.

75 GA 31, 203/140.

76 GA 31, 157/112 and 168/119, respectively. Heidegger refers the reader to the Kant book where these criticisms are present but downplayed.

77 GA 31, 159n25/114n38.

78 GA 31, 205/142 and 288/197, and 264/183, respectively.

79 GA 31, 203/141.

80 Though he says "not—as is often thought—in order to deny the meaning of phenomenology, but in order to let my path of thinking be nameless." *Unterwegs zur Sprache* (Pfullingen: Verlag Günther Neske, 1959) [*On the Way to Language*, trans. Peter D. Hertz (New York: Harper & Row, Publishers, 1971)], 121/29.

81 In *Sein und Zeit*, he says phenomenology is a recovery of the ancient Aristotelian insight into the subordination of *logos* to phenomena. See §§ 7, 33, and 44. Recalling the sense of the Greek terms, Heidegger observes that phenomenon is "that which shows itself in itself, the manifest," and *logos* in turn "makes manifest" (SZ 32/56). Together phenomenon and *logos* let "that which shows itself be seen from itself in the very way in which it shows itself from itself" (34/58). *Logos* is in service to the self-showing of phenomenon.

82 GA 41, 137/135.

83 GA 41, 138/135.

84 GA 41, 190/186–7. In the 1961 essay, Heidegger repeats this claim but puts more emphasis on its partial subjectivizing in transcendental apperception, GA 9i, 459/347 and 462/350.

85 GA 41, 182/179.

86 "[T]his *between* as a pre-conception reaches beyond the thing and likewise back behind us. Pre-conception is thrown-back [*Vor-griff ist Rück-wurf*]" (GA 41, 245/243).

87 GA 41, 131/129.

88 GA 41, 188/184.

89 GA 41, 244/242.

90 GA 41, 181–2/178.

91 Letter to William J. Richardson, April 1962, in "Preface / Vorwort" to William J. Richardson, *Heidegger: Through Phenomenology to Thought*, 2d ed (The Hague: Martinus Nijhoff, 1967), xiv.

92 Letter to Richardson, xiv. As we have seen, Heidegger's interpretation of Kant has been guided by the phenomenological principle of evidence, which Heidegger takes to be pre-theoretical. On Heidegger's "l'approfondissement" of Husserl's principle of principles in the context of this letter, see Klaus Held, "Heidegger et le Principe de la Phénoménologie," in *Heidegger et l'Idée de la Phénoménologie*, ed. Franco Volpi et al (Dordrecht: Kluwer Academic Publishers, 1988), 239–63.

93 *Schellings Abhandlung über das Wesen der menschlichen Freiheit (1809)*, ed. Hildegard Feick (Tübingen: Max Niemeyer Verlag, 1971) [*Schellings's Treatise on the Essence of Human Freedom*, trans. Joan Stambaugh (Athens, Ohio: Ohio University Press, 1985)], 45/37.

94 GA 20, 73/55.

95 Husserl, "Letter to Alexander Pfänder, January 6, 1931," in *Confrontation with Heidegger*, 482.

96 Dahlstrom says that the lecture courses of 1925–26 and 1927–28 offer "a far more extensive interpretation" of the *Critique of Pure Reason* than the 1929 book on Kant. While his observation is true regarding breadth, those courses are less *intensive* and follow the external rather than the internal architectonic of the book. This is a critical distinction as this chapter will make clear, for Heidegger reads the internal architectonic as an analysis of transcendence. See Dahlstrom, "Heidegger's Kant-Courses," 293.

97 GA 26, 89/72. Cf. GA 26, 91–2/74.

98 GA 26, 81/65. The categories can thus be real determinations of objects without being empirical properties of them. Though they are not ontic

determinations, they are transcendental ones: "Their reality, their belonging to essential content, is a transcendental reality, a finite, horizonal-ecstatic reality."

99 See GA 26, 245/168 and following. "Freedom" becomes a favorite formal indication for that which transcendence and being-in-the-world likewise indicate. The terms are dropped in the 1930s in favor of "openness."

100 (a) Leibniz: "Our exposition of the monadology was already guided by the interpretation of Dasein as timeliness, especially by an insight into the essence of transcendence." GA 26, 271/209. (b) Kant: "To be sure, this concept of transcendental science does not coincide directly with the Kantian; but we are certainly in a position to explicate by means of the *more original concept of transcendence* the Kantian idea of the transcendental and of philosophy as transcendental philosophy in their basic tendencies." GA 24, 460/323.

101 GA 26, 210/165 and GA 3, 201/141.

102 GA 26, 88/71. "The actuality of what has been resides in its possibility. The possibility becomes in each case manifest as the answer to a living question that sets before itself a futural present in the sense of 'what can we do?' The objectivity of the historical resides in the inexhaustibility of possibilities, and not in the fixed rigidity of a result." GA 26, 88/72.

103 Quoted from Kant's tract against the Leibnizian Eberhard, entitled "On a Discovery According to which Any New Critique of Pure Reason Has Been Made Superfluous by an Earlier One," at GA 3, 201–2/141.

104 GA 26, 10/9. The projected articulation of *Being and Time* into two parts, one systematic and one historical, reflects their interdependence.

105 GA 26, 27/21. Schalow helps clarify the relation between *Being and Time* and the study of Kant in particular. Heidegger's hermeneutic method requires that he explicitly appropriate the historical presuppositions of his analyses in *Being and Time*. Kant's overcoming of rationalism in terms of the ecstatic horizon of time brings the whole tradition into focus. In this way, Schalow argues that Heidegger's adoption of the hermeneutic method sets the stage for the dialogue with Kant. See *Heidegger-Kant Dialogue*, 15, 52, 70, and 192.

106 GA 26, 7/6.

107 GA 26, 127/103 and GA 3, xvi/xix.

108 GA 26, 35–6/27–8. Heidegger refers to Russell's *A Critical Exposition of the Philosophy of Leibniz* (Cambridge: Cambridge University Press, 1900) and Couturat's *La Logique de Leibniz. D'après des documents inédits* (Paris: Presses Universitaires de France, 1901). Couturat notes that Russell "par une interprétation toute différente d'ailleurs" came to the same conclusion, namely that "la métaphysique de Leibniz repose uniquement sur les principes de sa Logique." *La Logique*, x. In Russell's preface to the second edition (1937), he says his thesis, "that Leibniz's philosophy was almost entirely derived from his logic," "received overwhelming confirmation from the work of Louis Couturat." *A Critical Exposition*, 2nd ed., v.

109 GA 9b, 25/367.

110 GA 26, 8/6.

111 GA 26, 7/6 and GA 26, 17–8/14.

112 GA 26, 24/19.

113 GA 26, 25/19–20.

114 *Philosophical Papers and Letters*, trans. Leroy E. Loemker (Dordrecht, Holland: D. Reidel Publishing Co., 1969), 291–4.

115 GA 26, 72/58.

116 GA 26, 78/63.

117 Thus Leibniz can write: "There is no other knowledge than intuitive of a distinct primitive concept, while for the most part we have only symbolic thought of composites." *Philosophical Papers and Letters*, 292.

118 GA 26, 76/61.

119 GA 26, 80/65. Leibniz writes, "Whenever our knowledge is adequate, we have a priori knowledge of a possibility, for if we have carried out the analysis to the end and no contradiction has appeared, the concept is obviously possible." *Philosophical Papers and Letters*, 293.

120 "Under the heading, 'the objective reality of the categories,' Kant tries to understand the essence of categories in such a way that categories can be real determinations of objects (of appearances) without having to be empirical properties (of appearances). If determinations of being are not ontic properties of the things that are, in what way do they still belong to *realitas*, to the what-content of objects? Their reality, their belonging to essential content, is a transcendental reality, a finite, horizonal-ecstatic reality." GA 26, 81/65.

121 GA 26, 82/67.

122 GA 26, 82/67.

123 GA 26, 82/67.

124 In a puzzling passage, he writes: "By suspending what is actual (in the phenomenological reduction) the what is set forth—but, in suspending the actual, the actuality, i.e., the *modus existendi*, and its essential connection [*Wesenszusammenhang*] with the essential content in the narrower sense, is not suspended. Essence has here a double meaning: it means the a priori of *essentia* and of *existentia*!" GA 26, 229/178. My sense is that what comes in for criticism here is Husserl's divide between the transcendental and empirical egos; somehow they are the same but Husserl is without resources to talk about their identity; Heidegger's Dasein, by contrast, is introduced principally to solve this problem, as the last chapter showed.

125 GA 26, 234/182.

126 GA 26, 84/68. This is the core methodological insight that Heidegger finds in Leibniz. In this regard, Daniel Selcer's development of an "abyssal interpretation of philosophical method" based on this lecture course seems misguided. For him, Heidegger's interpretation of Leibniz opens up a reading of Leibniz in which method generates itself and so is not grounded on subjectivity. "Heidegger's Leibniz and Abyssal Identity," *Continental Philosophy Review* 36 (2003): 319. And yet, provocative as this reading is, it seems counter to Heidegger's core principle that method gives way to matter, which he calls transcendence in the period of the lecture course. As corroboration with the Kant book suggests, real definition is the methodological insight most relevant for Heidegger's project, since it is grounded in being and thus not in itself.

127 GA 26, 84/68.

128 GA 26, 126–7/102.

129 Heidegger does admit Leibniz's ambivalence on the score, noting that Leibniz's "inclination to develop logic out of itself and metaphysics, as it were, out of logic repeatedly comes through." GA 26, 127/103. Though Leibniz never made the metaphysical foundation of logic explicit, Heidegger's analysis has made a case that it implicitly entails just such a foundation.

130 GA 26, 89/72. Cf. GA 26, 91/74: "His metaphysical-ontological purpose always accompanies the physical-ontic intent without a clear division of domains, without difference in kind of problem and proof."

131 GA 26, 89/72.

132　This is due to Leibniz's obscurity on the matter; for a list of problems, see GA 26, 135/109.

133　GA 26, 142/114. Heidegger cites the treatise *De rerum originatione radicali* (1697) in this regard: "Hence it is very clearly understood that out of the infinite combinations and series of possible things, one exists through which the greatest amount of essence or possibility is brought into existence. There is always a principle of determination in nature which must be sought by maxima and minima; namely, that a maximum effect should be achieved with a minimum outlay, so to speak." *Philosophical Papers and Letters*, 487.

134　GA 26, 143/115-6.

135　GA 26, 384/219. Heidegger acknowledges that the idea of creation is the "backdrop and center" of the principle; however, he distinguishes the problematic itself from Leibniz's motivation for posing and solving it; he thinks that the problematic remains even when the theological reference is set aside. GA 26, 142-3/115. On Heidegger's puzzling reduction of the philosophical theme of creation *ex nihilo* to making *ex possibili*, see Prufer, *Recapitulations*, 74, 81. Heidegger's question concerning the possibility of experience remains other than the question of creation not only in terms of motivation but also in terms of the philosophical problematic.

136　GA 3, 14/9.

137　GA 3, 15/10.

138　GA 3, 12-3/8-9.

139　See Schalow, *Heidegger-Kant Dialogue*, 58-59.

140　GA 3, 13-8/9-12.

141　KRV A 11, B 25 and GA 3, 16/10. Heidegger notes that Kant even mentions the "transcendental philosophy of the ancients." KRV B 113.

142　A 19, B 34.

143　GA 3, 21/15.

144　KRV A 320, B376f.

145　GA 3, 25/17.

146　GA 3, 21-3/15-6.

147　GA 3, 25/18.

148　KRV A 19, B 33.

149　GA 3, 26/19.

150　Though Kant sometimes seems to undercut the precedence of intuition by indifferently correlating intuition and thought, content, and form, Heidegger insists that the precedence of intuition is central "if we want to come closer to the innermost course of the Kantian problematic." GA 3, 35-6/25. See KRV A 277, B 333, and A 51, B 75.

151　GA 3, 29/20. Heidegger continues: "[Understanding's] presenting requires the detour of a reference to a universal by means of and according to which the several particulars become conceptually presentable. This detour-characteristic (discursiveness) which belongs to the essence of understanding is the sharpest index of its finitude."

152　KRV A68, B 93.

153　Heidegger thinks this manifests the genuine character of understanding's "pre-senting" (*Vor-stellen*), namely it "helps to set forth [*beistellen*] the content of an object." Heidegger does not think that Kant's "spontaneity" rightly conceives the core of this "productive" (*herstellenden*) character. GA 3, 30/21.

154　GA 3, 28-9/20.

155　For predicate synthesis, Heidegger cites the following passage from Kant's *Logic: A Manual for Lectures*, § 17: "A judgment is the presentation of the unity of the consciousness of various presentations, or the presentation of their relation insofar as they constitute a concept."

156 GA 3, 38/27.
157 GA 3, 31/22.
158 GA 3, 34/24.
159 GA 3, 32/22.
160 Quoted by Heidegger at GA 3, 32/23.
161 GA 3, 43/30. Cf. GA 3, 38–9/27. Heidegger repeats this assessment in the winter semester 1935–36 lecture course on Kant, which we will examine in the next chapter. GA 41, 244/242.
162 GA 3, 43/30.
163 Heidegger cites two passages from the *Critique of Pure Reason* that point to a common source of intuition and thought. (1) In the introduction, Kant writes, "By way of introduction or anticipation we need only say that there are two stems of human knowledge, namely, *sensibility* and *understanding*, which perhaps spring from a common, but to us unknown, root. Through the former, objects are given to us; through the latter, they are thought" (KRV A 15, B 29). (2) In the conclusion, Kant writes, "We shall content ourselves here with the completion of our task, namely, merely to outline the *architectonic* of all knowledge arising from *pure reason*; and in doing so we shall begin from the point at which the common root of our faculty of knowledge divides and throws out two stems, one of which is *reason*. By reason I here understand the whole higher faculty of knowledge, and am therefore contrasting the rational with the empirical" (KRV A 835, B 863). GA 3, 37/ 25–6.

Dieter Henrich offers a reading contrary to Idealism, on the one hand, and Heidegger, on the other; by reconstructing Kant's milieu, he shows that Kant has good reason to think that the unknown root is unknowable in principle and that the subject cannot be resolved into a unity: "Moreover, the unknown is for Kant . . . something entirely closed to us, which can disquiet us only as long as we are not certain of its unattainability." "On the Unity of Subjectivity," trans. Guenter Zoeller, in *The Unity of Reason: Essays on Kant's Philosophy*, ed. Richard L. Velkley (Cambridge, MA: Harvard University Press, 1994), 33. If this is so, Heidegger's interpretation errs in thinking that Kant is committed to the fundamental phenomenological principle that knowledge is primarily intuition, for, as we noted above, his interpretation is geared toward showing that the inner architectonic reveals the unfolding structure of transcendence in such a way that regressing to some unknown foundational principle is rendered impossible.
164 "It is true that pure intuiting, as finite, is an accepting presenting. However, what should now be accepted, where it concerns the knowing of being and not entities, cannot be an on-hand entity which gives itself. On the contrary, the pure accepting presenting must give itself a presentable. Pure intuition, therefore, must in a certain sense be 'creative.'" GA 3, 44/31.
165 GA 3, 43/30.
166 Heidegger offers three reasons why Kant analyzes the unity of knowledge within a subdivision of the Transcendental Logic, namely, the Analytic of Concepts: (1) the Transcendental Logic is privileged precisely because pure thinking has an essentially "servile relationship to intuition" and thus must involve the relationship to intuition essentially within its problematic; (2) Kant brings to bear the thinking in general of traditional formal logic so retains the "logical" designation; and (3) the "orientation toward logos and ratio" are marks of the Western metaphysical tradition which "comes to be expressed as a *Critique of Pure Reason*." GA 3, 67–8/47–8.

167   For a detailed commentary on the five stages, see Sherover, *Heidegger, Kant and Time*, 48–130.

168   GA 3, 44/31.

169   GA 3, 45/32. "In a preliminary glimpse, what is intuited in pure intuition is [*steht*] nonobjective [*ungegenständlich*] and moreover unthematic. Nevertheless, in this way what is glimpsed in the unified whole makes possible the ordering according to [which things can be] beside-, under-, and in back of one another." GA 3, 47/33.

170   Heidegger notes that Kant's argument for the primacy of time here rests on an ambiguity in the words "intuition" and "presentation." "On the one hand, the expressions mean states of mind, but at the same time they mean that which they, as such states, have as their objects." Consequently, Kant can reason from the psychic succession of external intuitions to the succession of what is intuited in those intuitions. GA 3, 50/35.

171   GA 3, 48/34.

172   GA 3, 49/34.

173   GA 3, 54/38.

174   Heidegger quotes an important passage of Kant at length: "All concepts generally, no matter from where they may take their material, are reflected, i.e., presentation[s] raised to the logical relation of general applicability. Yet there are concepts, the entire sense of which is to be nothing other than one reflection or another, to which occurring presentations can be subject. They can be called concepts of reflection (*conceptus reflectentes*); and because every kind of reflection occurs in judgments, so they become the mere action of the understanding which, in the judgments applied to the relation, are apprehended absolutely in themselves as grounds for the possibility of judging." *Kants handschriftlicher Nachlaß*, vol. V, no. 5051. GA 3, 54–5/38–9.

175   GA 3, 58/41.

176   GA 3, 59/41.

177   GA 3, 63/45.

178   KRV A 78, B 103. Béatrice Longuenesse, in her study on the doctrine of judgment in Kant, agrees with Heidegger that every judgment involves synthesis, but she disagrees that it is the result of the imagination; instead, she insists it is but "a function of thought." *Kant and the Capacity to Judge: Sensibility and Discursivity in the Transcendental Analytic of the 'Critique of Pure Reason'*, trans. Charles T. Wolfe (Princeton, NJ: Princeton University Press, 1998), 204. As we will see in the next chapter, Heidegger will come to downplay the role of imagination, but at the same time he will continue to distinguish Kant's project from the rationalism suggested by Longuenesse's interpretation.

179   GA 3, 65/45. Of the triad of intuition, imagination, and thought, Kant writes: "What must first be given—with a view to the *a priori* knowledge of all objects—is the *manifold* of pure intuition; the second factor involved is the *synthesis* of this manifold by means of the imagination. But even this does not yet yield knowledge. The concepts which give *unity* to this pure synthesis, and which consist solely in the presentation of this necessary synthetic unity, furnish the third requisite for the knowledge of an object; and they rest on the understanding." KRV A 78–9, B 104.

180   Cf. KRV A 79, B 104–5: "The same function which gives unity to the various presentations *in a judgment* also gives unity to the mere synthesis of various presentation *in an intuition*; and this unity, its most general expression, we entitle the pure concept of the understanding. The same understanding, through the same operations by which in concepts, by means of analytical unity, it produced the logical form of a judgment, also introduces

a transcendental content into its presentations, by means of the synthetic unity of the manifold in intuition in general."

181 GA 3, 65/45–6.

182 KRV A 88, B 121.

183 GA 3, 69/49.

184 GA 3, 71/50.

185 "Only if the letting-stand-against of . . . is a holding oneself in the nothing can the presenting allow a not-nothing, i.e., something like an entity if such a thing shows itself empirically, to be encountered instead of and within the nothing." GA 3, 72/51.

186 Kant writes, "Now we find that our thought of the relation of all knowledge to its object carries with it an element of necessity; the object is viewed as that which prevents our modes of knowledge from being haphazard or arbitrary, and which determines them *a priori* in some definite fashion." KRV A 105. The object accords unity, and unity is the special provenance of concepts. Kant interprets concepts as rules, that is, "the presentation of a universal condition according to which a certain manifold can be posited in uniform fashion." KRV A 113. The pure understanding then becomes further determined as the faculty of rules, and so understanding has a unique role in the unity of an object.

187 GA 3, 76/53.

188 Rather, as Kant makes clear, deduction is a *quaestio juris* prosecuted against rationalist metaphysics. Heidegger brings together some of Kant's imagery: "Pure reason must 'open the trial,' the 'witnesses' must be interrogated. Kant speaks of a 'tribunal' (KRV A 669, B 697; A 703, B 731). The legal action falling within the problem of ontological knowledge requires the deduction, i.e., the proof for the possibility of the a priori ability of pure concepts to refer to objects." GA 3, 85–6/60. The pure possibility is shown in the unveiling of the essence of the categories in their essential relation to imagination and time. This unveiling at the same time shows the "reality" or "fact-ness" (*Sachheit*) of the essence, not its actuality or existence.

189 KRV A 116–20 and A 120–8, respectively.

190 GA 3, 78/55.

191 Kant characterizes the mediating role of imagination as follows: "A pure imagination, which conditions all *a priori* knowledge, is thus one of the fundamental faculties of the human soul. By its means we bring the manifold of intuition [into connection] on the one side, into connection with the condition of the necessary unity of pure apperception on the other. The two extremes, namely sensibility and understanding, must stand in necessary connection with each other through the mediation of this transcendental function of imagination." KRV A 124. Heidegger added the bracketed text for clarification.

192 KRV A 99.

193 GA 3, 84/59.

194 KRV A 110.

195 GA 3, 89/63.

196 GA 3, 90/63.

197 Imagination both creates and images the horizon: "The pure power of imagination [*die reine Einbildungskraft*] carries out the forming of the look of the horizon [*das Bilden des Horizontanblickes*]. But then it does not just 'form' ['*bildet*'] the intuitable perceivability of the horizon [1] in that it 'creates' [this horizon] as a free turning-toward. Although it is formative in this first sense, it is so in yet a second sense as well, namely, in the sense that [2] in general it provides for something like an 'image' [*ein 'Bild'*]." GA 3, 90/64.

198 This use of schemata is analogous to Heidegger's in *Being and Time*. As we saw in chapter 1, the schemata unite the self and world in terms of timelines. Schalow points out that the Kantian schematism, by exposing the centrality of imagination, prepares for Heidegger's project of disclosing timeliness. See *Heidegger-Kant Dialogue*, 156–7 and 183–4.

199 "This presentation of a universal procedure of imagination in providing an image for a concept, I entitle the schema of this concept." KRV A 140, B 179–80.

200 "Still less is an object of experience or its image ever adequate to the empirical concept; for this latter always stands in immediate relation to the schema of imagination, as a rule for the determination of our intuition, in accordance with some specific universal concept." KRV A 141, B 180.

201 GA 3, 92–4/65–6. Heidegger underscores that the empirical image contains still more than the concept but it contains it differently; the empirical image presents "one from among many" and the concept presents "one which applies to many." GA 3, 98/69.

202 GA 3, 98/69.

203 "Thus in the immediate perception of something on-hand, this house for example, the schematizing prelook [*Vorblick*] of something like house in general is of necessity already to be found. It is from out of this pre-senting alone that what is encountered can reveal itself as house, can offer the look of an 'on-hand house.' So the schematism occurs of necessity on the grounds of our knowing as a finite knowing." GA 3, 101/71.

204 GA 3, 98/69.

205 KRV A 142, B 181. In light of this difference, Heidegger reads Kant as downplaying the question of "subsumption" with which Kant begins the section. The logical action of subsumption applies properly to sensible concepts, whether empirical or pure, where it is a question of subsuming an object under a concept. Kant then notes the difference between sensible concepts and categories, since categories are not homogeneous with appearances; consequently "the subsumption of intuitions under pure categories" or "the application of a category to appearances" is problematic (KRV A 138, B 177). Kant has raised the question of mediation, though, and the answer will prove to be time. GA 3, 109–12/77–9. As Sherover points out, Heidegger is not alone among Kant interpreters in finding the language of "subsumption" problematic. See *Heidegger, Kant, and Time*, 108–10.

206 KRV A 142, B 182. Cf. A 320, B 377.

207 Heidegger characterizes the self-regulation and articulation of schemata as follows: "Through internal self-regulation in time as pure look, the schemata of the notions pass their image off from this and thus articulate the unique pure possibility of having a certain look into a variety of pure images." GA 3, 104/74.

208 KRV A 145, B 184–5.

209 KRV A 145, B 184–5.

210 KRV A 138, B 177. On time's mediating role, see Schalow, *Heidegger-Kant Dialogue*, 180.

211 GA 3, 108/76.

212 GA 3, 108/76. Heidegger interprets the "transcendental object" as "the terminus of the preliminary turning-toward," namely the contrariety of objectivity which forms the horizon of transcendence. "This horizon is indeed not object but rather a nothing, if by object we mean an entity which is apprehended thematically." GA 3, 121–3/85–7.

213 KRV A 154–8, B 193–7.

214 GA 3, 114/81.

215 KRV A 154, B 193–4. Emphasis mine.

216 GA 3, 115/82.
217 KRV A 155, B 194.
218 For this distinction, Heidegger refers to two telling notes in the *Critique*, namely KRV B 302 and KRV A 596, B 624, in addition to § 106 of Kant's lectures on logic.
219 KRV A 156, B 195.
220 GA 3, 117–8/83.
221 KRV A 157, B 196–7.
222 KRV A 158, B 197.
223 GA 3, 119/84.
224 GA 3, 119/84.
225 GA 3, 119/84.
226 KRV A 146, B 185. See GA 3, 123/87. Without ontological truth, our ontic truth is rendered void: "For no knowledge can contradict it without at once losing all content, that is, all relation to any object, and therefore all truth." KRV A 63–4, B 87.
227 "Anthropology does not pose the question of transcendence at all." GA 3, 133/93. Heidegger will say that Kant's project points to a pure, i.e., philosophical anthropology, something that Kant himself does not undertake. The first *Critique*'s articulation of human interest into three questions—namely What can I know? What ought I to do? What may I hope?—are in the introduction to the lectures on logic rooted in the question, What is man?" GA 3, 207/146. Heidegger's metaphysics of Dasein fulfills this anticipated analysis of human finitude. GA 3, 231/162. See KRV A 804–5, B 832–3, and *Lectures on Logic*, trans. J. Michael Young (Cambridge: Cambridge University Press, 1992), 538.
228 "It is easily seen that the pure intuition of the pure succession of nows cannot be the taking-in-stride of a presence [*Anwesenden*]. If it were, then at most it would be able to 'intuit' just the current now, and never the sequence of nows as such and the horizon formed in it." GA 3, 173/122.
229 Kant expressly says that apprehension is a mode of imagination (KRV A 120), and he expressly identifies reproduction with imagination (KRV A 100). Recognition proves more difficult. Heidegger cites a passage from Kant's lectures on metaphysics in which he speaks of "forming power" as the faculty that "produces presentations" of the past, present, or future; it takes a likeness, reproduces, and prefigures. Based on this passage, Heidegger takes the synthesis of recognition to be a power of the imagination: "Insofar as Kant allocates the modes of taking a likeness, reproduction, and prefiguration to the empirical imagination, then the forming of the preliminary attaching as such, the pure preparation, is an act of the pure power of the imagination." GA 3, 186/130. See Pölitz, I. *Kants Vorlesungen über die Metaphysik*, 2d ed., newly edited according to the edition of 1821 by K. H. Schmidt (1924), 88.
230 KRV A 102.
231 KRV A 103. The bracketed text is Heidegger's. GA 3, 186/130.
232 GA 3, 186/130.
233 GA 3, 191/134.
234 KRV A 77, B 102: "Space and time contain a manifold of pure *a priori* intuition, but at the same time are conditions of the receptivity of our mind—conditions under which alone it can receive presentations of objects, and which therefore must also always affect the concept of these objects."
235 GA 3, 190/133.
236 KRV B 67–8.
237 Heidegger notes that Kant uses the same essential predicates to discuss the two: fixed and perduring. "The 'fixed and perduring' I goes so far as to

mean: the I, in the original forming of time, i.e., as original time, forms the letting-stand-against of . . . and its horizon." GA 3, 193/135. See KRV A 123; A 143, B 183; A 182, B 224–5.

238 GA 3, 196/137.
239 GA 3, 196–7/137.
240 GA 3, 149/104.
241 GA 3, 149/105.
242 Cf. KRV A 126.
243 GA 3, 151/106.
244 GA 3, 151/106.
245 GA 3, 153/107.
246 GA 3, 155/109.
247 GA 3, 155/109.
248 GA 3, 160/112.
249 KRV A 94 and A 115.
250 GA 3, 167/117.
251 See Dahlstrom, *Concept*, 131–8.
252 GA 3, 137/96–7.
253 GA 3, 197/138 and 244/171. Heidegger quotes a passage from Hegel to confirm his interpretation of German Idealism: "Accordingly, logic is to be understood as the system of pure reason, as the realm of pure thought. This realm is truth as it is without veil and in its own absolute nature. It can therefore be said that this content is the exposition of God as he is in his eternal essence before the creation of nature and a finite mind." *Science of Logic*, trans. Arnold V. Miller (London: Allen & Unwin, 1969), 50. In this regard, Henrich says the Kant book is "secretly a counterproposal to Hegel's Kant-interpretation and that of speculative Idealism in general." On his interpretation, both Heidegger and Hegel go beyond the historical Kant to grasp the unity of the subject, but Heidegger avoids Hegel's idealism by insisting on the equiprimordiality of the subject's structure in such a way that understanding cannot be absolute. "On the Unity of Subjectivity," 18 and 48. For Heidegger's account of the transition from Kantian finitude to German Idealism, see the winter semester 1930–31 lecture course, "Hegel's *Phenomenology of Spirit*," (GA 32, 146–61/101–12), and our fourth chapter.
254 GA 3, 197/138.
255 Stephan Käufer advances the thesis that Heidegger unsuccessfully attempts to marry two heterogeneous accounts of judgment: what Käufer calls the "derivation from practice" presented in § 33 of *Being and Time* and what he calls the "derivation from synthesis" made in the Kant interpretations of the late 1920s. He thinks this leads Heidegger to develop a failed analogy between "the temporal preconditions of care" and "the transcendental preconditions of the threefold synthesis." See his "Schemata, Hammers, and Time: Heidegger's Two Derivations of Judgment," 79–91. I think the analogy is troubled but not failed; Heidegger takes both accounts, the derivation from world in *Being and Time* and the derivation from temporal synthesis in Kant, to be essentially phenomenological. The account in *Being and Time* traces the origin of the apophantic synthesis to hermeneutic synthesis and this to the synthetic bringing forth of timeliness; the account in *Kant and the Problem of Metaphysics* traces ontic synthesis to the synthetic activity of original time. So, both accounts concern the ultimate phenomenological origin of derivative syntheses. The problem with the marriage, then, is that Kant bypasses the handy and pre-predicative experience. Consequently, his account of judgment has a critical lacuna that Heidegger attempts to work around.

256 GA 3, 86–7/61. Accordingly, Heidegger distinguishes between two kinds of assertions: ontic (existentiell) ones concerning fact and ontological (existential) ones concerning essence. GA 26, 217/169–70.

257 GA 3, 2/2. This unveiling grounds all assertions about what is unveiled. GA 3, 10/7.

258 GA 3, 87/61–2. cf. GA 3, 205/144. The disclosure of finitude is crucial. Traditional ontology "raises itself to an a priori ontic knowledge which can only come to an infinite creature." GA 3, 124/88.

259 GA 3, 12/8.

260 In 1930, while discussing transcendental freedom in Kant, Heidegger alludes to the role of formal indication in realizing the concreteness of essence: "Essence remains closed off to us as long as we ourselves do not become essential in our essence." That is, we can access our essence only "in the actual willing of [our] ownmost essence." GA 31, 301/204, 303/205.

261 Sherover, *Heidegger, Kant, and Time*, 5. In partial support of his thesis, Sherover points to a passage from *Being and Time* which, as Crowell persuasively argues, is mistranslated. Macquarrie and Robinson render the key text: "Nevertheless, our way of exhibiting the constitution of Dasein's being remains only *one way* which we may take. Our *aim* is to work out the question of being in general." The passage, though, should read: "Nevertheless, our way of exhibiting the constitution of Dasein's being remains only *a way* [*ein Weg*]. Our *aim* is to work out the question of being in general." On the mistranslation, see Crowell, *Space of Meaning*, 297.

262 Sherover does point to some passages in which Kant glosses his projects as a "phenomenology," but he does not explicate what this could mean for Kant, nor does he explicate Heidegger's explicit attribution of a phenomenological method to him. See *Heidegger, Kant and Time*, 7 and 228n13.

Part II

The Attempt to Leap Over the Shadow

3   The Revised Kant Book (1935–36)

> Through Kant's critical determination of judgment and of thought in general, *intellectus*, the presumption of uprooted understanding is metaphysically overcome for the first time in a more grounded manner. That we today still have not yet actually adopted this overcoming, speaks not against an apparent rationalism of Kant's, rather it speaks only against us.
> —Martin Heidegger[1]

With *Being and Time* and *Kant and the Problem of Metaphysics*, Heidegger embraces the transcendental turn in philosophy with Kant serving as its historical motivation. The shadow, we can say, is cast. But soon two problems arise. First, Heidegger comes to doubt the adequacy of transcendentalese and its real definition for expressing the dynamic bringing forth at the heart of experience; hence Heidegger's own transcendental project becomes transfigured in terms of a more dynamic vocabulary centered on the changing affectivity of historical dispositions. Second, Heidegger realizes that his efforts to motivate others to follow him on his path fail for several reasons. The first of these reasons has to do with the inherent prejudice of the scholar who endeavors always to understand the new as merely a restatement of the old. In the *Contributions*, Heidegger expresses frustration at his reception, "No one understands what 'I' think here . . . because everyone tries to explain 'my' attempt merely historiographically and appeals to the past, which he thinks he grasps because it seems already to lie behind him."[2] The second of these has to do with his historiographical discovery that the book on Kant had misconstrued the authentic horizon of questioning operative for the historical Kant. Heidegger did not much care about the distortion of Kant per se; his worry instead was the way his own thought appeared to his contemporaries as distorted due to the native constraints of Kant's horizon of questioning. Again, Heidegger writes in the *Contributions*, "But, if one contends—and rightfully so—that historically Kant here is distorted, then one must also avoid presenting as Kantianism the basic position from which and into which the distortion took place."[3] Heidegger cannot be pigeonholed as a Kantian. This chapter details Heidegger's attempt to work out a new historical motivation for his transfigured philosophy, one that will be mindful of the distance between his own thought and Kant's, and yet one in which again Kant plays a privileged role.

In the *Contributions*, he writes, "What is happening everywhere here is really *history*, which remains out of the reach of what is merely historiographical, because this history is not a matter of allowing the past to come up but rather is in all respects the momentum over to what is to come."[4] For Heidegger, the central concern is to motivate his philosophical project, and that means engaging the philosophical tradition according to a double hermeneutic: namely, he turns to the tradition to render his own novel position intelligible, but this can only be accomplished by means of measuring the tradition against a problematic largely foreign to it. Hence, his interpretation remains violent and inevitably so: he is not interested in repeating the tradition but of transcending it. At the same time, this double strategy of making the new intelligible in terms of the old and the old in terms of the new pays greater dividends in his interpretation of Kant than any other figure in the tradition. This is because, like Heidegger, Kant is a rigorous conceptual thinker concerned with the movement of experience. The difference is that Kant concerns himself narrowly with justifying scientific experience of objects and Heidegger concerns himself broadly with exposing the experience of the entire domain of intelligibility—scientifically, poetically, and philosophically. Kant is the figure in the history of philosophy that Heidegger can interpret with the least amount of violence, because his inquiry is closest to Heidegger's own.

If the purpose of a historical interpretation is to motivate inquiry, it has to have some plausibility as an interpretation; otherwise, it will attract attention to itself rather than to the matter to be thought; instead of a way into thinking, it will become an obstacle to thinking. Heidegger repents of his misreading of Kant by taking on the foreign yoke of Kantian thinking in order to show a new way in which Kant leads into Heidegger's thought. In 1962, Heidegger issues two publications in an attempt to "make up for what the writing *Kant and the Problem of Metaphysics* . . . lacked."[5] One is the winter semester 1935–36 lecture course, "Fundamental Questions of Metaphysics," published as *What Is a Thing? Toward Kant's Doctrine of the Transcendental Principles*, and the other a 1961 lecture, "Kant's Thesis about Being." While both seek to interpret Kant from within the horizon of his own manner of questioning, the course differs markedly from the 1961 lecture, which acknowledges that Kant makes strides in judgment and method yet focuses instead on Kant's shortcomings. Hence, a question concerns whether the two texts offer compatible interpretations. To this question, Heidegger gives an unequivocal yes. In a preliminary note to a 1965 republication of *Kant und das Problem der Metaphysik* (1929), Heidegger characterizes both of these writings, the 1961 lecture and the 1935–36 lecture course, as supplements to the interpretation of that book. In 1973, he writes that both writings retract the Kant book's overinterpretation: "In later writings . . . I attempted to retract the overinterpretation without at the same time writing a correspondingly new version of the Kant book itself."[6] So, the chronology is as follows: in 1961 he delivers a lecture on Kant; in 1962 he publishes that lecture as an essay, and he also publishes the lecture course from 1935–36; in 1965 he points to these two writings together as supplements; in 1973 he calls the two writings retractions of portions of the Kant book. At no time did he present the 1961 lecture as a correction of the 1935–36 lecture course; instead both writings correct, supplement, and retract aspects of the 1929 book. All this suggests that in Heidegger's own mind the lecture and the lecture course offer compatible though not identical interpretations. And yet, the result is "not new discoveries in Kant philology" but an interpretation that finds a path into Heidegger's own manner of questioning.[7]

Of these two texts, the most extensive and intensive is the 1935–36 lecture course, and it comes at a pivotal moment in Heidegger's development; I will discuss the 1961 lecture in its proper context in the concluding chapter. Now, in 1935, on the eve of composing the *Contributions*, the text in which he attempts to leap over his transcendental shadow, Heidegger returns to Kant's *Critique of Pure Reason* in a sustained and sympathetic effort to interpret Kant faithfully and fruitfully against the backdrop of his own later philosophy. *Faithfully*, in that Heidegger intends to get Kant right rather than imposing on him a foreign horizon of questioning, as he came to realize he did in the 1929 *Kant and the Problem of Metaphysics*: "Henceforth, only Kant shall speak."[8] In the course, Heidegger does not set himself against transcendental philosophy, but he takes up a position *within* the transcendental way of questioning: "When, in this lecture, we constantly ask about the thingness of the thing and endeavor to place ourselves into the realm of this question, it is nothing else than the exercise of the transcendental point of view and position of questioning."[9] Heidegger now reads Kant as asking the question "What is a thing?" rather than the question "How is the domain of experience possible?" *Fruitfully*, because the Kant that emerges is one that leads to the threshold of Heidegger's own later thinking. Kant's transcendental thinking traces judgment and the thing—and thus logic and science—back to the pre-subjective and pre-objective context opened up in the encircling happening of experience. He shows that the transcendental mode of questioning grounds knowledge in intuition and consequently enables Kant to overcome the insufficient understanding of judgment characteristic of rationalism.[10] Kant's transcendental distinction between analytic and synthetic judgments provides a more adequate understanding of thinking as essentially in service to the givenness of intuited entities. His highest principle of synthetic judgment uncovers the context in which entities can stand opposite us and be apprehended as they are in themselves. Heidegger's own later thinking recapitulates this Kantian context in terms of the deeper connection of Dasein and being. The question "What is a thing?" naturally leads beyond itself to the question, "How is the domain of experience possible?"

His new reading of Kant, focusing as it does on the transcendental overcoming of rationalism in the novel distinction of analytic and synthetic judgment, originates in a seminar on Kant that he delivered in the summer of 1931.[11] With this new interpretation, Kant plays a privileged historical role in motivating for us today the broadly phenomenological thinking that Heidegger aims to inaugurate. While Heidegger no longer thinks Kant is interested in the givenness of the ontological itself, he still thinks Kant is broadly phenomenological in his concern for the condition for the possibility of judgment and experience. Heidegger aims to disrupt the contemporary obviousness of either judgment or facts as the theme of philosophical reflection. He wants to motivate a decision for the proper topic of thinking, namely the site presupposed by every judgment and every fact. Heidegger recalls Kant in order to invite his contemporaries to achieve a more adequate, that is, transcendental, understanding of judgment and thereby to lead them to the threshold of Heidegger's own later thinking. Among contemporary positions, he singles out scientific positivism and mathematical logic as two standpoints that do not adequately—that is, transcendentally—grasp the essence of judgment. The former focuses only on the object of the judgment and the latter only on the form of the assertion. Both pass over the more fundamental relation of assertion and object given in intuition, and it is this relation that Kant analyzes in his transcendental manner of consideration.[12] Heidegger's reenactment gives us a Kant on the scent of more and more fundamental relations culminating in a context of relations that makes experience possible.

Kant stands apart from other figures in the tradition, because he symbolizes the transcendental turn in philosophy; he represents, for Heidegger, ambiguously either the highpoint of modern thought or more intimately, one of the two figures in "transcendental phenomenology"— either Husserl's phenomenology or Heidegger's own work in *Being and Time*. In the 1920s, Heidegger tells us that he "was trying to think the nature of phenomenology in a more originary manner, so as to fit it in this way back into the place that is properly its own within Western philosophy."[13] Where was that home? First with Augustine, then Aristotle, and finally Kant. In the 1930s, he adjusts the historical register of his phenomenology by connecting it to the pre-Socratics and by offering Kant as the mode of access to this ancient tradition; working through Kant's critical philosophy affords the means for us moderns to disavow our rationalism and recover that pre-Socratic beginning. Heidegger stops talking about Husserlian phenomenology; he had come into his own and now had his own philosophy to work with and against. He later insists that his suppression of the name, "phenomenology," does not mean that he stopped being thoroughly phenomenological.[14] Having found the proper historical place of phenomenology in Kant, the thinker from Königsberg serves as a kind of representative or privileged anticipation of Heidegger's peculiar "transcendental phenomenology." Having understood Kant thanks to Husserl, Heidegger replaces Husserl with Kant in his self-represented genealogy. Kant symbolizes the advent of transcendental phenomenology, its great promise as well as its inherent limits.

The significance of the revised Kant book stems not only from its proximity to the *Contributions* but also from its relation to the three lecture courses that surround it. The previous semester, Heidegger had sketched the uniform oblivion of being characteristic of Western philosophy. In the lecture course on Kant, Heidegger offers Kant and transcendental philosophy as a path out of the oblivion of being. Central to Heidegger's interpretation is a careful and sympathetic reading of the methodological critique of the logical and mathematical prejudices as well as its disclosure of what Heidegger provocatively calls "the between" as the highest principle of synthetic judgment.

In the next chapter I will turn to Heidegger's *Contributions to Philosophy*, written from 1936–38. There we discover that transcendental philosophy in its Heideggerian and Kantian forms provides an essential transitional role in leading from the oblivion of being to the thinking of being. Both grasp some measure of human finitude by recognizing that our thought is subordinate to the givenness of being. This chapter, then, details Heidegger's account of a historical overcoming of rationalism through transcendental philosophy, and the next details the transitional role accorded transcendental philosophy in Heidegger's own thinking. In the lecture courses and in the *Contributions*, Heidegger aims to motivate the overcoming of the Western oblivion of being by repeating more fundamentally the Kantian overcoming of modern rationalism. At the same time, he wants to distance himself from the limits inherent in the transcendental project as such, including the preliminary question of *Being and Time*. The transcendental program is necessary—there is no other entrance to Heidegger's path of thinking—but it needs to be reconfigured radically. Heidegger proposes we first think transcendentally in order to get a glimpse of the domain to be thought and then "leap" over the limitations of transcendence by experiencing the reciprocal interplay of Dasein and being.

1 The Immediate Context for the Revised Kant Book

The 1935–36 lecture course interprets Kant as a critical figure in overcoming rationalism through transcendental philosophy. Heidegger delivered his individual lecture courses in the 1930s as part of a larger project: "Perhaps at a later time some may succeed in experiencing . . . that which is kept silent [in the lecture courses] and from there in setting within its limits what is explicitly said."[15] Situating the Kant course in its immediate context helps bring to light the full implication of its thesis concerning transcendental philosophy. The course is framed by a famous overview of Western metaphysics before and an extensive treatment of Schelling after. When situated between a discussion of metaphysics in general and German Idealism in particular, the overcoming of rationalism takes on its full sense. Kant's transcendental philosophy proves to be an indispensable though ambiguous path out of the oblivion of being, because Kant's manner of questioning discloses the original place of truth. Since rationalistic prejudices again predominate in the systems of German Idealism and biologism, Heidegger bids us to return to Kant's finite ground and there begin anew.

Heidegger identifies the rationalistic disjunction, "being and thought," in the famous lecture course, "Introduction to Metaphysics," which he delivered the semester before the 1935–36 lecture course. There he charts various restrictions of being, such as being and seeming, being and becoming, being and the ought. The dyad, "being and thought," appears alongside these others but he highlights its importance: this dyad constitutes the "fundamental attitude" (*Grundhaltung*) and "fundamental position" (*Grundstellung*) of the Western spirit.[16] It was foreshadowed by the first philosophers, received definition with Plato and Aristotle, but "takes on its authentic form at the beginning of modernity."[17] For this dyad, thinking does not stand in service of being in the manner of phenomenological *logos*; rather it sets itself *against* being—thereby making being its *object*—and it forms the basis for interpreting being in general.[18]

Heidegger's analysis seeks to show the originary junction of the present disjunction. "Here we insist that the disjunction between being and thinking, if it is an inner and necessary disjunction, must be founded on an originary belonging of what is divided."[19] Demonstrating this junction does not supplement the traditional disjunction but instead undermines it. In fact, he outlines a twofold approach to overcome it. (1) The first is to show its *limits* originally. "In the seemingly irrelevant division *being and thinking* we have to recognize that fundamental position of the spirit of the West that is the real target of our attack. It can be overcome only *originally*—that is, in such a way that its inceptive truth is shown its own limits [*Grenzen*] and thereby founded anew."[20] (2) The second is to *think more rigorously* by thoughtfully returning to its origin.

> The misinterpretation of thinking and the misuse of misinterpreted thinking can be overcome only by a genuine and originary thinking, and *by nothing else*. In order to provide a new foundation for such thinking, we must above all else return to the question of the essential relation of thinking to being—but this means unfolding the question of being as such. Overcoming traditional logic does not mean the abolition of thinking and the rule of mere feelings. Instead, it means a more originary, rigorous thinking that belongs to being.[21]

The overcoming of Western rationalism, then, does not occur through a flight into irrationalism. Thinking does not yield to feeling or dissolve into mysticism. Rather traditional logic and its objectification of being is overcome through a new, more rigorous thinking that belongs to being by returning to its origin. Consequently, Heidegger returns to the beginning and shows how, for the first thinkers, thinking belonged to being.

For both Heraclitus and Parmenides, there is an originary unity of φύσις and λόγος, being and thinking. Here λόγος means gathering or relating and not discourse or assertion; φύσις means "the emerging sway" (*das aufgehende Walten*).[22] Heidegger especially focuses on Parmenides' famous saying, τὸ γὰρ αὐτὸ νοεῖν ἐστίν τε καὶ εἶναι.[23] Indeed this becomes a focal point for him throughout subsequent decades. According to his gloss, the saying does not mean, "Thinking and being are the same," but instead, "Belonging-together reciprocally are apprehension and being."[24] Apprehension here names the fundamental happening in which humans enter history. Consequently, Parmenides's fragment identifies the originary belonging together of the human and being from which the disjunction "being and thinking" can first arise: "In the belonging-together of being and the human essence, their disjunction comes to light. The division 'being and thinking,' which has long since become pale, empty and rootless, no longer allows us to recognize its origin unless we go back to its inception."[25] In the beginning, then, human beings belonged to being.

Heidegger's account of the decline and end of this inceptive beginning is well known.[26] With Plato, the emerging sway of φύσις gives way to what is present, ἰδέα.[27] With Aristotle, λόγος as gathering gives way to discourse about what is present, a discourse that can be true or false; upon this interpretation of truth as correctness, the categories are founded.[28] The subsequent history of Western philosophy takes its bearings from the end of the Greek beginning instead of from the origin of the beginning in Heraclitus and Parmenides. Consequently, for subsequent philosophy, thought determines being rather than originally belonging to it. And this, it seems, is despite the work of the greatest of modern thinkers. Leibniz, Kant, and Hegel, each in their own way, make "decisive efforts to overcome traditional logic"—and its objectification of being—but apparently to no avail.[29] Later in the course he writes, "For despite Kant and Hegel, logic has not taken a single step farther in what is essential and inceptive. The only possible step remaining is to unhinge it . . . from the *ground* up."[30]

2 The Historical Significance of Kant's *Critique*

The next semester course, devoted to Kant, constitutes a significant qualification to this general historical thesis. In the 1935–36 lecture course on Kant, Heidegger says that Kant brings the traditional fundamental position into an explicit foundation, and what makes this possible is the transcendental attitude.[31] Heidegger divides the course into two parts. In the second part of the course, he revises his Kant book by undertaking a lengthy and sympathetic interpretation of the first *Critique*. In the first part, he sketches a history of inquiry into the question, "What is a thing?" The aim is to show that the so-called natural perspective is in fact historically constituted, because just what a thing is appears differently for ancient and modern thought. He thinks Kant's *Critique of Pure Reason* diagnoses and critiques the prejudices that constitute the trajectory of Western philosophy, ancient and modern: "In the title, 'pure reason,' lies the λόγος of Aristotle, and in the 'pure' above all a determinate formation of the mathematical."[32] Both prejudices mask the way things encounter us in our everyday experience. Rationalism follows these prejudices, and Kant unfolds the prejudices in such a way that they are overcome in principle. Kant's transcendental philosophy does limit the rationalistic position, "being and thought," though it does not do so originally, that is historically.

Heidegger endeavors to make questionable what he dialectically calls the "natural interpretation of the world" (*natürliche Weltauffassung*). According to this view, a thing is an on-hand bearer of on-hand properties.[33] In *Being and Time* he had claimed that this is a derivative mode of interpretation in which the timely world-horizon has dimmed down, leaving just the bare, present entity; the relation of the thing to the world retreats, thereby leaving only a relation of subject and predicate. Heidegger here identifies and diagnoses this interpretation as a prejudice dominating our everyday, scientific, and philosophical ways of thinking.

He thinks the justification for this prejudice is the correspondence theory of truth. Something is true when it fits itself to things. The essence of truth, *a fortiori*, must fit itself to the essence of things and vice versa. "It is necessary from the essence of truth as fitting [*Anmessung*] that the structure of things be reflected in the structure of truth."[34] The unfolding interdependence of on-handness and correspondence also entails a third member, assertion, as the place of truth. Since truth is the correspondence to things, the assertion must emerge as that which corresponds correctly or incorrectly, as that which can be true or false.[35]

Assertion has a threefold structure: "[1] A proposition [2] giving information [3] which, when carried out vis-à-vis others, becomes communication."[36] Assertion is the site of truth in the narrower sense of proposition. That is, it can be true or false, because it conveys predicative information. The proposition itself has a threefold structure: the subject or object of the proposition, the predicate or assertion of the proposition, and the copula or connective. "The structure and the structural parts of the truth, that is, of the true proposition (object of proposition and assertion of the proposition), are exactly fitted to that by which truth as such guides itself to the thing as the bearer and to its properties."[37] The structure of the proposition, in accordance with the essence of truth, reflects the structure of things.

In the "natural" view, then, we have a constellation of three interdependent interpretations: the thingness of the thing as on-handness, correctness as the essence of truth, and the assertion as the place of truth.[38] Heidegger provides substantially the same analysis that was found in *Being and Time* except that he no longer exonerates Aristotle from this view. Such a difference in interpretation is assuredly related to the emerging emphasis on history and prejudice. Though we may call the everyday, scientific, and philosophical views of the thing "natural," they are in fact historical with a demonstrable origin in Plato and Aristotle.[39] Indeed, the term *natural* has its own history and means something different for the Greeks, for the medievals, and for the moderns.[40] Though this prejudice is seemingly obvious, it in fact leads us to misconstrue things as they present themselves: "So it could be that in our natural worldview we have been dominated by a centuries-old interpretation of the thingness of the thing, while things actually encounter us quite differently."[41]

As in § 33 of *Being and Time*, Heidegger underscores the ontological importance of this doctrine of truth. The Greeks called the proposition κατάφασις, because it asserts something "down" to something that underlies it. The proposition, then, asserts both a determination and something already present that is determined. The general ways assertions determine things are called κατηγορία. According to this interpretation, then, modes of assertedness are the determinations of being.[42] "The modes of assertedness guide the view in the determination of presence [*Anwesenheit*], that is, of the being of the entity."[43] The Greek term for assertion, λόγος, becomes translated into Latin as *ratio*, and in the translation the thing becomes determined by the basic forms of thinking. Finally, *ratio* becomes translated into German as *Vernunft* (reason), and the prejudice takes its place in the title of Kant's *Critique of Pure Reason*.

Our everyday experience of things is filtered through the logical prejudice, but another prejudice has a still greater hold on us. Heidegger says that modern natural science, as a universal way of thinking, is "what most holds us captive and makes us unfree in the experience and determination of things."[44] Drawing on Greek etymology, he terms this prejudice "mathematical," with a signification more fundamental than the discipline of mathematics. "Mathematical" encompasses two Greek expressions, μάθησις, the manner of learning what one already knows, and τὰ μαθήματα, what is learned and can be learned only through this manner.[45] There is no presuppositionless science, Heidegger says, because the essence of science consists in presupposing.[46] Biology presupposes the animate and botany the vegetative. The index of the scientific character of a science is the degree to which it acts according to its pre-judgments. Heidegger here goes beyond his analysis of the modern scientific project given in *Being and Time* by rooting it in the essence of the mathematical prejudice. In doing so, he lays the ground for his critique of technology as

the fulfillment of modern science. In view of this, William Barton's suggestion that Heidegger's analysis is but "a concession to the mathematical-
physical assumptions of the *Critique*" misses the point.[47] Bringing to light
this prejudice determinative of the modern world is, on Heidegger's interpretation, the great merit of the *Critique*.

Heidegger illustrates the manner of learning characteristic of the mathematical by asking us to consider the way we might come to know a rifle.[48]
Through practice we take possession of how to deal with it by learning to
load it, aim it, etc., and through this we come to know the thing in a general and indefinite way. We can also learn ballistics and mechanics, and
thus know more about the thing in general. But something essential still
remains to be learned, namely, the thing's "involvement" (*Bewandtnis*).
When we come to know the involvement, we take possession of what we
already in some sense have.[49] Involvement enables us to see a weapon as
such; it goes before our particular dealings and makes them possible. We
can deal with something without the involvement being explicit, but we
can produce it only if we have such knowledge.[50]

What is most difficult to learn is the whole of what we already know;
when we know that we have taken possession of the presupposition of
our knowledge of things: "The mathematical is that fundamental position [*Grundstellung*] to things in which we take up [*vor-nehmen*] things,
as already given to us, and as they must and should be given. Therefore,
the mathematical is the fundamental presupposition [*Grundvorausset-
zung*] of the knowledge of things."[51] This is no small prejudice, then, but
one that gets to the heart of all of knowledge.

Though Heidegger gives it a Greek name, he thinks it is a decidedly
modern prejudice. It receives its metaphysical foundation in Descartes
and achieves its scientific elaboration in Newton. Heidegger thinks that
Kant intends this specific sense of the mathematical when he writes,
"I assert, however, that in any special doctrine of nature there can be only
as much *proper* science as there is *mathematics* therein."[52] The essence of
modern science and modern thought in general does not lie in its concern
for facts, nor in its experiments, nor even in its measurements; indeed
ancient and medieval investigations of nature had these as well.[53] Rather,
the essence of modern science is its mathematical projection.

Heidegger offers a prolonged analysis of Newton to clarify the mathematical character of modern science. Turning to Newton's *Principia:
Mathematical Principles of Natural Philosophy*, he focuses on the most
important principle of that work, the law of motion: "Every body perse-
veres in its state of being at rest or of moving uniformly straight forward,
except insofar as it is compelled to change its state by forces impressed."[54]
Heidegger contrasts this definition with Aristotle's doctrine of motion.
Though Newton and Aristotle agree that the standard of knowledge is
the way things appear, what appears and how it is understood differ
greatly. Aristotle's nature is a capacity for motion intrinsic to bodies,

but Newton's nature is the changing positions of bodies within a neutral framework of space-time positions. This difference becomes clearer once the essence of the mathematical has been outlined.

The mathematical prejudice projects thingness and thereby opens a realm for things to appear as facts.[55] The project sets up what and how things will be evaluated, and these determinations are called ἀξιώματα, from the Greek word to evaluate, ἀξιόω. Following the logical prejudice, they take the form of "propositions" (*Sätze*) and so are "principles" (*Grund-sätze*). The project is the "prior conception" (*Vorausgriff*) of the essence of things that maps out the structure of things and their relations to other things and thus the plan of the realm of things. This axiomatic project and the realm it opens calls for a particular "manner of access" (*Zugangsart*) to things that now show themselves only according to the plan projected in advance. This manner of access is the modern experiment, which asks questions in accord with the project. Moreover, the project calls for a uniform measure, which gives rise to a mathematics in the narrow sense. Paradoxically, then, modern science is experimental and mathematical only because it is based on an axiomatic project that at first "leaps over" (*Überspringen*) every measurable fact. "Bodies have no concealed qualities, powers, and capacities. . . . Things now show themselves only in the relations of places and time points and in the measures of mass and working forces. How they show themselves is prescribed in the project."[56] Newton's mathematical project of axioms or principles marks a radical departure from Aristotle's interpretation of nature.

The mathematical prejudice is at work not only in modern natural science but also in modern mathematics and metaphysics as well. Heidegger turns to modern metaphysics to see how the mathematical is grounded. Descartes's early work, *Regulae ad directionem ingenii*, shows a specific concern for the mathematical as the basis of all knowledge.[57] The title itself indicates this concern: *Regulae* are "guiding principles" (*Grund- und Leitsätze*) by which the mathematical follows its own essence; *ad directionem ingenii* suggests a "ground-laying" (*Grundlegung*) of the mathematical so that it can serve as the measure of the mind doing research. Heidegger quotes the third through fifth rules and focuses on the fifth. There Descartes writes:

> The whole method consists entirely in the ordering and arranging of the objects on which we must concentrate our mind's eye if we are to discover some truth. We shall be following this method exactly if we first reduce complicated and obscure propositions step by step to simpler ones, and then, starting with the intuition of the simplest ones of all, try to ascend through the same steps to a knowledge of all the rest.[58]

The simplest propositions, then, provide the basis for the whole of knowledge. Heidegger connects the priority of these first propositions with their role as foundation: "To the essence of the mathematical as project belongs the axiomatical, the application of fundamental propositions or principles [*Grundsätzen*] upon which everything further is founded [*gründet*] in insightful order."[59] To ground the mathematical prejudice, Descartes needs to articulate the founding propositions. The propositions in question must be intuitively certain and must project the thingness of things.

Now, the logical prejudice determined the being of the entity by following the assertion, and the mathematical prejudice does not depart from this tradition. It does, however, transform the nature of the assertion which performs this ontological function. Traditionally, the assertion or proposition was something on-hand that presented something as "underlying" (*vorliegenden*) and "on-hand" (*vorhanden*). The mathematical prejudice, however, cannot admit something "pre-given" (*vorgegebenen*) as its basis but must provide such a foundation out of itself. The proposition sought, then, must bring forth its own *subjectum* in being posited. The mathematical posits positing itself as this subject and thereby fulfills its inner requirement of taking explicit possession of something it necessarily already has.

If anything is given at all, it is only the *proposition* in general *as such*, that is, the positing, the position, in the sense of thinking that asserts. The positing, the proposition, only has itself as that which can be posited. Only where thinking thinks itself, is it absolutely mathematical, that is, a taking cognizance of that which we already have.[60]

The mathematical prejudice takes over the logical prejudice's demand for an underlying subject, but in accord with its peculiar essence finds in the act of thinking or positing itself, in the *ego cogito*, the *subjectum* of its first, intuitively evident proposition: "In the essence of positing lies the proposition: I posit. That is a proposition which does not depend upon something pre-given, but only gives to itself what lies within it."[61]

The mathematical project is founded on something itself projected in the project. A new sense of freedom as being bound by self-imposed obligations emerges in such a projection. "According to this inner march, a liberation to a new freedom, the mathematical drives out of itself to lay its own essence as the ground of itself and thus of all knowledge."[62] The self-grounding ground, founded in the posited subject, is the essential thrust of this prejudice. With this new freedom, the subject provided by mathematical prejudice becomes *the* subject par excellence: "In the 'I posit' the 'I' as the positer is co- and pre-posited as that which is already present [*das schon Vorliegende*], as the entity. The being of entities determines itself out of the 'I am' as the certainty of positing."[63] Every other entity, a *subjectum* according to the logical prejudice, now becomes an object that stands in essential relation to the newly determined subject. The being of things is likewise an object opposite the subject, and thus thought is disjoined from being.[64] The pure unfolding of reason's principles now determines the thingness of the thing, and the prejudice takes its place in the title of Kant's *Critique of Pure Reason*.

A critique delimits what is decisive and peculiar, and a critique of pure reason exhibits the proper essence or inner construction of pure reason by "a lifting out of different possibilities of the uses of reason and their corresponding rules."[65] The survey of reason refers to principles and not facts; it determines "the whole essence of pure reason out of its own principles."[66] The architectonic accomplishes this survey by exhaustively exhibiting the principles of pure reason.[67] It thereby exposes rationalism to its limits: "In the enactment of the 'critique' of pure reason so understood, the 'mathematical' in the principled [*grundsätzlich*] sense first comes to its unfolding and, at the same time, to its sublimation [*Aufhebung*], that is, to its own limit."[68] Kant exhaustively unfolds the principles of pure reason and in doing so limits the dominance of the logical and mathematical prejudices. Being is no longer determined from thought alone, and the disjunction, "being and thought," becomes more of a conjunction in which thought is returned to being.

3 The Movement of Kant's *Critique*

Heidegger's analysis moves in two stages. First, he shows that Kant initiates a "revolution" regarding the understanding of judgment by placing it essentially in service to intuition. This new understanding of judgment necessitates the novel distinction between analytic and synthetic judgments. The analytic judgment refers to the object through the mediation of the subjective concept, and it therefore can clarify knowledge but not expand it. The synthetic judgment has immediate recourse to the intuitively given object itself, and it therefore enlarges knowledge. Judgment and thought are now understood in terms of their subordination to intuitive givenness. Consequently, Heidegger can conclude that with Kant's new "characterization of judgment, the originary sense of λόγος as *gathering*, though dimmed, shines through."[69] The second stage of Heidegger's reading focuses on the possibility of synthetic judgments. This is established in the section, "The Highest Principle of All Synthetic Judgments." Heidegger shows that the rationalistic hegemony of the principle of non-contradiction is overcome by the new articulation of synthetic judgment and its principle. The principle of non-contradiction is no longer the sufficient ground of all truth as it was for modern rationalists; instead, it is but a negative condition, a *conditio sine qua non*.[70] Heidegger labors for sixty-one pages in the German text to show that Kant's exposition of the highest principle of synthetic judgment, the new sufficient ground of truth, opens the pre-subjective and pre-objective "between" in which humans can encounter things.[71] I will follow the text carefully for several reasons. First, the Niemeyer edition on which the English translation is based is without a useful textual division, and this lack of editorial apparatus obscures Heidegger's careful reconstruction of Kant. The *Gesamtausgabe* edition rectified this shortcoming, but it is still not readily available.[72] Second, it is in the detail of his reading that that his affinity to transcendental philosophy can come to light; in reenacting Kant, Heidegger creates a momentum toward the enactment of his own later thinking.

Reenacting the Transcendental Method

Kant is misunderstood, Heidegger says, when we approach him in our everyday or scientific attitude that wants to understand everything as something on-hand.[73] Instead we must adopt the transcendental "viewpoint and position of questioning" (*Blick- und Fragestellung*), which brings to light the originary relation of experience and the object of experience.[74] Kant's transformation of judgment is overlooked when we approach the first *Critique* without realizing the reorientation our own thought must undergo. "The chief difficulty in understanding this basic section of the *Critique of Pure Reason* and the whole work lies in the fact that we approach it from our everyday or scientific mode of thinking and read it in that attitude [*Haltung*]."[75] Our everyday or scientific habit of mind discloses only part of the entire structure of judgment. Our account of judgment is either psychological or logical; that is, it attends either to how the object is experienced or the logical form of its articulation. To comprehend judgment, however, we cannot simply add together psychological and logical accounts. Instead, we have to move into a new domain of reflection. Kant includes his new definition of judgment in the title of § 19, "The logical form of all judgments consists in the objective unity of the apperception of the concepts which they contain."[76] Heidegger says this title shows the interplay of judgment and method: "To read this as a methodical directive means that all discussion of the essence of the judgment must arise from the entire essential structure of judgment as it is established, in advance, from the relations to the object and to the knowing human."[77] When we enact Kant's transcendental consideration, we can see that judgment emerges from a pre-subjective and pre-objective domain.

Heidegger clarifies what "transcendental" means for Kant by pointing out that people usually think the difference between engaging in a science and thinking about that science is one of content. However, as Heidegger observes, we "cannot deal biologically with biology" by employing the methods of biology. Rather the shift from engaging in a science to talking about a science entails a qualitative difference, namely, "in the essence, in line of sight, in concept-formation and in demonstration."[78] In our everyday or scientific attitude, we are directed straightaway toward relations among entities and so do not grasp assertions about them as such. We can also, with the logician, maintain ourselves in this attitude while directing ourselves toward the assertions themselves, leaving aside the relation to the object. The assertion is then grasped as a subject-predicate relation. But we can also adopt a wholly new attitude that grasps "the relation" (*der Bezug*) between the assertion and the object.[79]

> We are now not only not directed to [1] the object of the assertion, but also not to [2] the form of the assertion as such, but rather to [3] how the object is the object of the assertion, how the assertion presents [*vorstellt*] the object in advance, how our knowledge passes over to the object, *transcendit*, and how, thereby, and in what objective determination the object encounters. Kant calls this way of considering transcendental.[80]

In this third way, we bring to light what was overlooked in the two poles of the everyday attitude. In transcendental philosophy, we consider the entity "in regard to how this object is an object *for us*, in which respect it is meant, that is, how our thought thinks it."[81] Heidegger notes that Kant himself explicitly calls transcendental "a determination of a thing with regard to its essence (as thing)."[82]

Central to the account of these various ways of inquiry is the relation that shows up in each. The everyday and scientific attitude registers relations among objects themselves. Heidegger gives Kant's example, "The sun warms the rock." The scientific turn to the assertion as such takes it as an object. We consider the sentence simply as a subject-predicate relation. In the shift to the transcendental position the relation that becomes manifest is the relation of the object to the knowing human, which Heidegger elsewhere terms the intentional relation. "Transcendental consideration [*Betrachtung*] is not directed upon objects themselves nor upon thought as the mere presentation [*Vorstellen*] of the subject-predicate relationship, but upon the passing over and the relation to the object *as this relation*."[83] Transcendental reflection does not take a psychological account together with a logical account. Rather this viewpoint and position of questioning discloses "something more original [*etwas Ursprünglicheres*], from which these two sides have been separately lifted out."[84]

Heidegger maintains that all reflection on the sciences must move in the transcendental domain. Otherwise, reflection will isolate a part of the phenomenon and take it as the whole. Mathematical logic's attempt to be "the scientific logic of all sciences" will meet with frustration until it traces the form of the assertion back to its ground in experience.[85] Similarly, positivism's "idolization of facts" (*Tatsachenvergötterung*) will continue until scientists become philosophical and recognize that prejudgments are essential for us to be able to encounter objects.[86] Both positions can accomplish their aim only by entering the transcendental viewpoint: "But just as we cannot take one reasonable or fruitful step in any science without being familiar with its objects and procedures, so also we cannot take a step in reflecting on the science without the right experience and practice in the transcendental point of view."[87] Heidegger does not deny the validity of logic and science. He only denies the adequacy of the average contemporary interpretation of that validity, because it artificially isolates a part and does not grasp the whole phenomenon.[88]

The shift into the transcendental habit of mind discloses a new interpretation of knowledge in the subordination of thought to intuition. Heidegger thinks this is evident in the very first line of the *Critique of Pure Reason*. The well-known sentence reads: "In whatever manner and by whatever means a mode of knowledge may relate to objects, *intuition* is that through which it is in immediate relation to them, and to which all thought as a means is directed."[89] Due to this transformation of knowledge, judgment, the traditional vehicle of knowledge, must itself be understood anew in terms of its subordination to intuition.[90] Kant's new interpretation of knowledge and judgment can be understood only when we shift from our everyday or scientific habit of mind and enter the transcendental attitude: "Therefore, when, from the first sentence onward, we read the *Critique of Pure Reason* in this attitude, from the start everything shifts into a different light."[91]

Synthetic Judgments and the Theme of Givenness

A judgment, according to the traditional definition, says something about something. Such a definition can be found in thinkers from Aristotle through Christian Wolff.[92] In his lectures on logic, Kant used the textbook of Georg Friedrich Meier, a student of a student of Wolff. Meier's *Summary of the Doctrine of Reason* flattens Wolff's definition by defining judgment as "a presentation of a logical relation of several concepts."[93] Kant declares his dissatisfaction with this definition at a critical juncture of the *Critique*, the Transcendental Deduction of the Pure Concepts of the Understanding:

> I have never been able to accept the interpretation which logicians give of judgment in general. It is, they declare, the presentation of a relation between two concepts. . . . I need only point out that the definition leaves undetermined wherein the asserted *relation* consists.[94]

As Heidegger underscores, Kant does not say this tradition is false but rather unsatisfactory.[95] It omits some of the essential moments that constitute the essence of judgment. Kant's new definition, by contrast, involves a fundamental clarification of the essence of judgment in light of the subordination of thought to intuition.

Judgment, Kant asserts, is "nothing but the manner in which given modes of knowledge are brought to the objective unity of apperception."[96]

Heidegger underscores that Kant no longer defines judgment in terms of concepts or presentations. Instead he defines judgment in terms of "given modes of knowledge," and the given in knowledge are intuitions. The essence of judging consists in bringing these intuitions to "objective unity." The unity of the intuitions belongs to the object itself. Registering this unity entails at the same time an awareness of the subject as the dative of the unity. In "apperception," this relation to the subject is perceived along with the object, and something like the intentional relation emerges.[97] When we take these aspects together, we see that the relation at issue has grown wider. No longer is judgment merely a relation between concepts; rather, such a relation itself is now situated within a larger whole, namely a relation between a knowing subject and a known object. Heidegger can thus write: "Here judging as an action of understanding is not only related to intuition and object, but its essence is defined from this relation and even as this relation."[98] Consequently, understanding itself is transformed from a faculty of connecting presentations to a faculty which relates to a known object.[99]

We may be tempted to think that Kant has offered a mere addendum to the traditional definition of judgment that rounds it out and makes it complete. Heidegger assures us, however, that Kant gives us a new definition that grasps the matter more fundamentally.[100] From the perspective of Kant's new definition, the traditional definition appears as an "artificial construct." It isolates the relation of concepts "from the supporting ground of the relations to the object and to the knowing I."

Heidegger thinks that the new definition of judgment shows itself in Kant's newly minted distinction between analytic and synthetic judgments. Heidegger notes that this distinction is regularly misunderstood by interpreters, because it is confused with a distinction that dates back to Aristotle. For this traditional distinction, analysis is separation and synthesis is unification. Heidegger argues that from the point of view of the traditional doctrine of judgment Kant's distinction between analytic and synthetic judgments is "nonsensical." Why? Because every judgment, in order to unite a subject and predicate, must also distinguish them. In this way, then, every judgment is both analytic and synthetic.[101] Kant's distinction, however, derives from his new delineation of judgment and can only be understood within this context.[102] Heidegger writes: "The various twisted, slanted, and fruitless attempts to come to terms with Kant's distinction all suffer in advance from being based on the traditional definition of judgment, but not on that attained by Kant."[103]

Both analytic and synthetic judgments concern the object. The difference between the two kinds of judgment is the manner in which the object is included. In an analytic judgment, the object is included only by means of a subjective concept, and the predicate is derived on the basis of that concept alone. The ground for the truth of the judgment, then, is not the object given in intuition; rather it is the concept alone. Kant writes that the ground of the analytic judgment is "that which as concept is contained and is thought in the knowledge of the object."[104] In an analytic judgment, then, our knowledge of the object is not enlarged but only elucidated. For example, the judgment, "The board is extended," is based exclusively on the concept of a material object; to this concept, extension necessarily belongs.

A synthetic judgment, by contrast, has immediate recourse to the object and its givenness. The ground of the relation between subject and object is the given object itself and not the subjective concept. Kant writes: "For the notion of synthesis clearly indicates that something outside of the given concept must be added as a substrate which makes it possible to go beyond the concept with my predicate."[105] Heidegger glosses this as follows:

> We have to step out of the subject and pass beyond the concept and go by way of the object itself. This, however, means that now in addition to the concept of the object, the object itself must be presented there. This presenting-with-that of the object is a synthesis. Such a judgment, where the predicate is added to the subject by passing through the X and having recourse to it, is *synthetic*.[106]

Since synthetic judgments involve a fresh encounter with the object, they do not merely elucidate the content of our knowledge but in fact enlarge it. For example, the judgment, "The board is black," cannot be based on the concept of board alone, which, as Heidegger reminds us, could be gray, white, or red; only recourse to the object itself grounds this relation of subject and predicate. The difference between analytic and synthetic judgments, then, trades on the new definition of judgment, which seeks to identify the ground of the relation of subject and object. If that ground is the concept of the object alone, the judgment is analytic. If that ground is the object and its givenness, then the judgment is synthetic.

The new formulation of judgment and its new distinction into analytic and synthetic entails at the same time a transformation of thinking itself. No longer is it, with the rationalists, a merely conceptual procedure; rather thinking is now subordinate to the truth of the object itself. Heidegger writes, "This distinction is only visible and able to be established, when thinking is grasped in its object-relation and thinking is no longer understood as reckoning with concepts, but rather as essential action of object-determination and, that is, as standing in the service of truth."[107] Kant therefore overcomes rationalism not by means of a flight into irrationalism but instead by means of a determination of thinking as thoroughly oriented toward truth.[108]

Judgment is no longer simply the combination of concepts, and therefore the understanding can no longer be grasped exclusively along these lines. Heidegger says the understanding is instead the unification of presentations "which grasps and constitutes this reference to an object as such."[109] Kant consequently calls the understanding the faculty of rules since it specifies the conditions for unification. He writes, "This distinguishing mark is more fruitful, and approximates more closely to its essential nature."[110] Kant also says that the understanding, as the source of rules, is the source of all truth. The rules allow an object to come to constancy in the appearances and so make the truth of correspondence possible. Heidegger suggests that the understanding's principles respond to the need to bring to constancy the appearances in which we are suspended.[111] Because Kant understands understanding on the basis of such metaphysical necessity, he thinks he "has understood the understanding in a way no thinker has before."[112]

We need only connect, with Heidegger, the new essence of judgment and its distinction into analytic and synthetic with the distinction between *a priori* and *a posteriori*. The *a priori* concerns the essence of something; it has priority in the order of nature but not the order of knowing, because it "enables the thing to be what it is."[113] How the priority of the *a priori* is determined follows from how the thingness of the thing and the being of the entity is conceived. In modern philosophy, the I-principle has priority. Consequently, assertions regarding it are all *a priori*: "The *a priori* is what belongs to the subjectivity of the subject. Everything else, on the contrary, which first becomes accessible only by going out of the subject and entering into the object, into perceptions, is—as seen from the subject—later, i.e., *a posteriori*."[114] Now, analytic judgments are all *a priori*, since they remain within the domain of thought, and synthetic judgments are *a posteriori*, since they go beyond thought to the givenness of the object.

Rational metaphysics sought, on the basis of thought alone, insight into the nature of God, the soul, and the cosmos. Because its basis was thought it was *a priori* but because it hoped to achieve knowledge of objects it was synthetic. Hence, Kant formulates the question concerning the possibility of rational metaphysics as: "How are a priori synthetic judgments possible?"[115] Heidegger observes that synthetic judgments *a posteriori* pose no problem and neither do analytic judgments *a priori*. Only this strange hybrid requires the great labors of a critique of pure reason. Curiously, Kant finds that such a hybrid is possible, but not in the form desired by rationalism. Synthetic judgments are possible *a priori* as articulations of the very possibility of experience and the thing experienced.[116]

The Basis of Judgment and the Essence of Experience

Kant's "System of All Principles of Pure Understanding" concerns the essence of experience.[117] On the one hand, experience designates the act of the subject, and on the other, it designates the object that is so experienced or able to be experienced. As we have already seen, knowing or experiencing has two essential components, intuition and thought. The "object" (*Gegen-stand*) is likewise twofold. In accord with intuition, the object stands *against*, and in accord with thought, it *stands*.[118] Kant uses "object" in a narrower sense and a broader sense. In the narrower sense, it designates "nature," the experiential judgment of science. In the broader sense, it designates the object of intuition alone, which includes merely perceptual judgments that do not rise to the level of categoriality via the concept. Kant is concerned exclusively with justifying the narrower sense and so leaves the pre-scientific undetermined and unexplored. Despite this phenomenological failing, Kant does bring judgment to greater givenness and he does grasp the essence of experience as something that is not an "on-hand" (*vorhanden*) thing or object.[119]

Kant's chapter on the essence of experience is divided into three sections. The first deals with the highest principle of analytic judgments, the second with the highest principle of synthetic judgments, and the third with the systematic presentation of all the synthetic principles of the pure understanding. The distinction between analytic and synthetic judgments, then, proves to be crucial, and Kant endeavors to ground the possibility of synthetic judgments in the essence of experience. Our analysis examines the systematic presentation of the principles of understanding in which we discover that what makes experience possible is a domain prior to subject and object.

In the first section of the "System of All Principles of Pure Understanding" Kant discusses the highest principle of analytic judgments. The first lines of the section, which Heidegger quotes in full, show that the principle of non-contradiction is no longer a sufficient ground for truth, as it was for the rationalists. Kant also is clear that the principle of non-contradiction is not a sufficient ground for truth at all but instead merely a negative condition of all judgments, whether they are analytic or synthetic. Kant writes:

> The universal, though merely negative, condition of all our judgments in general, whatever be the content of our knowledge, and however it may relate to the object, is that they be not self-contradictory; for if self-contradictory, these judgments are in themselves, even without reference to the object, null and void.[120]

If a principle is something that provides grounds for truth, the so-called principle of non-contradiction is now no longer a principle but merely a negative condition or as Kant calls it, a *conditio sine qua non* for the truth of a judgment.[121] The negative condition is not itself sufficient for truth. Kant continues:

> But even if our judgment contains no contradiction, it may connect concepts in a manner not borne out by the object, or else in a manner

for which no ground is given, either *a priori* or *a posteriori*, sufficient to justify such judgment, and so may still, in spite of being free from all inner contradiction, be either false or groundless.[122]

Heidegger points out that the negative condition applies to our judgments alone and not to our knowledge as such; this again indicates that judgment is but one of the components of knowledge.[123] Our knowledge always has some content and some relation to the object. Kant's new determination of knowledge and judgment forms the horizon for understanding this passage.[124]

Kant's discussion of the principle of non-contradiction occurs in a section that seeks to identify the highest principle of analytic judgments. Such judgments, we recall, are related to the object mediately through a concept. In such judgments, the content of our knowledge remains the same, for content can be expanded only through experience. But in such judgments we bring the knowledge we do have to greater clarity. What is the ground of the truth of such clarifying judgments? Kant seems to indicate it is the principle of non-contradiction, but as we have seen that "principle" is merely a negative condition of both analytic and synthetic judgments. Heidegger brings some clarity to Kant's discussion by distinguishing with Kant between a negative and a positive employment of the principle. Negatively, it is a condition for all judgments whatsoever, but in its positive employment it serves as the determining ground for analytic judgments. In its positive employment, it is called the principle of identity. Formally speaking the negative formulation, $A \neq$ non A, becomes positively stated as $A = A$.[125] Kant does not explicitly name the principle of identity in the present section but simply refers to the principle of non-contradiction in its positive employment. In the introduction, however, he identifies this employment with the principle of identity: "Analytic judgments (affirmative) are . . . those in which the connection of the predicate with the subject is thought through identity."[126] The self-sameness of the concept alone is at issue; the clarifying judgment is true if it says the same as the subjective concept. Only with the synthetic judgment, as we have seen, is the full structure of knowledge involved with its necessary immediate relation to the object of experience. The newly registered distinction between analytic and synthetic judgments thus allows Kant to determine the full range of the statement of non-contradiction: in its negative employment it is a condition for the truth of any judgment whatsoever, and in its positive employment it is the sufficient ground for the truth of an analytic judgment.[127] Through such determination formal logic is placed on the periphery of knowledge and judgment is put in the essential service of intuition and the expansion of knowledge.[128]

The second section of "The System of the Principles of Pure Understanding" exhibits the highest principle of synthetic judgments. Heidegger emphasizes the principle's importance: "Whoever understands this principle understands Kant's *Critique of Pure Reason*."[129] The section is the "deepest ground" of the whole work, because in it Kant determines "the essence of human knowledge, its truth and its object."[130] Synthetic judgments, as we have seen, reach beyond the mere concept of an object to the object itself. The ground of truth is not the selfsameness of the concept but the experienced object in the synthesis of intuition and thought. The principle of this judgment, then, cannot be merely the negative condition of non-contradiction or even the positively formulated principle of identity in the selfsameness of the concept. Rather, the principle must ground the possibility of going beyond mere thought to include what is wholly other to it. Such a relation of thought and intuition is a synthesis that alone allows an object to encounter us. Heidegger underscores the primacy of enacting this relation: "Only while we enter into this relation and maintain ourselves in it does an object encounter us. The inner possibility of the object, that is, its essence, is thus co-determined out of the possibility of this relation to it."[131] The highest principle of synthetic judgment must ground this relation between us and what we encounter and thereby serve as the ground of truth: "The condition of the possibility of all truth is grounded in this posited ground."[132]

Kant states the highest principle of all synthetic judgments as follows: "Every object stands under the necessary conditions of synthetic unity of the manifold of intuition in a possible experience."[133] Heidegger prefers the formulation Kant provides several lines later at the very end of the section. Here Kant is applying the principle of synthetic judgments to the problem of *a priori* synthetic judgments. For *a priori* synthetic judgments, the principle reads:

> The conditions of the *possibility of experience* in general are likewise conditions of the *possibility of the objects of experience*.[134]

Synthetic judgments *a priori* are indeed possible but not, as we have seen, in the manner of the rationalists. Rather, such judgments articulate the possibility of encountering things; they establish the belonging together of thing and knowing. Heidegger thus suggests that only the third section, which unfolds the relation of all the *a priori* synthetic principles of the understanding, will make this second section fully understandable.[135] "The sources of all truth are the principles of pure understanding. They themselves and therefore these sources of all truth go back to a deeper source, which is brought to light in the highest principle of all synthetic judgments."[136] Consequently, Heidegger's analysis of the third section, "Systematic Representation of All the Synthetic Principles of Pure Understanding," seeks to develop the highest principle of synthetic judgments.

In the 1929 Kant book, Heidegger intended to show that the transcendental imagination, as primordial time, mediated between the two elements of knowing, thought and intuition. Now, in the 1935–36 lecture course, Heidegger no longer thinks such mediation is required because

Kant rethinks understanding from the ground up as essentially related to intuition. Heidegger sees this expressed, above all, in the synthetic *a priori* principles, which each in their own way articulate the one principle of synthetic judgments. The synthetic *a priori* principles make experience and the object of experience possible. They thus articulate the necessary relation of intuition and thought.

The division of the table of principles into mathematical and dynamical reflects the distinction between intuition and thought. Mathematical principles articulate the otherness of the object as achieved in the intuition and so constitute the "against" of the object. Dynamical principles articulate the stability of the object and so constitute the "stand" or constancy of the object. The principles, then, together constitute the two dimensions of an object heard in the German *Gegen-stand*. In the principles of pure reason "the 'against' of the object and the 'stand' of the object are opened up in their primordial unity."[137] The principles, then, metaphysically make possible the mathematical and dynamical character of things, which serve as the subject of mathematics and physics, respectively. The names for these divisions originate with Leibniz, but only Kant demonstrates their inner unity.[138] He shows that these principles are but particular expressions of the one principle of synthetic judgment. That principle grasps the primordial unity of thought and intuition, and it does so by disclosing something like "world."

Heidegger focuses on the proofs as the key to understanding the principles. In the proof, the principle in question is exhibited in terms of its basis or ground.[139] The four proofs or elucidations follow the same schema: "All are constructed according to one definite schema, which coheres [*zusammenhängt*] with the essential content of these principles [*Grundsätze*]."[140] This schema is the interrelation between the possibility of experience and the possibility of the objects of experience, an interrelation expressed in the highest principle of all synthetic judgments. "The respective proof, however, does nothing other than to lift into the light the ground of these principles themselves, which finally must be ever one and the same and which we then encounter in the highest principle of all synthetic judgments."[141] Heidegger's analysis of these principles of the understanding aims to show that there is a more fundamental source of truth than the principles of the understanding. In particular, the circularity of the proofs serves to illustrate the nature of the domain brought to light in the highest principle of synthetic judgments.

The proofs of the first three principles exhibit what belongs to an object in order for it to be encountered and constant. They demonstrate that the categories of quantity, quality, and relation have objective reality. In doing so they "lay that as ground, through which a field of view is first formed at all, within which this and that and many can encounter and stand in context [*im Zusammenhang*] as something objective."[142] The final group, the Postulates of Empirical Thought in General, adds nothing to this ground; it does not determine the factuality of the object. Instead, it turns to the *relation* of the object to the knowing faculties in order to determine whether the object is possible, actual, or necessary.[143] Heidegger highlights the importance of this relation by pairing the three postulates with the first three principles; in this he brings out what is perhaps latent in Kant's presentation.[144] On the basis of the relation expressed by the postulates, Kant effects the decisive overthrow of rational metaphysics: being is no longer determined by thought alone.[145]

The Axioms of Intuition show that the encountering of an object requires that the pure concept, quantity, belong to the nature of the spatial object. In the second edition, Kant formulates the principle for the axioms as follows: "All intuitions are extensive magnitudes."[146] The proof of this principle takes the form of a syllogism in which Kant argues that the condition for the possibility of experiencing appearances is at the same time the condition of the possibility of an object of experience. In this case, Kant's major premise names the condition for experiencing, namely that all appearances contain an intuition in space and time. The minor premise states that such a manifold cannot be unified as an object of experience save through the concept of magnitude. The conclusion drawn is that appearances are magnitudes.[147] The proof is obviously circular, and Heidegger takes this as Kant's recognition of the circularity of experience, a point I will return to below. For now it remains to see the connection of the first principle of the pure understanding with the fourth. The corresponding postulate of empirical thought is possibility; if something satisfies this formal condition of experience, then its mode of being is *possible*. Possibility is no longer simply the absence of contradiction, as it was for rational metaphysics. We can think something that does not contradict itself, but it is a possible object only if it can appear in space and time.

The Anticipations of Perception show that the encountering of an object entails that the pure concept, quality, belongs to the sensation of the object.[148] Again, the proof consists in showing that intuition and thought, the determinable and the determining, must unite as the condition for the possibility of experiencing and of the object of experience; this time the concept of quality is placed into relation with the matter of intuition, namely sensation. The corresponding postulate of empirical thought is actuality; if something also satisfies the material conditions of experience, then its mode of being is *actual*. "What is called actuality is fulfilled and borne out for us only in the relation between presenting and the encountering of the real of sensation."[149] Rational metaphysics thought of the actual as something added to mere conceptual possibility. Kant, though, recognizes that the actual must not only be subject to space and time but it must also involve the reality of sensation. Reality, then, is not the same as actuality; the former is a condition for the givenness of the latter.

The Analogies of Experience show that the constancy of an object involves a preview of the context of relations in which the appearance stands, a preview rooted in time.[150] And again, the proof is circular. The corresponding postulate of empirical thought is necessity; if something also satisfies these universal conditions of experience, then its mode of being is *necessary*. Again, rational metaphysics determined necessary existence on the basis of possibility as conceivability, identifying the necessary with "what is unthinkable as nonbeing."[151] Kant shows, though, that "what we have to think need not for this reason exist." In fact, existence itself can never be grasped as necessary; rather, only states of objects in relation to others can be necessary.

The transformed essence of judgment, which led to the overcoming of the dominance of the principle of non-contradiction, now expresses itself in the synthetic principles of pure understanding. In this exhaustive elucidation of principles, Kant recovers some of the givenness of being, and logic thereby loses some of its dominance.

> Kant, in defining the modes of being, at the same time restricted being to the being of the object of experience. The merely logical clarifications of possibility, actuality, necessity, as in rational metaphysics, are rejected. In short, being is no longer determined out of mere thought.[152]

Just what determines being, then? Being is determined out of the *relation* of our capacity to know and the conditions for the possibility of known objects. The modes of being do not add to what is included in the object—being is not a *real* predicate—but they do add the *relation* to the knower. Kant writes: ". . . since they are nonetheless synthetic, they are so subjectively only, that is, they add to the concept of a thing (of something real) . . . the cognitive faculty from which it springs and in which it has its seat."[153] The first three principles establish the context of experience in the reciprocal relation of experience and object of experience, but the postulates clarify the reciprocal relation that thereby emerges. Accordingly, in the postulates Kant speaks of the modes of being as "what agrees with" (*was übereinkommt mit*) or "what coheres with" (*was zusammenhängt mit*) the conditions of experience, whether formal, material, or universal.[154]

To exhibit this relation, the proof and elucidation in each case is circular. It sets out to show that the synthetic principles of pure understanding are possible only on the ground of the interrelation of intuition and thought, and the principles themselves are what make such a ground possible. The circularity expresses the movement of experience:

> The proof consists in showing that the principles of pure understanding are possible through that which they themselves make possible,

through the essence of experience. This is an obvious circle, and indeed a necessary one. The principles are proved by going back [*Rückgang*] to that whose coming forth [*Hervorgang*] they make possible, because these propositions are to bring to light nothing else than this circular movement [*Kreisgang*] itself; for this constitutes the essence of experience.[155]

Such circularity demonstrates that Kant realizes that experience is not a thing but a happening that opens up the domain in which things can be encountered. He remarks in the Discipline of Pure Reason that each of the principles of understanding has this peculiarity: "But though it needs proof, it should be entitled a *principle*, not a *theorem*, because it has the peculiar character that it makes possible the very experience which is its own ground of proof, and that in this experience it must always itself be presupposed."[156] Though Kant notes this circularity of experience, he does not make it thematic.

A central theme of *Being and Time* was the independence of entities but the dependence of their intelligibility. At one point, Heidegger asks, "[H]ow are 'independent' ["*unabhangige*"] entities within-the-world 'connected' ["*hängt*" . . . "*zusammen*"] with the transcending world?"[157] Here in the later work on Kant this most difficult question becomes the guiding horizon of interpretation. Kant's transcendental articulation of experience aims to uncover the "context" (*Zusammenhang*) in which we can encounter and know things that are genuinely other than ourselves. Heidegger says that "what Kant hit upon and what he sought to grasp ever anew as the ground-happening is this: We humans are able to know entities, which we ourselves are not, even though we have not made these entities ourselves."[158] The synthetic principles of pure understanding disclose the possibility of such a genuine encounter. Heidegger says that together the principles articulate the full content of the essence of experience and the essence of the object of experience. The circular proofs exhaustively elucidate the highest principle of synthetic judgments.[159] We can encounter something other than ourselves, because intuition and thought, the conditions of experiencing, are also the conditions of the objectivity of the object of experience. Intuition as space and time and thought as the categories are conditions for both experience and the standing-against of the experienced object. "Leaping beyond" (*Überspringen*) things lets them encounter us and throw us back in the encounter.[160] Hence, objects can "stand against us as they themselves, even though this letting-encounter happens through us."[161] Truth, then, neither depends exclusively on the thing nor on us but is strangely in between.[162] "To be a being in the midst of an open opposition of entities is constantly strange."[163]

With the happening of experience, we come to the crux of Heidegger's revised Kant interpretation. Something like the clearing comes to light in Kant's efforts to account for our knowing things genuinely other than ourselves. Heidegger calls this the "open" or "between" and thereby translates Kant's project into the terminology of his own thinking:

> The ground which [the principles] lay, the nature of experience, is not an on-hand thing, to which we return and upon which we then simply stand. Experience is a happening circling in itself through which what lies within the circle becomes opened up [*eröffnet*]. This open [*Offene*], however, is nothing other than the between [*Zwischen*]—between us and the thing.[164]

The circularity of the proofs uncovers the "circular movement" (*Kreisgang*) of experience. The reciprocity of experience and object of experience opens up what Heidegger calls the "between." Strangely, we head out beyond things and only thereby encounter them in their otherness.[165] To articulate this interplay, Heidegger reaches into his past and deploys vocabulary from his earliest lecture courses concerning the reciprocity of experience. "[T]his *between* as a pre-conception reaches beyond the thing and likewise back behind us. Pre-conception is thrown-back [*Vorgriff ist Rück-wurf*]."[166] This original domain is open only while we move back and forth through the encircling movement of experience. This movement comes to light when we attend neither to the object nor to the proposition but instead to the between which emerges in transcendental questioning. Heidegger's translation of Kant's project into his own terminology signals the need to make the "between" the focus of philosophical investigation.[167] Kant uncovers what yet needs to be secured through thoughtful reflection.

Amid this positive appraisal, Heidegger does make two pointed criticisms. First, Kant continues to determine entities on the basis of principles and so in this way remains bound to the modern priority of the subject.[168] Second, under the spell of modern science, Kant fails to analyze what is most manifest, the thingness of surrounding things, and instead attends only to mathematical-physical nature. Heidegger maintains that the account of surrounding things cannot simply be appended to Kant's project, because fundamental presuppositions affect his sense of being in general.[169] The subjective starting point and the exclusive interest in objectivity mean that, while Kant illumines the open between in which alone judgments are possible, he does not fathom that the open in fact allows humans to be themselves. As Heidegger writes in 1938, "Openness is not only what makes this possible—i.e., a particular human comportment, the asserting and judging about objects—but is what makes man himself possible in the first place. . . ."[170] Because of this omission, the theme of thrownness and dispositions is lacking in Kant's thought, and there is no recognition that the opening does not merely stand open but it also conceals itself and unfolds differently for different epochs.

Despite these shortcomings of his project, shortcomings that are emphasized in the *Contributions* and the 1961 lecture, "Kant's Thesis about Being," Kant does pave the way for their overcoming. First, he undermines the modern priority of the subject by recognizing that the principle of non-contradiction is not a sufficient ground for truth; recourse to the givenness of intuition is necessary. Second, Kant limits the identification of being with on-handness by indicating that the context in which on-hand things are encountered is something that is not itself on-hand. We thereby learn that entities cannot be defined except by reference to a non-entitative context:

> If we do not otherwise admit it, indirectly we can at least learn this from Kant's determination of the thing, namely, that a single thing for itself is not possible and, therefore, the determination of things cannot be carried out with reference to single things. The thing as a natural thing is only determinable from the essence of one nature in general.[171]

To learn this is no small matter for Heidegger's thinking. Kant shows that the being of entities are definable only out of the "field of view" (*Gesichtskreis*) or "context" (*Zusammenhang*), which Heidegger also calls the "between" (*Zwischen*).[172] Though Kant equates being with objectivity, he shows that objectivity is understandable only against the backdrop of the pre-objective context. The exposition of the first three principles establish the context, and then the elucidation of the postulates concerns the relation that makes such a context possible. Heidegger connects this context with the phenomenological elucidation of our everyday encounter with things: "Accordingly and even more so, the thing, in the sense of what we encounter closest to us—before all theory and science—is adequately and first of all determinable out of a context [*Zusammenhang*] which lies *before* and *above* all nature."[173]

4 Returning to the Immediate Context of Courses

Heidegger's new reading of Kant becomes even more significant when we understand it in the context of the previous semester's course. Heidegger's interpretation of Kant's highest principle of synthetic judgment echoes his interpretation of Parmenides's saying about the reciprocal belonging together of apprehension and being.[174] But it is not enough for us simply to note Kant's Parmenidean-like originality. This similarity illustrates the thesis about Kant the 1935–36 lecture course advocates, namely, the transitional role Kant plays in overcoming the disjunction, "being and thought." We recall that in the 1935 lecture course, Heidegger specifies two requirements for the overcoming of the disjunction. (1) The first is to show the *limits* of its inceptive truth. As we have seen, Heidegger thinks that the tradition takes its bearing from the end of the inceptive beginning. The end of the beginning saw the emergence of the logical prejudice that becomes, in modernity, the mathematical prejudice. But Kant shows the limits of the mathematical prejudice and in doing so shows the limits of inceptive truth. As we quoted above, Heidegger writes in the 1935–36 course: "In the enactment of the 'critique' of pure reason so understood, the 'mathematical' in the principled [*grundsätzlich*] sense first comes to its unfolding and, at the same time, to its sublimation [*Aufhebung*], that is, to its own limit [*Grenze*]."[175] (2) The second requirement is to think more originally the belonging of thought to being. But Kant's "Postulates of Empirical Thought in General" restrict the sense of being to the object of experience:

> Kant, in defining the modes of being, at the same time restricted being to the being of the object of experience. The merely logical clarifications of possibility, actuality, necessity, as in rational metaphysics, are rejected. In short, being is no longer determined out of mere thought.[176]

Moreover, Kant accomplishes the critique by thinking more rigorously: "Kant did not overcome intellectualism through mere renunciation, rather through a more originary essential determination of thinking."[177] Kant does not replace thought with feeling, but he puts thought in service to the givenness of intuition.

The two requirements for overcoming the disjunction, then, (1) showing the limits of the beginning and (2) thinking more rigorously the belonging of thought to being, are thus met in part by Kant. Consequently, Heidegger can write: "Through Kant's critical determination of judgment and of thought in general, *intellectus*, the presumption of uprooted understanding is metaphysically overcome for the first time in a more grounded manner."[178] But this overcoming is something that does not remain in the past but is a challenge for us today: "That we today still have not yet actually adopted this overcoming, speaks not against an apparent rationalism of Kant's, rather it speaks only against us."[179] Kant discloses the "between," and it remains for us today to bring it to thought.[180] Repeating Kant's transcendental philosophy prepares us to overcome rationalism in our own thinking.

Though Kant overcomes rationalism in principle by no longer determining being from thought *alone*, he nonetheless continues to determine being *from* thought instead of experiencing the originary unity of being and thought. That is, he thinks thought's relation to intuition.[181] The fact that the union of thought and intuition happens on the basis of understanding's principles points to a continued dominance of thought. Moreover, Kant does not think the prejudices in their historical origination, and by consequence his limiting them does not go deep enough.

Introducing historical questioning would bring Kant's unfolding of the prejudices and the discovery of the between to life. The between not merely stands open, but it also conceals itself. In this sense, Kant limits understanding in a way that prepares us to be determined in a fundamental disposition in which being and thought are unified. Kant limits the modern project in a way that prepares us to be thrown; he readies us to be moved from "fundamental position" (*Grundstellung*) and its variants, *Vorstellung* and *Ge-stell*, to a new "fundamental disposition or attunement" (*Grundstimmung*).[182] He thus serves as a crucial transitional figure for Heidegger's later thinking.

This transitional role becomes even clearer when we examine the following semester course, delivered in the summer semester 1936 and entitled, "Schelling, *On the Essence of Human Freedom*." There Heidegger comes to terms with Kant's foundation and the interpretation German Idealism gives it. "What German Idealism understands as philosophy is just Kant's concept thought through to the end in one direction."[183] In a seminar from the early 1940s, Heidegger repeats this assessment of Kant. "German Idealism does not skip over Kant. But it begins where Kant brought philosophy to. It begins there immediately and in terms of the whole. And *here the true and sole appreciation of Kant reveals itself.*"[184] Heidegger, it seems, wants to think transcendental philosophy in another direction. Namely, he wants to hold to Kantian finitude against Idealism's absolutism while at the same time cultivating the philosophical concern for history. Such concern is found not in dialectical teleology but in fundamental dispositions. Now there was no mention of fundamental dispositions in the 1935–36 lecture course on Kant, but in the 1936 lecture course on Schelling, Kant reappears as the transitional figure whose thinking on freedom prepares the way for fundamental dispositions. Kant, then, ambiguously forms the transition to absolute knowing and to being-historical thinking.

The demand for system in modern philosophy flows from the mathematical prejudice. In the previous semester, Heidegger showed that Kant's system of principles in fact illuminates a finite domain that reigns in the mathematical prejudice. Now, Heidegger points to the emerging problematic that leads German Idealism beyond Kant and back to the mathematical prejudice. Kant criticized rationalism and limited knowledge to experience, but he failed to achieve explicit foundation of the critique itself. "Kant did succeed in a critique, that is, at the same time a positive essential determination of knowledge as experience, but he neglected the foundation of the essence of that knowledge which was carried out as critique. The critique as critique was itself not founded."[185] Heidegger points to two places where Kant struggled with his methodology, namely in "The Amphiboly of Concepts of Reflection" and "The Architectonic of Pure Reason." The first presents transcendental reflection, and the second presents philosophy as the *teleologia rationis humanae*.[186] Especially in the latter, philosophy is presented as being concerned with the whole—that is, with system. Nonetheless, the fundamental problem is that Kant's ideas of reason, God, world, and the human being, are without origin and thus without foundation, so the system of ideas remains problematic.[187]

The post-Kantian demand for system involved a new appreciation for the creativity of human reason, and it is Kant's fundamental reflection on reason that first makes this possible.[188] German Idealism is not a return to dogmatism, for its ideas arise on the basis of the givenness of pure intuition, albeit in an expanded form. Kant, moreover, never demonstrated that what the ideas presented were objects subject to the limits of cognized objects. Against Kant, German Idealism shows that "what is non-objective is still not nothing at all."[189] It grasps the original unity of knower and known.[190] Being becomes in becoming known, and this becoming is nothing other than absolute Being.[191] "En route through Kant's philosophy," German Idealism fulfills the hidden demand for the total realization of the mathematical prejudice by grounding it mathematically in the Absolute:

> The interpretation of true knowing as "intellectual" intuition . . . makes evident the innermost presupposition, until now hidden, which is placed at the beginning of system in the sense of the mathematical system of reason. For only from that moment on when this presentation of system as the absolute system of reason knows itself in absolute knowledge is system absolutely founded in terms of itself, that is, really mathematically certain of itself, founded on absolute self-consciousness and comprehending all realms of entities.[192]

Kant limited the mathematical project and so grounded it in the finitude of the open between. Rather than curbing the prejudice German Idealism fulfills it by grounding it according to its ownmost demand for totality. The Absolute, as the totality of entities, absolves every relation since there is nothing outside it. "This absolute *relationlessness* to anything else, this absolutely absolved is called the *Ab-solute*."[193] It would be hard to imagine a position more antithetical to Heidegger's own thinking.[194]

With the theme of history, however, the thinking of the Absolute does uncover—albeit in an inappropriate way—something that accords with the finitude of Heidegger's thinking. Accordingly, Heidegger wants to understand history philosophically but not absolutely:

> Only from this standpoint of absolute knowing does it become possible, but necessary, too, to understand the previous stages of the formation of system in their conditioned and conditioning role. Now the idea of a system according to preliminary forms and transitional forms, all oriented towards the absolute system, is searched for in the whole history of Western philosophy.[195]

Kant is clearly a transition to the standpoint of absolute knowing, but he also proves to be a transition for Heidegger's own path of thinking. Heidegger interprets Kant in a way that retains finitude and yet still finds its way into history.

Heidegger's later, historical thinking focuses on fundamental dispositions. Heidegger thinks Schelling's introduction to *On the Essence of Human Freedom* has the aim of forming "a readiness for a unique attitude of seeing and questioning."[196] The move beyond common sense to philosophical thinking involves "a transformation of our real thinking and questioning."[197] This was likewise the theme of the whole course on Kant the previous semester. What is new is that with Schelling Heidegger explicitly ties this transformation to fundamental dispositions: "This transformation is in itself, and not just subsequently, a conversion to an originary fundamental disposition."[198] There is something other than the Absolute at work in Schelling, and it is the fundamental disposition of Schelling's old friend and Heidegger's new collaborator in the art of thinking: "There is throughout Schelling's treatise something of the fundamental disposition of Hölderlin."[199]

Schelling treats this fundamental disposition as human freedom. Heidegger says that it is this freedom that allows history to happen: "The knowledge of freedom is certain of its highest necessity because it alone makes that position of receptivity possible in which the human being stands, and is able as a historical being to encounter a destiny, to take it upon himself and to transcend it."[200] But how does Schelling come to this fundamental ground of freedom? By way of Kant.

This turn to the theme of freedom in Kant may appear peculiar since the previous lecture course explicitly focuses on the first *Critique*, making no mention of freedom. And yet the theme of freedom had been a topic for Heidegger since the late 1920s. His 1930 lecture course, "On the Essence of Human Freedom: Introduction to Philosophy," was devoted to Kant's *Second Critique* and the concept of freedom, even though it proved to be largely a criticism of the ontic causality at work in it.[201] Now the criticism is made in view of the fundamental disposition: in Kant freedom still stands opposed to nature, so it does not embody the unity of a fundamental disposition. Nonetheless, Kant forms the transition to the total freedom of Schelling: "Kant's philosophy creates and forms the transition from the inappropriate to the appropriate concept of freedom. For him freedom is still mastery over sensuousness, but not this alone, but freedom as independence in one's own ground and self-determination as self-legislation."[202] Moreover, Heidegger says that Schelling confirms Kant's fundamental position on freedom, namely, that we comprehend only its incomprehensibility. "And freedom's incomprehensibility consists in the fact that it resists com-prehension [*Be-greifen*] since it . . . transposes us into the enactment of be-ing [*Vollzug des Seyns*], not the mere pro-posing [*Vor-stellen*] of it."[203] Not only, then, does Kant lead to the between, but he also provides some positive characterization of it as incomprehensible and thus open to the enactment of being, the very unfolding of history.[204]

Heidegger seizes on the mathematical prejudice grounded in the critique and grasps it as a prejudice. Rather than going the route of German Idealism's Absolute, which seeks to fulfill the mathematical prejudice beyond Kant in the form of absolute knowing, Heidegger insists with Kant on the finitude of knowing. But he borrows from German Idealism the concern for history, though in a new key. No longer is it the completion of absolute knowing in the end, but following the theme of freedom in Schelling (and Kant), it is being determined by the happening of being.

As we have seen, the 1935–36 lecture course focused on the heart of the first *Critique*, which Heidegger takes to be the center of Kant and modern philosophy in general, and the 1936 lecture course on Schelling alludes to Kant's *Second Critique* as anticipating fundamental dispositions. To complete the triptych, then, we might expect some discussion of Kant's *Third Critique* in the context of the 1936–37 lecture course on Nietzsche, "Will to Power as Art," and that is exactly what we find.[205] Even more so than the course on Schelling the treatment of Kant belongs to the margins of the lecture course. While trying to interpret Nietzsche's doctrine of the aesthetic state, Heidegger defends Kant's doctrine of the beautiful from its misinterpretations by Schopenhauer, Nietzsche, and Dilthey. That Heidegger does so is all the more remarkable because he reports that he merely wants to "provide a possibility of grasping what Nietzsche himself says about beauty on the basis of its own original, historical context."[206] The proper interpretation of Kant is decidedly beyond his intention in the course. Heidegger shows that Kant's understanding of beauty, grasped rightly, is quite compatible with Nietzsche's.

The controversy concerns Kant's definition of beauty as that which we like "devoid of all interest."[207] The dominant interpretation mistakes lack of interest to mean indifference. Heidegger says this interpretation misses Kant on two counts. First, it wrongly takes this brief indication as Kant's full exposition of the concept of beauty, and second, it overlooks the essential *relation* that emerges only when an object is stripped of every interest.

> The misinterpretation of "interest" leads to the erroneous opinion that with the setting aside of interest every essential relation to the object is suppressed. The opposite is the case. Precisely by means of the "devoid of interest" the essential relation to the object itself comes into play. The misinterpretation fails to see that now for the first time the object comes to light as pure object and that such coming to light is the beautiful. The word "beautiful" means appearing in the radiance of such coming to light.[208]

When we suppress every sought advantage and enjoyment, we allow the object to be as it is in itself instead of dominating it according to our will. As in previous courses, Heidegger insists that to grasp these concepts we must understand them "in terms of the Kantian philosophical task and its transcendental advance, not flattened out according to everyday notions."[209] When we understand Kant in terms of his transcendental method the essential relation to the object becomes accessible for the first time.

Kant characterizes the fundamental comportment to the beautiful as the "pleasure of reflection."[210] With this characterization, his method unfolds the fullness of the human essence: "Kant's interpretation of aesthetic behavior as 'pleasure of reflection' propels us toward a fundamental state of human being in which the human being for the first time arrives at the well-founded fullness of his essence."[211] Thus, Heidegger here repeats the interpretation of Kant developed in the 1935–36 lecture course on the first *Critique*, but he is extending the importance of the particularly transcendental way of questioning and the manner of relation that comes to the fore in it to the *Third Critique*. Along with this praise of Kant's philosophy, Heidegger also repeats the criticism that he still remains constrained by the mathematical prejudice: "Even Kant, who because of his transcendental method possessed a larger number of more determinate possibilities for interpreting aesthetics, remained trapped within the limits of the modern concept of the subject."[212]

These four lecture courses from 1935–37 clarify the transitional role of transcendental philosophy. On the basis of transcendental questioning, the everyday attitude that reduces everything to something on-hand is overcome toward the opened between, which is not itself on-hand. Such reflection establishes the limits of reason by contextualizing it within a domain of givenness. The disjunction "being and thought," then, becomes more a conjunction, although it does not achieve the original unity that Heidegger saw in Heraclitus and Parmenides. Transcendentally, Kant overcomes Western rationalism in principle by disclosing the presupposition of finitude.[213] By grounding projection in what makes projection possible, he clears the way to understand history's different epochs of interpretation, and he thereby readies us for the overcoming of Western rationalism.

In the *Contributions*, Heidegger sketches the sense and aim of his lectures on figures in the history of philosophy.[214] They constitute a coordinated effort make manifest the need for the other beginning. The "historical" lectures belong to the sphere of this task:

> to make visible *Leibniz's* unfathomable manifold shaping of the onset
>   of the question but to think Da-sein instead of monads;
> to re-enact *Kant's* main steps but to overcome the "transcendental"
>   approach through Da-sein;

to question thoroughly *Schelling's* question of freedom and nevertheless to place the question of "modalities" on another ground;

to place *Hegel's* system in the commanding view and then to think in
a totally opposite direction;

to dare to come to grips with *Nietzsche* as the one who is nearest
but to recognize that he is farthest removed from the question of
being.[215]

At first glance the place of Kant in this list appears unremarkable, for
all five thinkers are affirmed in some fashion and denied in another. But
an important difference between Kant and the others is apparent: while
Kant's thought is to be entered into and "reenacted," the others are
viewed from the outside; he uses verbs such as "made visible," "question," and "oppose." Moreover, Heidegger specifies that the purpose of
all the lecture courses is "to coax into knowing awareness what is always
only *sole and unique*, namely that the essential swaying of be-ing needs
the grounding of the *truth* of be-ing and this grounding must be enacted
as *Da-sein*." The description of Kant's course is the only one that uses the
same verb as the task he is readying for: "to reenact" (*nachvollziehen*)
Kant prepares us "to enact" (*vollziehen*) this grounding as Dasein. In our
reenactment we must overcome the "approach" (*Ansatz*) of transcendental philosophy rather than the enactment of transcendental philosophy.
The approach for transcendental philosophy is the question concerning
the thing and judgment worked out in terms of principles, but its terminus is the between or here of being-here (Da-sein); Heidegger's enactment
thus begins exactly where Kant's enactment ends.

The historical lectures, then, show that Heidegger provides not only a
critique but also an affirmation of Kant and transcendental philosophy.
Heidegger lauds Kant's contextualization of judgment. It is not merely
the combining of concepts since something wholly other is involved—
namely, the thing given in intuition. Kant's analysis in terms of the fundamental principles of understanding brings to light the between as the
context for the inclusion of the thing in the judgment. So, Kant anticipates Heidegger by situating rationalism within its limits and context.
But along with this positive appraisal, Heidegger makes two pointed criticisms. The first qualifies the praise given Kant's view of judgment in that
it does remain finally subject to the dominance of thought even though
it makes great strides in overcoming it. The second situates Kant's project of tracing judgment back to its context within a still further context
that transcendental philosophy did not grasp: history. The proposition
of the judgment, traced back to the between, ultimately rests on the fundamental disposition granted in history. That is, to make a "determination" (*Bestimmung*) requires first being determined/disposed by history's
"fundamental disposition" (*Grundstimmung*). Put in the poetic terms
of Heidegger's later philosophy, we can say that Kant glimpsed world,

but missing history, he could not fathom earth.[216] But even world was not thought rightly, because it was not thought on the basis of earth. So, returning to Kant, Heidegger holds to finitude and thinks history. Doing so, he is able to overcome the rationalistic disjunction, "being and thought."

Conclusion

Michael Friedman argues that Ernst Cassirer can serve as a bridge between analytic and continental philosophy, because he held on to the Kantian architectonic before it split into "scientific" (Carnap) and "humanistic" (Heidegger) camps.[217] When we turn to Heidegger's own reading of Kant, however, we discover not the abolishment of scientific logic in favor of humanistic interests but its contextualization within its domain of sense. Heidegger does not reject the rigor of scientific logic; rather, he moves deeper within the pre-judicative domain presupposed by everyday life, science, and logic. The interesting thing, for him, is how this domain is itself given.

Kant's transcendental exposition of judgment, according to Heidegger's 1935–36 lecture course, can perhaps be outlined according to the following theses. With synthetic judgments, Kant recovers some measure of the original Greek sense of *logos* as "gathering" (*Sammlung*).[218] As the highest principle of synthetic judgment, Kant uncovers a pre-judicative "togetherness" (*Zusammenhang*) in which such gathering is possible.[219] In contrast to the abstraction of mathematical logic and scientific positivism, Kant's transcendental exposition shows that judgments and things presuppose such a context; we can know and make judgments about things because things encounter us within a pre-objective and pre-subjective domain. To be sure, Heidegger is no Kantian: Kant articulates such a context by means of the principles of subjectivity and he introduces it as the context for objectivity, thereby overlooking the being of everyday things. Nonetheless, his discovery of the contextual between remains significant: "Whoever grasps this does not only know a book among the writings of philosophy, but masters a fundamental position of our historical Dasein, which we can neither avoid, nor leap over, nor in any way deny. But we have to bring this by an appropriate transformation to decision in the future."[220] Returning to Kant, we can expand and secure the context he left ungrounded, and thereby safeguard the turning relation of Dasein and being. Heidegger does not think we can abandon transcendental philosophy, because it remains crucially relevant for his own later thinking. The transcendental domain is something "we can neither avoid, nor leap over, nor in any way deny." Instead, we have to bring it to completion.

Kant's analysis identifies and limits the prejudices which Heidegger sees characteristic of the Western philosophical tradition. Heidegger reads Kant's critique as lifting into the light of day the form of philosophy itself: namely, a reflection from an entity out onto an entity. Kant reaches behind the modern *mathesis universalis* to recover something of the Greek beginning with the self-showing of entities, and in doing so he situates the assertion and the principle within a larger context. The highest principle of synthetic judgment accordingly decenters the *mathesis universalis* by subordinating projection to the reciprocity of subject and intuited object. At the same time, Kant's critique obliquely illumines something even more radical than Kant himself proposes: the context of such reciprocity.

There is, then, a qualified sense, which Heidegger clearly acknowledges, of the continued relevance of transcendental philosophy for his later thinking. Transcendental philosophy shows the way for us to go beyond the limitations of the tradition and ultimately, too, beyond the traditional limitations of transcendental philosophy. Strictly speaking, then, it is not true to say that Heidegger rejects transcendental philosophy, though it is true to say that he no longer thinks it adequate on its own terms. As Heidegger emphasized in his interpretation of Kant's critique of the logical definition of judgment, the difference between acceptance-rejection on the one hand and relative adequacy on the other is important. Commentators are wrong to frame the issue of Heidegger's relation to transcendental philosophy in terms of the either-or of acceptance or rejection. To be inadequate or insufficient is not to be false, and therefore insufficiency provides a point of departure and ingredient for one's own search for a satisfactory account. Kant, representing transcendental phenomenology, affords the path into Heidegger's later thought.

Notes

1 GA 41, 249.
2 GA 65, 8/6–7.
3 GA 65, 253/179.
4 GA 65, 9/7.
5 Heidegger inserted the following statement just before the 1935–36 lecture course's exposition of the system of principles: "The following interpretation makes up for what the writing *Kant and the Problem of Metaphysics* (1929) lacked. Compare the preface to the second edition, 1950," GA 41, 127/125. The statement was obviously added after 1950 and likely just before the lecture course was published in 1962.
6 GA 3, xiv/xviii.
7 Hansgeorg Hoppe presents a good overview of this transformation of the horizon of questioning from the essence of transcendence to the essence of a thing. The second book on Kant operates "unter einem ganz anderen Vorgriff" and moves "an innerhalb eines ganz anderen Horizonts als im Kant-Buch," and thus Kant appears "in ganz anderem Licht." "Wandlungen in der Kant-Auffassung Heideggers," in *Durchblicke. Martin Heidegger zum 80. Geburtstag*, ed. Vittorio Klostermann (Frankfurt am Main: Klostermann, 1970), 304, 305, 307. Hoppe criticizes the first Kant book for distorting

Kant's question about the possibility of the lawfulness of nature in favor of *Being and Time*'s transcendence, but he thinks that the second book is more faithful to Kant: "die Auseinandersetzung Heideggers mit Kant unter dem Gesichtspunkt einer geschichtlichen Fragestellung also zu einer sehr viel sachlicheren und gerechteren Auslegung der KRV als im Kant-Buch führt" (311).

8 GA 41, 56/56.

9 GA 41, 182–3/179.

10 GA 41, 188/184.

11 See GA 84.1, 19 and 76.

12 For mathematical or symbolic logic, see GA 41, 159–60/156; for positivism, see GA 41, 59/59 and 67/67; for both, see GA 41, 178–83/175–9.

13 *Unterwegs zur Sprache*, 95/9.

14 He says he stops using the term "not—as is often thought—in order to deny the meaning of phenomenology, but in order to let my path of thinking be nameless." *Unterwegs zur Sprache*, 121/29.

15 GA 66, 421/372.

16 GA 40, 153/154 and 125/123.

17 GA 40, 102/100.

18 "Thinking sets itself against being in such a way that being is pre-sented [*vorgestellt*] to thinking, and consequently stands against thinking like an ob-ject [*Gegen-stand*]." GA 40, 124/123. Thinking and reason thus form the horizon for the determination of being. GA 40, 154/154.

19 GA 40, 131/130.

20 GA 40, 125/123–4.

21 GA 40, 131/129–30.

22 GA 40, 132–4/130–3.

23 H. Diels and W. Kranz, *Die Fragmente der Vorsokratiker* (Berlin: Weidmann, 1974), B3.

24 GA 40, 154/155. See Susan Schoenbohm, "Heidegger's Interpretation of *Phusis*," in *A Companion to Heidegger's 'Introduction to Metaphysics*, ed. Richard Polt and Gregory Fried (New Haven: Yale University Press, 2001), 156–7.

25 GA 40, 149–50/150.

26 Dahlstrom provides a detailed overview of the fall. See his "The Scattered Logos: Metaphysics and the Logical Prejudice," in *A Companion to Heidegger's 'Introduction to Metaphysics*, ed. Richard Polt and Gregory Fried (New Haven: Yale University Press, 2001), 90–7.

27 GA 40, 189–94/192–8. See GA 9c, 203–38/155–82.

28 GA 40, 194–7/198–202.

29 GA 40, 129/128.

30 GA 40, 197/201.

31 "With it Kant moved into a new fundamental position of the human being in the midst of entities, or more precisely he lifted [*gehoben*] one always persisting in the ground expressly into metaphysical knowledge and brought it to grounding." GA 41, 137–8/135.

32 GA 41, 108/108.

33 Heidegger gives various terms to illustrate the distinction between thing and properties: ὑποκείμενον and συμβεβηκός, *substantia* and *accidens*, *Träger* and *Eigenschaften*, and subject and predicate. GA 41, 33/34.

34 GA 41, 34/36.

35 GA 41, 35/36.

36 GA 41, 36/37. Heidegger likewise outlines a threefold structure of the assertion in § 33 of *Being and Time*. There his intention was to demonstrate

judgment's derivative character; it is rooted in the primary interpreting and understanding constitutive of being-in-the-world. Instead of a predicating that gives information, he spoke there of a determining pointing out that lets something be seen. In the present analysis, then, Heidegger holds in reserve the phenomenological recovery of judgment and instead exhibits the structure of the seemingly "natural" point of view. The first analysis aims to recover judgment, the second to show that it stands in need of such a recovery.

37 GA 41, 36/38.

38 GA 41, 44/45.

39 GA 41, 38/40. Heidegger attempts to demonstrate the logical prejudice's origin with Plato and Aristotle in his famous "Plato's Doctrine of Truth" and in his "On the Essence and Concept of Φύσις in Aristotle's *Physics* B, 1." See GA 9c and GA 9d, respectively.

40 GA 41, 37–8/39.

41 GA 41, 39/40.

42 GA 41, 62–3/62–3. Heidegger underscores the centrality of the proposition in this relationship: "We cannot lay this fact too often and too emphatically before our eyes—namely, that those determinations which constitute the being of an entity, thus of the thing itself, have their name from assertions about the thing." GA 41, 63/63.

43 GA 41, 64/64.

44 GA 41, 49/51.

45 The mathematical relates to things according to a "definite respect" (*Hinsicht*), namely, insofar as they are learnable. Heidegger contrasts this with other ways of relating to things. τὰ φυσικά: the things as they emerge from themselves; τὰ ποιούμενα: the things as they are produced by us; τὰ χρήματα: the things, natural or artificial, as they are in use; τὰ πράγματα: the things as we deal with them at all, which includes the previous senses. τὰ μαθήματα is yet a fifth sense, which is yet more encompassing. GA 41, 70/70.

46 GA 41, 184/180.

47 "An Introduction to Heidegger's 'What Is a Thing?'" *Southern Journal of Philosophy* 21 (1973): 23.

48 GA 41, 71–3/71–2.

49 In this way, numbers are a particular form of the mathematical, and we can only count three apples if we already have the number "three."

50 Thus Heidegger seems to have in mind something akin to Aristotle's distinction between "knack" (ἐμπειρία) and "know-how" (τέχνη). With knack, we can handle something through familiarity, but only with know-how do we appropriate that knowledge so that we can make the thing and teach others about it. *Metaphysics*, 980b26–981b13. Heidegger himself takes up this distinction in the winter semester 1924–25 lecture course, "Plato's *Sophist*," during an Aristotelian propaedeutic to the study of the dialogue; knack establishes the referential connection and know-how explicitly sees the whatness. See GA 19, 69–78/48–54 and 91–4/62–5.

51 GA 41, 76/75. In order to do academic work, one "must grasp that the fundamental condition for the proper possibility of knowing is the knowledge of the fundamental presuppositions of all knowledge and the attitude [*Haltung*] we take based on such knowledge." GA 41, 76/75–6.

52 *Metaphysical Foundations of Natural Science*, trans. Michael Friedman (Cambridge: Cambridge University Press, 2004), 6. Cf. GA 41, 68–9/68.

53 GA 41, 66–9/66–8.

54 *Principia*, trans. I. Bernard Cohen and Anne Whitman (Berkeley: University of California Press, 1999), 416.

55 GA 41, 92–4/92–4.

56 GA 41, 93/93.
57 It is worth going beyond Heidegger to quote from the passage in which Descartes is most explicit about his concern: "I began my investigation by inquiring what exactly is generally meant by the term 'mathesis'. . . . When I considered the matter more closely, I came to see that the exclusive concern of mathematics is with questions of order or measure and that it is irrelevant whether the measure in question involves numbers, shapes, stars, sounds, or any other object whatever. This made me realize that there must be a general science which explains all the points that can be raised concerning order and measure irrespective of the subject-matter, and that this science should be termed *mathesis universalis*." In *The Philosophical Writings of Descartes*, vol. 1, trans. John Cottingham, Robert Stoothoff, and Dugald Murdoch (Cambridge: Cambridge University Press, 1985), 19.
58 Ibid., 20.
59 GA 41, 103/102.
60 GA 41, 104/104.
61 GA 41, 105/104.
62 GA 41, 97/97.
63 GA 41, 104–5/104.
64 Heidegger claims, for instance, that with the mathematical prejudice "the truth concerning what things are in their thingness determines itself from the principles of pure reason." GA 41, 119/118.
65 GA 41, 122/120. Cf. Kant, KRV A 768, B 796 and B xxiii.
66 GA 41, 123/121.
67 GA 41, 123/121. For the connection of principles and architectonic, Heidegger refers to Baumgarten, *Metaphysica*, § 4, and Leibniz, *De primae Philosophiae Emendatione*.
68 GA 41, 123/121.
69 GA 41, 190/186-7.
70 KRV A 152, B 191. In other words, that a judgment is not contradictory does not mean it is not "false or groundless." KRV A 150, B 190.
71 61 pages in the *Gesamtausgabe* edition, 47 pages in the 1962 Niemeyer edition, and 63 pages in the English translation.
72 Thankfully Roman and Littlefield has a new English translation in the works.
73 GA 41, 245/243.
74 GA 41, 182–3/179, 245/243.
75 GA 41, 245/243.
76 KRV B 140.
77 GA 41, 163/160.
78 GA 41, 177/181. Earlier in the course, Heidegger remarks that Kant's contemporaries were baffled by the *Critique of Pure Reason*, because it "went beyond anything customary by the elevation of its question-posing, by the rigor of its concept-formation, by the far-seeing organization of its questioning, and by the novelty of the language and its decisive goal." GA 41, 57/57–58.
79 GA 41, 182/179.
80 GA 41, 182/178-9.
81 GA 41, 181–2/178.
82 *Kants gesammelte Schriften*, XVIII (Berlin: Walter de Gruyter, 1928), no. 5738. See GA 41, 179/176.
83 GA 41, 179/176.
84 GA 41, 182/179.
85 GA 41, 159/156.

86 GA 41, 60/60. See also GA 41, 183–4/180.

87 GA 41, 182/178.

88 He does, for instance, say that Werner Heisenberg and Niels Bohr are two contemporary scientists who are philosophically minded and whose work thus opens up new ways of posing questions. GA 41, 67/67.

89 KRV A 19, B 33. Heidegger thinks that this passage announces a new orientation of human beings: "With it Kant moved into a new *fundamental position* of the human being in the midst of entities, or more precisely he lifted [*gehoben*] one always persisting in the ground expressly into metaphysical knowledge and brought it to grounding." GA 41, 137–8/135. Emphasis mine.

90 GA 41, 152/149: "Thought has experienced a new characterization through Kant's essential definition of human knowledge: It enters into the essential service of intuition. Therefore, the same must also be valid for the act of thought of the judgment."

91 GA 41, 245/243.

92 See Aristotle, *De Anima*, V.6, 430a26, and *De Interpretatione*, 6, 17a25, and Wolff, *Logica*, *Opera* I (Verona: Apud Haeredes Marci Moroni, 1779), §§ 39, 40, and 201.

93 *Auszug aus der Vernunftlehre*, available in *Kants gesammelte Schriften*, XVI, 2nd ed. (Berlin: Walter de Gruyter, 1924), § 292. Heidegger notes the empty circularity of this definition of *logos*: "It is particularly 'logical' that in this definition *logos* is defined as a presentation of a logical relation." GA 41, 157/154. Heidegger characterizes Meier's definition as a "trite" reproduction of Wolff's definition in his logic, which still includes a relation to the object. Heidegger cautions against looking for Kant's own doctrine in his logic lectures, since there he follows the scholarly tradition so closely. GA 41, 154–5/152. On the importance of Meier for Kant, see Riccardo Pozzo, "Prejudices and Horizons: G.F. Meier's *Vernunftlehre* and its Relation to Kant," *Journal of the History of Philosophy* 43 (2005): 185–202.

94 KRV B 140–1.

95 "The characterization of the assertion as the connection of representations is correct but unsatisfying." GA 41, 159/156.

96 KRV B 141.

97 In a dense passage, Heidegger explains that the opposition of the object requires the anticipation of a subject, and this subject is present to itself but not as an object: "The opposition of the object [*Die Entgegenstehen des Gegenstandes*] as such is not possible unless that which encounters, in its opposition is present [*gegenwärtig*] for a pre-senting representing [*für ein Vor-stellendes, Repräesentierendes*], which thereby at that same time has itself present [*präsent*] *with*, although not as an object." GA 41, 161–2/158.

98 GA 41, 160/157.

99 Kant writes, "*Understanding* is, to use general terms, *the faculty of knowledge.* This knowledge consists in the determinate relation of given presentations to an object; and an *object* is that in the concept of which the manifold of a given intuition is *united.*" KRV B 137.

100 "It looks as though Kant only added something to the definition of judgment which had been omitted up till then. But it is not a question of a 'mere extension,' but of a more original grasp of the whole." GA 41, 162/158-9.

101 GA 41, 163–4/160 and SZ 159/201. See Aristotle, *De Anima*, III.5, 430 b1–5, and Thomas Sheehan, "*Hermeneia* and *Apophansis*: The Early Heidegger on Aristotle," 78.

102 Regarding the novelty of the distinction, Kant remarks that it "perhaps . . . has never previously been considered." KRV B19. In a 1790 polemical

essay, Kant defends this position against Johann August Eberhard's counter claim; after surveying the texts of his predecessors, Kant concludes: "No one therefore has conceived this distinction in its universality with regard to a critique of reason in general." *Kants gesammelte Schriften*, VIII (Berlin: Walter de Gruyter, 1912), *The Kant-Eberhard Controversy: 'On a Discovery According to which Any New Critique of Pure Reason Has Been Made Superfluous by an Earlier One,'* ed. and trans. Henry E. Allison (Baltimore: Johns Hopkins University Press, 1973), 246/156. Allison offers a defense of the distinction's novelty in his essay, "The Originality of Kant's Distinction between Analytic and Synthetic Judgments," in *The Philosophy of Immanuel Kant*, ed. Richard Kennington (Washington, DC: The Catholic University of America Press, 1985), 15–38. Heidegger thinks the distinction is new in Kant, because it trades on his new determination of judgment enabled by the disclosive power of transcendental questioning.

103 GA 41, 162/159.
104 KRV A 151, B 190.
105 *Kants gesammelte Schriften*, VIII, *The Kant-Eberhard Controversy*, 245/155.
106 GA 41, 166/163.
107 GA 41, 249–50.
108 "Kant did not overcome intellectualism through mere renunciation, rather through a more original essential determination of thinking." GA 41, 249.
109 GA 41, 190/186.
110 KRV A 126.
111 GA 41, 192–3/189.
112 GA 41, 249.
113 GA 41, 169/165.
114 GA 41, 170/166.
115 KRV B 19.
116 "In the Kantian sense, we encounter things first and only in the domain of synthetic judgments; and, accordingly, we first encounter the thingness of the thing only in the context of the question of how a thing as such and in advance is possible as a thing, i.e., at the same time how synthetic judgments *a priori* are possible." GA 41, 184/181.
117 Heidegger thinks that it "is nothing other than a sketch of the essence and essential structure of experience." GA 41, 128/126.
118 Heidegger notes that Kant employs a complex of terms to designate these two aspects of knowing. When he intends the presented as such in the object, he terms them intuition and thought. When he has in view the modes of comporting operative in the presentings, he terms them receptivity and spontaneity. When naming the character of the presented—whether happening or result—he terms them affection and function. Finally, as capacities or sources of knowledge, he calls them sensibility and understanding. GA 41, 146/144.
119 In *Being and Time*, Heidegger argues that Dasein or the experiencing human being must have a wholly different way of being than the entities that it understands within the world it discloses. These entities are either isolated objects of curiosity as with on-hand things, or they are nested within the world's network of significance as with handy things. The specimen under the microscope is on-hand, but the microscope in use is handy. The biologist viewing the specimen with the microscope is neither on-hand nor handy. See especially §§ 15, 44, and 69.
120 KRV A 150, B 189.

121 KRV A 152, B 191. Heidegger writes that "a principle [*Grundsatz*], in contrast to a mere negative condition, is a proposition [*Satz*] in which there is posited the ground [*Grund*] for possible truth, that is, something sufficient for supporting the truth of the judgment." GA 41, 176/173.

122 KRV A 150, B 190.

123 As is well known, Kant modifies the traditional formulation of the principle of non-contradiction by deliberately omitting its temporal reference. It now reads, "No predicate contradictory of a thing can belong to it" (A 151, B 190). Kant justifies this omission by saying that the principle is merely formal or logical and so does not include the content of knowledge, namely the temporal object of experience. For two important traditional formulations of the principle, see Aristotle, *Metaphysics,* IV.3, 1005b19, and Wolff, *Ontologia, Opera* V (Verona: Apud Haeredes Marci Moroni, 1779), §28.

124 Heidegger observes that in the determination of the so-called principle of non-contradiction Kant speaks about human knowledge in particular and leaves open the question of an infinite mind. He also stands in sharpest contrast with Hegel and Schelling, who dissolve the negative condition into absolute and not merely human knowing.

125 GA 41, 177/174.

126 KRV A 7, B 10. Heidegger also points to the second section of the chapter in which Kant says that the relation to the object included in the synthetic judgment is "never a relation either of identity or of contradiction." Consequently, "from the judgment, taken in and by itself, the truth or falsity of the relation can never be discovered." KRV A 154–5, B 194. The truth of an analytic judgment, then, is based on identity or contradiction.

127 GA 41, 176/173.

128 Formal logic does not suffice for knowledge, but it does play a guiding role in Kant's transcendental researches. Kant, for instance, borrows the categories from the table of logical judgments. There seems, then, to be an omission in Heidegger's presentation of Kant. While it is true that formal logic does not have the dominance it has in rationalism, it also has an important place in Kant's program. As Henri Declève rightly asks, "Pourquoi Heidegger ne thématise-t-il pas le rôle positif de la logique conceptuelle dont il laisse apercevoir à tout moment comment elle guide la recherche transcendentale?" *Heidegger et Kant* (The Hague: Nijhoff, 1970), 292. For an account of the guiding role of logic in Kant, see Richard L. Velkley, "Kant on the Primacy and Limits of Logic," in his *Being after Rousseau: Philosophy and Culture in Question* (Chicago: The University of Chicago Press, 2002), 81–9.

129 GA 41, 186/183.

130 GA 41, 186/182–3.

131 GA 41, 185/182.

132 GA 41, 186/182.

133 KRV A 158, B 197.

134 KRV A 158, B 197.

135 "The second section also takes precedence over the third, which by comparison is only the unfolding of the second. Therefore a complete and definite understanding of this decisive second section is possible only if we already know the third one." GA 41, 186/183. Correcting the translation.

136 GA 41, 186/182.

137 GA 41, 193/190.

138 GA 41, 195/191. See *Die philosophischen Schriften von Gottfried Wilhelm Leibniz*, IV, ed. C.I. Gerhardt (Hildesheim: Olms Verlagsbuchhandlung, 1960–61), 394–5.

139 "The understanding of the principles [*Grundsätze*] is gained only by going through their proof; for this proof is nothing other than the exhibition of the 'principle' ['*Prinzip*'], of the ground, on which they ground, from which they hence create that which they themselves are. Accordingly, everything depends on these proofs." GA 41, 196/192.

140 GA 41, 196/192. Correcting the translation.

141 GA 41, 197/193.

142 GA 41, 239/237. See also GA 41, 228/226 and KRV A 216, B 263.

143 KRV A 219, B 266.

144 Kant links possibility, actuality, and necessity to conditions of intuition and of concepts, perception, and universal conditions of experience, respectively. The Axioms of Intuition, the Anticipations of Perception, and the Analogies of Experience seem to account for each of these three conditions though Kant does not explicitly say so in this connection. See in particular KRV A 218, B 265-7 and A 234, B 286-7.

145 GA 41, 242/240. Heidegger's treatment of the synthetic principles of pure understanding is quite extensive, running some forty-five pages in the German text. Here we can provide only a summary of the exposition of each principle. A somewhat longer summary can be found in Declève, *Heidegger et Kant*, 276-89.

146 KRV B 202.

147 Heidegger glosses Kant's proof, given at A 162, B 202-3, as follows: "Because objectivity as such is the unity of the collection of a manifold in a presentation of unity and preconception, but this manifold encounters in space and time, the encountered itself must stand against in the unity of quantity as extensive size." GA 41, 207-8/205.

148 Heidegger observes that Kant's recognition of the priority of sensation is especially astonishing given his commitment to the mathematical tradition of Newtonian physics and Cartesian subjectivity, neither of which are "suited to promote the free view of this unusual anticipation in the receptivity of perception." GA 41, 224/222.

149 GA 41, 241/239.

150 Kant here roots the community of substances in space and time, so Heidegger notes that the analogies of experience manifest Kant's departure from Leibniz's windowless monads. GA 41, 238/235.

151 GA 41, 242/240.

152 GA 41, 242/240. See also GA 41, 179/176: "Logic cannot be the fundamental science of metaphysics."

153 KRV A 234, B 286.

154 KRV A 218, B 265-6. See GA 41, 242-3/240.

155 GA 41, 244/241-2.

156 KRV A 737, B 765.

157 SZ 351/402.

158 GA 41, 244/242. This repeats a key claim of the Kant book. GA 3, 43/30.

159 The circularity in the proof "means nothing other than this: Fundamentally these principles always express only the highest principle, but in such a way that in their belonging together [*Zusammengehörigkeit*] they explicitly cite all that which belongs to the full content of the essence of experience and the essence of an object." GA 41, 245/243.

160 GA 41, 246/244. This repeats a key claim from his thought in the late 1920s. He writes in 1928, "Only because, in our factical intentional comportment toward entities of every sort, we, outstripping in advance, return to and arrive at entities from possibilities, only for this reason can we let entities themselves be what and how they are." GA 26, 279/216.

161 GA 41, 244–5/242.
162 Cf. GA 41, 30/31.
163 GA 41, 244/242.
164 GA 41, 244/242.
165 GA 41, 222/220.
166 GA 41, 245/243. In 1919 he anticipates the dynamism expressed here, writing, "The experienced 'something' is not a concept but is *identical* with the motivational process of life as such and its tendency; therefore not a concept, but a *recept* [Rückgriff]." GA 56/57, 219/187.
167 Theodore Kisiel is one of the few commentators who grasps the significance of the 1935–36 course for interpreting Heidegger: "Kant's transcendental reflection, which first found its locus in the movement of thought to its object, now finds itself drawn into a movement of reciprocal grounding between the subjectivity of the subject and the objectivity of the object, where the 'between' suggests the ground of a more original unity as the essence of transcendence (experience). Going *back* to this ground would then be a more basic transcendental reflection, one which Heidegger assumes as his own task." "The Mathematical and the Hermeneutical: On Heidegger's Notion of the Apriori," in *Martin Heidegger: In Europe and America*, ed. Edward G. Ballard and Charles E. Scott (The Hague: Martinus Nijhoff, 1973), 113.
168 GA 41, 188/184. In the *Contributions*, Heidegger says that the subject in Kant is subjective "in the best sense"—namely it is a metaphysical subject and not egoistically or epistemologically. GA 65, 448/315.
169 GA 41, 131/129. Kant "skips that sphere of things in which we know ourselves immediately at home, the things as the painter shows them to us." GA 41, 214/211.
170 GA 45, 227/188. See GA 65, 239/169.
171 GA 41, 131/129. Among other passages, Kant writes: "Taken together, the analogies thus declare that all appearances lie, and must lie, in *one* nature, because without this *a priori* unity no unity of experience, and therefore no determination of objects in it, would be possible." KRV A 216, B 263. Such a unity involves space as well as time. Kant distinguishes himself from Newton on the one hand and Leibniz on the other, both of whom had similar ontological commitments. Newton took space itself to be an on-hand thing, and Leibniz took space to be a web of relations rooted in on-hand things. For Kant, space is not anything on-hand but is instead a constitutive element of our experiencing. Heidegger observes, though, that Kant problematically attributes space to human subjectivity whose being is left unclarified. In this regard, Heidegger refers to his own attempt to articulate the non-subjective problematic of space in *Sein und Zeit*, §§ 19–24 and §70. GA 41, 203–4/199–200.
172 GA 41, 239/237.
173 GA 41, 131/129.
174 At the end of the 1952 lecture course Heidegger makes the connection explicit: "The most magnificent variation [of Parmenides' saying], which, despite all the variance of its fundamental metaphysical position, matches in its greatness the majesty of early Greek thinking, is that proposition of Kant which he thinks as the supreme principle of all *a priori* synthetic judgments." *Was Heißt Denken?* (Tübingen: Max Niemeyer Verlag, 1954) [*What is Called Thinking?* trans. J. Glenn Gray (New York: Harper & Row, Publishers, 1968)], 148/242–3. Due to this similarity, Heidegger says both in the 1935–36 lecture course and the 1961 lecture that in Kant's understanding of judgment the originary senses of λόγος and φύσις dimly shine through. GA 41, 190/186–7, and GA 9i, 459/347.

175 GA 41, 123/121.

176 GA 41, 242/240. See also GA 41, 179/176: "Logic cannot be the fundamental science of metaphysics."

177 GA 41, 249.

178 GA 41, 249.

179 GA 41, 249. In the following semester lecture course on Schelling, after discussing modernity's mathematical prejudice, Heidegger writes, "In everything recounted just now, an inner context is betrayed, a *change* of European existence in terms of a *ground* which remains in the *dark* for us up until today." *Schellings Abhandlung*, 38/32.

180 Kisiel is thus justified in saying that "by way of the transcendental, the mathematical ripens into the hermeneutical." "The Mathematical," 113.

181 Kant's transcendental logic is "a logic which considers thought inclusive of its relation to the object." GA 41, 179/176.

182 Cf. Hans-Georg Gadamer, "Martin Heidegger's One Path," trans. P. Christopher Smith, in *Reading Heidegger from the Start: Essays in His Earliest Thought*, ed. Theodore Kisiel and John van Buren (Albany, NY: State University of New York Press, 1994), 27.

183 *Schellings Abhandlung*, 60/50. Heidegger thus changes his mind from the previous semester when he had insisted that German Idealism merely sidesteps Kant's foundation. Cf. GA 41, 58/59.

184 *Schellings Abhandlung*, 235/194. Emphasis mine.

185 *Schellings Abhandlung*, 49/41.

186 KRV A 260, B 316, and A 839, B 867.

187 *Schellings Abhandlung*, 50/41. "On the one hand, Kant showed the necessity of system in terms of the essence of reason. On the other hand, that same Kant left system in essential difficulties." *Schellings Abhandlung*, 54/44.

188 "Although Kant himself never took the fundamental position of German Idealism, as far as German Idealism went beyond Kant, it is certain that this could happen *only* on Kant's foundation and following the lead of the fundamental reflection he accomplished on the essence of human reason." *Schellings Abhandlung*, 42–3/35.

189 *Schellings Abhandlung*, 55/45.

190 *Schellings Abhandlung*, 57/47.

191 *Schellings Abhandlung*, 55/45.

192 *Schellings Abhandlung*, 57–8/47–8.

193 *Schellings Abhandlung*, 53/43.

194 Cf. *Schellings Abhandlung*, 194–5/161–2. In the 1930–31 lecture course, "Hegel's *Phenomenology of Spirit*," Heidegger observes, "If reading the problematic of *Being and Time* into some other text is ever nonsensical, then this is the case with Hegel. For the thesis that *the essence of being is time* is the exact opposite of what Hegel tried to demonstrate in his entire philosophy." GA 32, 209/145. Later, Heidegger found in the *Phenomenology of Spirit* the echo of a thought closer to his own. An essay based on a seminar from 1942–43 attempts to show that there is a hint of "appropriation" (*Ereignis*) in Hegel's concept of experience, for the unfolding of the dialectic moves through the realm between (διά) ontic and ontological consciousness and gathers (λέγειν) the truth of its nature. See GA 5b, 183–4/138.

195 *Schellings Abhandlung*, 58/48.

196 *Schellings Abhandlung*, 126/105.

197 *Schellings Abhandlung*, 126/105.

198 *Schellings Abhandlung*, 126/105.

199 *Schellings Abhandlung*, 198/164.

200 *Schellings Abhandlung*, 196/162.

201 On this course, see Schalow, *Heidegger-Kant Dialogue*, 267–304.
202 *Schellings Abhandlung*, 101/84.
203 *Schellings Abhandlung*, 196/162.
204 Heidegger repeatedly mentions Leibniz too as central for Schelling's path though he does not explicitly develop this dependence. See, for instance, *Schellings Abhandlung*, 102–3/84–5.
205 In *Nietzsche*, vol. 1 (Pfullingen: Verlag Günther Neske, 1961), *Nietzsche*, vol. 1, trans. David Farrell Krell (New York: Harper & Row, Publishers, 1979).
206 *Nietzsche*, vol. 1, 131/111.
207 For this definition, see *Kritik der Urteilskraft*, §§ 2–5.
208 *Nietzsche*, vol. 1,130/110.
209 *Nietzsche*, vol. 1,133/112.
210 *Kritik der Urteilskraft*, § 39.
211 *Nietzsche*, vol. 1,133/113.
212 *Nietzsche*, vol. 1,145/123.
213 Cf. *Nietzsche*, vol. 1, 133/113: "Kant's interpretation of aesthetic behavior as 'pleasure of reflection' propels us toward a basic state of human being in which man for the first time arrives at the well-grounded fullness of his essence. It is the state that Schiller conceives of as the condition of the possibility of man's existence as historical, as grounding history."
214 In the 1930s, Kant is the subject of the 1935–36 lecture course, Schelling is the subject of the 1936 lecture course, Hegel is the subject of the 1930–31 lecture course, and Nietzsche becomes the subject of the 1936–1937, 1937, 1939, and 1940 lecture courses. Additionally, Leibniz, Kant, and Hegel are subjects of numerous seminars.
215 GA 65, 176/123–4. Nietzsche, subject of the most lecture courses, is certainly "nearest" in the sense of coming last and representing for Heidegger the close of the metaphysical tradition. He may also be "nearest" in his critique of Platonism and recognition of its implicit nihilism. Heidegger thinks that Nietzsche sensed the effects of Western rationalism but misdiagnosed its causes; hence, he is "farthest removed from the question of being." The numerous courses on Nietzsche afford Heidegger the opportunity to traverse the whole history of philosophy with Nietzsche as its termination.
216 See, for example, GA 65, 391/273.
217 *A Parting of the Ways*, 157.
218 GA 41, 190/186–7. In the 1961 lecture, Heidegger still thinks Kant puts thought in essential relation to intuition, but he no longer suggests that thought is subordinate to intuition. GA 9i, 459/347.
219 Rather than this pre-subjective "between," the 1961 lecture grounds judgment in transcendental apperception, which "is unifying-gathering, λόγος in the original sense, but transferred to and relocated in the I-subject." GA 9i, 462/350.
220 GA 41, 186/183.

4   *Contributions* (1936–38)

Such a task exceeds even the capacity of a great thinker. It demands nothing less than to leap over one's own shadow. No one can do this. However, the greatest effort in attempting this impossibility—that is the decisive ground-movement of the action of thought.
—Heidegger, 1935–36[1]

By Heidegger's own admission, the *Contributions* is his attempt to do the impossible and leap over his own shadow. Just what he had in mind can be discovered by carefully reviewing his account of Kant's shadow. Having completed the *Critique*, Kant was in a position to make an entirely new beginning on the basis of the ground opened up in the analytic, but this he could not do. The failure was nothing psychological or personal; the failure was rooted in the very finitude of the philosopher. One's trajectory of thinking remains specified by one's beginning. As far as one may go on the path of thinking, one remains bound to one's origins. Applied to Heidegger's own path, what is he suggesting? Having finished *Being and Time*, Heidegger was then in a position to begin again where it left off, to rupture the horizon of that work on the basis of the progress that it had made. Heidegger echoes the same thought twenty years later, again in the context of interpreting Kant:

The greater the work of a thinker—which in no way coincides with the breadth and number of writings—the richer is what is *unthought* in this work, which means, *that which emerges in and through this work* as having not yet been thought. Of course this unthought has nothing to do with what a thinker has overlooked or not mastered which wiser descendants would then have to make good on.[2]

Heidegger's mature understanding of motivation comes from the necessity of philosophy, a necessity rooted in the impossible attempt to overcome the finitude of the philosopher. The unthought is normative for us. The unthought, discovered, commends itself to us as obligatory. The unthought is not merely absent but instead privative. It is something that *should* be there, and it is the force of this *should* that motivates the philosopher. This is nothing like the Cartesian appeal to authenticity. Rather it is a will rooted in the binding character of what is given, the tradition that, in illuminating, simultaneously casts shadows, shadows that are for us there to be illuminated.

Philosophy is not a domain of problems, some of which remain unresolved, so that that those who have gone before us contribute nothing to our attempts to solve what remains. Philosophy rather is a path in which those who have gone before us have made essential progress, progress that we have to as it were appropriate for ourselves, but a progress that cannot be merely repeated, but must be repeated with this difference: by means of traversing the previous path we acquire the means to penetrate yet further into the domain of investigation. In a notebook entry from the same time as the 1935 course on Kant, he reaffirms the impossibility of a philosopher's leaping over his own shadow and then specifies that to leap over one's shadow would mean "to build originally on the freshly placed ground."[3] Applied to Heidegger's own itinerary, what Heidegger attempts in the *Contributions* is possible only due to the success of *Being and Time* in arriving at the domain to be thought. Only "in and through this work" can one appreciate what he later attempts to do.[4] Hence, it is false to say that Heidegger disavows the transcendental thought of *Being and Time* precisely because such a claim rests upon a falsification of Heidegger's own understanding of the nature of philosophy and his own understanding concerning his path of thinking.

In another notebook entry from the same period, Heidegger employs the metaphor of leaping to illustrate the larger historical ambition of his later work.

> Whoever wants to accomplish a *big leap* needs a big *start*. For this big start, he must go far *back*. This going back must go to the first beginning—if it values the second beginning in the leap.[5]

These two images of leaping, one concerning the impossible task of transcending one's own origins, the other concerning the great difficulty of inaugurating a new tradition in philosophy by retrieving and thereby exceeding the prior tradition, in the end are both operative in the *Contributions*. Heidegger remains doubly bound by the transcendental tradition historically and personally but endeavors the impossible task of going back in order to go forward to a new tradition. That he is aware of both the impossibility, and the felt need to do so is manifest in the juxtaposition of these two telling images.

The *Contributions* constitutes Heidegger's attempt to leap over his own shadow, to shift from the transcendence of experience to the experience of transcendence. Transcendental thought is oblivious to the givenness of the domain as such and so is closed to the history of different domains founded on different fundamental dispositions. Transcendental thought needs to be rethought and deepened historically; this is the task of the later Heidegger. In his self-understanding, his own shadow is the transcendental entrance to the domain to be thought; now that he finds himself there, he grasps its final inadequacy, but he cannot disavow it since it is what first enabled him to enter to the domain. The *Contributions* is also his attempt to transition from what he takes to calling the first beginning to the other beginning of philosophy. Hence, the attempt to transcend his own transcendental heritage becomes the attempt to transcend the entire philosophical tradition, under the motto: "Always in the transition and leaving!"[6]

This chapter concerns Heidegger's heroic efforts in the late 1930s to twist free of his transcendental heritage while acknowledging the impossibility of doing so. I first identify just what it is that the later Heidegger finds troublesome about transcendental philosophy; Heidegger finds problematic the idea that the subject transcends objects, because he thinks that, prior to such transcendence, the subject must dwell within a transcendental domain. The problem, then, does not have to do with the dimension that opens up with the transcendental turn; the problem has to do with the suggestion that a prior subject subsequently transcends entities, a movement that overlooks what is in fact more fundamental: the openness of the domain in which such transcendence is possible in the first place. In other words, Heidegger gives a transcendental critique of transcendence. Second, I compare the kind of Kantian transcendence explored in the third chapter with the kind of Heideggerian transcendence of *Being and Time* and the *Contributions*. Kant's transcendence approaches but does not obtain the transcendence of *Being and Time* and the transcendence of *Being and Time* approaches but does not obtain the "transcendence" of the *Contributions*. Third, I come to the center of this chapter and discuss the theme of "fundamental dispositions" *(Grundstimmungen)* that runs throughout the *Contributions* and the accompanying 1937–38 lecture course, *Basic Questions of Philosophy*. Heidegger deploys what I call a "rhetoric of being" to motivate the requisite pathos out of which philosophers can attend to the proper subject matter of philosophy. Fundamental dispositions open up an affective transcendence that stands in contrast to his earlier projective transcendence; before Dasein can be in a position to go beyond entities, Dasein must in the first place be brought into the open domain in some manner or another. Fundamental dispositions specify just how the transcendental domain opens up. The first thinkers were enthralled by wonder before the presence of entities, but today Heidegger thinks we rather experience, in terror, the absence of any awareness of the domain of experience—entities still "are" but the interplay of presence and absence has tragically fallen from view. Heidegger thinks the transition from wonder to terror is in a certain sense inevitable; displaying this inevitability is a tragic device aimed to evoke the pathos of terror and the givenness of the domain of experience. The rhetoric of being proves to be Heidegger's affective antidote to the unilaterally projective dimension of the transcendental tradition. Finally, I show that Heidegger cannot shake the transcendental tradition despite his best efforts to do so, because he makes sense only by means of that tradition and its inherent limitations.

1 The Transcendental Approach to Transcendence

Daniela Vallega-Neu is correct to observe, "In *Contributions*, Heidegger's critique of the transcendental approach to the question of being is severe."[7] Yet, the critique of transcendence applies only *in part* to Heidegger's own transcendental philosophy. In the context of a general Nietzsche-inspired critique of "Platonism," Heidegger iterates various senses of transcendence. This is particularly important, for he includes his own transcendental program of *Being and Time* among the senses. He takes pains to distinguish the various traditions of transcendental philosophy from his own, and he does so by maintaining that other transcendental programs, stemming from Plato, involve a "representation" of transcendence, determined by a unilateral relation of thought and being. But he insists that the transcendental program of *Being and Time* did not employ such a "representation." For ease of reference, I have numbered the passages.

> The "fundamental ontological" transcendence in *Being and Time*. [1] Here the word's originary meaning is returned to it: surpassing as such; and it is grasped as the distinctive mark of Da-sein, in order thus to indicate that Da-sein always already stands within the openness of entities. [2] This joins and, at the same time, determines more precisely "ontological" "transcendence," insofar as transcendence is grasped here in accord with "Dasein, i.e., originarily as *understanding of being*. [3] *But* because now understanding is also grasped as thrown projecting-open, transcendence means: standing in the truth of be-ing, indeed without initially knowing this or questioning it.
> [4] But now since Da-sein as Da-*sein* originarily sustains the openness of the sheltering-concealing, strictly speaking one cannot speak of a transcendence of Da-sein; in the context of this approach representation of "transcendence" in *every* sense must *disappear*. . . .
> [5] This representation [of transcendence] is still frequently used in "epistemological" observation which, beginning with Descartes, primarily hinders the "subject" from going out and going over to the "object" or makes this relation doubtful. [6] Even this kind of "transcendence" is overcome with the onset of Da-sein in that this transcendence is left behind in advance.[8]

Heidegger disavows the *representation* of transcendence as a going beyond, but it is not a disavowal of the *opening up of the transcendental domain* disclosed in *Being and Time*, which, he says in [1] is the "original meaning" of transcendence. In [2], Heidegger takes care in his formulation: he knows he cannot and should not reject the opening up of the transcendental domain in *Being and Time*, which does appropriate something of the previous transcendental tradition. In [3], he makes clear that, in adopting the transcendental approach of understanding, he nonetheless transforms it by rooting it in the affectivity of being thrown. In [4] he identifies a problem in the presentation of *Being and Time* and chastens the philosophical mode of access that, on the model of the modern sciences and thus on the model of the mathematical character of projection, understands itself as research. The dynamic is not Dasein's resistance of its tendency toward falling. Heidegger rather sees the dynamic as prior to Dasein, as determining the character of the domain in which Dasein finds itself. *Being and Time* was right to identify the transcendental domain, but it was wrong to think that the domain can be most originally accessed through research or transcendence, and it was wrong to think this because, as Heidegger already then realized, the domain is not constituted in this manner. Rather, only insofar as the domain is already opened up in a fundamental disposition, whether that be wonder or terror, can it then be possible to do something like research. The more original philosophical access to the constitution of the domain, then, must be attentive to the original disclosive power of fundamental dispositions and their manner of givenness. The dynamic of history is not rooted in the falling tendency of Dasein. It is rooted in the changes of fundamental dispositions. In [4] and [5], he rejects the *representation* of transcendence, but in [1] and [6], he affirms the original sense of transcendence in terms of the opening up of the transcendental domain. There is no disavowal of the transcendental program of *Being and Time*, but only a disavowal of the sort of transcendental program that is anchored either in the mathematical or logical prejudices; in other words, Heidegger simply becomes more critical of the tradition that had already come in for critique in *Being and Time*. Already in 1925, he wrote, "This is the very reason why, strictly speaking, Dasein cannot be taken as a 'between,' since the talk of a 'between' subject and world always already presupposes that two entities are given between which there is supposed to be a relation."[9] The *Contributions* constitute his efforts to purge the transcendental domain disclosed in *Being and Time* of its residual associations with the unwanted sense of transcendence by shifting from research to affectivity.

Heidegger's newfound qualms with transcendental thinking become intelligible by recalling some characteristically transcendental passages from the ambit of *Being and Time*. In the 1927 summer lecture course, *Die Grundprobleme der Phänomenologie*, which he says belongs to the domain of SZ I.3, Heidegger distinguishes Plato the sober researcher into being from Plato the enthusiast. With Kant, he identifies himself with the former while excoriating the latter.[10] After decrying the contemporary forgetfulness of being, Heidegger notes that no progress has been made in this question, the cardinal question of philosophy, since Plato:

> We, too, with this apparently quite abstract question about the conditions for the possibility of the understanding of being, want to do nothing but bring ourselves out of the cave into the light, but in all sobriety and in the complete disenchantment of purely objective inquiry.
> What we are in search of is the epekeina tes ousias.[11]

Though indicating his distance from Plato's unscientific lack of objectivity and sober-mindedness, Heidegger indicates here fundamental agreement with Plato's own concern. He draws out two characteristics of the idea of the good in Plato: (1) Hardly to be seen, it is the end to which all cognition runs back or from which all cognition begins (7.517b8f); (2) It renders knowledge and truth possible (cf. 517c3f). Heidegger does indicate uncertainty as to what the "beyond" means or what the good that is "supposed to render knowledge and truth possible" signifies in Plato, for it is "in many respects obscure."[12] Rather than enter more deeply into the text, he simply offers the thesis that Plato's conception somehow remains mired within the productive ontology of ancient thought.[13] Heidegger instead focuses on his own understanding of the question concerning the condition for the possibility of the understanding of being. His answer, temporality, brings us to the question of the *a priori*, for all possibilities have the character of the *earlier*, and *"time is earlier than any possible earlier . . .* because it is the basic condition for an earlier as such."[14] Now, Plato is the discoverer of the *a priori*. Plato, according to Heidegger, recognized in the doctrine of anamnesis that the possibility for clarifying being can be pursued only as a coming back to what was earlier and already understood.[15] To substantiate this reading, he cites two passages from Plato: (1) A soul that does not see the truth cannot take on human form (*Phaedrus*, 249c5-c6); and (2) Learning itself is nothing but recollection (*Phaedo*, 72e5).[16] In light of these passages, Heidegger returns briefly to the allegory of the cave and says that the liberation of the prisoners and their turning around to see back into the light is the recollection of the *prius*. In this *prius* "there lies enclosed the enabling of understanding being itself."[17]

Heidegger closes the lectures with a stinging rebuke of the "philosophy of feeling" by reading an extended quotation from Kant: "What Kant, the first and last scientific philosopher in the grand style since Plato and Aristotle, had to say against the philosophy of feeling may well close these lectures. If our own course never attained it, Kant's example may nevertheless summon us to sobriety and real work."[18] Kant's quotation distinguishes between two Platos: one the objective, sober researcher into the *a priori*, and the other the "father of all enthusiasm in philosophy," whose contemporary followers, emphasizing the subjective, border on "rapturous gush" and speak of intimations rather than deliberating concerning explanations.[19] At this juncture, Heidegger prizes the analytical *a priori* over historical affectivity, but that changes decisively in the ambit of the *Contributions*. In the *Letter on Humanism*, he reiterates the claim that *Being and Time* opened up the transcendental domain but remains mired in the mathematical.

> In the poverty of its first breakthrough, the thinking that tries to advance thought into the truth of being brings only a small part of that wholly other dimension to language. This language even falsifies itself for it does not yet succeed in retaining the essential help of phenomenological seeing while dispensing with the inappropriate concern with "science" and "research."[20]

The problem with the transcendental approach is its remaining within the ambit of the *a priori* as the correlate or horizon of the researcher. What remains unthought in such an approach is the original relation in which a secondary relation such as research is possible. Heidegger must break ranks with Kant's sobriety and embrace the intimations of the enthusiasts to make sense of this relation. He becomes enamored with the erotic character of philosophy and the sort of divine madness Plato sometimes celebrated.[21]

2 From Kantian to Heideggerian Transcendence

Heidegger bemoans the fact he is persistently misunderstood: "No one understands what 'I' *think* here: to let *Da-sein* emerge from within the *truth of be-ing* . . . in order to ground entities in the whole and as such and to ground man in the midst of them."[22] Why this pervasive misunderstanding of Heidegger's project? Because scholars try to explain the new in terms of the old. "No one grasps this, because everyone tries to explain 'my' attempt merely historiographically and appeals to the past, which he *thinks* he grasps because it seems already to lie behind him." And yet, alongside such a distancing of the tradition, there is recognition that Kant's transcendental thinking happens upon something enduringly questionable: "Kant's *Critique of Pure Reason*, in which since the Greeks once more an essential step is taken, has to presuppose this context [*Zusammenhang*] without being able to grasp it as such and to bring it fully to a ground (the turning relation of Dasein and being)."[23] Heidegger says that the fact that this context, initially approached in the encircling of us and thing, was not thought

as such in terms of the relation of being and Dasein led to the absolutism of German Idealism and its subsequent collapse into positivism. To
overcome this later tradition, we do well to recall Kant: "According to
a familiar habit we think of these projections as forms of presentation
which enable the encountering of objects: Kant's transcendental condition. And we do well to practice thinking of entities as such by way
of this interpretation of entity-ness as objectivity."[24] Heidegger recommends that we "re-enact *Kant's* main steps" as a way to prepare for
the enactment of Da-sein as guardian of the truth of being.[25] We have
to invoke the transcendental way and then revoke the metaphysical
subjectivity and exclusive concern with objectivity, and what remains
is the finite context.

Indeed, Heidegger seems to be suggesting an elaborate analogy. The
relation thematized in the rationalist or merely logical account of judgment appears artificial from the point of view of the transcendental
between, which thematizes the object-relation itself as well as its context. That is, the subject-predicate relation can take place only within
the subject-object relation, and this can take place only within the pre-
judicative between. In the same way, the transcendental account itself
appears to be artificial and insufficient from the context of Heidegger's
later thinking. The "between" signaled in Kant's thought can be hidden
from view. Even though we make judgments and relate to things, we
can be oblivious to the context in which such access is possible. Thus,
there emerges a still deeper relation: our wakeful relation to the us-thing
between. In the *Contributions* he calls this relation itself the "between"
or "appropriation" (*Ereignis*).[26] "Every saying of be-ing . . . must name
ap-propriation, . . . always decisively *interpretive of the between*."[27] As
we have seen, Kant notably interprets being in terms of the experiential
between, though he interprets it as objectivity and overlooks the precat-
egorial. Heidegger suggests, then, that just as Kant interprets being from
the reciprocity of us and thing, so should we interpret being out of our
reciprocal relation to being.[28] Kant's shortcoming is that he was limited
to the question of the thingness of the thing rather than the question
of our relation to being, but in attending to his question something of
the site for our relation to being comes to light. The pre-subjective and
pre-objective relation that emerges in Kant now becomes enveloped in
a still more fundamental relation. As Kant traces the account of judgment to the between, so Heidegger traces the transcendental between to
appropriation. In this way, Kant is a "distant prelude" for Heidegger's
later thinking.[29]

As Heidegger emphasizes, Kant thinks the logical account of judgment is unsatisfactory but not false. In the same way, we can see that
the transcendental between is not false but simply insufficient. Indeed
if it were false, he would not recommend it as that mode of inquiry
that the sciences must invoke to comprehend themselves. "There is no

presuppositionless science, because the essence of science consists in such presupposing, in such pre-judgments about the object. Kant has not only affirmed all this, but has also shown it, and not simply shown but also grounded it."[30] Transcendental questioning uncovers a "happening that does not lie somewhere aloof from us in the dim and distant past but is here in every proposition and in each everyday opinion, in every approach to things."[31] Rather than false, the manner of questioning is insufficient, for something more original is happening than it grasps: humans are pulled open by the opening up of the open itself, and only thereby are they capable of entering into the transcendental manner of questioning that thinks the subject-object relation. We do transcend objects, but such transcendence is founded on a prior relating. Appropriation opens up the open; the movement of transcendence presupposes the movement of appropriation.

A further ambiguity in Heidegger's Kant interpretation stems from the fact that Kant does not quite attain Heidegger's transcendental philosophy. "In Kant [the ontological difference] is known in the concept of the 'transcendental'—and *yet not* known, because on the one hand entity-ness is grasped as object*ivity* and on the other hand it is precisely this interpretation of entity-ness that cuts off any *questioning of being*."[32] Since Kant's project does not quite attain Heidegger's own transcendental thinking, some adjustment is required in order to make Kant a transitional figure.[33]

> But what if "subjectivity," and thus the relation to the *objectivity* of the object, is grasped transcendentally (as in Kant); and what if, beyond this, the object "nature" counts as the solely experienceable entity—and thus objectivity coincides with entity-ness—is there not here an opportunity, even an historically [*geschichtlich*] singular fundamental position in which—in *spite of all essential differences*—for the first time to render accessible to those of today that relation of Da-sein and be-ing out of what has gone before? Of course.[34]

Heidegger says that the 1929 book *Kant and the Problem of Metaphysics* attempted just such a project but to succeed could not avoid doing scholarly violence to Kant.[35] In this passage, he does not refer to the 1935–36 lecture course on Kant in which he tries to interpret Kant from his own horizon of questioning.

The 1929 book on Kant sought to make accessible the relation of Dasein and being from out of Kant. The 1935–36 lecture course seeks to make manifest the presupposition of projection, but Heidegger worries this way will be taken as mere Kantianism.

> As long as "be-ing" is grasped as entity-ness, as what is somehow "general" and thus as a condition for entities inserted behind entities,

that is, condition for their presentedness and objectivity, and finally for their being "in-themselves," be-ing is lowered to the truth of entities, to the correctness of presentation.

Because all of this is accomplished in its purest form in Kant, one *can* attempt to make manifest with his work something even more originary and thus not derivable from that work, something totally other, but at the risk that such an attempt will be read again in a Kantian way and be misinterpreted and made harmless as an arbitrary "Kantianism."[36]

Heidegger does venture the risk, as we have seen, and he shows that Kant implicates the opened between through the reciprocal relation of the condition for the possibility of experience and the object of experience. "Kant's *Critique of Pure Reason*, in which since the Greeks once more an essential step is taken, has to presuppose this context without being able to grasp it as such and to ground it fully (the turning relation of Dasein and being)."[37] The fact that Kant did not ground this ground made it possible for German Idealism to become absolute knowing and subsequently collapse into positivism and biologism. Though German Idealism repeats Leibniz on the basis of Kant's transcendental philosophy, Heidegger says "there is no bridge from here to the other beginning."[38]

As we saw in the last chapter, Heidegger recommends that we "reenact [*nachvollziehen*] *Kant's* main steps" as a means to prepare us to "enact" (*vollziehen*) the grounding of the *truth* of be-ing as Da-sein and thereby overcome the tradition of metaphysics.[39] This reenactment means that we try our hand at thinking of the being of entities in the manner that Kant did: "And we do well to practice thinking of entities as such on the basis of [Kant's] interpretation of entity-ness as objectivity."[40] And yet we must "overcome the 'transcendental' approach through Da-sein."[41] This means that we do not try to understand originary time-space metaphysically simply by means of the schematism or transcendental imagination, since these overlook the fact that the origin withdraws.[42] The movement of the transcendental imagination is the expression of the deeper movement of appropriation: "*As thrown projecting-open grounding, Da-sein is the highest actuality in the domain of imagination*, granted that by this term we understand not only a faculty of the soul and not only something transcendental (cf. Kantbook) but rather *appropriation* itself, wherein all *transfiguration* reverberates."[43] Heidegger's phrase "not only" suggests that here transcendental imagination is deepened and not simply set aside. The deepening occurs as follows: "We succeed in doing that at all only if we basically already read Kant no longer 'subjectively' but rather reassess him in view of Da-sein."[44] Now, Kant is already subjective "in the best sense." This means that *subjectum* is understood metaphysically as presupposed and is not taken to be epistemological or egological.[45]

Reenacting Kant non-metaphysically leads one toward that which withdraws in projecting.

> On a historical path, this is a step for coming closer to *that* thinking which understands projecting-opening, no longer as condition for presentation but rather as Da-*sein* and as the thrownness of a clearing that takes a foothold and above all grants shelteredness and thus reveals the not-granting.[46]

This transitional and ambiguous character is captured in Heidegger's claim that Kant is "a distant prelude" for the other beginning—provided, that is, that we understand him from within the other beginning.[47] Why is Kant a *prelude*? Heidegger suggests two reasons. The first is that Kant holds to "*an* experience as *the* experience . . . so that Kant could initially point to that which the 'transcendental' kind of knowledge was to grasp." Similarly, in the other beginning there is need to hold to the experience of the "the abyss (cf. truth) as belonging to appropriation." The second is that Kant treats the modalities at the end of the principles "thus pre-determining everything that has gone before." In this way, Kant oriented his whole inquiry toward the being of entities. Analogously, Heidegger aims to think being as such and analyzes everything else, including the ontological difference, in light of it. "For truth is the between for the essential sway of be-ing and the entity-ness of entities. This between grounds the entity-ness of entities in being."[48] Kant's overcoming of modern rationalism sets the stage for Heidegger's overcoming of Western rationalism and its disjunction, "being and thought."

Despite this positive assessment of Kant, and in accord with the continual ambiguity of the assessment, Heidegger insists on the uniformity of the oblivion of being:

> Whatever the magnitude of Kant's step might be, whatever again the difference between absolute idealism of post-Kantian philosophy and Kant might continue to be, and however confusingly then everything is reduced to the half and groundless character of "logical" and "biological" interpretation of the *a priori*, which in this shape reappears again in Nietzsche—all of these differences cannot hide the simple cohesion of the whole history of this inquiry into being (into entity-ness, in the shape of the question of what an entity is). History of *this* question concerning entities is the history of metaphysics, history of the thinking that thinks being as the being of an entity *from out of and unto an entity.*[49]

Here Heidegger suppresses the nuances of his interpretation in order to insist on the need for a wholly new kind of inquiry. For the interpretation to function in its intended role as a motivation, it must both establish an identity as a point of departure and introduce a decisive difference as the terminus, to provoke the motivating movement. Heidegger must therefore both identity with the transcendental tradition and yet emphasize the limits of that tradition to achieve the desired effect of introducing his own immanent transformation of that tradition.

3 Motivating Philosophy Through Affective History

Heidegger entitles section 17 of the *Contributions* "The Necessity of Philosophy." To do justice to the between, he shifts from analytic to disposition, from projection to affectivity.[50] In Richard Polt's felicitous expression, the *Contributions* has philosophy arise in response to "the emergency of being."[51] What compels philosophy is the experience of need. Heidegger distinguishes two fundamental needs: the sort of experience of the presence of entities that aroused wonder in the hearts of the first philosophers, and the sort of absence of the significance of entities that instills terror in the hearts of today's philosophers. Kant represents the nodal point of the modern tradition insofar as his analyses hearken back to the end of the Greek beginning in the wonder of present entities while implicating the context of being that the first beginning neglected. What is needed is a pathos with a broader scope than wonder that is attentive to what withdraws in the Greek beginning and in the Kantian transcendental recovery of the end of that beginning. He seeks to motivate the requisite disposition by sketching the movement from the wonder of the beginning through the terror of today to the anticipated deepened wonder of another beginning.

The editor of the *Contributions* points to the winter semester 1937–38 lecture course as the indispensable starting point for understanding the difficult project of the *Contributions*.[52] The lecture course is pivotal in Heidegger's thought, and in his famous letter to Father Richardson, Heidegger quotes from the draft of the course to illustrate the shift in his manner of thinking.[53] Both Plato and Aristotle tell us that philosophy begins in the πάθος of wonder, and in the course, Heidegger subjects the *Grundstimmung* of wonder to a prolonged analysis, showing how, within this disposition, the philosopher first found himself faced with entities as entities. Heidegger's analysis finds in the basic structure of wonder a tension that inevitably yields to the unrestrained curiosity of modern science and technology—a tension that inevitably effaces the wondrousness of entities: that they are. Curiously, wonder carries within itself the seeds of its own dissolution. Heidegger bases the reflection on the very logic of disclosure: when entities are given, their givenness necessarily yields to what is given, and what is entirely forgotten is what withdraws in every granting and thereby makes the granting possible. Heidegger gives his analysis of wonder in order to clear the ground for the thinking of that which necessarily withdraws, the mystery that lies at the heart of the "space" or clearing in which entities are given and come to presence. In the first beginning, wonder disclosed entities, and now in the called-for other beginning, a new *Grundstimmung* discloses the mystery that is self-withdrawing.[54] These two beginnings, the first and the other, and the leap from the first to the other, are at the center of Heidegger's later, historical thinking.[55] The interrogation of the first beginning can be understood only in light of what Heidegger understands the other beginning to be. The question of the nature of wonder is the question of the nature of philosophy, past and future,[56] and for Heidegger, the question of the nature of philosophy is nothing other than the question of what is most worthy of thought. The 1937–38 lecture course, *Basic Questions of Philosophy*, deploys an analysis of the tragic limitation of the wonder of the first beginning, which leads to the manifold disposition of the *Contributions*. Wonder inspires the desire to preserve entities in their presence, which simultaneously effects a neglect of the context in which presence occurs and necessarily leads to a decadence in which entities are abandoned by the context of being.

The Affectivity of Thought

In the analysis of wonder in the *Basic Questions* lecture course, Heidegger points to two texts for a greater elaboration of fundamental dispositions. The first is *Being and Time*, but "above all," he says, one should consult his winter semester 1934–35 lecture course on Hölderlin, and it is to this latter text that we now turn.[57] Heidegger warns that a fundamental disposition is no mere feeling or physical lived experience. Neither can it be understood based on traditional anthropology, because such determinations can be made only *within* a fundamental disposition.[58] Rather, fundamental dispositions transport Dasein, placing it into the opening of entities as a whole, and thereby grounding it: "The opening of the world happens in the fundamental disposition. The transporting, inserting, and such opening power of the fundamental disposition is with this simultaneously *grounding*, i.e., it stands Dasein in its ground and before its abyss."[59] Heidegger indicates that the ground is "the expanse of entities" and the abyss is "the depth of be-ing."[60] These four essential components—transporting, inserting, opening, and grounding—are in the simplicity of their unity what Heidegger calls "suspendedness" (*Ausgesetzheit*) [61] in the midst of manifest being as a whole, which itself simultaneously requires "preservation" (*Bewahrung*) of this openness.

In *Basic Questions* three years later, Heidegger identifies "displacement" (*Versetzung*) as the essential character of a disposition.[62] He thinks fundamental dispositions in terms of the "event of appropriation" (*Ereignis*) and need. This need is not a need of "misery and complaint." Rather it is an overflowing gift, which itself gives rise to the highest form of necessity. This need arises from the "distress of not knowing the way out or the way in."[63] There is no *way out* of the whole of entities, since it is all encompassing, and no *way in* to this whole, since it is undifferentiated and precludes focus on any one being in particular. Instead, thinkers stand in this irreducible *between* that opens the place for thought and grounds history: "We call it the fundamental disposition because in disposing man it displaces him into that toward which and in which word, work, and deed, as happenings, can be founded and history can begin."[64]

The new emphasis on affectivity takes on its full significance by contrasting it with his treatment of the topic some ten years earlier in the 1925 summer course, which Kiesel regards as the second, phenomenological draft of *Being and Time*. Heidegger says that the fact that both Husserl and Scheler neglected the question of being was "not accidental," because it was rooted in the falling tendency of Dasein. To pose the question of being, then, amounts to a rebellion: "This means that Dasein in this mode of being of *falling* [*Verfallen*], from which it does not escape, first really comes to its being when it rebels [*aufbäumt*] against this tendency."[65] What motivates this rebellion? "There is a neglect [of the question of being] only because Dasein is defined as *care*."[66] Dasein has within itself concern for its own being. The authentic researcher comes into his or her own by seizing upon this concern and resisting the falling tendency. The structure of care, however, derives normativity from various existential sources and is itself derived from the dynamism of time.[67] In other words even in the ambit of *Being and Time* Heidegger intended to show that the normativity of philosophy derives not from care but from that which constitutes care, what he came to call temporality and then, after the change in approach, the event of appropriation. The problem is that he presents the philosophy as something we choose rather than as something that happens to us. The beginning of philosophy is not a choice rooted in the structure of Dasein; it is the experience of a fundamental disposition. Alongside this choice, phenomenological research undertakes a staged investigation of its phenomenon that implicates its reader into its momentum. Speaking of Husserl's *Logical Investigations*, Heidegger makes a comment equally applicable to the about-to-be-written *Being and Time*:

> Even more unusual than the subject matter and totally contrary to the customary way of philosophizing is the kind of penetration and appropriation which the work demands. It proceeds in a thoroughgoing investigative fashion. It calls for a step-by-step, expressly intuitive envisaging of the matters at issue and a verifying demonstration of them. Accordingly, one cannot, without subverting the entire sense of the investigations, simply pull out results and integrate them into a system. Rather, the whole thrust of the work serves to implicate the reader into pressing further and working through the matters under investigation.[68]

Instead of this step-by-step form of research aimed at unveiling the essence of transcendence, Heidegger now deploys a step-by-step deepening of pathos. The thrust of the work is now not a ground-laying analytic of fundamental ontology but instead the happening of fundamental dispositions.

Each of the stages of the *Contributions* has its own guiding disposition: In the echo stage, "terror" (*Schrecken*) discloses being's abandonment, and "awe" (*Scheu*) occurs before the resonating appropriation. In the playing-forth stage, "delight" (*Lust*) happens in surpassing the beginning in questioning. In the leap stage, "awe" (*Scheu*) sustains nearness to the mystery. In the grounding stage, there is "reservedness" (*Verhaltenheit*) from which all guiding dispositions flow. In contrast to wonder's tragic shortcoming, the fundamental disposition of reservedness heeds the necessary withdrawal of the context of being that enables the presence of entities.

Historical Reflection as Motivation

What is essential to history in Heidegger's mind is not a series of occurrences but the granting of an epoch, a granting that is appropriated by Dasein, and this appropriation alone determines the essence of Dasein. In view of the question of motivating philosophy, Heidegger distinguishes between "historiographical consideration" (*historische Betrachtung*) and "historical reflection" (*geschichtliche Besinnung*). *Historie* belongs to the nonessential sense of (ἀρχή as a beginning, *Beginn*. *Geschichte* corresponds to the fullest sense as an origin, *Ursprung*. Heidegger links *Historie* to its Greek roots in ἱστορεῖν, which means "to explore," and indicates that *Historie* is haunted by a certain arbitrariness, because the past is explored in terms of the present. The past thereby becomes timely, but due to the fleetingness of the present, this timeliness is transitory. As Heidegger expresses it, "the present soon again turns into an other, and timeliness remains the most inconstant."[69] Consequently, every achievement of historiographical science soon becomes dated, and every generation fancies its own historiography to be markedly superior to what has come before. *Historie*, then, is a matter of projection upon the past by the present. By contrast, historical reflection seeks to discern the hidden necessity of the past, a necessity that leaps ahead, as it were, into the future. The former understands the past out of the present, the latter the future out of the past. Historical reflection discerns the *Ursprung* of the past that also determines the future; by discerning this necessity and creatively responding to it, truly historical happenings come to pass.[70] Heidegger's reflection on wonder is an example of it.[71] Historical reflection is Heidegger's way to awaken the *Grundstimmung* of the other beginning by displaying the law or λόγος of that beginning.

Heidegger develops the notion of historical reflection with three basic theses: (1) Historical reflection is futural, because the future itself is original and the source of history; (2) as a source, it is hidden, because it withdraws behind what flows from it; (3) consequently, what is required is a revolutionary stance that unearths the hidden law of the beginning and sets it free for a new beginning. I will explicate each point in turn. First, all happenings are enclosed in the "beginning" *(Anfang)* and this beginning flows out of the future. *"The future is the origin [Ursprung] of history. What is most futural, however, is the great beginning [Anfang], that which—withdrawing itself constantly—reaches back the farthest and at the same time reaches forward the farthest."*[72] Insofar as the *Anfang* is no mere *Beginn*, it does not belong to the past, but in its continual dominance it determines history and stretches forth into the future. In historical reflection we return to the beginning in such a way that we turn to the future and act out of the genuinely futural.

Second, the withdrawing beginning conceals within it a law. The beginning, as inexhaustible and withdrawing, is hidden behind the usual and the habitual that follows upon it. "The ordinary character of what is henceforth the ordinary becomes the lord over what is forever the extraordinary character of the beginning."[73] Creative activity plumbs the depths, reveals the law, and succumbs to its force. Goals of creative activity are decisive if they flow from the inner law of the historical beginning: "The greatness of creative activity takes its measure from the extent of its power to follow up the innermost hidden law of the beginning [*dem innersten verborgenen Gesetz des Anfanges*] and to carry the course of this law to its end."[74] Because it is founded in law, Heidegger can thus say that historical reflection is necessary and is "bound to the past in an essentially more rigorous way than historiography is."[75] Historiography is quite arbitrary and chiefly serves the end of the development of historiographical science and related cognitions. But historical reflection follows the innermost law of the beginning. To the extent that it lives up to its essence historical reflection sounds out the innermost law of the beginning and is seized by its necessity.

Third, we must understand this creative experiencing of the hidden law as revolutionary. The hidden law must be experienced in order to manifest its necessity and enable its creative accomplishment. "The *beginning* is only *acquired* when we *creatively experience [erfahren] its law*, and this law can never become a rule but remains specific and particular, the uniqueness of the necessary. The uniqueness of the necessary is that which, as the most difficult, must ever and again be accomplished completely anew."[76] This experience breaks up the usualness of the usual, which follows in the wake of the beginning and obscures it in its originary greatness. The original relation to the beginning is not preservation or conservation but revolution that overturns the ordinary and unusual and returns to the hidden law of the beginning. Heidegger cautions against a possible misunderstanding: this is no mere destruction but is rather a constructive revolution because it frees the hidden law of the beginning: "Thus the original and genuine relation to the beginning is the revolutionary, which, through the upheaval of the habitual, once again liberates the hidden law of the beginning."[77] To be revolutionary, then, does not mean to attempt something new, but to reattempt what is original and thus futural. It is to tap into the source of the beginning in order to begin again by breaking through the ossification of what trails in the wake of the beginning. To begin *(Anfangen)* "means: to think and to act from the perspective of the future and of what is extraordinary, and from the renunciation of the crutches and evasions of the habitual and the usual."[78] To begin is no mere imitation but because it is originary it is unique and yet the same: "And because the original [*Ursprüngliche*] belongs to the beginning [*Anfang*], the restructuring of the beginning is never the poor imitation of what was earlier; it is entirely other and nevertheless the same."[79] Historical reflection aims to experience the original law of the beginning and thereby experience the necessity of effecting another beginning. Man is historical because in freedom he can respond to the necessity: "Only man is historical—as that being which, exposed [*ausgesetzt*] to entities as a whole, and in commerce with these entities, sets himself free in the midst of necessity."[80] The breaking up of the usual and habitual and the initiation of a beginning form some of the core features of wonder. Wonder is the revolutionary *Grundstimmung* that enables the first beginning.

What is critical for historical reflection is the open region of happening, which is the very meaning of history. In "reflection" *(Be-sinnung)*, Heidegger thinks together "historical" *(geschichtlich)* and "happening" *(das Geschehen)* on the basis of their unity in the open region.

> The word "historical" [*geschichtlich*] means "happening" [*das Geschehen*], history itself as an entity. . . . We will not speak here of historical "considerations" but "reflection." For reflection [*Be-sinnung*] is a looking for the meaning [*Sinn*] of a happening, the meaning of history. "Meaning" refers here to the *open region* [offenen Bereich] of goals, standards, impulses, decisive possibilities, and powers—all these belonging *essentially* to happening.[81]

The centrality of openness roots historical reflection within the reflection on *Grundstimmung* as the opening of the "*Da*" of *Da*-sein. Those who creatively grasp the hidden law of the past and thus the future—the poet, architect, thinker, and statesman—"accomplish the opening up [*Eröffnung*] and the new foundation [*Neugründung*] of history."[82] Heidegger sees reflection as a way of awakening *Grundstimmungen*.[83] We now turn to his attempt to awaken the needed *Grundstimmung* by a reflection on the *Grundstimmung* of the first beginning: wonder.

As Heidegger has it, the beginning was so taken by the unconcealedness of being that the interplay of concealedness and unconcealedness or ἀλήθεια as such, could not be brought explicitly to thought:

> The question of the Greeks, the primordial question about entities, is of such a kind that it precludes the questioning of ἀλήθεια as such. For unconcealedness is the determination of entities that in general and in advance constitutes the horizon [*Gesichtskreis*] within which become possible the manifestation [*Herausstellung*] of the characters of entities we mentioned and hence the fulfillment of the question of entities. In order to bring into view what resides in a horizon, the horizon itself must precisely light up first, so that it might illuminate what resides within it; however, it cannot and may not be seen explicitly. The horizon, ἀλήθεια, *must* in a certain sense be overlooked.[84]

Recollecting the first beginning, we are prepared for a new beginning because the need for a newer and deeper beginning has come to view; this new beginning will be given the task of thinking ἀλήθεια as such and thereby safeguarding its essence and truth. Just as in the first beginning the horizon had to be missed, today the horizon *must* be made explicit, a necessity that can be felt only within a prolonged reflection on the necessity and need of the first beginning in the *Grundstimmung* of wonder.

The Rhetoric or Poetics of Being

Heidegger deploys the reflection on wonder in order to initiate his audience into the other beginning. Only by situating the reflection on wonder within the problem of initiation will its multiple components be fully understood.[85] In this section, I will understand Heidegger's analysis of wonder in the context of his project to bring about a philosophy faithful to philosophy's true subject matter. Within this context, I argue that the categories of rhetoric of being and tragedy are helpful for the elucidation of Heidegger's project of initiation into the disposition that will disclose that subject matter. I show that the effectiveness of both the rhetoric of being and the tragic rely on the law of the beginning, which is the logic of disclosure, ἀλήθεια.

What both rhetoric and the tragic have as an end is the evocation of πάθος in the listener or the spectator.[86] Rhetoric has as one of its devices the swaying of the passions so that the auditor might be properly disposed to the speaker's judgments. In the rhetoric of being, a similar change must be effected insofar as it is a question of being properly disposed to the subject matter. The tragic, too, ignites the passions, and the tragic in Heidegger's thought serves the *Grundstimmung* that discloses the matter to be thought; the rhetoric of being is at the same time the *poetics* of being.[87] It is with this focus on πάθος that we speak of Heidegger's rhetoric of being and the tragic character of the *Grundstimmung* of wonder that he presents. Heidegger's aim is to make needful within a new disposition the other beginning that will finally be adequate to the true matter of thinking. Both terms, the rhetoric of being and the tragic, go beyond what Heidegger himself said in an attempt to make sense of his thought.[88]

The rhetoric of being is necessary because a *Grundstimmung* cannot be willed by Dasein but must happen beyond and before the initiative of Dasein.[89] The rhetoric of being regards the manner of initiation into the matter of thinking, an initiation that must come about through the highest necessity. The tragic regards the character of what is given to thinking in the first beginning, marked as it is by an inner tension between φύσις and τέχνη that inevitably leads to a "falling off" *(Abfall).*[90] However great the first beginning was, Heidegger discloses an inevitability within its very logic or law that leads to a decadence. The tragic is a device Heidegger deploys to serve his overall project of a rhetoric of being. Indeed, in his analysis of the tension that leads to the falling off of Greek wonder and the consequent task for today, he asks rhetorically whether this shift from the past to the present occurred in the course of the reflection or whether the reflection did not concern the present and only the present from the beginning.[91] What we call the tragic serves to make us ready for the disposition needed today.

The Tragedy of Wonder's Inevitable Decadence

In *Basic Questions*, §§36–38, Heidegger discerns a tension between intentionality and its ground—or as he now calls it, τέχνη and φύσις—a tension that inevitably leads to the decadence of "wonder" *(Er-staunen)* in philosophy's beginning.[92] Heidegger discloses this tension in his articulation of wonder's essence in order to awaken the necessary need and fundamental disposition of the other beginning. Allow me to trace briefly the movement of the thirteen-point exposition of wonder. In the first six points, he exhibits the character of wonder phenomenally. In wonder the usual becomes no longer obvious but universally *unusual.* The uprooting of the usual in turn gives rise to the philosophical "between" as a domain. In the seventh point, he notes that wonder *places* human beings into the domain it opens. In subsequent points, he exhibits several characteristics of wonder that follow from its role as the grounding disposition. Since it first opens up the possibility of bringing entities into presence, wonder itself is inexplicable, unconscious, necessary, and beyond human agency.[93]

In the final two points, the analysis culminates in the tension between (1) preservation of entities in presence by means of τέχνη and (2) φύσις's own character as presencing *and* absencing. In wonder itself there lies the "danger" *(Gefahr)* of its own dissolution into arbitrariness. Φύσις is such that τέχνη must work against it, and within this basic opposition lies the possibility of breaking out of the necessity and primordial need of the fundamental disposition.[94] Truth then becomes understood as correctness—the agreement of present things—instead of the full interplay of unconcealing and concealing indicated by the Greek term for truth, ἀ-λήθεια. Wonder's decadence is unavoidable, because the experienced interplay of presencing and absencing is not thought as such and so cannot be preserved.

In the *Contributions*, Heidegger addresses the tension between τέχνη and φύσις in greater detail.[95] Τέχνη is essentially related to φύσις but in a subordinate and complementary fashion.[96] Τέχνη is founded upon φύσις and takes for its own what originally belongs to φύσις: "φύσις is not τέχνη, i.e., now what belongs to τέχνη; the well-versed look ahead into εἶδος and *re*-presenting and bringing before oneself of the outward look is precisely what happens *by itself* in φύσις, in ὂν ᾗ ὄν."[97] Τέχνη constitutes the necessary response to the surging forth into presence of entities, where ὄν is experienced as φύσις, emergence. Τέχνη names the basic relation to entities as such, and this relation is a human "anticipation" *(Vorgriff)*.[98] Along with assertion and certainty, τέχνη determines in advance the horizon for the interpretation of the beingness of things. Heidegger calls for "the great turning around" *(die große Umkehrung)* of the fundamental orientation of humans in τέχνη toward entities so that humans no longer ground entities, but rather humans are grounded in terms of being.[99] This will require a complete transformation of the relations to entities and being as well as strength for creating, suffering, and questioning. In short, this entails a new fundamental disposition.

The decadence of the first beginning is unavoidable: "In this way, the beginning contains in itself the unavoidable necessity that, in unfolding, it must surrender its originality."[100] What makes it unavoidable is that ἀλήθεια itself remains by necessity unquestioned and thus able to be forgotten. In this decadence, entities become determined according to their appearances, which as ideas become the standard for judging the entities themselves:

> In the beginning, the question of entities stays within the clarity of ἀλήθεια as the basic character of entities. Ἀλήθεια itself, however, remains by necessity unquestioned. But the sustaining of the beginning position in the sense of τέχνη leads to a falling away [*Abfall*] from the beginning. Entities become, to exaggerate somewhat, objects of representations conforming to them.[101]

What is noteworthy is the uncharacteristic admission "to exaggerate somewhat" that is missing from his more public works, such as "Plato's Doctrine of Truth." Nevertheless, the brunt of the claim remains despite its exaggeration: because ἀλήθεια could not at first be thought as such it inevitably become calcified as conformity of correct representations and not as unconcealedness and emergence. There is, then, an unmistakably *tragic* character of wonder as the first beginning, when thought in terms of the necessity of the decadence. Buried within wonder as the first beginning is the tragic flaw that leads to its own dissolution. The wondrous emergence of entities fatefully and inevitably yields to pure on-hand entities. Heidegger will maintain this tragic assessment of wonder through his last seminars. Thirty years later, in the 1969 seminar at Thor he says: "In the Greek climate, the human is so overwhelmed by the presencing of what presences, that he is compelled to the question concerning what presences *as* what presences. The Greeks name the relation to this thrust of presence θαυμάζειν."[102]

Heidegger recollects this tension as part of his rhetoric of being with the intention of evoking the needed disposition by making it needful. Heidegger also turns to the beginning to offer an alternative to Nietzsche's understanding of the root causes of nihilism. This is the reason why in the midst of his Nietzsche lectures that span from 1936–1942, Heidegger takes a semester to sound out the history of truth and the necessity of its decadence. The end we experience today in the fall from unconcealedness to correctness in truth was precipitated by a corresponding fall, a necessary fall, into the forgetfulness of being. We can turn from man's forgetfulness to what founds it—the granting and withdrawal—and say that today we face the complete abandonment of entities by being. Nietzsche did not fully understand nihilism and interpreted the phenomenon superficially:

> What if the abandonment of entities by being were the most hidden and most proper ground, and the essence, of what Nietzsche first recognized as "nihilism" and interpreted in terms of "morality" and the "ideal," in the fashion of the philosophy of Plato and Schopenhauer, but did not yet understand *metaphysically?*[103]

Heidegger tells us that by "metaphysically" he means according to the essential happenings of Western thinking, which alone is the site where nihilism can be surpassed. The lack felt today is the result of this falling off, and the task today is not to duplicate the fall by reestablishing ourselves in wonder. Rather, the task today is to think in such a way that all falling off is precluded. Ἀλήθεια must be thought as such; or if ἀλήθεια belongs more to the essence of entities than to truth,[104] we must instead think the clearing that enables ἀλήθεια, the one that was "hardly surmised or heeded" in wonder.

The Affective Need to Counter Wonder's Tragic End

Heidegger says our age is unique in that there is no need or necessity to propel us into a fundamental disposition. We carry on philosophical reflection out of an obligation to the past and a tradition we could not initiate today.[105] In an age in which all is obvious and nothing is questionable, philosophy itself becomes by necessity a mere curiosity.[106] Heidegger does propose, however, that our lack of need could itself be the need that could found the necessity and fundamental disposition of a new beginning.

> What if the abandonment of entities by being, that entities still "are" and yet being and its truth remain denied to entities and consequently to man . . . what if this event [*Ereignis*] which proceeds out of entities as a whole were the concealed ground of the still veiled fundamental disposition which compels us into another necessity of another original questioning and beginning?[107]

In *Basic Questions*, terror (radicalized as *Er-schrecken*) along with awe, reservedness, and intimating, names the one fundamental disposition of the new beginning. In the *Contributions* as in *Basic Questions*, Heidegger identifies "reservedness" as the primary designation for the new fundamental disposition: "What does it mean to be placed before *self-concealing*, refusal, hesitation, and to be steadfast in its *open*? [It means] *reservedness* and thus fundamental disposition: terror, reservedness, awe."[108] He cautions that the manifold of names should not be seen as undermining the simplicity of the fundamental disposition but rather as indicating the incomprehensibility of all that is simple.[109] Terror, awe, and intimation are guiding dispositions that belong essentially to the one grounding disposition of reservedness.[110] In *Basic Questions* and *Contributions*, Heidegger's analysis of these dimensions of the fundamental disposition is quite cursory and not on the level of the careful analysis of angst in *Being and Time* or even the reflection on wonder. But as he writes in *Contributions*, "This fundamental disposition is not to be described so much as to be effected."[111]

1. Terror (*Erschrecken*). Terror discloses the opening in such a way that the withdrawal can be grasped *as* withdrawal (i.e., as mystery). It is thus essentially deeper than wonder, which could never bring the withdrawal to thought and focused only on what was granted in the withdrawal, namely the presencing of entities into presence. There is no simple opposition here but rather a kind of complementarity and mutual penetration:

> It would be a very extrinsic conception of these various fundamental dispositions if we would see in wonder [*Er-staunen*] only inclination [*Lust*] and jubilation and seek terror [*Erschrecken*] in the nebulous

realm of aversion [*Unlust*], grief, and despair. Just as wonder bears in itself its own sort of terror [*Schrecken*], so does terror involve its own mode of self-composure, calm steadfastness, and new wonder [*Staunen*].[112]

Wonder's terror is the threat of the absencing of what has come to presence, which leads to the great labor to keep present what presences. Terror's wonder is not yet evident, and we should turn to Heidegger's development of the disposition in order to bring it to light.

Wonder discloses entities and lets them stand in their form. Such a disclosure inevitably leads to curiosity and our domination of entities. Terror breaks through such a preoccupation and shows the meaninglessness of such an orientation. What becomes wondrous is that entities can be at all while the truth of being is forgotten.[113] How can entities be if abandoned by being? How can they continue to be without being grounded? Moreover, why is it that such a ground is everywhere thought to be superfluous? Terror, then, harbors wonder at the lack of genuine wonder and concern for being in our preoccupation with entities. What remains unquestioned because obvious is the nature of the primal openness: "No one thinks to ask how entities as entities come into the open and what this opening might be."[114] Thus terror opens upon deeper ground than wonder's ontology. Here the subject matter is not Aristotle's entities as entities. Rather, the subject matter is the primal opening in which entities as entities can be disclosed.

In terror there is a sort of inversion[115] from wonder's presence of presencing (which degenerates into sheer presence of what is present) to the presence of absencing—but this inversion is not an inversion in being but the unfolding of its own essence along with humanity's entering deeper into its mystery. "The *first* beginning thinks being as presence from within a presencing which manifests the first flash of *the one* essential swaying of be-ing."[116] Terror, like wonder, is attuned to the giving of being, but it recognizes in the withdrawal the highest gift.

2. Awe *(Scheu)*. Terror discloses being's abandonment, and awe preserves and conserves what is continually disclosed in terror. Awe is a way of drawing near and remaining near to the distant as such. It discloses "what is remotest, namely that in entities, and before each being, be-ing holds sway [*das Seyn west*]."[117] In the 1943 essay on Hölderlin's poem "Remembrance," Heidegger devotes a full page to awe. Hölderlin's "many / are awed in going to the source" provokes Heidegger's reflection. To be in awe is to be patient and to let the origin be:

> Awe is that reserved, patient, astonished remembrance of that which remains near in a nearness which consists solely in keeping something distant in its fullness, and thereby keeping it ready for its arising from its source. This essential awe is the disposition of a homecoming

which *thinks and remembers* the origin. Awe is the knowledge that the origin cannot be directly experienced.[118]

Awe opens itself to the mystery and cherishes its mysteriousness as such.[119] It is not rushed or eager but slow and reserved: "It is the fundamental disposition of the holidays for the slow paths."[120]

3. Intimating *(Er-ahnen).* In *Basic Questions*, Heidegger does not specifically mention intimation as a dimension of the new fundamental disposition, but nonetheless it plays an important role in evoking the disposition in its fullness: "Only after our thinking has undergone this transformation of attitude [i.e., the leap] by means of historical reflection, will we intimate [*ahnen*], in an auspicious moment, that already in our discussions another essence of truth, and perhaps indeed only that, was at issue."[121] Intimation, then, is a kind of insight into the hidden nature of essential happenings: "There are only a very few who in the course of this history of the dissolution of the beginning have remained awake and intimate what has transpired."[122] We could perhaps say, then, that what was wondrously experienced in the unfolding of the first beginning will now be understood: instead of wondering at what is present, intimation understands what withdraws.[123] Heidegger says that intimation opens up the expanse of the concealing.[124] It is "the hesitant *sheltering* of the unconcealing of the hidden as such, of the refusal."[125] It can therefore understand philosophy's proper subject matter without the threat of decadence.

4. Reservedness *(Verhaltenheit).* In reservedness, the dominant name for the grounding disposition, terror is not overcome but is preserved in awe.[126] Reservedness determines the style for the thinking that is to come,[127] a thinking in which the mystery of the essential sway of truth becomes the most worthy of questioning.[128] Reservedness is the "predisposing of preparedness for refusal as gifting."[129] This preparedness is the strongest and gentlest readiness for standing within the essential sway of truth, "the turning in the event of appropriation" *(der Kehre im Ereignis).*[130] The steadfastness of the turning in the event *(Er-eignis)* is "ownhood" *(Eigen-tum),* and it is this ownhood that grounds reservedness.[131] "What does it mean, to 'stand' ['*stehen*'] in the clearing of concealing and to sustain [*ausstehen*] it? It means *fundamental disposition of reservedness, the outstanding and historical uniqueness of this inabiding* [Inständigkeit], that here above all 'what is true' is decided."[132] Reservedness, Heidegger says, is the very ground of care, now specified as *for the sake of being* rather than humans.[133] It serves as such a ground because it is attuned to stillness: the stillness of the passing of the last god, the stillness of the sheltering of truth, the stillness of strife between the clearing and the concealing, the world and the earth.[134] In reservedness, humans are the guardians of the stillness that was not grasped in wonder.

Even though Heidegger sees in the original form of wonder a critical shortcoming, the fundamental disposition that discloses the mystery hidden by that wonder, the fundamental disposition of the other beginning, is also a kind of wonder. What is thought in the other beginning was in fact experienced—however obliquely—in wonder's beginning. Because it avoids the necessary decadence of the first wonder, the fundamental disposition adequate to the mystery of the withdrawal is in fact a deepened wonder: "In the other beginning, the first is experienced more originally and is restored to its greatness."[135]

Heidegger indicates the continuity of the first and the other beginning in a number of places, and it is worth noting some of these, for they show that Heidegger does not reject the first beginning but in transcending it, he retains and deepens it.[136] Discussing Hölderlin, Heidegger has occasion to identify the fundamental disposition of the other beginning as wonder. With the setting aside of work in human celebration and in keeping to ourselves, we can be transported into a realm opened by terror, awe, and wonder *(Erstaunen)*.[137] Again, while meditating on the event of appropriation and language in Heraclitus, Heidegger asks whether Heraclitus, in his questioning way, has glimpsed the essential relations of gods, humans, and the clearing.

> In this case the fragment, with its questioning, could give voice to the thoughtful wonder [*das denkende Erstaunen*], which stands expectantly before that relation wherein the clearing takes the essential sway of gods and men unto itself. The questioning saying would then correspond to what remains ever and again worthy of thoughtful wonder and remains preserved in its worth by thoughtful wonder.[138]

Heidegger thereby indicates the continued vitality of a "thoughtful" wonder—that is, an authentic wonder that is adequate to the mystery of the event of appropriation. Wonder, then, has not been superseded but finally given its authentic form. As he writes in *Basic Questions*, "To say philosophy originates in wonder means philosophy is wondrous in its essence and becomes more wondrous the more it becomes what it really is."[139] To glimpse the tragic character of the original wonder is to feel the pull of a deeper wonder.

4 The Ambiguity of Transcendental Philosophy

Both Heidegger's own transcendental philosophy and Heidegger's interpretation of Kant's transcendental philosophy are needed to lead to the domain of Heidegger's later thinking, but both fall short of Heidegger's later being-historical thinking. Kant approaches, but does not attain, Heidegger's transcendental project in *Being and Time*, and Heidegger's transcendental project in *Being and Time* approaches, but does not attain,

Heidegger's later historical thinking. Kantian transcendental philosophy arrives at the domain of presence, but due to its neglect of fundamental dispositions, it cannot fathom and safeguard the necessary withdrawal that enables the presence of entities; it brings only part of the domain to light. It successfully leads to the domain but is finally inadequate for the domain. Heidegger's transcendental philosophy attends to fundamental dispositions but accords them only a methodological significance in terms of unveiling the transcendental structures of Dasein through the resolve of the philosophical researcher. It successfully leads to the affective domain, but it brings only part of the domain to light. It does in fact grant entrance to the domain to be thought, but there remains the need to shift from analytic to disposition, recognizing that philosophy happens thanks to something that happens to the philosopher, not thanks to something he or she can initiate.

As we have seen, the predominant view is that in the 1930s Heidegger's thinking makes a decisive "turn," and this turn is *away* from transcendental philosophy in either its Heideggerian or Kantian forms *toward* being-historical thinking. The preceding chapter demonstrates, however, that according to Heidegger's own way of thinking, Kantian transcendental philosophy fulfills a crucial transitional role. Precisely because it is transitional, though, it is treated by Heidegger in an ambiguous fashion: in some contexts it is lauded and in others rejected. On the one hand, Kant takes a "transcendental step beyond Descartes," and on the other hand, the "transcendental" motif seems to be in the tradition of Descartes.[140] This plays out in Heidegger's assessment of his own transcendental philosophy and in his assessment of Kant's. Kant proves to be a transition to the transitional form of Heidegger's transcendental thinking.

After *Being and Time*, Heidegger aimed to think the ontological difference between being and entities and to think its origin. In the *Contributions*, he says that it is transcendental thinking that discloses the ontological difference. But he also says that transcendentally thinking the difference does not disclose the truth of be-ing; instead it projects merely the entity-ness of the entity. "Therefore, the effort was needed to come free of the 'condition for the possibility' as going back into the merely 'mathematical' and to grasp the truth of be-ing from within its *own* essential sway (appropriation)."[141] Heidegger also insists that transcendental projection's ontological difference is *essential* for beginning the inquiry into being. Transcendental philosophy, then, has the ambiguity of being both necessary and limiting: "For as necessary as this distinction is (to think in traditional terms), in order to provide at all a preliminary perspective for the question of be-ing, just as disastrous does this distinction continue to be."[142]

To cut this Gordian knot, Heidegger proposes the figure of the "leap" (*Sprung*). The task is no longer to think transcendence as the surpassing of entities but instead to "leap over this distinction" and "to inquire inceptually into be-ing and truth."[143] The leap thereby settles an ambiguity in *Being and Time*. There "understanding of being" means both the transcendental thinking of entity-ness and the thrown openness of "being-here" (Da-sein).[144] In the leap, then, the first sense dissolves into the second; transcendental projection yields to being appropriated as the thrown openness of Da-sein.[145] Now, it is tempting to focus on the terminus of the leap instead of its start. But the start proves to be indispensable, and Heidegger recognizes that both the ontological difference and the transcendental thinking that registers the distinction play crucial preparatory roles.

Heidegger explicitly says that the transcendental way is provisional and preparatory: "The *transcendental* way (but another 'transcendence') only provisionally, in order to prepare the reversing-momentum and leaping-into."[146] And yet this is an unavoidable transition: "When coming from the horizon of metaphysics, there is at first no other way even to make the question of being graspable as a task."[147] Having followed transcendence and that means the understanding of being to the end, Heidegger now stands in the turning of the truth of being and being of truth. Since, however, Da-sein "originally sustains the openness of sheltering-concealing," there is no longer any need to speak of surpassing entities and thus "strictly speaking one cannot speak of a transcendence of Da-sein; in the vicinity of this approach presentation of transcendence in *every* sense must *disappear*."[148]

Transcendental philosophy's ontological difference is especially important in reading the history of philosophy. The purpose of the ontological difference is to show that "the attempt at a more originary question of being must be a more essential adoption of the history of metaphysics."[149] In this case, the guiding question about entities can, on the basis of the ontological difference, become the grounding question about being. " 'Ontological difference' is a passageway that becomes unavoidable if the necessity of asking the grounding question out of the guiding question is to be made manifest."[150] Ontological difference, then, primarily names the task of engaging the philosophical tradition in a transitional way, and not surprisingly the center of that engagement will be transcendental philosophy where the distinction first emerges.

In sum, transcendental philosophy and its ontological difference is transitional, and consequently Heidegger ambiguously insists both on its necessity and on the importance of leaping over it:

> But in thinking in the crossing, we must sustain this ambiguity: *on the one hand* to begin an initial clarification with this distinction and *then* to leap over this very distinction. But this leaping over occurs along with the *leap* as the grounding of the ground of the truth of be-ing, by leaping into the appropriation of Da-sein.[151]

The transition between these two ways and the resulting ambiguity form the backdrop for understanding the still further level of ambiguity operative in the hermeneutic of his Kant interpretations.

Conclusion

Even in the throes of Herculean efforts to leap over the shadow of his earlier embrace of the transcendental tradition, Heidegger remains ensnared. For the leap to another beginning must be motivated, and the best motive turns out to be an engagement with the transcendental tradition including Kant and especially the Heidegger of *Being and Time*. Both are necessary to lead into the later thinking, but both fall short. Heidegger recommends Kant to lead beyond isolated judgment to its context and thereby motivate a philosophy that experiences the unity of being and thought; for our contemporary way of thinking, beholden as it is to the modern, mathematical manner of apprehending things, Kant's transcendental turn is the gateway to Heidegger's thinking. Heidegger recommends the published portion of *Being and Time* to lead beyond the subject-object relation to the transcendental between constituted by care and disclosed by angst. But in keeping with the original intention of *Being and Time*, he calls for a turn from transcendence as a movement originating with Dasein to a movement that is anterior to Dasein. He takes transcendence up within a more comprehensive understanding of the dynamic interplay of Dasein and its domain.

The 1946 *Letter on Humanism* again invokes the "between" in the very sense developed in the revised Kant book: "[T]he human being in his essence is ek-sistent into the openness of being, into the open region that first clears the 'between' within which a 'relation' of subject to object can 'be.' "[152] The quotation marks indicate that such language is not "strictly speaking" adequate, for our essence does not lie in the subject-object relation as such but derives from the opening up of the open itself.[153] It is important to note that Heidegger is careful to qualify his criticisms of transcendental philosophy. He distances himself "from every merely *transcendental* way of knowing" and suggests that transcendental philosophy "has not yet been thought being-historically."[154] The "strictly speaking," "merely," and "not yet" say that transcendental philosophy is not opposed to being-historical thinking but only that it can and must be rethought from within the experience of being appropriated.

This chapter warrants the following conclusion: Heidegger does not disavow transcendental philosophy. He knew quite well he could not, because transcendental questioning is necessary for arriving at the domain of thinking; the Kantian return of judgment to the between undermines the logical and mathematical prejudices and readies for the analytic of Dasein; the Heideggerian return of the between to the context of world and its constitution through ecstatic timeliness readies for the experience of appropriation. The final domain, first disclosed transcendentally, is richer than transcendental philosophy could fathom, but it still remains a domain arrived at by transcendental thinking.

When *Being and Time* was at the printer's, the founder of phenomenology said something about the relation of the book to Heidegger that was so insightful it proved to be prophetic: ". . . you are blessed with the great fortune of having in press the book with which you grow into what you are and, as you well know, have given your own being as a philosopher its first realization. Beginning with this book you will blossom into new dimensions."[155] Husserl saw right away that this book was both deeply personal and transitional: only the *first* realization which as a beginning will in time afford him the possibility of seeing beyond its necessary limitation in a second realization. Husserl's prescient suggestion, this chapter demonstrates, became Heidegger's own. Heidegger's shadow is the first realization that both opens up new avenues and binds him to a determinate beginning. "For every great thinker always *thinks* one leap more originally than he directly *speaks*."[156] To leap over the shadow means to try to catch up in speech to the thought that always outstrips it. Books are written to be transgressed, such that the transgression fulfills rather than undermines the work.

Notes

1 GA 41, 153/150.
2 GA 10, 105/71, my emphases. Merleau-Ponty uses Heidegger's discussion of the unthought in other philosophers in order to characterize a movement in Husserl from rationalism to the embodied lifeworld. See "The Philosopher and His Shadow," in *Signs*, trans. Richard C. McCleary (Northwestern, IL: Northwestern University Press, 1964), 159–81.
3 GA 94, 219.
4 GA 10, 105/71.
5 GA 94, 234.
6 GA 94, 235.
7 *Heidegger's 'Contributions to Philosophy': An Introduction* (Bloomington, IN: Indiana University Press, 2003), 28. Dahlstrom and Malpas provide instructive overviews of Heidegger's criticisms of transcendental philosophy in the *Contributions*. See "Heidegger's Transcendentalism," 37–44, and "Heidegger's Topology," 126–34, respectively.
8 GA 65, 217–18/110.
9 GA 20, 347/252.
10 GA 24, 468/329.
11 GA 24, 404/285. Beierwaltes rightfully observes that the transcendence of Dasein is not compatible with the authentic Platonic transcendence. Werner Beierwaltes, "*Epekeina*. A Remark on Heidegger's Reception of Plato," trans. Marcus Brainard, *Graduate Faculty Philosophy Journal* 17 (1994): 83–99.
12 GA 24, 405/285–6.
13 "What could the idea of the good have to do with production? Without entering further into this matter, we offer only the hint that the idea agathou is nothing but the demiourgos, the producer pure and simple. This lets us see

already how the idea agathou is connected with poiein, praxis, techne in the broadest sense." GA 24, 405/286.

14 GA 24, 463/325.

15 GA 24, 463–4/326.

16 GA 24, 464–5/326.

17 GA 24, 465/327.

18 GA 24, 467–8/328.

19 GA 24, 468–9/329–30.

20 GA 9f, 357/271.

21 I agree with Robert Dostal that Heidegger's Plato misses the mark: "But Heidegger does not see that, rather like his own notion of transcendence that grounds intentionality, so too Plato's notion of *eros* grounds *logos*. In the 'erotic mania' of philosophy one comes to stand outside oneself and in the truth. Heidegger would call this the ecstatic character of Dasein." "Beyond Being: Heidegger's Plato," *Journal of the History of Philosophy* 23 (1985): 96.

22 GA 65, 8/6–7.

23 GA 65, 315/221.

24 GA 65, 447–8/315.

25 GA 65, 176/123–4.

26 See GA 65, 470–1/331 among other passages.

27 GA 65, 484/341.

28 "What does it mean that at the end of the analytic of principles the 'modalities' are dealt with, thus pre-determining everything that has gone before?" GA 65, 279/196.

29 GA 65, 279/196.

30 GA 41, 184/180. In 1955, Heidegger will say that Heisenberg arrived at this same view somewhat independently of Kant and yet in such a way that his insight can only be thought by means of "the transcendental realm." See GA 9g, 402/304.

31 GA 41, 47/49.

32 GA 65, 468/330. As a consequence of this reference to subjectivity, Kant's interpretation of space and time as intuitions is "a weak attempt to rescue what is ownmost to space and time." GA 65, 70/49. See also GA 65, 208/145 and 373/261.

33 Cf. GA 65, 217/151.

34 GA 65, 253/178.

35 In the *Contributions*, Heidegger thinks that Kant's great virtue is that he brings being into relation with time, but he finally remains bound to the logical and mathematical prejudices so the truth of be-ing is "unquestionable." GA 65, 254/179. He takes thinking as "presentation of something in general" on the basis of categories and the table of judgments. GA 65, 215/150.

36 GA 65, 93–4/64–5.

37 GA 65, 315/221.

38 GA 65, 202–3/142.

39 GA 65, 176/123.

40 GA 65, 448/315. See Schalow, *Heidegger-Kant Dialogue*, 318.

41 GA 65, 176/123. Heidegger says that we need to understand Kant's determination of appearance as object in order that we may leave objectivity behind and thereby "experience the appearing of the appearance . . . originally." *Unterwegs zur Sprache*, 132–3/37–8. This happens by means of our returning to the Greeks and more originally thinking the clearing as such.

42 GA 65, 448/315 and 379–88/264–71.

43 GA 65, 312/219.

44 GA 65, 448/315.

45 In Kant and German Idealism, the solipsistic ego is already reshaped in "a referential dependence on the 'we'." GA 65, 68/47.

46 GA 65, 448/315–6.

47 GA 65, 279/196.

48 GA 65, 10/12.

49 GA 65, 425–6/300.

50 See Robert E. Wood, "The Fugal lines of Heidegger's *Beiträge*," *Existentia* 9 (2001): 253–66.

51 *The Emergency of Being: On Heidegger's* Contributions to Philosophy (Ithaca: Cornell University Press, 2006).

52 "Among the lecture courses of the 1930s whose study is a prerequisite for the necessary enactment of *Contributions to Philosophy*, the *Basic Questions of Philosophy: Selected 'Problems' of 'Logic'* (from WS 1937–38) towers above everything else. For, by unfolding in this lecture course the question of truth as the preliminary question for the grounding question of being, Heidegger communicates an essential thought process of *Contributions to Philosophy*—in lecture style, thus meeting the demands of academic teaching. Thus the study of this lecture text . . . is the most important and immediate preparation for understanding *Contributions to Philosophy*." GA 65, 364/513.

53 See William Richardson's *Heidegger: Through Phenomenology to Thought*, 2nd ed. (The Hague: Martinus Nijhoff, 1967), xx–xxi. The drafts for the course are included as an appendix to the lecture course in GA 45.

54 Richard Velkley fruitfully situates Heidegger's call for a new beginning in the modern tradition, inaugurated by Rousseau, of searching for the unitary ground of prediscursive wholeness. See his *Being after Rousseau*, especially 6–8, 26–7, and 138–50.

55 George Seidel traces Heidegger's distinction between a "first beginning" and "another beginning" to Schelling and German Idealism. There the "first beginning" is creation and the other is the Incarnation. "Heidegger's Last God and the Schelling Connection," *Laval Théologique et Philosophique* 55 (1999): 95–6.

56 Aristotle recognizes the connection of wonder and the nature of philosophy and in his introduction to first philosophy he helps to delineate philosophy's nature and subject matter as theoretical by appeal to the nature of wonder. Philosophy, as truly theoretical science, proceeds to relieve the pangs of ignorance and has no practical utility. *Metaphysics*, 982b12ff.

57 Heidegger speaks of the specific task of the poet—that is, Hölderlin, who must awaken the fundamental disposition of holy sorrow *(heilige Trauer)* at the flight of the gods. This is not the task of the thinker, a task Heidegger here passes over: "If philosophy is ready for a task, then it can only be determined out of its ownmost necessity, i.e., in the Graeco-German sending, out of which thinking steps forth from its own origin in the original dialogue with poetry and its need. Our interpretation here serves only the poet; it leaves the thoughtful and his necessities, i.e., his need, knowingly unsaid." GA 39, 151. Heidegger's deferral will later be fulfilled with his analysis of philosophy's beginning in the fundamental disposition of wonder.

58 GA 39, 139.

59 GA 39, 141.

60 GA 39, 142. *Die Weite des Seienden* and *die Tiefe des Seyns*, respectively.

61 Michel Haar translates this term into French as "*exposition.*" "*Stimmung et pensée,*" in *Heidegger et l'idée de la phénoménologie* (Dordrecht: Kluwer Academic Publishers, 1988), 272.

62 GA 45, 161/139.
63 GA 45, 160/139 and 153/133.
64 GA 45, 170/147. Translation modified.
65 GA 20, 179–80/130.
66 GA 20, 185/136.
67 GA 20, 440–2/318–20.
68 GA 20, 32/26.
69 GA 45, 35/33. Translation slightly modified.
70 But this is not to ignore the value of historiography, which is indispensable if determined out of historical reflection: "Historiographical considerations are essential only insofar as they are supported by a historical reflection, are directed by it in their very way of questioning, and are determined by it in the delimitation of their tasks. But this also implies the converse, that historiographical considerations and cognitions are indeed indispensable." GA 45, 50/46.
71 GA 45, 49/45.
72 GA 45, 40/38.
73 GA 45, 40/38.
74 GA 45, 36–37/35.
75 GA 45, 49/45.
76 GA 45, 41/39.
77 GA 45, 37/35.
78 GA 45, 41/38.
79 GA 45, 41/39.
80 GA 45, 36/34.
81 GA 45, 35–36/34.
82 GA 45, 43/40.
83 Historical reflection stands between optimism and pessimism and seeks to prepare for the authentic reception of a fundamental disposition: "[H]istorical reflection works toward the preparation of a historical existence which lives up to the *greatness* of fate, to the peak moments of being." GA 45, 55/50.
84 GA 45, 147/127–28. Translation modified.
85 This does not seem to be a theme that other commentators have identified. See Klaus Held, "Fundamental Moods and Heidegger's Critique of Contemporary Culture," trans. Anthony J. Steinbock, in *Reading Heidegger: Commemorations*, ed. John Sallis (Bloomington: Indiana University Press, 1993), 287–303; Michel Haar, *Heidegger and the Essence of Man*, trans. William McNeill (Albany, NY: State University of New York Press, 1993); Haar, *The Song of the Earth: Heidegger and the Grounds of the History of Being*, trans. Reginald Lilly (Bloomington: Indiana University Press, 1993); Haar, "*Stimmung* et pensée"; John Sallis, "Imagination, Metaphysics, Wonder," in *American Continental Philosophy: A Reader*, ed. Walter Brogan and James Risser (Bloomington: Indiana University Press, 2000), 15–43; and John Llewelyn, "On the Saying that Philosophy Begins in *Thaumazein*," in *Post-Structuralist Classics*, ed. Andrew Benjamin (London: Routledge, 1998), 173–91.
86 Indeed, as Gadamer rightly points out, what is most striking about Aristotle's definition of the tragic is that it involves the spectator. *Truth and Method*, 2nd rev. ed., trans. Joel Weinsheimer and Donald G. Marshall (New York: Continuum, 1998), 130–1.
87 Cf. Aristotle, *Poetics*, 1453a13–16. Note the tragic passions are fear and pity, 1453b13, and one of the leading properties of the new *Grundstimmung* is terror.

88 Heidegger never calls his project a "rhetoric of being," and he does not call the tension in the first beginning "tragic." The latter is surprising insofar as the tragic was a popular theme for his immediate predecessors and contemporaries. Following Friedrich Nietzsche (1844–1900), both Wilhelm Dilthey (1833–1911) and Max Scheler (1874–1928), among others, focused on the tragic.

89 We borrow the term "rhetoric of being"—though not its exact sense—from Prufer. For Prufer, phenomenological ontology is a rhetoric of being insofar as it must speak of the fullness of being from the appearances of being. "Because philosophy speaks about being by means of the appearances of beings, in which being appears, it is the rhetoric of being, if rhetoric is the use of the means of speech which are available for speaking about that which cannot be spoken of as it is in itself." Prufer, "The Philosophical Act," *International Philosophical Quarterly* 2 (1962): 594. For Prufer, it is not a question of initiation into the proper, revelatory fundamental disposition.

90 GA 45, 181/156. See his comments in "Brief über den *Humanismus*" on falling away *(Verfallen)* from authenticity: "Forgetting the truth of being in favor of the pressing throng of entities unthought in their essence is what 'falling' [*Verfallen*] means in *Being and Time*." GA 9f, 332/253.

91 "The reflection leaped over to *our* need. Did the reflection only leap to this at the end, or did it not constantly concern us and *only* us ourselves?" GA 45, 187/161.

92 In his epilogue, the editor of the volume says that §§ 36–38, which constitute the analysis of wonder, were subject to a subsequent "reworking" that "does not exceed the level of the reflection inherent in the lectures as delivered." GA 45, 230/190. Heidegger clearly thought the analysis of wonder was important.

93 On the difficulty of interrogating wonder, a separate but related issue, see John Sallis, "Imagination, Metaphysics, Wonder," 36. All questioning already moves within the space opened by wonder; there is consequently no way to question wonder except within wonder.

94 GA 45, 180/155.

95 See especially § 97, written between 1936–37, "φύσις (τέχνη)." GA 65, 190/133.

96 GA 65, 193/135, 190/133.

97 GA 65, 191/133–34.

98 GA 65, 184/129.

99 GA 65, 184/129.

100 GA 45, 181/156.

101 GA 45, 181/156.

102 GA 15, 331/38.

103 GA 45, 185–86/160. See also comments from the first draft, GA 45, 196/168.

104 GA 45, 189/162.

105 GA 45, 213/180.

106 GA 45, 185/159–60.

107 GA 45, 186/160.

108 GA 65, 341/239. Translation modified. "This fundamental disposition can hardly be named with *one* word, unless it be with the word reservedness." GA 65, 395/277.

109 GA 65, 22/16.

110 Each of the stages of the *Contributions* has its own guiding disposition and purpose: a) Echo's guiding dispositions are terror *(Schrecken)*, which discloses being's abandonment, and awe *(Scheu)* before the resonating

appropriation; b) Playing-forth's guiding disposition, delight *(Lust)*, in surpassing the beginning in questioning; c) Leap's awe *(Scheu)* to sustain nearness to the mystery; d) Grounding's reservedness from which all guiding dispositions flow. Note that *delight*, which does not seem to disclose anything, is suddenly introduced but not developed. On this division, see GA 65, 396/277, 107/75, 396/277, 169/119, and 227/161.

111 GA 65, 396/277.

112 GA 45, 197/169. Translation slightly modified.

113 GA 45, 197/169–70. John Caputo captures the thought well: "If the early Greeks were tuned to Being in wonder, the wonder is for us that we do not wonder." *Demythologizing Heidegger* (Bloomington: Indiana University Press, 1993), 20. See also GA 65, 484/340.

114 GA 45, 198/170.

115 Cf. Michel Haar, *The Song of the Earth*, 45. Also, in the *Contributions*, Heidegger remarks that terror is best clarified by being contrasted with wonder, though characteristic of the rough form of the *Contributions*, Heidegger does not follow through with the suggestion. GA 65, 15/11.

116 GA 65, 31/22.

117 GA 45, 4/2.

118 GA 4a, 131/153.

119 Cf. Klaus Held, "Fundamental Moods," 291.

120 GA 4a, 132/153.

121 GA 45, 188/162.

122 GA 45, 195/168.

123 In the *Contributions*, Heidegger sets up a contrast between wonder and intimation: "In the first beginning: wonder [*Er-staunen*] / In another beginning: intimation [*Er-ahnen*]." Like many of his suggestions in the work, this contrast is left undeveloped. GA 65, 20/15.

124 GA 65, 22/16.

125 GA 65, 22/16.

126 GA 45, 4/2.

127 GA 65, 15/12.

128 GA 45, 4/2.

129 GA 65, 15/12. Translation modified.

130 GA 65, 34/24.

131 GA 65, 320/225.

132 GA 65, 352–3/247. Translation modified.

133 GA 65, 35/25.

134 GA 65, 17/13, 34–35/25.

135 GA 45, 199/171.

136 The "Postscript" (1943) to the essay "What Is Metaphysics?" brings together the new fundamental disposition with the first wonder: *that* entities *are*: "Readiness for anxiety is a Yes to assuming a stance that fulfills the highest claim, a claim that is made upon the human essence alone. Of all entities, only the human being, called upon by the voice of being, experiences the wonder of all wonders [*das Wunder aller Wunder*]: *that* entities *are*. The being that is thus called in its essence into the truth of being is for this reason always attuned in an essential manner. The lucid courage for essential anxiety assures us the enigmatic possibility of experiencing being. For close by essential anxiety as the terror of the abyss dwells awe. Awe clears and cherishes that locality of the human essence within which humans remain at home in that which endures." In GA 9e, 307/234. Cf. GA 45, 197/169.

137 GA 4a, 102/126.

138 GA 7c, 286/121. Translation modified.

139 GA 45, 163/141. At the beginning of the *Contributions*, Heidegger speaks of the necessity of experiencing the primal wonder of questioning: "Here everything is geared toward the sole and single *question* of the truth of being, i.e., toward *questioning*. So that this attempt turns into an impulse, the *wonder* [Wunder] of enactment of questioning must be experienced and made effective for awakening and strengthening the force of questioning." GA 65, 10/7–8. Translation slightly modified. See also GA 94, 225.

140 GA 65, 202/142. Cf. GA 65, 337/236.

141 GA 65, 250/176. The "condition for the possibility" is "in Kant, the transcendental concept of essence." GA 65, 289/203. This, too, takes its bearing from entities and not being as such. GA 65, 426/300. cf. GA 65, 478/336.

142 GA 65, 250/176–7.

143 GA 65, 251/177.

144 GA 65, 455/320.

145 GA 65, 239/169: "[The leap] is the enactment of projecting-open the truth of be-ing in the sense of shifting into the open, such that the thrower of the projecting-open experiences itself as thrown—i.e., as appropriated by be-ing. The opening in and through projecting-open is such only when it occurs as the experience of thrownness and thus of belongingness to be-ing. That is the essential difference from every merely *transcendental* way of knowing with regard to the conditions of possibility."

146 GA 65, 305/215.

147 GA 65, 450/317.

148 GA 65, 217/152. In this way, Heidegger can insist that his intended overcoming of metaphysics is not transcendental. GA 65, 504/354.

149 GA 65, 468/329.

150 GA 65, 467/328.

151 GA 65, 251/177.

152 "Brief über den *Humanismus*," 180–1/266.

153 "But now since Da-sein as Da-*sein* originarily sustains the open of the sheltering-concealing, strictly speaking [*streng genommen*] one cannot speak of a transcendence of Da-sein; in the vicinity of this approach presentation of transcendence in *every* sense must *disappear*." GA 65, 217/152.

154 GA 65, 239/169 and "Die Metaphysik als Geschichte des Seins," in *Nietzsche*, vol. 2 (Pfullingen: Verlag Günther Neske, 1961) ["Metaphysics as History of Being," in *The End of Philosophy*, trans. Joan Stambaugh (New York: Harper & Row, Publishers, 1973)], 415/14–5.

155 "December 1926: Edmund Husserl to Martin Heidegger (draft)," trans. Thomas Sheehan, in *Becoming Heidegger*, 378–9.

156 *Nietzsche*, vol. 1, 158/134.

Conclusion
Heidegger's Finitude

Hegel alone apparently succeeded in leaping over this shadow, but only in such a way that he eliminated the shadow, i.e., the finiteness of man, and leaped into the sun itself. Hegel skipped over the shadow, but he did not, because of that, surpass the shadow. Nevertheless every philosopher *must* want to do this. This 'must' is his vocation.

—Heidegger[1]

Was ist der Sinn von Heidegger? The thinker provides several metaphors for making sense of his thought. The most pervasive and influential is the metaphor of way or ways. In the last section of *Being and Time*, Heidegger calls the work *ein Weg*.[2] In doing so, he recalls his earlier provisional description of phenomenology as the way into the subject matter of ontology, and he echoes Kant, who, on the last page of the *Critique of Pure Reason*, refers to the work and its method as the only *Weg* that remains open for philosophy.[3] The metaphor of way persists into the late writings. Heidegger entitles his two major anthologies, *Wegmarken* and *Holzwege*, and he publishes his collected works under the motto, *Wege, nicht Werke*. The metaphor takes on a different meaning in the singular and plural. As a *way*, Heidegger's writings are variations on a single theme relentlessly pursued. As *ways*, however, his writings appear as a collection of heterogeneous wanderings.[4] The advantage of the metaphor is that it invites readers to approach his corpus not as a doctrine to master but as a question to pursue; in this respect the image captures some of the movement expressed earlier in terms of the method of formal indication and later in the rhetorical turn toward inducing the requisite fundamental dispositions. The disadvantage of the metaphor is that, especially in the plural form, it obscures the unity of his philosophical itinerary, and it leaves unexplained the relation between his earlier and later approaches. It obscures what motivated Heidegger to tread the paths he did, and thus it obscures what might motivate us, his readers, to follow in his footsteps. It is here that Heidegger's metaphor of a star recommends itself. The significance of this image can be inferred from the fact he had it chiseled on his gravestone in the place of a cross. The star recalls his earlier poetic expression: "To think is to confine yourself to a / single thought that one day stands / still like a star in the world's sky."[5] The metaphor of a single star corrects the misperception fostered by the plural ways. It suggests that the thinker zeroes in relentlessly on a single topic, as the Magi followed a single star: "To head toward a star—this only." The image underscores the unity of his path, the sublime character of his topic, and the significance of his thought for others, yet again it does not help us understand the tortuous difficulty found in the course of his life's thought, including the truncation of *Being and Time* and his motive for attempting to complete it with a new beginning. This is where the value of a third metaphor, the motif of this book, shows itself. Heidegger says that philosophy is the attempt to leap over one's shadow, *über den eigenen Schatten springen*. This German expression means doing something that directly contradicts one's essence or nature.[6] Heidegger takes shadow to designate the intrinsic limits of a given philosopher *qua* philosopher.[7] While the ordinary German idiom suggests a kind of conversion that, while difficult, is nonetheless possible, Heidegger takes the idiom literally. No matter how hard one may try to leap over one's shadow, the shadow will always follow. Heidegger takes the folly of the attempt to be the glory of the philosopher who challenges his finitude, knowing what Hegel did not know: the challenge is doomed to fail. The tension between the necessity and the impossibility of the task explains the violent contortions of the Heideggerian corpus. No sooner had Heidegger projected a horizon for *Being and Time* than he grew unsettled with its terminus and point of departure. His other writings push further into the domain opened up in *Being and Time*. At the same time, the later thinking does not simply complete the transcendental framework; it also marks a new beginning. Heidegger's shadow is the transcendental tradition.

Transcendental thought has a twofold significance in Heidegger's writings. On the one hand, it accounts for how Heidegger, through Husserl, came to his own lasting topic. On the other hand, it accounts for how Heidegger, through Kant, seeks to lead others to his own lasting topic. He offers a historical path into his thought that is otherwise than the one he personally trod. For, as we have seen, it is only in light of Husserl that Heidegger comes to embrace Kant and not vice versa. As I showed in the introduction, both Husserl and Heidegger first attempt to introduce the transcendental by appeal to the authenticity of the researcher. The problem that both discover is that one cannot just will to philosophize transcendentally; one has to be as it were drawn slowly and unknowingly into making the turn by wrestling with the nature of experience and discovering that it cannot, on pain of absurdity, be explained by psychological, biological, or physical principles. In their own paths of thinking, both Husserl and then Heidegger fell into the transcendental turn in this manner. Heidegger offers Kant to motivate transcendental phenomenology by inviting others to think through the topic of judgment's givenness. Heidegger's reading of Kant is the attempt to convince non-phenomenologists that Kant was in effect Husserlian in rediscovering the interplay of intuition and thought in the constitution of things. Kant's transcendental innovation regarding judgment anticipates the Husserlian breakthrough accomplished in the *Logical Investigations*. Heidegger's engagement with Kant aims to lead to (Husserlian) phenomenology and thus to Heidegger's personal point of departure. Heidegger became a transcendental phenomenologist through Husserl; he offers not Husserl but Kant as the motivated path into his thinking; but insofar as he stylizes Kant as a Husserlian transcendental phenomenologist, he does not obscure topically but only nominally his own point of departure.

As the shadow, transcendental thought holds an ambivalent place in Heidegger's philosophical itinerary. It proves crucial for motivating his thought but at the same time artificially constrains the discovered domain. "Even the clarification of transcendence on the basis of ecstatic timeliness was of no avail. And yet thinking must take this course, because it is the most proximate path [*der nächste Weg*] in the transition from metaphysics into the history of being."[8] Now, Heidegger accords philosophical prejudice a crucial role in motivating inquiry. Rationalism's mathematical prejudice motivated transcendental philosophy, which had the peculiar effect of undermining not just the mathematical prejudice but also the mathematical method adopted in the performance of the transcendental critique. Heidegger thinks that the discovered transcendental domain in turn undermines the horizon of the transcendental method that had discovered the domain. The contemporary intellectual landscape remains dominated by the mathematical prejudice, which is the modern form of the ancient orientation to judgment as the locus of truth. Both the ancient and modern forms of the prejudice neglect the pre-judicative domain of experience and instead treat logic and the modern subject as context-free entities. We think in the mode of representation operative in modern science and technology, and for such a mind-set, the transcendental way is the only way into philosophy. It invites someone to consider the condition for the possibility of things (and so the condition for the possibility of science and technology), and in doing so, one discovers the transcendence of Dasein as ground. The transcendental affords an alternative to logic and science as first philosophy; it defends the priority of phenomenology and experience.

Heidegger's various early analyses congeal in *Being and Time*'s radical appropriation of transcendental thought, an appropriation devoted to healing the Husserlian dichotomy of the transcendental and empirical subjects. In the Kant book, Heidegger presents his own thought as a more authentic repetition of Kant's analytic aimed at laying bare the ultimate origins of the movement of transcendence. Where Kant had shrunk back from the radicality of his analysis, Heidegger presses forward. Later, he retracts this charge of inauthenticity laid at Kant's feet and instead sees Kant as having grappled with the rootlessness of modern thought but in such a way that the full affective ground remains covered over. Kant remains bound not by inauthenticity but by the necessary limits of finitude, which constrain the horizon of a philosopher's inquiry.

The finitude of the philosopher expresses the thrownness and facticity of the philosopher, who is given to think what he finds unthought in others and himself. The finitude of philosophy, for Heidegger, concerns the domain of philosophy historically opened up in the sequence of fundamental dispositions. The finitude of the philosopher and the finitude of philosophy means that the philosopher will always be dependent on what is other for him to come into his own, whether that be the otherness of the philosophical tradition or the otherness of the affective dispositions that account for historical differences in that philosophical tradition.

Even though Heidegger keenly felt the need to do so, for good reason he could not extricate himself from the transcendental tradition. His difficulty is irresolvable: either *affirm* transcendental philosophy and thereby distort his goal or *deny* transcendental philosophy and thereby occlude his point of departure. Hence his writings reflect a conflicted attitude to transcendental philosophy in general and Kant and Husserl in particular. We should resist the tendency to over-simplification that would lead us to say that Heidegger rejects transcendental philosophy; he rather comes to realize its limitations while appreciating all the more his own inescapable entanglement with it. In this concluding chapter, I consider the significance of this entanglement for making sense of Heidegger. First, I review some later texts to show the persistence of the ambivalence to transcendental thought. Second, I argue that the persistence underscores his Husserlian heritage. Third, I reflect on the possibility for transcendental thinking that Heidegger opens up. Finally, I identify the limits of Heidegger's own horizon of inquiry.

1 Husserl, Kant, and Transcendence in Some Late Texts

Heidegger's ambivalence toward the transcendental tradition continues into his later writings. In "Conversation on a Country Path about Thinking," dating from the mid-1940s, Heidegger discusses the matter for thinking. In the course of the conversation, the relation of "releasement" (*Gelassenheit*) to that which regions is distinguished from the ontic relation of cause and effect on the one hand and the ontological relation of transcendental-horizonal making possible on the other. Instead it is called "regioning" (*Vergegnis*).[9] In a similar fashion, the relation of a thing to the regioning is neither ontic nor ontological but "thinging" (*Bedingnis*).[10] But determining these relations can occur only on the basis of the experience of thinking and releasement. Sheehan helpfully underscores the metaphor of countryside (*die Gegend*) in this account: "This countryside lies open *before* us without ever being an object (*Gegen-stand*) standing over "against" us as subjects. Heidegger's *Gegend*-metaphor evokes 'the already open countryside' in which we find ourselves and within which particular things are meaningfully present."[11] Regioning and thinging, then, are meant to evoke that sense of openness that lies at the basis of experience; it is an attempt to articulate experience outside the subject-object opposition. Now, even though the thinking in releasement is clearly contrasted with transcendental thinking, it is nonetheless true that transcendental thinking is indeed in the region for thought. Its shortcoming is that it grasps the open only in relation to us. "We are in that which regions when we present transcendentally and step out into the horizon. And again we are still not in it, insofar as we have not released ourselves for that which regions as such."[12] By means of awaiting, we are released from the transcendental relation and drawn to the horizon.[13] We are then appropriated and thereby related more originally to being. And yet there is also the hint that releasement to that which regions may not require the way through releasement from transcendental philosophy, since the source of releasement is regioning itself.

In the 1961 Kant lecture, "Kant's Thesis about Being," Heidegger focuses on Kant's determination of being and how he enacts "a far-reaching step," "effects a decisive turn," and brings about a "transformation."[14] This step, turn, or transformation regards in the first place the determination of being, but it also entails Kant's transformed understanding of judgment, because judgment is central to Kant's account of being. Heidegger says that for Kant the being of the entity means "positing as positing of an affection," and positing has the character of judgment.[15] Again, then, judgment is related to the sensuous given, although it is no longer clear that it is in service to intuition. Concepts alone are inadequate for an object of judgment, so the new definition of judgment's orientation to affection regains a hint of the originary relation between λόγος as gathering/revealing and being as self-revealing presencing.[16] In the 1961 lecture, though, Heidegger makes no mention of the "between" but sees instead a partial subjectivizing of judgment. Transcendental apperception, although related to the sensuous given, is what provides the unity of the object of judgment. It is the fundamental principle of judgment and "is unifying-gathering, λόγος in the inceptive sense, but transferred to and relocated in the I-subject."[17] But insofar as transcendental apperception is essentially related to intuition, Kant's doctrine of judgment is not fully enclosed within the subjectivity of rationalism and is therefore not fully subject to the disjunction, "being and thought." Even though Kant did take a tremendous step forward, he remains finally within the tradition that neglects the context of being.

In 1965, celebrating Eugen Fink on his birthday, Heidegger recalls how Fink, already a student of Husserl, began to follow Heidegger and thereby "entered another, and yet the same school of phenomenology."[18] A year earlier, in "The End of Philosophy and the Task of Thinking" (1964), Heidegger takes a more critical posture; he considers Husserl's phenomenological return to the things themselves and argues that it betrays a commitment to the priority of method over matter and thus a commitment to subjectivity that echoes Hegel. "The transcendental reduction to absolute subjectivity gives and secures the possibility of grounding the objectivity of all objects (the being of these entities) in their valid structure and consistency, that is, in their constitution, in and through subjectivity."[19] In this way, Heidegger repeats the criticism, already made in 1925, that Husserl neglects the being of transcendental subjectivity. At the same time, Heidegger continues to acknowledge that the reduction brings to givenness something of the being of entities that Parmenides was the first to fathom.[20] He introduces his own topic as bringing to experience the place in which we can meet with the being of entities. In the same essay, he revises the claim he had made since the 1920s that the Greek word for truth, *alētheia*, originally meant unconcealment. Instead, he acknowledges that the natural concept of truth was correctness. Heidegger writes:

> The natural concept of truth does not mean unconcealment, not in the philosophy of the Greeks either. It is often and justifiably pointed out that the word *alēthes* is already used by Homer only in the *verba dicendi*, in statements, thus in the sense of correctness and reliability, not in the sense of unconcealment. But this reference means only that neither the poets nor everyday linguistic usage, nor even philosophy, see themselves confronted with the task of asking how truth, that is, the correctness of statements, is granted only in the element of the clearing of presence.
>
> In the scope of this question, we must acknowledge the fact that *alētheia*, unconcealment in the sense of the clearing of presence, was originally experienced only as *orthotēs*, as the correctness of representations and statements. But then *the assertion about the essential transformation of truth, that is, from unconcealment to correctness, is also untenable.*[21]

What does this mean? It means that the fact that Parmenides experienced the being of entities cannot be accounted for in terms of Greek experience in general. But this also makes Parmenides much more puzzling; what motivated him to turn to the correlation of thought and being if it wasn't the richness of Greek experience? The turn Heidegger claims for Parmenides, the turn manifest in Husserl and Kant, remains essential but also deeply puzzling. The question of motivation only intensifies with this late retraction of the thesis about *alētheia*.

The last seminars are likewise significant for tracking the importance of the transcendental turn in Heidegger's thought. While Heidegger sharply criticizes Hegel and Marx, he treats Kant and Husserl more in keeping with his generous readings of Parmenides and Heraclitus. In the "Seminar in Le Thor 1968," Heidegger again places Kant in the sharpest opposition to Hegel. Kant expressly denies the possibility of a system because an absolute ground is lacking us: "Unconditioned necessity, which we so indispensably require as the last bearer of all things, is for human reason the veritable *abyss*."[22] Heidegger comments, "We can say that Fichte and Hegel are looking for a ground where for Kant there could only be an abyss. In thirty years everything will be reversed, so much so that in his Berlin discourse we can say that Hegel spoke in a way diametrically opposed to the text of the *Critique of Pure Reason* we just read."[23] In "Seminar in Le Thor 1969" and "Seminar in Zähringen 1973," Heidegger reiterates that Kant addresses the being of entities even while codifying its Cartesian reduction to the objectivity of objects: "Between Aristotle and Kant there lies an abyss. . . . For the Greeks, things appear. For Kant, things appear to me."[24] The subject provides the site for things to appear, and they accordingly do so as objects: "Precisely stated, objectivity is being-present in the dimension or 'space' of subjectivity, whether it is a matter of (with Kant) the subjectivity of a finite subject, or (with Hegel) the subjectivity of the absolute subject."[25]

In "Seminar in Zähringen 1973," Heidegger also discusses Husserl in a way that hearkens back to the discussions in the 1925 lecture course that set the stage for his Kantian turn the following year. Heidegger describes his relation to Husserl as the tale of two Brentanos. Husserl's point of departure was Brentano's 1874 scholastic treatises, *Psychology from an Empirical Standpoint*; Heidegger's point of departure was Brentano's 1862 treatise, *On the Manifold Meaning of Being in Aristotle*. "A strange and significant commonality between Husserl and Heidegger, who both took their first steps with the same philosopher, but not with the same book. My Brentano, Heidegger says with a smile, is the Brentano of Aristotle!"[26] At the same time, Heidegger acknowledges that it was Husserl's discovery of categorial intuition that enabled Heidegger to pose the question of being. Heidegger thinks categorial intuition arises out of a consideration of the object of experience: "It is thus a problematic of the theory of experience—through which Husserl again continues the Kantian heritage."[27] However, Husserl discovers something Kant did not. The categories are not deduced from the table of judgments; they are encountered in experience.[28] "With his analyses of the categorial intuition, Husserl freed being from its attachment to judgment."[29] Husserl, developing Kant, enabled Heidegger to get behind the logical prejudice. Despite this discovery, Husserl remains partially bound by the mathematical prejudice.

> The point that Husserl does not cross, however, is this: after having reached, as it were, being as *given*, he does not inquire any further into it. He does not unfold the question: "what does being mean?"

> For Husserl, there was not the slightest possibility of a question, since for him it goes without saying that "being" means being-object.[30]

Husserl, says Heidegger, does not fully escape the immanence of consciousness.[31] Accordingly, he ambiguously succumbs to Hegel's notion of science, is closed to a sense of history as tradition, and still retains the problem of sense data.[32] Husserl and Kant retain all their ambiguity in these last texts: on the one hand, they afford Heidegger access to the domain to be thought; on the other they remain impediments to its full enactment.

2 The Vindication of Husserl's Transcendental Turn

In the famous letter to Marcus Herz that announced the topic of the work that became the *Critique of Pure Reason*, Kant asked, "What is the ground of the relation of that in us which we call 'representation' to the object?"[33] Heidegger briefly mentions this passage in the 1928 Leibniz course to illustrate that his own question has been at work in philosophy from Parmenides through Kant. At the same time he thinks Kant and his successors up to the present fail to clarify the nature of the relation, what the relation is between, and its mode of being.[34] In the *Critique of Pure Reason*, Kant's question takes on the familiar form, "How are *a priori* synthetic judgments possible?"[35] He terms the inquiry concerned with this question *transcendental philosophy*.[36] Heidegger twice translates his project into Kantian terminology with somewhat different results. The first attempt in the late 1920s sees in Kant's doctrine of transcendental imagination and its schematism the mediation between thought and intuition and in this way finds in the phenomenological analytic of experience the condition for the possibility of experience. This interpretation has received much-deserved criticism; even in the book itself Heidegger admits it does a certain violence to Kant but necessarily so, and he would later retract some of its key claims.[37] As Dieter Henrich has argued, for Kant there is no sense in finding something to mediate between the two elements.[38] Heidegger's second major reading of Kant proceeds along different lines but continues the phenomenological theme of the possibility of experience. The essential elements of the reciprocal relation of the human qua subject and being qua objectivity of the object are articulated in the figure of the highest principle of synthetic judgments: "The conditions of the *possibility of experience* in general are likewise conditions of the *possibility of the objects of experience*."[39] These conditions reciprocally belong together as the circularity of the "proofs" make manifest. Those proofs all articulate the same "schema"[40] or "circular movement" (*Kreisgang*) by which "what lies within the circle becomes opened."[41] Things thereby become available in their being: "These wholly dissimilar pieces must come to an agreement [*übereinkommen*] in some respect in order to unify themselves at all as determinable and determining, and it must be in such a way that by virtue of this unification of intuition and thinking an object *is*."[42] Along with the being of entities, what emerges through this circular happening—which is elsewhere termed appropriation—is the open between. And since "every saying of be-ing . . . must name ap-propriation" and thereby be "always decisively *interpretive of the between*," we can see that Kant's circular hermeneutic, which comes to language as the highest principle of synthetic judgment, is an expression of Heidegger's lasting topic. Again, the positive evaluation is matched by a serious critique. Kant lacks the belonging of Dasein to being that is expressed in dispositions, although even on this point Heidegger suggests that it was Kant who paved the way for an ontological understanding of freedom and dispositions. Heidegger also thinks Kant remains subject to the limits of representational thinking and the presupposition of the on-hand. Despite the limitations of his starting point, Kant projects a horizon that leads to Heidegger's own point of departure. According to Heidegger, transcendental philosophy is that inquiry which happens upon the ground of the relation of dative and being and even brings to light its encircling reciprocity. In this sense, transcendental philosophy remains operative within Heidegger's later thinking.[43] Heidegger does not countenance psychologistic or naturalistic accounts. He does not try to explain the ontological in terms of the ontic. He subscribes to Husserl's refutation of psychologism and naturalism, even as he endeavors to bridge the real-ideal divide.[44] It is the transcendental approach that undermines both the logical prejudice and the mathematical prejudice.

Heidegger's phenomenological analyses trade on what he calls a "step back." He says that the move into philosophy is a "step back from a thinking that merely represents" and "into a questioning that experiences."[45] This "step back," Heidegger cautions, is not a change of attitude since attitudes are necessarily representational but instead a matter of responding to what is genuinely experienced. But what are we responding to? "Presencing of the present [*Anwesen des Anwesenden*], that is, the twofold of the two from out of their unity."[46] The presencing of the present is nothing other than what is at play in our everyday experience when freed of objectifying prejudices:

> Our everyday experience of things, in the wider sense of the word, is neither objectifying nor a placing over against. When, for example, we sit in the garden and take delight in a blossoming rose, we do not make an object of the rose, nor do we even make it something standing over against us in the sense of something presented thematically. . . . The rose stands in the garden, perhaps sways to and fro in the wind. But the redness of the rose neither stands in the garden nor can it sway to and fro in the wind. All the same we think it and tell of it

by naming it. There is accordingly a thinking and saying that in no manner objectifies or places things over against us.[47]

On the final day of his last seminar, Heidegger says that "phenomenology is a path that leads away to come before . . . , and it lets that before which it is led show itself."[48] This step back that leads away is a deepening of the transcendental turn. The Copernican revolution shifts from objects to what makes objects possible and in doing so limits objectivity to what fulfills its conditions; the transcendental turn thereby frees everyday experience from the specter of universal objectivism. The phenomenological step back is a further enactment of the transcendental turn, which *returns* us to the experience of experience in all its richness.

The persisting transcendental character of Heidegger's thought leads to some provocative implications for understanding his relation to Husserl. (a) It was Husserl who provided Heidegger with the genuine philosophical empiricism that was to issue in the affectivity of the *Contributions*; (b) it was Husserl who provided Heidegger with a compelling reading of Kant as a phenomenologist; (c) Kant and Husserl become entwined for Heidegger, and so the transitional role of the one must entail the transitional role of the other. I will take each of these in turn.

Genuine Empiricism

Heidegger adopts Husserl's phenomenology as something that is genuine but question-worthy. In *Being and Time* he writes, "But to disclose the *a priori* is not to make an 'a-prioristic' construction. Through Edmund Husserl, we have learned not only to understand once more the sense of every genuine philosophical 'empiricism' but also to handle the necessary tools for it."[49] In *Ideas I*, Husserl contrasts his approach with that of the naturalizing empiricists:

> We take our start from what lies *prior to* all standpoints: from the total realm of whatever is itself given intuitionally and prior to all theorizing, from everything that one can immediately see and seize upon—if only one does not let himself be blinded by prejudices and prevented from taking into consideration whole classes of genuine data.[50]

What becomes Heidegger's question is what follows the em dash. As he writes in 1925:

> It is easy and pleasant to make great projections after the barricades of prejudice have been breached, after the horizon has been laid open, but then one forgets that the decisive [*entscheidende*] work in

the field of philosophical research is always this first step, namely, the work of laying open and disclosing as such.[51]

The difficulty of this first step raises a host of questions: How is it that what is immediately given can at the same time be covered over by prejudices? Why is there need for the epoché to lead into the transcendental reduction? This is no inessential question for phenomenology. As Heidegger observes, there is need for phenomenology only because the phenomena often do not show themselves.[52]

In *Being and Time*, Heidegger accounts for the covering over of the phenomena through falling, which is rooted ultimately in a diminution of timeliness. By contrast, authenticity does not just neutralize prejudices, but it discloses the phenomena they miss. Later, Heidegger attempts to account for the blindness of prejudice in terms of historical destiny. This approach explains the great variety of philosophies developed by eminent thinkers who nonetheless do not quite have the same phenomena in view. It identifies the deeper identity through their differences as each deals with the same one domain as it has been disclosed to them under different aspects. Thus it could be said that the transcendental phenomenological reduction is different in different epochs but necessarily so. Husserl's philosophical empiricism remains, though it is now translated into a historical register.[53] Thinking through the question, "How do we experience the *a priori* of experience?" leads Heidegger to introduce the non-Husserlian theme of fundamental dispositions, but he does so because he applies the Husserlian method of phenomenology to the Husserlian topic of the basis of experience: we experience the *a priori* of experience thanks to fundamental dispositions that highlight different aspects of the *a priori* at different times; as such, the *a priori* has a kind of dynamism unforeseen by Husserl.

The Husserlian Kant

Heidegger acknowledges that Husserl enabled him to read Kant as a phenomenologist and hence as a collaborator in his research. Heidegger later distances himself from Husserl's Kant, partly under the chorus of accusations of violence it brought upon him, and partly due to his own growing dissatisfaction with the fittingness of its terms. However, Heidegger does not leave Kant behind but begins to characterize him as a central if ambiguous transitional figure in the historical motivation elaborately worked out in the *Contributions*. The reason Kant can serve in the capacity is that, from the province of Heidegger's later thinking, he can see that Kant uncovers the open between although he was still unable to appropriate it as such, and thus Kant left open the possibility for the subsequent falsification of his inquiry. To avoid Hegel's idealism and its aftermath in positivism and biologism, Heidegger proposes a return to Kant that finds in him a new trajectory for thought. In this way, Heidegger still remains indebted to Husserl's Kant.

Why Heidegger Needs Husserl and Kant

At the beginning of his "phenomenological decade" of the 1920s, Heidegger thinks Husserl shows the way to research the problem of constitution posed by Kant's thought; by the end of the decade, with Husserl's help, Heidegger can see Kant as a phenomenologist interested in the constitution of the ontological.[54] The fates of Husserl and Kant, both representing species of transcendental "phenomenology," are entwined in Heidegger's thought.

Because the later Heidegger still accords a central transitional role to Kant in virtue of the between that comes to light in his thinking, we are obliged to extend that transitional role to Husserl as well. Heidegger provides some clues that he thinks this is appropriate. The characterization of the transcendental attitude in the 1935–36 lecture course on Kant is framed in terms of Heidegger's earlier reading of Husserl. Heidegger says we misunderstand the *Critique* when we read it according to our everyday or scientific attitude. Instead, in the transcendental attitude we grasp the relation of the assertion to the object as such. We consider the entity "in regard to how this object is an object *for us*, in which respect it is meant, that is, how our thought thinks it."[55] It is this attitude that Heidegger says in the *Contributions* that we would do well to reenact.[56] When we do so we discover the open between. Heidegger's affection for the *Sixth Logical Investigation* is well known.[57] But it is there that Husserl moves from intentionality to categorial intuition to the *a priori*. As the lecture course in 1925, "History of the Concept of Time," endeavors to show, the phenomenological *a priori* thus disclosed is neither immanent nor transcendent but, Heidegger aims to show, a title for being.[58] Husserl's analysis of judgment, then, leads to the open between.[59] Consider, too, Husserl's admission of a "wholly irremovable defect" that undermines the systematic character of phenomenological investigation. Anticipating the hermeneutic circle, he writes, "We search, as it were, in zig-zag fashion, a metaphor all the more apt since the close interdependence of our various epistemological [i.e., phenomenological] concepts leads us back again and again to our original analyses, where the new confirms the old, and the old the new."[60] Here, in germ, is the toppling of the logical and mathematical prejudices. Husserl's zigzag and Kant's reciprocity serve to relativize the subject and its principles and bring the philosopher into the space that Heidegger identifies as the topic of thought. Finally, Heidegger's mature reading of Kant emphasizes the emergence of the context of experience in Kant's analysis. "Kant's *Critique of Pure Reason*, in which since the Greeks once more an essential step is taken, has to presuppose this context [*Zusammenhang*] without being able to grasp it *as such* and to bring it *fully* to a ground (the turning relation of Dasein and being)."[61] With this emphasis on pre-judicative context, Heidegger points to something that he first identified in Husserl back in 1925. Heidegger describes Husserl's development in *Ideas II*: "The main point now is not to view the context of lived experience as an appendage to physical things but to see that *experiential context as such* [*den Erlebniszusammenhang*] and the ego as a psychic ego-subject."[62] As we have seen, Heidegger reconfigures the ego-subject as Dasein but in doing so he retains the Husserlian focus on the experiential context as such.

The comments in this section are not meant to underplay the significant differences between Husserl and Heidegger. As Husserl saw it: "Philosophically I have nothing to do with this Heideggerian profundity, with this brilliant unscientific genius."[63] Despite the evident distance between the two philosophers, Heidegger yet remains bound to Husserl. Simon Critchley puts this well when he says that "Heidegger's contribution to philosophy is his radicalization of the basic idea of phenomenology, a radicalization that paradoxically shows the extent of his debt to Husserl, and, by extension, the radicality of Husserlian phenomenology."[64] Heidegger takes Husserl to be bound up with the logical and mathematical prejudices and to have a "specifically rationalistic orientation."[65] Heidegger wielded the phenomenological method against Husserl's one-sided emphasis on theoretical rationality. But he could do so only out of fidelity to the inner nature of phenomenology, as elaborated by Husserl, which enjoins us "to go from words and opinions back to the things themselves, to consult them in their self-givenness and to set aside all prejudices alien to them."[66] The remarks in this section serve only to relate Heidegger to *Heidegger's* Husserl, the version of Husserl we get from reading Heidegger's own works. Heidegger suppressed the deepest themes in Husserl, those matters closest to Heidegger's own thinking.[67]

3 Heidegger's Ways into Transcendental Philosophy

In the introduction, I pointed to the problem of introduction for transcendental philosophy, and I detailed Husserl's attempts to cope with the difficulty, an attempt that leads him to move away from Cartesian appeals to authenticity and instead to turn to history; I further noted that the appeal to history is other than the path that Husserl personally trod, for Husserl became Husserl by refuting psychologism and by wrestling with the way truth comes to experience. In the 1910s, Heidegger made Husserl's analysis of judgment his own, and then, in the 1920s, he deploys two sets of motives for making the transcendental turn that opens up his path of thought. Heidegger appeals to motivations of life and motivations of history. The first, preeminent in the published *Being and Time*, points to the authenticity of the researcher, who rebels against the falling tendency of everyday understanding. The second, belonging especially to *Kant and the Problem of Metaphysics*, finds in Kant a crucial failure of authentic resolve that led to the second edition of the *Critique of Pure Reason*, which shrank back from the abyss of the transcendental imagination; our task, then, is to return to Kant and be authentic where Kant was not. These twin paths are essentially heroic, a matter of being authentic in the face of the failures of other people and thinkers.

In the 1930s, Heidegger abandons these heroic paths as being infected with a problematical subjectivism. The difficulty is that the heroic resolve cannot explain the limits of the truly great past philosophers, nor can such appeals effectively motivate, because they do not specify the direction the new inquiry should take. Accordingly, in the 1930s, Heidegger presents a new suite of ways to the reduction. The focal strategy of this new approach, developed in the *Contributions* and related writings, is what I have called the "rhetoric or poetics of being," which aims to provoke the requisite pathos or fundamental disposition by pointing to the tragic flaw of the philosophical tradition. The decadence of wonder, at work in a Plato or Aristotle, or the terror of the contemporary abandonment of being, at work in Nietzsche, provokes us to a fundamental disposition geared toward the deeper withdrawal at the heart of experience. Alongside this rhetoric of being, which emphasizes the tragic limits of the tradition, Heidegger also develops a motive that seizes upon a positive movement intrinsic to the tradition that leads to its own surpassing. I might call this the Kantian or Husserlian way. In the lecture courses from the late 1930s and into the *Contributions*, Heidegger offers Kantian transcendental thinking as the immanent highpoint of modernity, the further development of which would lead us to transcend the problematical limits of the philosophical tradition, modern and ancient: for in the *Critique of Pure Reason* the modern mathematical prejudice and the ancient logical prejudice are limited in such a way that the pre-subjective and pre-objective between can emerge for reflection. Heidegger even prizes the second edition over the first insofar as the second edition is no longer the expression of a Kantian failure of resolve but instead a matter of Kant's deepening his understanding of the transformation that thought must undergo in terms of affectivity. Now, the Kantian way is historical and topical: it could be deployed historically in terms of Kant and his work in overcoming rationalism, a work in which the entire tradition comes into play, or it could be deployed topically in terms of making sense of judgment and its home in the context of experience.

What are we to make of these paths (the heroic, the tragic, and the Kantian)? As with Husserl's move from the Cartesian way to the reduction, Heidegger was right to distance himself from the heroic way to the reduction, for it fails to specify what is to be overcome or why the subject matter itself demands that we respond to it more adequately. As with Husserl's turn to history, Heidegger takes to telling sweeping stories

Table 5.1 Motivated Ways to the Transcendental Reduction

Phenomenologist	Kinds	Description
Husserl	Cartesian	Through authentic resolve
	Ontological/Historical	Through the tradition's fulfillment
	(Autobiographical)	Through wrestling with judgment and experience
Heidegger	Heroic	Through overcoming inauthenticity
	Tragic/Poetic	Through overcoming tragic limits of the tradition
	Kantian/Husserlian	Through overcoming inadequate accounts of judgment

about the tradition to motivate the turn to philosophy. The difference is that while Husserl gives a rational account of progress culminating in Husserlian phenomenology, Heidegger gives a poetic account of dispositions that deepen into Heideggerian thought. The affectivity of the philosopher comes to the fore, especially in the Heideggerian conception. However, both accounts suffer from a similar limitation: a gross overreach and simplification of every other philosophy that appears dogmatic and therefore off-putting rather than motivating. To be sure, Aristotle tells a historical narrative in which all of his predecessors fall short of his four causes, and Aquinas tells a story of the history of inquiry into being in which almost all his predecessors, including Plato and Aristotle, fail to inquire into being as being; these sorts of bold claims are common in philosophy and have a kind of legitimacy as motivational devices.[68] But the risk of such accounts is that they presuppose the truth of certain empirical propositions concerning the history of philosophy, the truth or falsity of which is relevant for whether or not the account can motivate the performance of phenomenology. Did wonder really have a necessary tension between presence and absence? We have to dig deeply into Plato and Aristotle to find out, and due to the nature of the claim, the texts might be inconclusive. Is the history of the inquiry into being reducible to an attempt to happen upon Heidegger's domain? A lot more work than Heidegger does would be necessary to begin to justify such a bold and ambitious claim.

The problem, then, with these broadly historical accounts of motivation, whether coming from Husserl or from Heidegger, is that they can easily appear dogmatic and therefore ineffective. Husserl and Heidegger of course are not interested in doing "the history of philosophy" but instead of motivating philosophy. They are both right, of course, to turn from authenticity and its implicit expression of the mathematical prejudice, unable as it is to explain how one could come to philosophize, but the turn to history suffers from the defect of appearing dogmatic and therefore incapable of motivating philosophizing. It is also the case that one can only see these historical motivations for what they are, accounts to motivate our philosophizing today rather than accounts about the past, from within the transcendental turn; thus they do not motivate the performance of the reduction. Instead they are accounts one can give after the fact for the legitimacy of the turn that has already been made. At best, they might motivate, within the already performed transcendental turn, a further enactment of the turn, but they appear incapable of motivating the initial performance of the turn. I will have more to say about the limits of history as a motivation in the final section of this chapter.

I think that the most effective way into philosophizing with transcendental phenomenologists, whether Husserl or Heidegger, is to retrace their own steps: both of them became what they were by returning to the things themselves, that is, by wrestling with the truth of judgment and its origin in experience. No one committed to the truth of the sciences can be indifferent to the origin of the truth of judgment, and no science can give an account of the truth of judgment. Wrestling with the phenomena themselves, rejecting absurd and self-defeating falsifications, makes one a convinced transcendental phenomenologist. The Kantian or Husserlian way into philosophy, recapitulating as it does Husserl's path and therefore Heidegger's own introduction, is the more compelling path. The topical question, illuminated by Kant's form of questioning, leads into the phenomenological terrain. The transcendental turn spirals inward, provoking ever deepening wonder concerning the unfolding logic of experience. It is important to underscore that "Kant" here becomes transformed; talk of the thing-in-itself drops out and the appearances of things become, in an Aristotelian fashion, an expression of their being. Thus, the transcendental path, for the phenomenologist, goes beyond the modern tradition to recover something of the ancient tradition, and it does so because of its obstinate desire to be faithful to how things really do show up in our experience.

4 Standing in Heidegger's Shadow

Heidegger's critical appropriation of the transcendental tradition casts shadows that become fruitful starting points for others. In this way, along with Husserl, he sets the terms of the conversation that is continental philosophy. Maxime Doyon argues that the subsequent continental thinking, rather than abandoning the transcendental turn, is in fact best understood as "numerous attempts at *enlarging* the scope of Kant's transcendental investigations."[69] Even for a figure such as Derrida "the transcendental method or attitude is not only a perfectly legitimate philosophical standpoint, but it is even a *necessary condition* for the practice of philosophy."[70] Heidegger's transcendentalism is no fixed possession. By engaging it and encountering its relentless self-questioning, new paths arise. Emmanuel Levinas, for example, rightly points to the neglect of the normativity of the other in Heidegger, and this lack motivates his own project.[71]

One of the more productive recent engagements with Heidegger's transcendental program comes from Jean-Luc Marion, who reads Heidegger as he wants to be read: in terms of the substantive issues themselves. By Marion's count, there are three phenomenological reductions. First, there is what he calls the Kantian or Husserlian transcendental reduction that uncovers the condition for the possibility of objects. Second, there is the Heideggerian existential reduction that deploys angst to uncover the condition for the possibility of understanding entities in terms of being. Beyond Heidegger, Marion calls for a third reduction that will seize upon the unthought in Heidegger and turn to pure givenness.[72] Marion overlooks the fact that Heidegger anticipated a more radical reduction in the very structure of *Being and Time*; writing in 1989, Marion was not in position to know that the thought of the *Contributions*, which likewise appeared that year, aimed precisely at motivating the requisite third reduction. Marion rightly shows that the transcendental, which approaches things as objects, organically develops into the ontological, which approaches things as entities, and it, in turn, organically develops into the properly phenomenological, which approaches things purely in terms of their manner of givenness. Due to the immanent development that Marion sketches, we are free to read the third reduction as a radicalization of the transcendental turn, as itself a species of transcendental thought. There is in this way an important contact between Marion's third reduction and Heidegger's own later thinking. The difference is that what Heidegger finds thought-provoking about the transcendental turn is not so much the theme of givenness as the emergence of the domain of givenness. Hence, his radicalization of the transcendental brings out the experience of the domain. Also, Heidegger remains, from first to last, a thinker engaged in making sense of the tradition of metaphysics or the history of being, who finds in that tradition the decisive motivations to philosophize. Marion, by contrast, does not appear to attend to the problem of motivating phenomenology, a problem which leads Husserl and Heidegger to turn to history. Rather, he accepts the phenomenological investigations of Husserl and Heidegger and aims to find within their programs the motivations to a further reduction. Husserl and Heidegger seek to motivate phenomenology by turning to history; Marion, taking phenomenology as a given, desires to motivate its radicalization by means of its immanent development. Marion remains one of the more innovative of recent phenomenologists. His development of phenomenology in part corresponds with Heidegger's own efforts to shift from a projective to an affective transcendentalism.

Heidegger ironically titles his second major work *Contributions*. He intends this "public title" as a criticism of the standard way of evaluating philosophical texts in terms of the unending advance of scientific knowledge.[73] By contrast, he wishes to call into question the conception of philosophy in terms of research. Heeding his warnings, we are nevertheless legitimately entitled to ask: What is Heidegger's contribution to philosophy? To what original truth does he bear witness? Why take his path or track his star rather than another's? In my view, Heidegger's most compelling contribution comes in terms of his engagement with the transcendental tradition. Specifically, he offers a naturalized, non-reductive transcendence, which is rooted in affectivity rather than the positing of the transcendental subject, and which is receptive to the essences of things.

Naturalized, Non-reductive Transcendence

Heidegger "naturalizes" transcendental thought by normalizing it. Always and everywhere experience occurs in some modality or another. The transcendental turn amounts to but one modality of such experience. In other modes, entities are thematized; in the transcendental mode the givenness of such entities becomes the focus. The modalization of experience contributes toward the domestication of transcendence; it is not some otherworldly change of perspective but the immanent change of focus from things to their givenness, a possibility native to experience itself. Heidegger makes transcendence palatable while not succumbing to naturalism, which would incoherently try to give an ontic account of the ontological, or to idealism, which would dissolve the ontic into the ontological. Moving beyond Husserl, he rejects the bifurcation of the self into transcendental and empirical egos, and his transcendental thought clarifies issues of normativity.[74] Steve Crowell, Jeff Malpas, and Daniel Dahlstrom demonstrate the continued relevance of the transcendental strain in Heidegger's thought. As I have shown, Heidegger does not disavow the transcendental elements they rightly prize; rather he acknowledges their essential role in motivating his later, more comprehensive approach to the same set of issues.

Affectivity and Motivation

Heidegger's version of transcendental philosophy hearkens back to Platonic *eros*, which opens up the human to what is pregiven and beyond the subject's control. It constitutes a genuine rupture of the modern subject. At the same time, Heidegger must do something Plato had no occasion to do: to make sense of the affectivity of the self in light of its subsequent neglect in the history of philosophy. In this way, Heidegger's transcendental thought undermines subjectivism. Commentators typically take subjectivity to be part and parcel of transcendentality.[75] However, as Sheehan rightly observes, "But at no stage in his thinking did Heidegger conceive of the 'opening up of the open' as an achievement of subjectivity."[76] In 1935, Heidegger writes that in *Being and Time*, transcendental "does not pertain to subjective consciousness; instead, it is determined by the existential-ecstatic temporality of Da-sein."[77] If Heidegger's transcendental philosophy had already dispensed with what is problematic about the subject, can we not speak of a "post-subjective" transcendental philosophy? It was Heidegger's transcendental impulses that led him further from the subject to think the between that comes to pass before the subject-object divide. Heidegger moves phenomenology beyond Husserl in a way he believes is more faithful to phenomenology's principles. Similarly, Heidegger's shift to a "post-subjective" transcendental philosophy is a purification of the transcendental turn that is more faithful to its original intent of grasping the ground of the relation.[78] Transcending as such names the finitude that is the site of disclosure, the open between in which we encounter entities.

If we can indeed conceive of the transcendental philosophy without the modern subject, Heidegger's contribution can be understood as an *affective transcendentalism*. What Heidegger sets out to do is to enact a transcendental account of transcendental philosophy. Whereas

Table 5.2 Species of Transcendental Questions in Heidegger

Type	Text	Question	Answer
Kant's Projective	*Kant and the Problem of Metaphysics*	How is the domain of experience possible?	Via the ground-laying of the transcendental imagination
	1935–36 Lecture Course	What (or how) is a thing?	Via a pre-subjective, pre-objective open between
Heidegger's Projective	SZ I.1	How are all comportments possible?	Via care for being-in-the-world
	SZ I.2	How is care for being-in-the-world possible?	Via ecstatic-horizonal timeliness
Heidegger's Affective	SZ I.3 and *Contributions*	How is timeliness possible?	*SZ:* Via the ground-laying of temporality *Contributions:* Via the affective experience of the domain's withdrawal (appropriation)
		How do we discover temporality or appropriation?	*SZ:* Via the authenticity of fundamental ontological research *Contributions:* Via the affective experience of the domain's withdrawal (appropriation)

transcendental thought is concerned with giving an account of everyday and scientific comportments, Heidegger wants to give an account of such an account: What does it presuppose? What is the condition for the possibility of thinking about transcendence? And to his mind the most satisfying answer comes in terms of being appropriated in fundamental dispositions; appropriation enables us to think about transcendence and determines the specific character of those comportments. Heidegger is a transcendental philosopher raised to the second power.

Heidegger's transcendentalism is based upon a normativity he finds in the robustness of experience. He criticizes subjective impositions that close us to experience's full wealth. The problem with modern natural science as a universal way of thinking is that it limits us in our experience; it closes us to its qualitative depth. The poetizing of the later Heidegger is his attempt to recover the richness of what is in fact there in our experience even though our ideologies make us unreceptive to it. Thanks to Husserl's radical widening of intuition over the categorial sphere, Heidegger has the impetus and courage to be attentive to all the contours of human experience. He goes beyond Husserl in widening "intuition," in the form of fundamental dispositions, over the contextual sphere in which categorial relations are given. The phenomenological puzzle concerns the fact that what is given can be closed thanks to prejudice. The phenomenological task, then, is to undermine prejudice and recover the breadth of experience. Heidegger's transcendentalism is his attempt to bring experience to experience without remainder. It is indeed strange and thought-provoking that in different ages different features of experience are taken for granted, are taken to be obvious. Heidegger aims to experience the amplitude of experience that shifts the focal points of philosophical investigation and human culture. It is in this way a highly speculative endeavor, but one rooted in a concrete enterprise: the radical return to the full wealth of experience. He aims to motivate the widening of experience over the domain of experience by deploying historical considerations to undercut our prejudices. He turns to what he regards as the necessary progression of the experience of experience: in wonder entities emerged into presence, but tragically, the wonder necessarily deadened, leaving entities exposed, with no thought of their presence and normativity. Today, struck with terror at the emptiness of our experience, we are to fathom the hidden presence that affords us entities. We renew the wonder not just before entities but before that which affords us entities, the opening up of the domain of experience.

Receptive to Essences

Heidegger sometimes has occasion to recognize that the transcendental tradition includes ancient and medieval representatives. For example, in

Being and Time, he writes that Aristotle's principle that the soul is in a way all things led Thomas Aquinas to discover the priority of Dasein, albeit inchoately:

> Aristotle's principle, which points back to the ontological thesis of Parmenides, is one which Thomas Aquinas has taken up in a characteristic discussion. . . . Thomas has to demonstrate that the *verum* is such a *transcendens*. He does this by invoking an entity which, in accordance with its very manner of being, is properly suited to "come together with" entities of any sort whatever. This distinctive entity, the *ens quod natum est convenire cum omni ente*, is the soul (*anima*). Here the priority of "Dasein" over all other entities emerges, although it has not been ontologically clarified. This priority has obviously nothing in common with a vicious subjectivizing of the totality of entities.[79]

Heidegger's own task is to clarify ontologically the priority of Dasein and then to clarify more radically the relation of Dasein to the place in which Dasein and be-ing emerge. Now, Aquinas derives transcendental truth and goodness from the correspondence of the nature of a thing (*res*) with the intellect that apprehends it.[80] Heidegger, not unlike modern thinkers such as Bacon and Nietzsche, regards natural forms as superficial.[81] Yet he does not, for that matter, follow them in regarding nature as raw material for the imposition of subjective purposes. Nor does he view the entity as an unknown x behind the appearances we constitute. In 1928, he writes that the "non-dependence [of an entity] precisely in relation to the subject is what is to be explained, to be made as such into a problem."[82] His objection to form is couched in phenomenological terms. He advocates a kind of letting be of entities, determined not simply by what the thing is, but also by its play of presence and absence and by the matrix of relations that constitute it. His later meditations on such things as a bridge, a temple, or a jug serve to highlight the contextual web of intelligibility operative in our experience.[83] The jug, for example, implicates the fourfold of earth, sky, mortals, and divinities; the water it bears comes from the spring that arises thanks to the interplay of weather and terrain, and it slakes the thirst of mortals as a gift not wholly in their control. He writes, "The jug's essence, so experienced and thought, is what we call *thing*."[84] The meaning of the jug is not imposed by us; it is genuinely given in experience. In letting things be as they are, we come into our own as the steward of intelligibility or shepherd of being.[85] The normativity of things, their essences, enhances rather than restricts our freedom. Heidegger, it is true, seems to restrict things to certain artistic and architectural features; the status of other sorts of things, such as animals and plants, remains obscure.[86]

Heidegger's own transcendental thinking opens up avenues of approaching Kant that avoid standard textbook presentations. Rather than focus on the Copernican revolution that constrains experience to our subjective imposition and closes us to what things really are in themselves, Heidegger risks an innovative reading that begins at the beginning of the *Critique*. There, Kant makes the basically phenomenological move of subordinating thought to intuition. The distinction between analytic and synthetic judgment, and Kant's focus on the latter, makes the theme of intuitive givenness central to Kant's program. This givenness and our response to it make sense, argues Heidegger, only in light of a pre-subjective domain or context. Heidegger has Kant point to what Husserl calls the lifeworld, and Heidegger unpacks under the rubric of world. Kant, of course, does not fathom what Heidegger calls "earth"—that is, the necessary hiddenness of this context. Heidegger's affective transcendentalism develops precisely this point.

Heidegger's conception of a thing, determined by our thoughtful experience of it in all its dimensions, fulfills the meaning of the transcendental in Kant. As Heidegger noted in the mid-1930s, Kant calls transcendental "a determination of a thing with regard to its essence (as thing)."[87] He then comments:

> If we do not otherwise admit it, indirectly we can at least learn this from Kant's determination of the thing, namely, that a single thing for itself is not possible and, therefore, the determination of things cannot be carried out with reference to single things. The thing as a natural thing is only determinable from the essence of one nature in general.[88]

At the time these lines were written, Heidegger was engaged in the task of writing the essay, "On the Origin of the Work of Art," in which he unveils an account of things in terms of the context that will later be developed into the fourfold. Heidegger regards his understanding of the thing as an organic development of Kant's, which widens its application beyond scientific objects and suppresses the residual commitment to the modern subject by emphasizing the affectivity of thought. Heidegger's transcendental thinking, taking its bearing from the normativity of entities as well as our changing relation to that normativity, stands outside the opposition of ancient and modern transcendentalism.

Taylor Carman calls Heidegger's position "ontic realism" to distinguish it from Kantian idealism about things on the one hand and what he calls Heidegger's idealism about being on the other.[89] By realism, of course, Carman does not mean to suggest that the world as described by modern natural science is the sole real world or that the ontic can explain the ontological. Rather, Carman means that for Heidegger we access a world populated by things that exist and have properties independent of our accessing them. Modern natural science is not a subjective construct; its project enables it to access real features of things. Similarly, the experience of a poet is not a subjective imposition on nature; it accesses real features of things. While I agree with "ontic realism," I do not agree with Carman that Heidegger is an idealist about being. First, in contrast to the rationalism of the idealists, Heidegger underscores the affectivity of being. Yes, "there is" no being independent of Dasein, but that does not make being into a projection of Dasein; rather Dasein only is thanks to the affectivity of being. Second, being realistic about entities entails the recognition that some complexions of the world are more illuminating than others. That is, Heidegger can bemoan the rootlessness of contemporary technology because he recognizes that a richer relation to things is possible and obligatory. The sort of new beginning he works toward is one in which our disposition would allow us to be beholden to the natures of things. Realism about entities entails realism about the context for interpretation. The meaning of being is not some thing independent of entities; it is the domain in which we meet with them. The domain and the entities can be distinguished but not separated.

5 The Shadow Heidegger Did Not See

As Heidegger sought the unthought in others, especially in his transcendental predecessors, did he adequately identify it in himself? In 1927, Heidegger remarks that Kant endeavored to understand his predecessors better than they understood themselves, and Heidegger takes this as justification for seeking to understand Kant better than he understood himself. The possibility of doing so, Heidegger is quick to add, is not an expression of our presumption; it rather expresses the necessary finitude of every philosopher:

> Every semblance of presumption disappears completely when we comprehend that even those who understand better are in need of a new interpretation, just when they understand appropriately and hit upon new foundations. Thus there is no reason to take oneself as absolute in the bad sense. There is a significant darkness in every philosophical endeavor, and even the most radical of these endeavors remains finite. Such an endeavor sees itself as absolute in the genuine sense only when it comprehends itself as finite.[90]

Working our way through Heidegger demands that we attempt to understand Heidegger better than he understood himself, that we attempt to illumine the darkness of Heidegger's project. In view of Heidegger's entanglement with transcendental philosophy, I would like to take a step back and identify three shortcomings of Heidegger's thinking. First, his transcendental program remains disconnected from the natural human concerns that Kant rightly thinks motivate philosophy in its origins. Second, the historical motivation he provides, to the degree to which it appears dogmatic, is to that degree unable to motivate the transcendental turn. Finally, he unnecessarily mystifies his subject matter by using language that appears to personify it.

The Limit of Heidegger's Inquiry

Philosophy, according to Heidegger, retains something of the sophistical. In 1925, he writes, "If all science and every form of research includes this possibility of falling, and necessarily so, it also goes without saying that philosophy is always necessarily a bit of sophistry, and that, as a form of enactment of Dasein, it carries this danger within itself."[91] In 1925, Heidegger says he avoids the sophist's curiosity by sticking resolutely to his one topic: " 'Are you still standing there,' condescendingly asked the much traveled Sophist of Socrates, 'and still saying the same thing about the same thing?' 'Yes,' answered Socrates, 'that I am. But you who are so extremely smart, you *never* say the same thing about the same thing.' "[92] Like Socrates, Heidegger always says the same thing about the same, and he always asks the same question of each one of his interlocutors. Accordingly, the analyses he gives us, say of art, technology, and thought, or readings of Aristotle, Leibniz, and Nietzsche, generally amount to little more than commentaries on his own unifying question of the experience of experience. If his task is simple, why is his corpus so complex? His restless spirit and prodigious productivity come from the paradox of his transcendental quest: to bring to speech and experience something heretofore unnamed using words that, strictly speaking, name other experiences. In 1951, he relates the paradox of this quest to Socrates, calling him "the purest thinker of the West":

> Once we are so related and drawn to what withdraws, we are drawing into what withdraws [*dann sind wir auf dem Zug in das Sichentziehende*], into the enigmatic and therefore mutable nearness of its appeal. Whenever man is properly drawing that way, he is thinking—even though he may still be far away from what withdraws, even though the withdrawal may remain as veiled as ever. All through his life and right into his death, Socrates did nothing else than place himself into this draft, this current, [*in den Zugwind dieses Zuges*] and maintain himself in it. This is why he is the purest thinker of the West. This is why he wrote nothing. For anyone who begins to write out of thoughtfulness must inevitably be like those people who run to seek refuge from any draft too strong for them. An as yet hidden history still keeps the secret why all great Western thinkers after Socrates, with all their greatness, had to be such fugitives.[93]

Heidegger thought of himself as just such a fugitive who, through the cacophony of his writings, tried to express the experience that led (Heidegger's) Socrates to remain silent. At play in all his writings is the continuous radicalization of the transcendental turn, the continuous attempt to speak of that which necessarily withdraws in making every experience possible.

Kant likewise relates his quest to that of Socrates. According to Kant, Socrates "gave an entirely new *practical* direction to the philosophical spirit and to all speculation. He stands almost alone among men as the one whose conduct came closest to *the idea of a wise man*."[94] Kant distinguishes the species of philosopher, exemplified by Socrates, from the philodoxus, represented by the theoretician:

> The mere theoretician or, as *Socrates* calls him, the *philodoxus*, strives only after speculative knowledge, without caring how much his knowledge contributes to the ultimate end of human reason; he gives rules for the use of reason to all kinds of ends. The practical philosopher, the teacher of wisdom through doctrine and examples, is the philosopher in the true sense. For philosophy is the idea of a perfect wisdom that shows us the ultimate ends of human reason.[95]

The philosopher, unlike the philodoxus, also concerns himself or herself with the human good. As is well known, Kant distills the Socratic search for wisdom into three (or four) questions:

1   What can I know?
2   What ought I to do?
3   What may I hope?
4   What is man?[96]

Heidegger addresses Kant's four questions in *Kant and the Problem of Metaphysics* in the context of defending the priority of Dasein for fundamental ontology; Kant, too, according to Heidegger, comes to see the priority of the question of man as a result of the foundations laid in the *Critique of Pure Reason*. In citing this text, he mentions that the four questions belong to Kant's cosmopolitan conception of philosophy.[97] Heidegger thinks that all four questions target human finitude and that it is the job of philosophy to highlight and safeguard it.[98] The finitude of the philosopher is that which the metaphor of leaping over one's shadow is meant to highlight. Now, Kant says that establishing "the limits of reason" is "the most urgent but also the most difficult task, of which the *philodoxus*, however, takes no notice."[99] In this way, Heidegger's insistence on finitude would seem to distinguish him from the philodoxus who neglects wisdom. Let us take a closer look at the scope of his questioning.

While Kant's Socrates poses three or four basic philosophical questions, Heidegger pursues but one: "In the age of *total lack of questioning anything*, it is sufficient as a start to inquire into the question of all questions."[100] He writes that "philosophizing" amounts to asking the question "What should we do?," which he construes according to four sub-questions:

> Who *are* we?
> Why should we *be*?
> What are entities?
> Why does being happen?[101]

Heidegger recasts Kant's question in the first-person plural rather than the first-person singular. One could say, of course, that this better expresses being-with others, but whatever reason one might assign to this difference, it opens up the danger of absolving the philosopher of individual responsibility for his or her actions. Moreover, Heidegger seems to regard all of these questions as a variation on acting, and yet the kind of acting at issue is not the kind of acting that involves the give and take of sharing the world with other people. Instead, he understands action along contemplative lines, as if action were merely a matter of having truth disclosed and not further a matter of performing the good that one perceives should be done. Finally, it is strange that Heidegger ignores the other Kantian questions of the good and of hope to prize the finitude of the *Critique of Pure Reason*. This is a point rightly pressed by Levinas: "The question *What may I know?* leads to finitude, but *What must I do?* and *What am I entitled to hope?* go farther and, in any case, elsewhere than toward finitude. These questions are not reducible to the comprehension of being; they concern the duty and salvation of man."[102]

For Heidegger, the question of experiencing experience is the most important question. But even were we to grant the centrality of his question, it would not follow that the question is the only one we might wish to pursue. To say that others have neglected this question and to say that others have asked questions that are unimportant are not equivalent claims. In this way, Heidegger's thought does not encompass the breadth of philosophical speculation illustrated by Socrates. Instead, Heidegger's greatness resides in the intensity with which he pursues a very constrained topic. He is the first one in the history of philosophy to have given such sustained attention to this issue, and he makes significant contributions to meta-philosophy and the transcendental tradition. But Heidegger is not what one might call a great philosopher. He is, as he puts it, a "thinker" (*Denker*) of the clearing and not a "philosopher" (*Philosoph*) as classically understood.[103] In light of his entanglement with transcendentalism, we might call him a great transcendental thinker. Heidegger's narrow focus on the experience of experience closes him to the more cosmopolitan interests of philosophers such as Plato, Aquinas, or Kant. Richard Velkley rightly observes that, in bracketing the question of the human good, "Heidegger strikingly separates himself not only from Kant but from the entire tradition of philosophy since Socrates."[104] In Kant's sense, then, he is a philodoxus, a theoretician, and not a philosopher. Hence, unlike Socrates, Heidegger's thought is separable from his life.

In "Heidegger's Apology," Kisiel argues that we should resist the ideology of separating Heidegger's life and thought, because the early Heidegger identified his project as a hermeneutics of facticity, thus implicating his biography into his philosophy. Accordingly, Kisiel thinks that, like Socrates, Heidegger's life and thought must be defended together.[105] It should be remembered, however, that the early Heidegger also summarizes the relevance of Aristotle's life for the understanding of his philosophy: "Regarding the personality of a philosopher, our only interest is that he was born at a certain time, that he worked, and that he died."[106] Kisiel warns us that the application of this reading of Aristotle to Heidegger in order to separate Heidegger's life and thought is "one of the most notorious examples of quotation out of context."[107] Kisiel emphasizes that the remarks occur within the development of Heidegger's hermeneutics of facticity such that a philosophy arises from out of the concrete experience of the philosopher. But why does Heidegger dismiss *Aristotle's* biography? Because, while each philosopher's biography is important for *that* person in furnishing the necessary motives to philosophize, no one else's motive may be my own. When we philosophize after the example of Heidegger, our own biography is central, but the biography of anyone else is not. We instead meet in the work we interpret in reference to our own experience. Heidegger says that in the course on Aristotle he has "the purpose of *gaining insight into the fundamental exigencies of scientific research*. Here, we offer *no philosophy*, much less a history of philosophy."[108] He aims to interpret the expressed conceptuality of Aristotle. Why should any of us care to follow along? That is something no one else can answer for us. The life of each of us is relevant in order to furnish motivations for each of us to philosophize, but the life of the philosopher we are engaging is not.

In 1927, in the context of discussing how his transcendental thought differs from Husserl's, Heidegger takes umbrage at the suggestion that his "work is Catholic phenomenology" because it takes seriously Thomas Aquinas and Duns Scotus: "But the concept of a Catholic phenomenology is even more absurd than the concept of a Protestant mathematics."[109] Philosophy is even more rigorously theoretical than mathematics; the affairs of the mathematician do not enter into mathematics; therefore, all the more so, the affairs of the phenomenologist do not enter into phenomenology. Similarly, he points out in the mid-1930s, that the philosopher's need to leap over his shadow "has nothing to do with a psychology of the creative personality. It concerns only the form of motion belonging to the work itself as it works itself out in him."[110]

Biography and philosophy are separable for a philodoxus, not a philosopher. Socrates, whom Heidegger regarded as the purest thinker because he wrote nothing, is someone whose significance is inseparable from his life. To a philosopher such as Socrates, character is not incidental but central. We cannot say of Socrates that our interest relates solely to the fact that he was born, worked, and died. Because Heidegger was a philodoxus, not a philosopher, our interest in his biography is limited to the following: he was born in 1889, wrote the volumes in the *Gesamtausgabe*, and died. Naturally, I am not excusing Heidegger the man at all. I am arguing that, according to the Socratic view of philosophy set forth by Kant, Heidegger is not a philosopher, and therefore his thought should be engaged and evaluated on its own merits independent of the overwhelming demerits of his life. We have no qualms about distinguishing the mathematics of an anti-Semitic mathematician from his anti-Semitism. It is only because we fail to distinguish the philodoxus from the philosopher that we balk at making the same distinction with Heidegger.

Heidegger is not alone in falling short of the classical ideal of philosophy; most philosophers in recent memory are likewise theoreticians. Quine, for example, embraces the restriction of philosophy to a purely theoretical interest.[111] Exceptions to this rule include Gabriel Marcel among continental authors and Thomas Nagel among analytic authors. The true *philosophical* significance of the Heidegger affair is not that it calls into question Heidegger's *Denkweg* but that it calls into question the status of the professional philosopher who is really at bottom a theoretician and not a philosopher in the classical sense.[112] There is something unsettling about the philosopher's disavowal of seeking wisdom for living life in the face of death. Historians may want to debate Heidegger's biography, but thinkers who wish to find reason to disagree with Heidegger ought not to invoke his biography; instead the evidence to appeal to is the evidence available to the thinker qua thinker. Heidegger was a species of transcendental phenomenologist whose thought admits of confirmation or disconfirmation. He offers us a way to make sense of the changing modalities of our experience of things, and it is up to us to turn to the field of experience in order to determine whether and to what extent his proposal illuminates it. What sort of character Heidegger had is irrelevant to his thought but relevant to the larger question of the nature of professional philosophy and the high calling of philosophy as classically understood.

Let me entertain an objection: Heidegger seizes upon philosophy as a radical possibility of life. At the beginning of his career, he writes, "It is hard to live as a philosopher—inner truthfulness toward oneself and toward those one is supposed to teach demands sacrifices, renunciation, and struggles that remain forever foreign to the academic 'tradesman.'"[113]

And he subsequently sought to reawaken a question that promises to renew our experience of things. He accordingly identifies and neutralizes prejudices that close us off from the full wealth of experience, and he develops ways such as the fourfold to articulate the complex play of presence and absence as well as the relationality woven into the fabric of human experience. Moreover, he seeks to reclaim the primacy of contemplation over technological manipulation by furnishing a new object for meditation: the mysterious domain of experience. In the interview with *Der Spiegel*, he says, "Thinking is not inactivity but is in itself the action that stands in dialogue with the fate of the world. It seems to me that the distinction, stemming from metaphysics, between theory and practice—as well as the notion of a transmission between the two—blocks the way to an insight into what I understand by thinking."[114] How can I maintain that a thinker so concerned with the rhythm of everyday being-in-the-world should be indifferent to the basic questions of life? And how can I think that one who so emphasizes the finitude of philosophers should somehow fail to be one?

Heidegger was mindful of the meaning intrinsic to experience, and he indeed underscored the fact that philosophy is conditional. But his discussions of authenticity and inauthenticity and his appeal to dispositions to motivate us are couched in terms of his theoretical question concerning our experience of experience. He brings out a practical dimension of philosophy, to be sure, but it is a practical dimension deployed to motivate his theoretical inquiry. In the *Contributions*, he firmly rejects attempts to find an ethical significance to questions of authenticity in *Being and Time*: "The danger of misinterpreting *Being and Time* in this direction, i.e., 'existentiell-anthropologically,' and of seeing the interconnection of disclosedness, truth, and Dasein from the perspective of a moral resolve . . . is basically excluded . . ., if, from the beginning we hold on to the grounding question of the 'meaning of be-ing' as the *only* question."[115] That's it. He has but one question; all other considerations are for the sake of this project. He therefore has little to say regarding what one as a person should do in life and what one may hope for, nor does he shed light on other sorts of questions that naturally arise in the pursuit of human and divine wisdom. Strictly speaking, Heidegger's thought is not philosophy or the pursuit of wisdom but a purely transcendental inquiry. I happen to think it is still valuable, but only for what it is, not for what it is not.

Provided that we understand the narrowness of Heidegger's project, we need not be scandalized that he was not a moral man. The value of his philosophical project is independent of the shocking debacle that was his life. Such crimes as his Nazism, his racism, his marital infidelity, and his betrayal of friends are atrocious failings, but they are his personal failings, because Heidegger does not overcome the specialist's opposition between philosophy and life. Heidegger is Socratic in prizing inquiry over results, but he is not Socratic in neglecting human concerns in his philosophizing. It is philosophically significant that Socrates did not sleep with Alcibiades;

it is not philosophically significant that Heidegger slept with Arendt. Transcendentalism, even as appropriated by Heidegger, does not exhaust philosophy; in fact, it leaves out much that is essential. For the finite being that philosophizes is one that was born and will die and until then, must live with himself and others. Transcendental philosophy seizes upon the finite being and its changing modalities of experience; philosophy upon the finite being who has questions about the ultimate causes of things and the form of the good life. Kant remains something more than a merely transcendental thinker; he is in touch with the Socratic heritage of philosophy. Heidegger remains merely a transcendental thinker concerned with the condition for the possibility of experiencing experience in all its richness.

Heidegger thinks he has good reason to focus on his one question of experience. The world is gripped by the mathematical prejudice; it takes for granted the modern worldview and it looks to the special sciences for information on the optimum way to conduct its affairs: "The sciences have today taken over the role that philosophy played up until now."[116] In such a situation, there is no "market" for philosophy as traditionally understood. In fact, Marcel, who celebrates Heidegger's thought, remarks, "For a philosopher worthy of the name there is no more important undertaking than that of reinstating experience in the place of such bad substitutes for it."[117] In calling into question such a state of affairs, in pointing to the non-scientific fundament of every science and the limits of the modern worldview, Heidegger prepares the way for something other than his own thought. Just what this thought is, however, remains undetermined by Heidegger. Those of us who follow after him remain free to surpass his shadow by asking a wider range of human questions. His recovery of experience aids in this quest.

Heidegger was only a philosopher in the sense the young Heidegger denied to Husserl: he inquired into being from out of his factical experience.[118] This is the Heideggerian version of transcendental philosophy. He was not, however, a philosopher in the classical sense, a philosopher in the sense of a Socrates, Kant, or Levinas, that is, a thinker for whom the question of the examined life was paramount. We can learn much positively from Heidegger qua transcendental philosopher, but concerning Heidegger qua philosopher we can glean only an example of what each of us ought not to be.

The Problem with History as Motivation

In the last section of the *Critique of Pure Reason*, Kant sketches the history of pure reason in which he speculates concerning the original motive for philosophizing. He maintains that transcendental inquiry necessarily develops later, in what Hegel would call philosophy's old age:

> It is a very notable fact, although it could not have been otherwise, that in the infancy of philosophy men began where we should incline

to end, namely, with the knowledge of God, occupying themselves with the hope, or rather indeed with the specific nature, of another world. However gross the religious concepts generated by the ancient practices which still persisted in each community from an earlier more barbarous state, this did not prevent the more enlightened members from devoting themselves to free investigation of these matters; and they easily discerned that there could be no better ground or more dependable way of pleasing the invisible power that governs the world, and so of being happy in another world at least, than by living the good life. Accordingly theology and morals were the two motives, or rather the two points of reference, in all those abstract enquiries of reason to which men came to devote themselves. It was chiefly, however, the former that step by step committed the purely speculative reason to those labours which afterwards became so renowned under the name of metaphysics.[119]

For Kant, the transcendental turn emerges as a kind of detour that necessarily comes after the war waged between dogmatic and skeptical approaches to metaphysics. The questions of death and life motivate metaphysics, and the consequent debate between philosophers such as Wolff and Hume make transcendentalism necessary. Heidegger's philosophy, in neglecting those human questions that inaugurate philosophy, leaves unexplained the remote ground for motivating the transcendental turn.[120] One begins to philosophize, begins to study the philosophical tradition, because one already has questions. And the sort of question that prompts philosophical inquiry is not the transcendental one. As he writes in 1920, "Philosophy as factical life experience requires a motive in which the worry about factical life experience itself remains."[121] Heidegger's question of motivation, then, should lead him to expand consideration of just what counts as a philosophical question.

The difficulty of entering into phenomenology concerns the difficulty of making the transcendental turn intelligible in a preliminary way. The trouble stems from the fact that the turn is intelligible only after it has been enacted. In grappling with this problem, Husserl and Heidegger shift from a Cartesian emphasis on research to a historically motivated movement. However, as I noted above, the historical shift engenders its own problems. Husserl's insistence that he is realizing the *telos* inborn in philosophy since its inception appears dogmatic and therefore unpersuasive. While Heidegger's discussion of fundamental dispositions does bring history to a kind of phenomenological exhibition, it too seems hounded by dogmatic assertions about the beginning of philosophy and its necessary decadence.

Heidegger sharply distinguishes history and historiography. History has to do with the thoughtful recollection of what has been so that we will be prepared to think what is unthought in these thinkers for ourselves. It belongs to what I have called the rhetoric or poetics of being.

Historiography is the study of what former thinkers have thought as such. Heidegger aims to do the first, not the second. But the way he talks about the history of being sometimes suggests that he is engaging in a theoretical reconstruction of the past rather than simply trying to find motivations to think in the present. Though Heidegger insists that the historical epochs are not necessary in the way they were in Hegel,[122] the unfolding of the logic of ἀλήθεια accords with the necessary logic of experience. The first philosophers, enthralled with entities, *necessarily* missed the horizon in which they were given. With Gadamer, then, we can recognize a "logically compulsive character" that approaches Hegel's.[123] But insofar as the complete decadence and oblivion of being to which we are led holds the promise of a new beginning free of the necessity of decadence, ἀλήθεια now being thought as such, we must disagree with Gadamer and move Heidegger even closer to Hegel: there is a kind of teleology built into Heidegger's history.[124]

Heidegger begins with the end, with an insight into the fundamental character of the domain of experience, which he then uses to contextualize ancient metaphysics. Where does "Heidegger"—naming, of course, not the person but the matter to be thought—himself then fit into the history of being? *Ereignis* does not belong in the genus of "being interpretation" in which being is understood in terms of entities as ἰδέα, ἐνέργεια, *actualitas*, *Wille zur Macht*, etc.,[125] but is precisely what grants the possibility for such interpretations. Philipp Rosemann is thus right in characterizing Heidegger's approach as "transcendental history."[126] However, Heidegger does seem to belong to the completion of the history of being. The telos of history has been achieved insofar as the mystery of the self-concealing, implicitly at work in every previous thinker, has been given to him to be thought by means of a recollection of the unthought in the tradition. There is, then, a kind of teleology built into Heidegger's history that allows Heidegger to view history from out of the origin of history. The history of being, determined by that which withdraws, can now give way to a reflection trained on that which withdraws as such. Given this end, Heidegger's history is not so much a tragedy as a comedy, but it is a comedy effected by means of a tragedy. It has something of the Christian *felix culpa* or happy fault of Adam that is happy because it brought about such a savior. Similarly, the tragic ending of the first beginning opens up the possibility of a bright new beginning.

Heidegger differs from Hegel in that for Heidegger the philosophers and epochs of philosophy do not emerge from a dialectic among entities, but each emerges from the unfolding logic of experience. Heidegger's meditation on Hegel in "Hegel and the Greeks" aims to show that behind and beyond Hegel's reach in the history of philosophy, the mystery of ἀλήθεια holds sway.[127] But if the mystery of ἀλήθεια is what determines history, to the extent that human beings are granted access to this mystery, they will be beyond history.[128] Haar rightly calls this point eschatological and post-historical.[129] John Caputo has isolated what he sees as the "mythological" dimension that emerges in his thought insofar as Heidegger gives historical instantiation to an antehistorical structure, ἀ-λήθεια.[130]

Emphasizing the fact that Heidegger is a transcendental thinker allows us to cut the history of being down to size. As with Kant, history is a heuristic device. Kant asks: "How, indeed, should it be possible to learn philosophy? Every philosophical thinker builds his own work, so to speak, on the ruins of another; never, however, has a work come about that would have lasted in all its parts. Merely for that reason one cannot learn philosophy, because *it is not yet given.*"[131] He adds, "He who wants to learn to philosophize must, on the contrary, regard all systems of philosophy only as the *history of the use of reason* and as objects for exercising his philosophical talent."[132] In a similar vein, we should not wonder how Heidegger fits into the history of being because the history of being concerns principally Heidegger's own program. In narrating history Heidegger aims to give an account of our own present experience and its deficiencies in order to motivate us to be more mindful of the thickness of our experience. Only within the transcendental domain can the logic of experience appear for confirmation or disconfirmation: the rush to presence that Heidegger locates historically among the Greeks can be registered in our own phenomenological experience today insofar as we allow our experience to be renewed. The inattention to presence and attention to that which is present can be experienced in our own phenomenological experience today insofar as we allow our experience to be deadened by the representation of the *mathesis universalis*. Transcendental phenomenology alone can justify the logic of presentation at work in the claims of Heidegger's history, and therefore transcendental phenomenology has a kind of priority in his account. For the claims about the past are immaterial; what counts for Heidegger are the claims about our experience today. History is there to motivate, not to represent. Heidegger chastises the tradition for not quite asking his own question, the question Heidegger proposes that each one of us ask today. Heidegger wants to show, again and again, that his question was not quite asked by those in the philosophical tradition. But this is different than showing that the questions they did pursue were not worthwhile. It is all too easy to regard his historical narrative as somehow dismissing or encapsulating the history of philosophy when in fact he cares only to motivate his philosophy. In this way, I think we would do well to downplay talk of "the history of being" and instead focus on what he wants us to think about: the domain of experience that necessarily withdraws from our attention in all our experiences of things.

Why should we give this topic thought? The reason is not that it has been unthought. That would be to regard as normative what is novel, which Heidegger would dismiss as empty curiosity. The normative rather comes from the subject matter itself and not the history of its interpretation. For example, Heidegger thinks the mathematical prejudice is "what most holds us captive and makes us unfree in the experience and determination of things."[133] The felt tension between the richness of experience and the inherited accounts of that experience gives rise to the normative pull that motivates us to philosophize afresh. In this way, I do not think transcendental phenomenology must choose between Cartesian research and dogmatic assertions about history. There is a third way. As the autobiographical path of Husserl or Heidegger's Kantian way show, the subject matter itself can furnish motivations. I have in mind here something like the "summoners" that Plato mentions in the *Republic*, which lead someone to turn from an enigma of jumbled intelligibility in the sensible realm (say a finger that is both large and small) to consideration of the intelligible realm of being.[134] In an analogous way, it would seem reasonable to suppose that we could find in the world of experience clues that would motivate the transcendental turn. I think the manifestation of the body in ostensive acts or the difference in presentation between an actor on stage and in real life can be such summoners.[135] In *Being and Time*, Heidegger points to the shift in presentation that happens when some element of our routine is missing or broken—perhaps our keys are not in their usual place—which causes our attention to turn from anticipating our day to concentrated consideration of what is missing. Such events can be the occasion for experiencing wonder concerning the play of presence and absence at work in all our experience, especially if someone else has indicated this dimension of experience to us before. As with judgment and experience, such presentational shifts as ostension and acting cannot be accounted for in terms of scientific or ontic modes of explanation. Therefore we must acknowledge a new dimension of experience that phenomenology gives us the means to analyze.

Ignoring such summoners exposes phenomenology to the danger that it might appear as an esoteric doctrine for the initiated rather than the proper philosophical standpoint for making sense of the logic of experience. What motivates transcendental philosophy best is the faithful confrontation with a phenomenon that manifestly cannot be explained in terms of the push and pull of physical forces and yet is fundamental to all experience. Truth, as the Husserl of the *Logical Investigations* and the Heidegger of *Being and Time* eloquently and compellingly demonstrate, cannot be accounted for in terms of psychology, biology, or physics; therefore, the transcendental turn is necessary.[136] Grappling with such things gives rise to the affectivity of wonder that brings about the turn.

Dispensing with Mystifications

Reappropriating transcendental terms may help to "demystify" the sometimes unnecessarily opaque vocabulary of the later Heidegger. Though he expressly denies the attributions, he sometimes appears as a prophet or a poet or a feigned Presocratic—not as a philosopher.[137] Gadamer in fact takes it as his chief task in *Heidegger's Ways* to work against this common misunderstanding: "Above all, these works are intended to prevent the reader from the error of supposing that a mythology or poetizing gnosis is to be found in Heidegger's renunciation of the customary."[138] The later Heidegger tends more and more to deny any continuity with the philosophical tradition. With this tendency, though, he seems to neglect a basic hermeneutical principle. As he points out in *Being and Time*, one must begin with semblance in order to lead to understanding; one cannot begin without some pre-understanding.[139] Even though the pre-understanding is to be radically challenged in the course of the investigation, it is nonetheless the case that pre-understanding serves as the necessary point of departure. In this case, the leap into the event of being appropriated requires a pre-understanding of what is to be transformed. Heidegger's occasional acknowledgment of his continual indebtedness to transcendental philosophy works against this neglect of hermeneutic principles and affords us the reader a way to make sense of him.

Critchley speaks of the need to clean up continental and analytic philosophy by steering discourse between the twin dangers of scientism with its language of causal explanation and obscurantism with its language of pseudo causation. He thinks phenomenology's language of clarification provides the route to engender understanding concerning those things that Wittgenstein says "are hidden because of their simplicity and familiarity."[140] Perhaps we can expand on Critchley's suggestion. Recourse to transcendental philosophy understood phenomenologically would do more to promote understanding than undermine it. The first step of philosophy is the recognition that our common understanding, which equates being with being on-hand, cannot handle every kind of knowledge—a recognition Heidegger attributes to transcendental philosophy. Having shifted into the philosophical manner of questioning, one finds oneself in the transcendental matrix of relations, which grounds all our comportments. At this point, Kant invokes principles to explain experience, but Heidegger follows Husserl in seeing the domain as one of phenomenological exploration rather than construction or what Critchley terms pseudo causation. Now, Heidegger does not remain here but continues further by inquiring into the givenness of this domain, which is ultimately accomplished in the reciprocal belonging together of given being and its dative. His project, while novel, is had by way of transcendental philosophy. The difference between everyday or scientific language and transcendental terms is greater than the difference between transcendental terms and the language of Heidegger's later thinking. Indeed, it remains questionable whether even the best of his later terminology (e.g., the "clearing") would be understandable unless it were first translated back into the phenomenological transcendentalese of *Being and Time* (ecstatic horizon of timeliness) before making the appropriate corrective adjustments. Formal indication may have introduced a distortion into the phenomena, but it did sometimes introduce others to the phenomena.

To be sure, these matters are intrinsically difficult and will never read as easily as a narrative and never have the clarity of mathematics.[141] Perhaps, though, Heidegger could learn something from Kant, whom he says "has something in common with the great Greek beginning, which at the same time distinguishes him from all German thinkers before and after him."[142] Just what is the rare virtue? "This is the incorruptible clarity of his thinking and speaking, which by no means excludes the questionable and the unbalanced, and does not feign light where there is darkness." Heidegger assuredly made this his goal as well, but it remains questionable whether he succeeded as well as Kant. In my view, the transcendental in his thought stands opposed to his more mythical strain as its corrective; the transcendental is the more compelling aspect of his thought.

I would like to flag two mystifications in Heidegger's thought as it concerns his attempt at self-critique concerning his transcendental involvement. I call these mystifications insofar as I think the way Heidegger expresses himself is unnecessarily misleading, and that we can clarify his path without any loss of meaning by changing its expression.

First, Heidegger rejects phenomenology as a transcendental research program when he discovers that the domain is not just hidden (and so amenable to research) but, as he says, "self-concealing." "Be-ing [*das Seyn*] is not merely hidden; it withdraws and conceals itself. From this we derive an essential insight: the clearing [*Die Lichtung*], in which entities are, is not simply bounded and delimited by something hidden but by something self-concealing [*Sichverbergendes*]."[143] In the experience of wonder, a Plato or Aristotle attended to present entities, thereby neglecting the experience of presence itself. Analogously, if we emerge from a thick woods into a clearing, we might very well feel the relief of the open space, but our attentions will likely focus on the beautiful deer grazing there rather than the clearing as such. What I find mystifying about the claim that the domain is self-concealing is that it suggests erroneously a personification of the domain insofar as it suggests a willful propensity. Naturally, Heidegger would reject such a suggestion. I think he has in mind what Aristotle says of nature when, in *Physics* II, he defines it as something with an inborn tendency to change and rest. Aristotle thought this was true of human beings but also animals, plants, and non-living things as well. Only with reason is there an ability to bring about contraries, is there willful propensity. In all other natural things, the tendency is determined by the kind of thing it is. In this way, Heidegger is suggesting that the domain, being the sort of the thing it is, naturally conceals itself.

Sheehan likewise turns to Aristotle to make sense of the self-concealing, but he takes it to be a point of logic; it does not make sense to look for a cause for the first principle.[144] But Heidegger's point is not logical or causal but phenomenological. Heidegger may not want to get behind the principle, but he does want to get to it. What is the mode of access to that which makes experience possible? Or in Sheehan's Aristotelian terms, how does the first principle of experience come to be experienced? I take it that what Heidegger wants to do is insist that the nature of Dasein and the activity of Dasein as transcendental philosopher simply cannot account for the fact that the horizon necessarily recedes to furnish us with entities, so that the experience of the principle would happen thanks to the authenticity of the researcher. It is not the falling of Dasein that makes the clearing pass unnoticed; this movement rather belongs to the very structure of experience itself. Polt goes further and suggests that the withdrawal simply cannot be given to experience. He writes:

> We could put it this way: the happening in which the being of beings is *given* cannot itself be given, because this event of be-ing sets the parameters for what givenness itself means. . . . When we hold and behold beings in their being, as a given gift, we are beholden to a giving that is itself self-withholding, that cannot give itself.[145]

Polt's reading suggests that Heidegger must abandon the goal of phenomenology. In *Being and Time*, Heidegger says that phenomenology is necessary precisely because certain primary phenomena do not ordinarily show up in experience:

> What is it that by its very essence is *necessarily* the theme whenever we exhibit something *explicitly*? Manifestly, it is something that proximally and for the most part does *not* show itself at all: it is something that lies *hidden*, in contrast to that which proximally and for the most part does show itself; but at the same time it is something that belongs to what thus shows itself, and it belongs to it so essentially as to constitute its sense and its ground.[146]

In *Being and Time*, he says the phenomena can be covered over in a number of ways, namely, if they are *undiscovered, completely covered up*, or *partially covered up* in the sense of "disguise" or semblance.[147] Heidegger's later discovery is that the phenomenological phenomenon can be hidden for a fourth reason: the opening up of the domain of experience can be hidden because it is *self-concealing*. Nonetheless, the newly discovered recalcitrance of the primary phenomenon does not compromise the phenomenological project of leading into the self-showing of that which for the most part remains hidden.[148] Polt's version would have him suppress the showing at the heart of the phenomenological enterprise, but Heidegger, I think, suggests a different strategy.[149] He continues to describe his project as a "phenomenology of the inapparent," which "leads away in order to come before . . ., and lets that before which it is led show itself."[150] The self-withholding is in fact given to experience, but it is shown in a way other than the way entities are experienced in their being. It is given to experience as that which is not experienced in and through every experience of entities. It is not simply that which is not experienced or self-withholding; it is that which is not experienced or withheld in every experience; it is the counterpart to the presencing of entities. Appropriation is genuinely given and so phenomenology is possible, but it is given through an experience of the counter-movement that makes presence and present entities possible.

With the phenomenology of the inapparent, Heidegger seems to have in mind an analogy with Husserl's categorial intuition, which he had described as follows: "When I see this book, I do see a substantial thing, without however seeing the substantiality as I see the book. But it is the substantiality that, in its non-appearance, enables what appears to appear. In this sense, one can even say that it is more apparent than what itself appears."[151] Husserl's great discovery, applauded by Heidegger, is to recognize the genuine givenness of substantiality even though it is not sensuously intuited. Analogously, the absencing of presence enables us to encounter present things; it is genuinely given and thus knowable even though it is not made present. Phenomenological showing is not limited to the presence of that which is present; it can bring to experience the self-effacing movement that constitutes experience, the self-effacing movement that makes possible the presencing of that which is present.

This first mystification is related to a second. Heidegger says that the clearing is not for the presence of entities but for the self-concealing of being.[152] Again, I do not think he means to personify being; rather he is making a teleological judgment, and as Aristotle argues, such judgments can be made about anything with a nature, even if such natural things are non-living, non-sensing, and non-rational. The clearing is for the sake of being's absencing rather than for the presencing of entities. But this seems like just a difference in perspective: entities come to presence by virtue of the horizon absencing and the horizon absences by virtue of entities presencing. Heidegger is characterizing one and the same movement from two perspectives. But the way up and the way down are one and the same. Why should we say that the telos is not the presence of entities but the absence of the domain as such? The argument seems to be that if we take the telos to be the presence of entities then entities themselves become obvious and open to the kind of positivistic, technological thinking that dominates the modern world. Instead, to safeguard our experience of things, we must say that the telos is what necessarily withdraws in every experience. However, this suggests that the real problem is our impoverished relation to things, which we can recover through attending to the domain of being.[153] It is mystifying to say that the clearing is somehow for the self-concealing. This seems to move it beyond the care of Dasein. Rather, I think the clearing is for the sorts of things that can show up within it: loved ones, other people, works of art, pets, other animals, plants, festivals, games, sunsets, and the like. To love is to desire the presence of loved ones, not in some degenerate way, but for the sake of communion.[154]

Conclusion

The conclusion of this work is twofold: first, Heidegger remains, in some sense, a transcendental thinker, and second, Heidegger himself acknowledges this fact. Now, because this conclusion is controversial, let me retrace the evidence against and the evidence for it.

It does seem that Heidegger disavows and abandons transcendental philosophy in his later thought, because he chastises transcendental philosophy as being ahistorical and his later thought is thoroughly historicized; instead of the *a priori* he identifies the changing complexion of being through history. However, while Heidegger does take up a critical distance toward transcendental philosophy, this is critical in Heidegger's sense of critical: to draw out what is essential in order to preserve it and to transcend its limits. Heidegger does not disavow or abandon transcendental thought, because he preserves what is essential to it, namely the sense of taking a step back from ordinary engagement with the world to begin thinking about the experience of having a world. Moreover, the *a priori* turns out to be the necessary first pass for approaching history; Heidegger's discussion of history avoids mythology only by being located within the transcendental turn. Most fundamentally, Heidegger puzzles long and hard over how to motivate his philosophical project, early and late. The transcendental program of *Being and Time* remains his recommended gateway to his path of thinking. Kant and Husserl, be it remembered, turned to history to motivate their transcendental philosophies; the movement from transcendence to historical considerations is native to transcendental thinking. And Heidegger criticized transcendental thinking for being "not yet" historical—not for being in essence opposed to these sorts of considerations; what might seem to be disavowals are in fact nuanced judgments that are the fruit of his development of transcendental thinking. Heidegger criticizes transcendental philosophy so severely because he remains entangled with it.

I think the above rejoinder to the anti-transcendental reading of Heidegger was amply defended in the course of the book. Let me append some ancillary considerations now. Why did the later Heidegger stand aloof from science? Was he merely anti-scientific? While Heidegger is prone to unilateral pronouncements about science, the transcendental strand of his thought allows us to make sense of his relation to science. Indeed, when he dialogues with scientists, he does not go deep into his later thought; instead he rehearses Kant's transcendental thinking and rehashes phenomenological analyses from *Being and Time*. "But just as we cannot take one reasonable or fruitful step in any science without being familiar with its objects and procedures, so also we cannot take a step in reflecting on the science without the right experience and practice in the transcendental point of view."[155] Heidegger has transcendental reasons for not embracing science and the facts of science as the starting point of philosophical consideration. Truth and manifestation cannot be accounted for by psychology, biology, or physics. It is this transcendental turn that separates Heidegger's program from that of someone like John Searle. But the difference is not that Heidegger is vague and Searle is clear; it is that Heidegger has reason to deploy a transcendental approach to philosophy, a reason that Searle does not so much refute as ignore.[156] The Heidegger of contemporary scholarship, the Heidegger shorn of his transcendental heritage, is a Heidegger that falls prey to Carnap's bald judgment: He is an artist without any talent, an artist whose words meaninglessly deviate from logical discourse.[157] Heidegger, by contrast, realizes that in this contemporary context the transcendental analysis of judgment is the place to begin and thereby show that there is more to λόγος than logic.

A second consideration. Why bother with Heidegger at all? Why not just read Rilke and Hölderlin, Heraclitus and Parmenides? Why not just let ourselves over to the fundamental dispositions of the moment, namely our terror or our boredom? Heidegger, I suggest, is mindful of the situation of philosophy in the contemporary world. The transcendental targets that mathematical prejudice that would make truth into a projection of the modern subject; it also undermines the ancient logical subject that handles everything, even the field of experience, as somehow a thing or collection of things. The transcendental vestige in Heidegger is that which he has to offer to us. It is his account of what in our present situation is demanded of philosophy. Poets and pre-Socratics alone will not help us here; only a transcendental renewal of experience, drawing on the witness of poets and pre-Socratics, allows us to diagnose and treat our situation.

What if we were to read Heidegger as he read others, by interposing our own horizon of questioning and finding the unthought in his work? Heidegger minded being, but in doing so he neglected the question of the human and the question of divine wisdom. He made what was merely interesting (the being of the between) into something ultimate for the sort of entity that we are. But his decision to do so is a function of a thought-provoking neglect of the human and its aspiration for the divine. Sheehan celebrates this reduction while likening it positively to Feuerbach.[158] But we can only follow Sheehan's Feuerbachian Heidegger to the extent to which we neglect the human quest for the good and the divine, to the extent to which we neglect the movement at work in figures such as Socrates, Augustine, and Levinas.[159] On my view, Heidegger's significance rather consists in a certain restraint, a return to the naive openness of human experience against rationalist constrictions;

he has not as it were stipulated what can or cannot appear, what can or cannot be revealed. He has not insulated us from the possibility of divine revelation, or even of doing something like metaphysics, albeit in a renewed sense.[160]

The transcendental is at the same time Heidegger's strength and his weakness: *strength*, insofar as it clarifies his itinerary and purifies it of "uninhibited word-mysticism," which he rightly censures in *Being and Time*,[161] and shows that his genuine contribution to philosophy consists of a certain radicalization of the transcendental program; *weakness*, insofar as his adoption of that tradition, even in the midst of an incisive criticism of the modern subject and its mathematical projection, nonetheless involves the adoption of the limits of the tradition with its separation of thought and life. Heidegger rejuvenates the transcendental tradition while exhibiting at the same time that such a tradition does not realize the full breadth of the philosophical project. The transcendental language of condition for the possibility of judgment, as misleading as it finally proves to be, nonetheless has a privileged role in motivating and preparing the way to think about something that exceeds its horizon of inquiry: our changing experience of the domain of experience in which we can, among other activities, comport ourselves to things. As I have argued, this is not the only question we might want to ask. This is not even the most important question we might want to ask. But it is a question eminently worth pursuing, one that holds the promise of renewing our relations to others, ourselves, and our world.[162] Alienated from experience, we are alienated from all those who show up in experience; at home in experience, we are at home among all those who show up in experience.

The phenomenological quest to return to the things themselves—and thereby run around the Neo-Kantian return to Kant—proved problematic insofar as it could not clarify (1) why such a return to the things themselves is necessary, (2) how it can be accomplished, or (3) what our motive for doing so might be. Oddly it was Husserl's phenomenological renewal of Kant's transcendental turn that began to answer these questions, and these are the very sorts of questions we too should like to know the answer to if indeed we too desire to return to the things themselves. What are Heidegger's answers? (1) Such a return is necessary, because we moderns have artificially constrained experience to objects, overlooking the original breadth and depth of human experience; (2) the return can be accomplished by inquiring into the condition for the possibility of the constitution of objects and by paying heed to the "between" that shows up in that analysis; and (3) we should want to return to the full breadth of experience because the artificial constraint on experience shuts us off from sources of meaning and makes it impossible for us to feel at home here and to know ourselves.

Notes

1 GA 41, 153/150–1.
2 SZ 436/487.
3 KRV A 856, B 884.
4 Consider the difference in meaning between the titles of two of Otto Pöggeler's books: *Martin Heidegger's Path of Thinking* and *The Paths of Heidegger's Life and Thought*, trans. John Bailiff (Amherst, NY: Humanity Books, 1998). The first emphasizes continuity; the second, discontinuity.
5 GA 13, 76/4.
6 See *Wer hat den Teufel an die Wand gemalt? Redensarten—wo sie herkommen, was sie bedeuten* (Berlin Duden Press, 2014), s.v. "*Schatten.*"
7 GA 41, 153/150 and GA 94, 219. Sheehan takes Heidegger's reference to apply not to the philosopher but to the person, and he therefore misconstrues the shadow in terms of Heidegger's limitations as a person, namely "his limited personal and cultural experience, his pinched worldview, his deep anti-modern conservatism." *Making Sense of Heidegger*, 290. In context, Heidegger applies the metaphor to Kant and his inability to understand the new beginning made possible by the conclusion of the *Critique of Pure Reason.* Heidegger clearly intends the metaphor, coming as it does while he is on the verge of writing the *Contributions* as the new beginning made possible by *Being and Time*, to apply to someone *qua* philosopher and in fact *qua* philosopher-who-has-written-an-original-work.
8 GA 71, 131–2/112.
9 *Gelassenheit* (Pfullingen: Verlag Günther Neske, 1959) [*Discourse on Thinking*, trans. John M. Anderson and E. Hans Freund (New York: Harper & Row, Publishers, 1966)], 55/76.
10 *Gelassenheit*, 56/77.
11 *Making Sense of Heidegger*, 222.
12 *Gelassenheit*, 51/73.
13 *Gelassenheit*, 51/73.
14 GA 9i, 446/338, 449/340, 462/350, respectively.
15 GA 9i, 458/346.
16 GA 9i, 459/347.
17 GA 9i, 462/350.
18 GA 29/30, 354/367.
19 "Das Ende der Philosophie und die Aufgabe des Denkens," in *Zur Sache des Denkens* (Tübingen: Max Niemeyer Verlag, 1969) ["The End of Philosophy and the Task of Thinking," in *Basic Writings*, rev. 2d ed., ed. David Farrell Krell (San Francisco: HarperCollins Publishers, 1993)], 70/440.
20 "Das Ende der Philosophie," 74/444.
21 "Das Ende der Philosophie," 77–78/447, emphasis mine.
22 KRV A 613/B 641.
23 GA 15, 300/18.
24 GA 15, 328–9/36.
25 GA 15, 378/67; cf. GA 15, 360/57.
26 GA 15, 385–6/72.
27 GA 15, 381/69. cf. GA 15, 306/22.
28 GA 15, 376/66.
29 GA 15, 377/67.
30 GA 15, 378/67.
31 GA 15, 382/70.
32 GA 15, 295/15, 297/16, and 374/65.
33 *Correspondence*, 133. This question unearths the hidden secret of metaphysics: "I noticed that I still lacked something essential, something that in my

long metaphysical studies I, as well as others, had failed to consider and which in fact constitutes the key to the whole secret of metaphysics, hitherto still hidden from itself."

34 GA 26, 163/130.

35 KRV B 19.

36 "I entitle *transcendental* all knowledge which is occupied not so much with objects as with the mode of our knowledge of objects in so far as this mode of knowledge is to be possible *a priori*. A system of such concepts might be entitled transcendental philosophy." KRV A 11–2, B 25.

37 He rejects the book as an adequate interpretation of *Kant* and *not* as a presentation of his own thinking.

38 *The Unity of Reason*, 33 and 53–4.

39 KRV A 158, 194.

40 GA 41, 196/192.

41 GA 41, 242.

42 GA 41, 208/206. Correcting the translation.

43 On various transcendental features of Heidegger's later thinking, see Dahlstrom, "Heidegger's Transcendentalism," 29–54.

44 Cf. GA 65, 460–1/324.

45 GA 7b, 183/181 and GA 9f, 343/261, respectively.

46 *Unterwegs zur Sprache*, 122/30.

47 GA 9a, 73/58. "Insight into the proper nature of thinking and saying comes only by holding phenomena in view without prejudice." GA 9a, 76/60.

48 GA 15, 137/80.

49 SZ 50/490.

50 *Ideas I*, 38–9. As we have seen, Heidegger says that modern natural science, as a universal way of thinking, is "what most holds us captive and makes us unfree in the experience and determination of things." GA 41, 49/51. But Husserl expressly saw something similar: "In fact, we allow *no* authority to curtail our right to accept all kinds of intuition as equally valuable legitimating sources of cognition—not even the authority of 'modern natural science.'" *Ideas* I, 37.

51 GA 20, 93–94/68–69. Translation modified.

52 SZ 36/60.

53 GA 15, 297/16.

54 See GA 60, 57/39 and GA 23, 83/57. In 1925 he tells us that for Husserl constitution means "*letting the entity be seen in its objectivity*." GA 20, 97/71.

55 GA 41, 181–2/178.

56 Von Herrmann recognizes the importance of phenomenology and Husserl in approaching Heidegger, although he fails to underscore the consequent centrality of transcendental philosophy: "In its manifold ways Heidegger's thinking can be appropriately and adequately interpreted only if each stage of interpretation heeds the *basic hermeneutic-phenomenological* character of this thinking. . . . Only one who has thoroughly mastered Husserl's phenomenology in the sense of its actual maxim 'to the things themselves' and who has worked through this phenomenology by enacting it—only such a one is called upon and capable of entering into a philosophical dialogue with Heidegger's thinking, as caretaker of this phenomenological-hermeneutic thinking and of the two ways of elaborating the question of being [namely, as fundamental ontology and as the history of being]." "Way and Method: Hermeneutic Phenomenology in Thinking the History of Being," in *Critical Heidegger*, ed. Christopher Macann (London: Routledge, 1996), 189.

57 It is true that Heidegger later speaks more wistfully of the *Logical Investigations* than the subsequent, explicitly transcendental works. But Heidegger does not criticize the transcendental turn that Husserl makes, nor does he

equate it with German Idealism. Instead the criticism he makes is that Husserl leaves the manner of being of the ego undeveloped. Heidegger's own interest is never in the intentionality of the *Logical Investigations* per se but rather in the transcendental horizon of its possibility.

58 GA 20, 101/74.
59 See Pöggeler, *Path*, 268. On this theme in Husserl, see Prufer, *Recapitulations*, 74–7.
60 *Logical Investigations*, vol. I, 260–1.
61 GA 65, 315/221. My emphases.
62 GA 20, 168/122. My emphasis.
63 Husserl's letter to Alexander Pfänder of January 6, 1931 in *Psychological and Transcendental Phenomenology and the Confrontation with Heidegger (1927–1931)*, ed. and trans. Thomas Sheehan and Richard Palmer (Dordrecht: Kluwer Academic Publishers, 1997), 482.
64 "Heidegger for Beginners," in *Appropriating Heidegger*, ed. James E. Faulconer and Mark A. Wrathall (Cambridge: Cambridge University Press, 2000), 103.
65 GA 20, 174/126.
66 *Ideas I*, § 19.
67 For example, Prufer thinks that Husserl's inaptly named "inner time-consciousness" is prior to the subject-object paradigm and so undermines Heidegger's attempts to reduce Husserl to "the self-objectification of transcendental subjectivity." *Recapitulations*, 76.
68 Aristotle, *Metaphysics*, 981b13–982a2, 993a11–23; Thomas Aquinas, *Summa Theologiae*, I, q. 44, a. 2.
69 Maxime Doyon, "The Transcendental Claim of Deconstruction," in *A Companion to Derrida*, ed. Zeynep Direk and Leonard Lawlor (Oxford: Wiley Blackwell, 2014), 132.
70 Doyon, "The Transcendental Claim," 133.
71 Levinas, "Is Ontology Fundamental?" in *Emmanuel Levinas: Basic Philosophical Writings*, ed. Adriaan Peperzak, Simon Critchley, and Robert Bernasconi (Bloomington, IN: Indiana University Press, 1996), 2–10; on Levinas and normativity, see Crowell, "Why is Ethics First Philosophy? Levinas in Phenomenological Context," *European Journal of Philosophy* 23 (2015): 564–88.
72 *Reduction and Givenness: Investigations of Husserl, Heidegger, and Phenomenology*, trans. Thomas A. Carlson (Evanston, Illinois: Northwestern University Press, 1998), 204–5. The third reduction has now been developed further in such works as *Being Given: Toward a Phenomenology of Givenness*, trans. Jeffrey Kosky (Stanford, CA: Stanford University Press, 2002) and *The Erotic Phenomenon*, trans. Stephen E. Lewis (Chicago: University of Chicago Press, 2006).
73 GA 65, 3/3.
74 See Chad Engelland, "Heidegger and the Human Difference," 175–93.
75 Dahlstrom thinks Heidegger turns from transcendental phenomenology to avoid its "unwanted suggestion that being-here is a transcendental subject." After this shift, what remains is the following: "Being-here is . . . the site of the disclosure itself." *Concept*, 403.
76 Sheehan, "*Kehre* and *Ereignis*," 16.
77 GA 40, 20/20.
78 Schalow observes that the "entire thrust" of Heidegger's Kant interpretation is to de-center the subject in favor of disclosedness. *Heidegger-Kant Dialogue*, 173–4 and 200–1.
79 SZ 14/34.

80 *De Veritate*, q. 1, a. 1. On Aquinas's conception of the transcendental, see Jan Aertsen, *Medieval Philosophy and the Transcendentals: The Case of Thomas Aquinas* (Leiden: Brill Academic Press, 1996). On the medieval transcendental tradition, see Aertsen, *Medieval Philosophy as Transcendental Thought: From Philip the Chancellor (ca. 1225) to Francisco Suarez* (Leiden: Brill Academic Publishers, 2012).

81 See Bacon, *Novum Organum*, I, § 51; Nietzsche, "On the Truth and Lies in a Nonmoral Sense," in *Philosophy and Truth: Selections from Nietzsche's Notebooks of the Early 1870's*, ed. and trans. Daniel Breazeale (Amherst, NY: Humanity Books, 1979), 83; and Heidegger, "Plato's Doctrine of Truth," 9c, 225/173, 230–1/176–7.

82 GA 26, 163/130.

83 See GA 7a, 154–60/152–8, GA 5a, 27–29/41–43, GA 7b, 168–76/166–74, respectively.

84 GA 7b, 176/174. Translation modified.

85 GA 7a, 153/151. For an example of a Heideggerian reflection on the essence of procreation, expressed in the language of Thomistic personalism, see Chad Engelland, "On the Personal Significance of Sexual Reproduction," *The Thomist* 79 (2015): 615–39.

86 For an alternative to the modern neglect of things that prizes the being of the things of nature, see Kenneth L. Schmitz, *The Recovery of Wonder: The New Freedom and the Asceticism of Power* (Montreal: McGill-Queen's University Press, 2005).

87 *Kants gesammelte Schriften*, XVIII (Berlin: Walter de Gruyter, 1928), no. 5738. See GA 41, 179/176.

88 GA 41, 131/129.

89 *Heidegger's Analytic*, 155–203.

90 GA 25, 4/3.

91 GA 20, 417/301.

92 Cf. GA 41, 74/73–74.

93 *Was Heißt Denken?* (Tübingen: Max Niemeyer Verlag, 1954) [*What Is Called Thinking?* trans. J. Glenn Gray (New York: Harper & Row, Publishers, 1968)], 52/17.

94 *Logic*, 34. On Kant and Socrates, see Richard Velkley, "On Kant's Socratism," in *Being after Rousseau*, 65–80.

95 *Logic*, 28.

96 KRV A 805, B 833. The fourth question appears only in the *Logic*, 29.

97 GA 3, 207/145.

98 GA 3, 216–17/152.

99 *Logic*, 29.

100 GA 65, 11/8.

101 GA 94, 5.

102 Emmanuel Levinas, *God, Death, and Time*, trans. Bettina Bergo, ed. Jacques Rolland (Stanford, CA: Stanford University Press, 2000), 59–60.

103 See "Das Ende der Philosophie," 66/436. In this essay, he reduces philosophy to metaphysics and thinks metaphysics has been completed by the special sciences.

104 Richard Velkley, *Heidegger, Strauss, and the Premises of Philosophy: On Original Forgetting* (Chicago: Chicago University Press, 2011), 89.

105 "Heidegger's Apology," in *Heidegger's Way of Thought*, ed. Alfred Denker and Marion Heinz (New York: Continuum, 2002), 2 and 13.

106 GA 18, 5/4.

107 *Genesis*, 287.

108 GA 18, 4/4.

109 GA 24, 28/20.

110 GA 41, 154/151.

111 "Has Philosophy Lost Contact with People?" in *Theories and Things* (Cambridge, MA: Harvard University Press, 1981), 190–3.

112 See Pierre Hadot, *Philosophy as a Way of Life: Spiritual Exercises from Socrates to Foucault*, ed. Arnold I. Davidson, trans. Michael Chase (Oxford: Blackwell, 1995).

113 "Letter to Engelbert Krebs on His Philosophical Conversion," trans. Thomas Sheehan, in *Becoming Heidegger*, 96.

114 GA 16b, 676/329.

115 GA 65, 87–88/60–61.

116 GA 16b, 673/327.

117 *The Mystery of Being*, vol. 1, trans. G. S. Fraser (South Bend, IN: St. Augustine's Press, 2001), 54. On Marcel and Heidegger, see Chad Engelland, "Marcel and Heidegger on the Proper Matter and Manner of Thinking," *Philosophy Today* 48 (2004): 91–106.

118 He wrote to his student Karl Löwith that "Husserl was never a philosopher, not even for one second of his life," presumably because the framework of the *Ideas* avoids Heideggerian emphases on factical life experience and the question of being. "Letter to Karl Löwith, February 20, 1923," trans. Theodore Kisiel, in *Becoming Heidegger*, 372.

119 KRV A 852–3, B 880–1.

120 On such human questions, see Chad Engelland, *The Way of Philosophy: An Introduction* (Eugene, OR: Cascade, 2016).

121 GA 59, 174/133.

122 See "Zeit und Sein," in *Zur Sache des Denkens* (Tübingen: Max Niemeyer Verlag, 1969) ["Time and Being," in *On 'Time and Being'*, trans. Joan Stambaugh (New York: Harper & Row, 1972), 9/9.

123 Gadamer, *Heidegger's Ways*, trans. John W. Stanley (Albany, NY: State University of New York Press, 1994), 157.

124 Gadamer writes: "Unlike Hegel's, [Heidegger's] was certainly not a teleological construction beginning with the end; rather, it was a construction based on a beginning, a beginning that already held the fate of Being [*Seinsgeschick*] of metaphysics. But 'necessity' was included, even if it existed only in the sense of εξ ὑποθέσεος ἀναγκαῖον [something necessary according to a hypothesis]." *Heidegger's Ways*, 157.

125 "Zeit und Sein," 22/21.

126 "Heidegger's Transcendental History," *Journal of the History of Philosophy* 40 (2002): 501–23.

127 See especially the final pages, GA 9h, 439–44/332–36.

128 Cf. Velkley, *Being after Rousseau*, 27.

129 *History of Being*, 46.

130 *Demythologizing Heidegger*, 28.

131 *Logic*, 29.

132 *Logic*, 30.

133 GA 41, 49/51.

134 *Republic*, 523a–525a.

135 See Chad Engelland, *Ostension: Word Learning and the Embodied Mind*; and "Unmasking the Person," *International Philosophical Quarterly* 50 (2010): 447–60.

136 See Chad Engelland, "Heidegger and the Human Difference," 175–93.

137 For example, Jürgen Habermas rails against what he calls Heidegger's "esoteric, special discourse, which absolves itself of the restrictions of discursive speech generally and is immunized by vagueness against any specific

objections." Habermas thinks this disguises a "performative contradiction" in Heidegger's approach: "He makes use of metaphysical concepts for purposes of a critique of metaphysics, as a ladder he casts away once he has mounted the rungs." *The Philosophical Discourse of Modernity: Twelve Lectures*, trans. Frederick Lawrence (Cambridge, MA: The MIT Press, 1987), 185.

138 *Ways*, viii.

139 SZ 36/60 and 150/191–2.

140 "Heidegger," 114.

141 Prufer observes that since the theme of "clearing" (*Lichtung*) goes beyond the interplay of presencing/absencing bringing it to speech is a special problem: "This expropriated and troped language strains to bring to speech what is beyond its resources." *Recapitulations*, 87.

142 GA 41, 55–6/56.

143 GA 45, 210/178.

144 *Making Sense of Heidegger*, 226–8.

145 *Emergency of Being*, 146.

146 SZ 35/59.

147 SZ 36/60.

148 See Chad Engelland, "The Phenomenological Motivation of the Later Heidegger," *Philosophy Today* 53 Supplement (2009): 182–9.

149 Polt, *Emergency of Being*, 103–4.

150 GA 15, 399/80.

151 GA 15, 377/67.

152 GA 65, 348–49/244.

153 On this point, see Polt, *Emergency of Being*, 146.

154 See Chad Engelland, "Absent to Those Present: Social Technology and Bodily Communion," in *Social Epistemology and Technology*, ed. Frank Scalambrino (London: Rowman & Littlefield International, 2015), 167–76; Chad Engelland, "The Play of Life in Art," *Journal of Aesthetics and Phenomenology* 2 (2015): 127–42.

155 GA 41, 182/178. Consider, for example, the seminars with psychologists that began in 1959. He begins the first session by discussing the analytic of Da-sein, the second and third by considering Kant and the ontological difference, and the fourth by discussing Kant's understanding of science. *Zollikoner Seminare*, ed. Medard Boss (Frankfurt am Main: Vittorio Klostermann, 1987) [*Zollikon Seminars*, ed. Medard Boss, trans. Franz Mayr and Richard Askay (Evanston, IL: Northwestern University Press, 2001)], 3/4, 5/4, and 31/25, respectively.

156 See Chad Engelland, "Heidegger and the Human Difference," 175–93; and Chad Engelland, *Ostension: Word Learning and the Embodied Mind*, 193–214.

157 Rudolf Carnap, "The Elimination of Metaphysics through the Logical Analysis of Language," trans. Arthur Pap, in *Logical Positivism*, ed. A.J. Ayer (Glencoe, IL: The Free Press, 1959), 80. For a restatement of Carnap's interpretation of Heidegger, see Paul Edwards, *Heidegger's Confusions* (Amherst, NY: Prometheus Books, 2004).

158 *Making Sense of Heidegger*, 294.

159 On Heidegger's entanglement with Augustine, which predates and postdates his close reading of Aristotle, see Ryan Coyne, *Heidegger's Confessions: The Remains of Saint Augustine in 'Being and Time' and Beyond* (Chicago: University of Chicago Press, 2015); Coyne shows, among other things, that Heidegger not only borrows the phenomenon of fundamental dispositions from Augustine (a fact known to every reader of *Being and Time*'s footnotes), but that his chosen disposition of the new beginning, reservedness, is

the disposition Heidegger locates in the *Confessions*. This is not to say that Heidegger's project is theological; it is to say that it is highly questionable to say that it has disqualified the sorts of questions that animate the *Confessions*. Further evidence comes from Jean-Luc Marion's potent phenomenological exhibition of the *Confessions*, which aims to show that Augustine operates in a more fundamental phenomenological reduction than can be found in Heidegger. *In the Self's Place: The Approach of Saint Augustine*, trans. Jeffrey Kosky (Stanford, CA: Stanford University Press, 2012).

160 On divine revelation, see Hans Urs von Balthasar, *Glory of the Lord: A Theological Aesthetics*, vol. 5, *The Realm of Metaphysics in the Modern Age*, trans Oliver Davies, Andrew Louth, Brian McNeil, John Saward, and Rowan Williams (San Francisco, Ignatius Press, 1991), 613–45; Robert Sokolowski, *The God of Faith and Reason: Foundations of Christian Theology* (Notre Dame: University of Notre Dame Press, 1982); and Jean-Luc Marion, *Givenness and Revelation*, trans. Stephen Lewis (Oxford: Oxford University Press, 2016). On metaphysics, see Sokolowski, *Presence and Absence: A Philosophical Investigation of Language and Being* (Bloomington, IN: Indiana University Press, 1978), 157–81; Engelland, *Ostension: Word Learning and the Embodied Mind*, 193–214; and Robert E. Wood, *The Beautiful, the True, and the Good: Studies in the History of Thought* (Washington, DC: The Catholic University of America Press, 2015).

161 SZ 220/262.

162 In this connection, see Capobianco, *Heidegger's Way of Being*, 96–8.

Bibliography

Works by Heidegger, Husserl, and Kant

Heidegger, Martin. GA 1a: "Das Realitätsproblem in der modernen Philosophie." In *Frühe Schriften*. Edited by Friedrich-Wilhelm von Herrmann. Frankfurt am Main: Vittorio Klostermann, 1978. "The Problem of Reality in Modern Philosophy." Translated by Philip J. Bossert and Aaron Bunch. In *Becoming Heidegger: On the Trail of His Early Occasional Writings, 1910–1927*, ed. Theodore Kisiel and Thomas Sheehan. Evanston, IL: Northwestern University Press, 2007. (Book review, 1912)

———. GA 1b: "Neuere Forschungen über Logik." In *Frühe Schriften*. Edited by Friedrich-Wilhelm von Herrmann. Frankfurt am Main: Vittorio Klostermann, 1978. "Recent Research in Logic." Translated by Theodore Kisiel. In *Becoming Heidegger: On the Trail of His Early Occasional Writings, 1910–1927*, ed. Theodore Kisiel and Thomas Sheehan. Evanston, IL: Northwestern University Press, 2007. (Review essay, 1912)

———. GA 1c: "Schluss: Die Kategorienproblem." In *Frühe Schriften (1912–1916)*. Edited by Friedrich-Wilhelm von Herrmann. Frankfurt am Main: Vittorio Klostermann, 1978. "Conclusion: The Problem of Categories." Translated by Roderick M. Steward and John van Buren. In *Supplements: From the Earliest Essays to* Being and Time *and Beyond*, ed. John van Buren. Albany, NY: State University of New York Press, 2002. (Habilitation conclusion, 1916)

———. GA 3: *Kant und das Problem der Metaphysik*. Edited by Friedrich-Wilhelm von Herrmann. Frankfurt am Main: Vittorio Klostermann, 1991. *Kant and the Problem of Metaphysics*, 4th ed. Translated by Richard Taft. Bloomington: Indiana University Press, 1996. (Book, 1929)

———. GA 4a: "Andenken." In *Erläuterungen zu Hölderlins Dichtung*. Edited by Friedrich-Wilhelm von Herrmann. Frankfurt am Main: Vittorio Klostermann, 1981. "Remembrance." In *Elucidations of Hölderlin's Poetry*. Translated by Keith Hoeller. New York: Humanity Books, 2000. (Essay, written in 1942)

———. GA 5a: "Der Ursprung des Kunstwerkes." In *Holzwege*. Edited by Friedrich-Wilhelm von Herrmann. Frankfurt am Main: Vittorio Klostermann, 1977. "The Origin of the Work of Art." In *Poetry, Language, Thought*. Translated by Albert Hofstadter. New York: Harper & Row, 1971. (Lectures, from 1935 and 1936)

———. GA 5b: "Hegels Begriff der Erfahrung." In *Holzwege*. Edited by Friedrich-Wilhelm von Herrmann. Frankfurt am Main: Vittorio Klostermann,

1977. "Hegel's Concept of Experience." In *Off the Beaten Track*. Edited and translated by Julian Young and Kenneth Haynes. Cambridge: Cambridge University Press, 2002. (Essay, based on seminars from 1942–1943)

———. GA 7a: "Bauen Wohnen Denken." In *Vorträge und Aufsätze*. Edited by Friedrich-Wilhelm von Herrmann. Frankfurt am Main: Vittorio Klostermann, 2000. "Building Dwelling Thinking." In *Poetry, Language, Thought*. Translated by Albert Hofstadter. New York: Harper & Row, 1971. (Essay, 1951)

———. GA 7b: "Das Ding." In *Vorträge und Aufsätze*. Edited by Friedrich-Wilhelm von Herrmann. Frankfurt am Main: Vittorio Klostermann, 2000. "The Thing." In *Poetry, Language, Thought*. Translated by Albert Hofstadter. New York: Harper & Row, 1971. (Essay, 1950)

———. GA 7c: "Aletheia (Heraklit, Fragment 16)." In *Vorträge und Aufsätze*. Edited by Friedrich-Wilhelm von Herrmann. Frankfurt am Main: Vittorio Klostermann, 2000. "Aletheia (Heraclitus, Fragment B 16)." In *Early Greek Thinking*. Translated by David Farrell Kr   ell and Frank A. Capuzzi. New York: Harper & Row, 1975. (Essay, 1954)

———. GA 9a: "Phänomenologie und Theologie: Anhang." In *Wegmarken*. Edited by Friedrich-Wilhelm von Herrmann. Frankfurt am Main: Vittorio Klostermann, 1976. "Phenomenology and Theology Appendix." Translated by James G. Hart and John C. Maraldo. In *Pathmarks*. Edited by William McNeill. Cambridge: Cambridge University Press, 1998. (Appendix, 1964)

———. GA 9b: "Vom Wesen des Grundes." Edited by Friedrich-Wilhelm von Herrmann. Frankfurt am Main: Vittorio Klostermann, 1976. "On the Essence of Ground." Translated by William McNeill. In *Pathmarks*. Edited by William McNeill. Cambridge: Cambridge University Press, 1998. (Essay, 1929)

———. GA 9c: "Platons Lehre von der Wahrheit." In *Wegmarken*. Edited by Friedrich-Wilhelm von Herrmann. Frankfurt am Main: Vittorio Klostermann, 1976. "Plato's Doctrine of Truth." Translated by Thomas Sheehan. In *Pathmarks*. Edited by William McNeill. Cambridge: Cambridge University Press, 1998. (Essay, 1940)

———. GA 9d: "Vom Wesen und Begriff der Φύσις. Aristoteles, Physik B, 1." In *Wegmarken*. Edited by Friedrich-Wilhelm von Herrmann. Frankfurt am Main: Vittorio Klostermann, 1976. "On the Essence and Concept of Φύσις in Aristotle's *Physics* B, 1." Translated by Thomas Sheehan." *In Pathmarks*. Edited by William McNeill. Cambridge: Cambridge University Press, 1998. (Essay, 1939)

———. GA 9e: "Nachwort zu 'Was ist Metaphysik?' " In *Wegmarken*. Edited by Friedrich-Wilhelm von Herrmann. Frankfurt am Main: Vittorio Klostermann, 1976. "Postscript to 'What Is Metaphysics?' " Translated by William McNeill. In *Pathmarks*. Edited by William McNeill. Cambridge: Cambridge University Press, 1998. (Essay, 1943)

———. GA 9f: "Brief über den *Humanismus*." In *Wegmarken*. Edited by Friedrich-Wilhelm von Herrmann. Frankfurt am Main: Vittorio Klostermann, 1976. "Letter on 'Humanism'." Translated by Frank A. Capuzzi. In *Pathmarks*. Edited by William McNeill. Cambridge: Cambridge University Press, 1998. (Letter, 1946)

———. GA 9g: "Zur Seinsfrage." In *Wegmarken*. Edited by Friedrich-Wilhelm von Herrmann. Frankfurt am Main: Vittorio Klostermann, 1976. "On the

Question of Being." Translated by William McNeill. In *Pathmarks*. Edited by William McNeill. Cambridge: Cambridge University Press, 1998. (Essay, 1955)

———. GA 9h: "Hegel und die Griechen." In *Wegmarken*. Edited by Friedrich-Wilhelm von Herrmann. Frankfurt am Main: Vittorio Klostermann, 1976. "Hegel and the Greeks." Translated by Robert Metcalf. In *Pathmarks*. Edited by William McNeill. Cambridge: Cambridge University Press, 1998. (Essay, 1958)

———. GA 9i: "Kants These über das Sein." In *Wegmarken*. Edited by Friedrich-Wilhelm von Herrmann. Frankfurt am Main: Vittorio Klostermann, 1976. "Kant's Thesis about Being." Translated by Ted E. Klein, Jr., and William E. Pohl. In *Pathmarks*. Edited by William McNeill. Cambridge: Cambridge University Press, 1998. (Lecture, 1961)

———. GA 10: *Der Satz vom Grund*. Edited by Petra Jaeger. Frankfurt am Main: Vittorio Klostermann, 1997. *The Principle of Reason*. Translated by Reginald Lilly. Bloomington: Indiana University Press, 1991. (Lecture course, WS 1955–56)

———. GA 13: *Aus der Erfahrung des Denkens*. Edited by Hermann Heidegger. Frankfurt am Main: Vittorio Klostermann, 1983. "The Thinker as Poet." In *Poetry, Language, Thought*. Translated by Albert Hofstadter. New York: Harper & Row, 1971. (Meditation, 1947)

———. GA 15: *Seminare*, 2d ed. Edited by Curd Ochwadt. Frankfurt am Main: Vittorio Klostermann, 2005. *Four Seminars*. Translated by Andrew Mitchell and François Raffoul. Bloomington: Indiana University Press, 2003. (Seminars, from 1951–1973)

———. GA 16a: "Lebenslauf (Zur Habilitation 1915)." In *Reden und andere Zeugnisse eines Lebenswege* 1910–1976. Edited by Hermann Heidegger. Frankfurt am Main: Vittorio Klostermann, 2000. "Curriculum Vitae." In *Becoming Heidegger: On the Trail of His Early Occasional Writings, 1910–1927*, ed. Theodore Kisiel and Thomas Sheehan. Evanston, IL: Northwestern University Press, 2007. (C.V., 1915)

———. GA 16b: "Spiegel-Gespräch mit Martin Heidegger (23. September 1966)." In *Reden und andere Zeugnisse eines Lebenswege* 1910–1976. Edited by Hermann Heidegger. Frankfurt am Main: Vittorio Klostermann, 2000. "*Der Spiegel* Interview with Martin Heidegger." In *The Heidegger Reader*. Edited by Günter Figal. Translated by Jerome Veith. Bloomington: Indiana University Press, 2009. (Interview, 1966)

———. GA 18: *Grundbegriffe der aristotelischen Philosophie*. Edited by Mark Michalski. Frankfurt am Main: Vittorio Klostermann, 2002. *Basic Concepts of Aristotelian Philosophy*. Translated by Robert D. Metcalf and Mark B. Tanzer. Bloomington: Indiana University Press, 2009. (Lecture course, SS 1924)

———. GA 19: *Platon: Sophistes*. Edited by Ingeborg Schüßler. Frankfurt am Main: Vittorio Klostermann, 1992. *Plato's 'Sophist'*. Translated by Richard Rojcewicz and André Schuwer. Bloomington: Indiana University Press, 1997. (Lecture course, WS 1924–25)

———. GA 20: *Prolegomena zur Geschichte des Zeitbegriffs*. Edited by Petra Jaeger. Frankfurt am Main: Vittorio Klostermann, 1979. *History of the Concept of Time: Prolegomena*. Translated by Theodore Kisiel. Bloomington: Indiana University Press, 1985. (Lecture course, SS 1925)

————. GA 21: *Logik: Die Frage nach der Wahrheit.* Edited by Walter Biemel. Frankfurt am Main: Vittorio Klostermann, 1976. (Lecture course, WS 1925–26)

————. GA 24: *Die Grundprobleme der Phänomenologie.* Edited by Friedrich-Wilhelm von Herrmann. Frankfurt am Main: Vittorio Klostermann, 1975. *The Basic Problems of Phenomenology,* rev. ed. Translated by Albert Hofstadter. Bloomington: Indiana University Press, 1982. (Lecture course, SS 1927)

————. GA 25: *Phänomenologische Interpretation von Kants Kritik der reinen Vernunft.* Edited by Ingtraud Görland. Frankfurt am Main: Vittorio Klostermann, 1977. *Phenomenological Interpretations of Kant's* Critique of Pure Reason. Translated by Parvis Emad and Kenneth. Bloomington: Indiana University Press, 1997. (Lecture course, WS 1927–28)

————. GA 26: *Metaphysische Anfangsgründe der Logik im Ausgang von Leibniz.* Edited by Klaus Held. Frankfurt am Main: Vittorio Klostermann, 1978. *The Metaphysical Foundations of Logic.* Translated by Michael Heim. Bloomington: Indiana University Press, 1984. (Lecture course, SS 1928)

————. GA 27: *Einleitung in die Philosophie.* Edited by Otto Saame and Ina Saame-Speidel. Frankfurt am Main: Vittorio Klostermann, 1996. (Lecture course, WS 1927–28)

————. GA 29/30: *Die Grundbegriffe der Metaphysik. Welt—Endlichket—Einsamkeit.* Edited by Friedrich-Wilhelm von Herrmann. Frankfurt am Main: Vittorio Klostermann, 1983. *The Fundamental Concepts of Metaphysics.* Translated by William McNeill and Nicholas Walker. Bloomington: Indiana University Press, 1995. (Lecture course, WS 1929–30)

————. GA 31: *Vom Wesen der menschlichen Freiheit: Einleitung in die Philosophie. Gesamtausgabe* 31. Edited by Hartmut Tietjen. Frankfurt am Main: Vittorio Klostermann, 1982. *The Essence of Human Freedom: An Introduction to Philosophy.* London: Continuum, 2002. (Lecture course, SS 1930)

————. GA 32: *Hegels Phänomenologie des Geistes.* Edited by Ingtraud Görland. Frankfurt am Main: Vittorio Klostermann, 1980. *Hegel's Phenomenology of Spirit.* Translated by Parvis Emad and Kenneth Maly. Bloomington: Indiana University Press, 1988. (Lecture course, WS 1930–31)

————. GA 38: *Logik als die Frage nach dem Wesen der Sprache.* Edited by Günter Seubold. Frankfurt am Main: Vittorio Klostermann, 1998. (Lecture course, SS 1934)

————. GA 40: *Einführung in die Metaphysik.* Edited by Petra Jaeger. Frankfurt am Main: Vittorio Klostermann, 1983. *Introduction to Metaphysics.* Translated by Gregory Fried and Richard Polt. New Haven: Yale University Press, 2000. (Lecture course, SS 1935)

————. GA 41: *Die Frage nach dem Ding: Zu Kants Lehre von den transzendentalen Grundsätzen.* Edited by Petra Jaeger. Frankfurt am Main: Vittorio Klostermann, 1984. *What Is a Thing?* Translated by William Barton and Vera Deutsch. Chicago: Henry Regnery Co., 1967. (Lecture course, WS 1935–36)

————. GA 45: *Grundfragen der Philosophie: Ausgewählte 'Probleme' der 'Logik.'* Edited by Friedrich-Wilhelm von Herrmann. Frankfurt am Main: Vittorio Klostermann, 1984. *Basic Questions of Philosophy: Selected 'Problems' of 'Logic.'* Translated by Richard Rojcewicz and André Schuwer. Bloomington: Indiana University Press, 1994. (Lecture course, WS 1937–38)

————. GA 56/57: *Zur Bestimmung der Philosophie*, 2d ed. Edited by Bernd Heimbüchel. Frankfurt am Main: Vittorio Klostermann, 1999. *Towards the Definition of Philosophy*. Translated by Ted Sadler. London: The Athlone Press, 2000. (Lecture courses, 1919)

————. GA 58: *Grundprobleme der Phänomenologie*. Edited by Hans-Helmuth Gander. Frankfurt am Main: Vittorio Klostermann, 1993. *Basic Problems of Phenomenology*. Translated by Scott M. Campbell. London: Bloomsbury, 2013. (Lecture course, WS 1919–1920)

————. GA 59: *Phänomenologie der Anschauung und des Ausdrucks*. Edited by Claudius Strube. Frankfurt am Main: Vittorio Klostermann, 1993. (Lecture course, SS 1920)

————. GA 60: *Phänomenologie des religiösen Lebens*. Edited by Matthias Jung, Thomas Regehly, and Claudius Strube. Frankfurt am Main: Vittorio Klostermann, 1995. *The Phenomenology of Religious Life*. Translated by Matthias Fritsch and Jennifer Anna Gosetti-Ferencei. Bloomington: Indiana University Press, 2004. (Lecture courses, WS 1920–21 and SS 1921)

————. GA 61: *Phänomenologische Interpretationen zu Aristoteles: Einführung in die phänomenologische Forschung*. Edited by Walter Bröcker and Käte Bröcker-Oltmanns. Frankfurt am Main: Vittorio Klostermann, 1985. *Phenomenological Interpretations of Aristotle: Initiation into Phenomenological Research*. Translated by Richard Rojcewicz. Bloomington: Indiana University Press, 2001. (Lecture course, WS 1921–22)

————. GA 65: *Beiträge zur Philosophie (Vom Ereignis)*. Edited by Friedrich-Wilhelm von Herrmann. Frankfurt am Main: Vittorio Klostermann, 1989. *Contributions to Philosophy (From Enowning)*. Translated by Parvis Emad and Kenneth Maly. Bloomington: Indiana University Press, 1999. (Book, 1936–38)

————. GA 66: *Besinnung*. Edited by Friedrich-Wilhelm von Herrmann. Frankfurt am Main: Vittorio Klostermann, 1997. *Mindfulness*. Translated by Parvis Emad and Thomas Kalary. New York: Continuum, 2006. (Book, 1938–39)

————. GA 71: *Das Ereignis*. Edited by Friedrich-Wilhelm von Herrmann. Frankfurt am Main: Vittorio Klostermann, 2009. *The Event*. Translated by Richard Rojcewicz. Bloomington: Indiana University Press, 2013. (Book, 1941–42)

————. GA 84.1: *Seminare: Kant—Leibniz—Schiller*. Edited by Günther Neumann. Frankfurt am Main: Vittorio Klostermann, 2013. (Seminars, SS 1931 through WS 1935–36)

————. GA 94: *Überlegungen II-VI (Schwarze Hefte 1931–1938)*. Edited by Peter Trawny. Frankfurt am Main: Vittorio Klostermann, 2014. (Notebooks, 1931–38)

————. "Das Ende der Philosophie und die Aufgabe des Denkens." In *Zur Sache des Denkens*. Tübingen: Max Niemeyer Verlag, 1969. "The End of Philosophy and the Task of Thinking." Translated by Joan Stambaugh. In *Basic Writings*, rev. 2d ed. Edited by David Farrell Krell. New York: HarperCollins Publishers, 1993. (Essay, 1964)

————. *Gelassenheit*. Pfullingen: Verlag Günther Neske, 1959. *Discourse on Thinking*. Translated by John M. Anderson and E. Hans Freund. New York: Harper & Row, Publishers, 1966. (Conversation, mid-1940s)

————. "Letter to Engelbert Krebs on His Philosophical Conversion." Translated by Thomas Sheehan. In *Becoming Heidegger: On the Trail of His Early Occasional Writings, 1910–1927*, ed. Theodore Kisiel and Thomas Sheehan. Evanston, IL: Northwestern University Press, 2007. (Letter, 1919)

———. "Die Metaphysik als Geschichte des Seins." In *Nietzsche*. Vol. 2. Pfullingen: Verlag Günther Neske, 1961. "Metaphysics as History of Being." In *The End of Philosophy*. Translated by Joan Stambaugh. New York: Harper & Row, Publishers, 1973. (Treatise, 1941)

———. *Nietzsche*. 2 vols. Pfullingen: Verlag Günther Neske, 1961. *Nietzsche*. 4 vols. Translated by David Farrell Krell. New York: Harper & Row, Publishers, 1979. (Lecture courses and essays, 1936–1946)

———. *Schellings Abhandlung über das Wesen der menschlichen Freiheit (1809)*. Edited by Hildegard Feick. Tübingen: Max Niemeyer Verlag, 1971. *Schelling's Treatise on the Essence of Human Freedom*. Translated by Joan Stambaugh. Athens, Ohio: Ohio University Press, 1985. (Lecture course, SS 1936)

———. *Sein und Zeit*, 18th ed. Tübingen: Max Niemeyer Verlag, 2001. *Being and Time*. Translated by John Macquarrie and Edward Robinson. New York: Harper & Row, Publishers, 1962. *Being and Time*. Translated by Joan Stambaugh. Albany, NY: State University of New York Press, 1996. (Book, 1927)

———. *Unterwegs zur Sprache*. Pfullingen: Verlag Günther Neske, 1959. *On the Way to Language*. Translated by Peter D. Hertz. New York: Harper & Row, Publishers, 1971. (Essays from the 1950s)

———. *Was Heißt Denken?* Tübingen: Max Niemeyer Verlag, 1954. *What Is Called Thinking?* Translated by J. Glenn Gray. New York: Harper & Row, Publishers, 1968. (Lecture courses, WS 1951–52 and SS 1952)

———. "Zeit und Sein." In *Zur Sache des Denkens*. Tübingen: Max Niemeyer Verlag, 1969. "Time and Being." In *On 'Time and Being.'* Translated by Joan Stambaugh. New York: Harper & Row, 1972. (Lecture, 1962)

———. *Zollikoner Seminare*, ed. Medard Boss. Frankfurt am Main: Vittorio Klostermann, 1987. *Zollikon Seminars*. Edited by Medard Boss. Translated by Franz Mayr and Richard Askay. Evanston, IL: Northwestern University Press, 2001. (Seminars, 1959–1969)

Husserl, Edmund. *Cartesian Meditations: An Introduction to Phenomenology*. Translated by Dorion Cairns. The Hague: Martinus Nijhoff, 1977.

———. *The Crisis of European Sciences and Transcendental Phenomenology*. Translated by David Carr. Evanston, Illinois: Northwestern University Press, 1970.

———. Husserliana XV. *Zur Phänomenologie der Intersubjektivität*. Texte aus dem Nachlass. Dritter Teil. 1929–35. Edited by Iso Kern. The Hague, Netherlands: Martinus Nijhoff, 1973.

———. *The Idea of Phenomenology*. Translated by William P. Alston and George Nakhnikian. The Hague: Martinus Nijhoff, 1964.

———. *Ideas Pertaining to a Pure Phenomenology and to a Phenomenological Philosophy. First Book: General Introduction to a Pure Phenomenology*. Translated by F. Kersten. Dordrecht: Kluwer Academic Publishers, 1998.

———. *Logical Investigations*. Translated by F. N. Findlay. Amherst, NY: Humanity Books, 2000.

———. *On the Phenomenology of the Consciousness of Internal Time (1893–1917)*. Translated by John Barnett Brough. Dordrecht: Kluwer Academic Publishers, 1991.

———. *Psychological and Transcendental Phenomenology and the Confrontation with Heidegger (1927–1931)*. Edited and translated by Thomas Sheehan and Richard Palmer. Dordrecht: Kluwer Academic Publishers, 1997.

Kant, Immanuel. *Correspondence.* Translated and edited by Arnulf Zweig. Cambridge: Cambridge University Press, 1999.

———. *The Kant-Eberhard Controversy: 'On a Discovery According to which Any New Critique of Pure Reason Has Been Made Superfluous by an Earlier One.'* Translated by Henry E. Allison. Baltimore: Johns Hopkins University Press, 1973.

———. *Kants gesammelte Schriften.* Preußische Akademie der Wissenschaften. Berlin: Walter de Gruyter, 1902.

———. *Kritik der reinen Vernunft. Kants gesammelte Schriften.* Vols. 3 and 4. Preußische Akademie der Wissenschaften. Berlin: Walter de Gruyter, 1903 and 1904. *The Critique of Pure Reason.* Translated by Norman Kemp Smith. New York: St. Martin's Press, 1965.

———. *Lectures on Logic.* Translated and edited by J. Michael Young. Cambridge: Cambridge University Press, 1992.

———. *Logic.* Translated by Robert S. Hartman and Wolfgang Schwarz. Indianapolis: The Library of Liberal Arts, 1974.

———. *Metaphysical Foundations of Natural Science.* Translated by Michael Friedman. Cambridge: Cambridge University Press, 2004.

———. *Opus Postumum.* Edited with an introduction and notes by Eckart Förster. Translated by Eckart Förster and Michael Rosen. Cambridge: Cambridge University Press, 1993.

Other Texts

Aertsen, Jan. *Medieval Philosophy and the Transcendentals: The Case of Thomas Aquinas.* Leiden: Brill Academic Press, 1996.

———. *Medieval Philosophy as Transcendental Thought: From Philip the Chancellor (ca. 1225) to Francisco Suarez.* Leiden: Brill Academic Publishers, 2012.

Allison, Henry E. "The Originality of Kant's Distinction between Analytic and Synthetic Judgments." In *The Philosophy of Immanuel Kant,* ed. Richard Kennington, 15–38. Washington, DC: The Catholic University of America Press, 1985.

Balthasar, Hans Urs von. *Glory of the Lord: A Theological Aesthetics,* vol. 5, *The Realm of Metaphysics in the Modern Age.* Translated by Oliver Davies, Andrew Louth, Brian McNeil, John Saward, and Rowan Williams. San Francisco: Ignatius Press, 1991.

Barton, William. "An Introduction to Heidegger's *What Is a Thing?*" *Southern Journal of Philosophy* 21 (1973): 15–25.

Beierwaltes, Werner. "*Epekeina.* A Remark on Heidegger's Reception of Plato." Translated by Marcus Brainard. *Graduate Faculty Philosophy Journal* 17 (1994): 83–99.

Blattner, William D. *Heidegger's Temporal Idealism.* Cambridge: Cambridge University Press, 1999.

Braver, Lee, ed. *Division III of Heidegger's* Being and Time: *The Unanswered Question of Being.* Cambridge, MA: The MIT Press, 2015.

———. *A Thing of This World: A History of Continental Anti-Realism.* Evanston, IL: Northwestern University Press, 2007.

Cairns, Dorion. *Conversations with Husserl and Fink.* The Hague: Marinus Nijhoff, 1976.

Capobianco, Richard. *Engaging Heidegger*. Toronto: University of Toronto Press, 2010.

———. *Heidegger's Way of Being*. Toronto: University of Toronto Press, 2014.

Caputo, John D. *Demythologizing Heidegger*. Bloomington: Indiana University Press, 1993.

Carman, Taylor. *Heidegger's Analytic: Interpretation, Discourse, and Authenticity in 'Being and Time'*. Cambridge: Cambridge University Press, 2003.

Carnap, Rudolf. "The Elimination of Metaphysics through the Logical Analysis of Language." Translated by Arthur Pap. In *Logical Positivism*, ed. A. J. Ayer, 60–81. Glencoe, IL: The Free Press, 1959.

Couturat, Louis. *La Logique de Leibniz. D'après des documents inédits*. Paris: Presses Universitaires de France, 1901.

Coyne, Ryan. *Heidegger's Confessions: The Remains of Saint Augustine in 'Being and Time' and Beyond*. Chicago: University of Chicago Press, 2015.

Critchley, Simon. "Heidegger for Beginners." In *Appropriating Heidegger*, ed. James E. Faulconer and Mark A. Wrathall, 101–18. Cambridge: Cambridge University Press, 2000.

Crowell, Steven Galt. "Does the Husserl/Heidegger Feud Rest on a Mistake? An Essay on Psychological and Transcendental Phenomenology." *Husserl Studies* 18 (2002): 123–40.

———. *Husserl, Heidegger, and the Space of Meaning*. Evanston, IL: Northwestern University Press, 2001.

———. *Normativity and Phenomenology in Husserl and Heidegger*. Cambridge: Cambridge University Press, 2013.

———. "Why Is Ethics First Philosophy? Levinas in Phenomenological Context." *European Journal of Philosophy* 23 (2015): 564–88.

Crowell, Steven Galt and Jeff Malpas. *Transcendental Heidegger*. Stanford, CA: Stanford University Press, 2007.

Dahlstrom, Daniel. *Heidegger's Concept of Truth*. Cambridge: Cambridge University Press, 2001.

———. "Heidegger's Kant-Courses at Marburg." In *Reading Heidegger from the Start: Essays in His Earliest Thought*, edited by Theodore Kisiel and John van Buren, 293–308. Albany, NY: State University of New York Press, 1994.

———. "Heidegger's Transcendentalism." *Research in Phenomenology* 35 (2005): 29–54.

———. "The Scattered *Logos*: Metaphysics and the Logical Prejudice." In *A Companion to Heidegger's 'Introduction to Metaphysics'*, ed. Richard Polt and Gregory Fried, 83–102. New Haven: Yale University Press, 2001.

Declève, Henri. *Heidegger et Kant*. The Hague: Nijhoff, 1970.

Descartes, René. *The Philosophical Writings of Descartes*. Vol. 1. Translated by John Cottingham, Robert Stoothoff, and Dugald Murdoch. Cambridge: Cambridge University Press, 1985.

Diels, H. and W. Kranz. *Die Fragmente der Vorsokratiker*. Berlin: Weidmann, 1974.

Dostal, Robert J. "Beyond Being: Heidegger's Plato." *Journal of the History of Philosophy* 23 (1985): 71–98.

Doyon, Maxime. "The Transcendental Claim of Deconstruction." In *A Companion to Derrida*, ed. Zeynep Direk and Leonard Lawlor, 132–49. Oxford: Wiley Blackwell, 2014.

Dreyfus, Hubert. *Being-in-the-World: A Commentary on Heidegger's 'Being and Time,' Division I.* Cambridge, MA: The MIT Press, 1991.

Drummond, John. "Husserl on the Ways to the Performance of the Reduction." *Man and World* 8 (1975): 47–69.

———. *Husserlian Intentionality and Non-Foundational Realism: Noema and Object.* Dordrecht: Kluwer, 1990.

Edwards, Paul. *Heidegger's Confusions.* Amherst, NY: Prometheus Books, 2004.

Engelland, Chad. "Absent to Those Present: Social Technology and Bodily Communion." In *Social Epistemology and Technology*, ed. Frank Scalambrino, 167–76. London: Rowman & Littlefield International, 2015.

———. "Heidegger and the Human Difference." *Journal of the American Philosophical Association* 1 (2015): 175–93.

———. "Marcel and Heidegger on the Proper Matter and Manner of Thinking." *Philosophy Today* 48 (2004): 91–106.

———. *Ostension: Word Learning and the Embodied Mind.* Cambridge, MA: MIT Press, 2014.

———. "On the Personal Significance of Sexual Reproduction." *The Thomist* 79 (2015): 615–39.

———. "The Phenomenological Motivation of the Later Heidegger." *Philosophy Today* 53 Supplement (2009): 182–9.

———. "The Play of Life in Art." *Journal of Aesthetics and Phenomenology* 2 (2015): 127–42.

———. "Unmasking the Person." *International Philosophical Quarterly* 50 (2010): 447–60.

———. *The Way of Philosophy: An Introduction.* Eugene, OR: Cascade, 2016.

Friedman, Michael. *A Parting of the Ways: Carnap, Cassirer, and Heidegger.* Chicago: Open Court, 2000.

Gadamer, Hans-Georg. *Heidegger's Ways.* Translated by John W. Stanley. Albany, NY: State University of New York Press, 1994.

———. "Martin Heidegger's One Path." Translated by P. Christopher Smith. In *Reading Heidegger from the Start: Essays in His Earliest Thought*, ed. Theodore Kisiel and John van Buren, 19–34. Albany, NY: State University of New York Press, 1994.

———. *Truth and Method*, rev. 2d ed. Translated by Joel Weinsheimer. New York: The Continuum Publishing Company, 1998.

Gardner, Sebastian and Matthew Grist, ed. *The Transcendental Turn.* New York: Oxford University Press, 2015.

Gelven, Michael. *A Commentary on Heidegger's 'Being and Time'*, rev. ed. DeKalb, IL: Northern Illinois University Press, 1989.

Gordon, Peter E. *Continental Divide: Heidegger, Cassirer, Davos.* Cambridge, MA: Harvard University Press, 2010.

Haar, Michel. *Heidegger and the Essence of Man.* Translated by William McNeill. Albany, NY: State University of New York Press, 1993.

———. *The Song of the Earth: Heidegger and the Grounds of the History of Being.* Translated by Reginald Lilly. Bloomington: Indiana University Press, 1993.

———. "*Stimmung et pensée.*" In *Heidegger et l'idée de la phénoménologie*, ed. Franco Volpi, Jean-François Mattéi, Thomas Sheehan, Jean-François Courtine, Jacques Taminiaux, John Sallis, Dominique Janicaud, Arion L. Kelkel, Rudolf

Bernet, Robert Brisart, Klaus Held, Michel Haar, and Samuel Ijsseling, 265–83. Dordrecht: Kluwer Academic Publishers, 1988.

Habermas, Jürgen. *The Philosophical Discourse of Modernity: Twelve Lectures*. Translated by Frederick Lawrence. Cambridge, MA: The MIT Press, 1987.

Hadot, Pierre. *Philosophy as a Way of Life: Spiritual Exercises from Socrates to Foucault*. Edited by Arnold I. Davidson. Translated by Michael Chase. Oxford: Blackwell, 1995.

Hegel, Georg Wilhelm Friedrich. *Science of Logic*. Translated by Arnold V. Miller. London: Allen & Unwin, 1969.

Heinämaa, Sara, Mirja Hartimo and Timo Miettinen, ed. *Phenomenology and the Transcendental*. New York: Routledge, 2014.

Held, Klaus. "Fundamental Moods and Heidegger's Critique of Contemporary Culture." Translated by Anthony J. Steinbock. In *Reading Heidegger: Commemorations*, ed. John Sallis, 287–303. Bloomington: Indiana University Press, 1993.

———. "Heidegger et le Principe de la Phénoménologie." In *Heidegger et l'Idée de la Phénoménologie*, ed. Franco Volpi, Jean-François Mattéi, Thomas Sheehan, Jean-François Courtine, Jacques Taminiaux, John Sallis, Dominique Janicaud, Arion L. Kelkel, Rudolf Bernet, Robert Brisart, Klaus Held, Michel Haar, and Samuel Ijsseling, 239–63. Dordrecht: Kluwer Academic Publishers, 1988.

Henrich, Dieter. *The Unity of Reason: Essays on Kant's Philosophy*. Edited with an introduction by Richard L. Velkley. Cambridge, MA: Harvard University Press, 1994.

Hermann, Friedrich-Wilhelm von. "Way and Method: Hermeneutic Phenomenology in Thinking the History of Being." In *Critical Heidegger*, ed. Christopher Macann, 171–90. London: Routledge, 1996.

Hoppe, Hansgeorg. "Wandlungen in der Kant-Auffassung Heideggers." In *Durchblicke. Martin Heidegger zum 80. Geburtstag*, ed. Vittorio Klostermann, 284–317. Frankfurt am Main: Klostermann, 1970.

Jones, Mitchell P. "Transcendental Intersubjectivity and the Objects of the Human Sciences." *Symposium* 4 (2000): 209–19.

Käufer, Stephan. "Schemata, Hammers, and Time: Heidegger's Two Derivations of Judgment." *Topoi* 22 (2003): 79–91.

Kern, Iso. "The Three Ways to the Transcendental Phenomenological Reduction in the Philosophy of Edmund Husserl." In *Husserl: Expositions and Appraisals*, ed. Frederick A. Elliston and Peter McCormick, 126–49. Notre Dame, Indiana: University of Notre Dame Press, 1977.

Kisiel, Theodore. "The Demise of *Being and Time*: 1927–1930." In *Heidegger's 'Being and Time': Critical Essays*, ed. Polt, 189–214. Lanham: Rowman & Littlefield, 2005.

———. *The Genesis of Heidegger's 'Being and Time'*. Berkeley: The University of California Press, 1993.

———. "The Genetic Difference in Reading *Being and Time*." *American Catholic Philosophical Quarterly* 69 (1995): 171–87.

———. "Heidegger's Apology: Biography as Philosophy and Ideology." In *Heidegger's Way of Thought*, ed. Alfred Denker and Marion Heinz, 1–35. New York: Continuum, 2002.

———. "The Mathematical and the Hermeneutical: On Heidegger's Notion of the Apriori." In *Martin Heidegger: In Europe and America*, ed. Edward G. Ballard and Charles E. Scott, 109–20. The Hague: Martinus Nijhoff, 1973.

Leibniz, Gottfried Wilhelm. *Philosophical Papers and Letters*. Translated by Leroy E. Loemker. Dordrecht, Holland: D. Reidel Publishing Co., 1969.

————. *Die philosophischen Schriften von Gottfried Wilhelm Leibniz*, IV, ed. C. I. Gerhardt. Hildesheim: Olms Verlagsbuchhandlung, 1960–61.

Lenkowski, William Jon. "What Is Husserl's *Epoche?*" *Man and World* 11 (1978): 299–323.

Levinas, Emmanuel. *God, Death, and Time*. Translated by Bettina Bergo. Edited by Jacques Rolland. Stanford, CA: Stanford University Press, 2000.

————. "Is Ontology Fundamental?" In *Emmanuel Levinas: Basic Philosophical Writings*, ed. Adriaan Peperzak, Simon Critchley, and Robert Bernasconi, 2–10. Bloomington, IN: Indiana University Press, 1996.

Llewelyn, John. "On the Saying that Philosophy Begins in *Thaumazein*." In *Post-Structuralist Classics*, ed. Andrew Benjamin, 173–91. London: Routledge, 1998.

Longuenesse, Béatrice. *Kant and the Capacity to Judge: Sensibility and Discursivity in the Transcendental Analytic of the 'Critique of Pure Reason'*. Translated by Charles T. Wolfe. Princeton, NJ: Princeton University Press, 1998.

Madison, Laurel. "Have We Been Careless with Socrates' Last Words? A Rereading of the *Phaedo*." *Journal of the History of Philosophy* 40 (2002): 421–36.

Malpas, Jeff. *Heidegger's Topology: Being, Place, World*. Cambridge, MA: The MIT Press, 2006.

————. ed. *From Kant to Davidson: Philosophy and the Idea of the Transcendental*. New York: Routledge, 2003.

Marcel, Gabriel. *The Mystery of Being*, vol. 1. Translated by G. S. Fraser. South Bend, IN: St. Augustine's Press, 2001.

Marion, Jean-Luc. *Being Given: Toward a Phenomenology of Givenness*. Translated by Jeffrey Kosky. Stanford, CA: Stanford University Press, 2002.

————. *The Erotic Phenomenon*. Translated by Stephen E. Lewis. Chicago: University of Chicago Press, 2006.

————. *Givenness and Revelation*. Translated by Stephen Lewis. Oxford: Oxford University Press, 2016.

————. *Reduction and Givenness: Investigations of Husserl, Heidegger, and Phenomenology*. Translated by Thomas A. Carlson. Evanston, IL: Northwestern University Press, 1998.

————. *In the Self's Place: The Approach of Saint Augustine*. Translated by Jeffrey Kosky. Stanford, CA: Stanford University Press, 2012.

McGrath, Sean J. "Heidegger and Duns Scotus on Truth and Language." *Review of Metaphysics* 57 (2003): 339–58.

Merleau-Ponty, Maurice. "The Philosopher and His Shadow." In *Signs*. Translated by Richard C. McCleary. Northwestern, IL: Northwestern University Press, 1964.

Mohanty, J. N. *The Possibility of Transcendental Philosophy*. Dordrecht: Martinus Nijhoff, 1985.

Moyle, Tristan. *Heidegger's Transcendental Aesthetic: An Interpretation of the 'Ereignis'* Aldershot: Ashgate Publishing, 2005.

Newton, Isaac. *The Principia: Mathematical Principles of Natural Philosophy*. Translated by I. Bernard Cohen and Anne Whitman. Berkeley: University of California Press, 1999.

Nietzsche, Friedrich. "On the Truth and Lies in a Nonmoral Sense." In *Philosophy and Truth: Selections from Nietzsche's Notebooks of the Early 1870's*, ed. and trans. Daniel Breazeale, 79–97. Amherst, NY: Humanity Books, 1979.

Pöggeler, Otto. *Martin Heidegger's Path of Thinking*, trans. Daniel Magurshak and Sigmund Barber. Atlantic Highlands, NJ: Humanities Press International, 1987.

———. *The Paths of Heidegger's Life and Thought*, trans. John Bailiff. Amherst, NY: Humanity Books, 1998.

Polt, Richard. *The Emergency of Being: On Heidegger's Contributions to Philosophy*. Ithaca: Cornell University Press, 2006.

———. *Heidegger: An Introduction*. Ithaca, NY: Cornell University Press, 1999.

Pozzo, Riccardo. "Prejudices and Horizons: G. F. Meier's *Vernunftlehre* and Its Relation to Kant." *Journal of the History of Philosophy* 43 (2005): 185–202.

Prufer, Thomas. "The Philosophical Act." *International Philosophical Quarterly* 2 (1962): 591–4.

———. *Recapitulations: Essays in Philosophy*. Washington, DC: The Catholic University of America Press, 1993.

———. "Reduction and Constitution." In *Ancients and Moderns*, ed. John K. Ryan, 341–3. Washington, DC: The Catholic University of America Press, 1970.

Quine, W. V. "Has Philosophy Lost Contact with People?" In *Theories and Things*, ed. Quine, 190–3. Cambridge, MA: Harvard University Press, 1981.

Richardson, William J. *Heidegger: Through Phenomenology to Thought*, 2d ed. The Hague: Martinus Nijhoff, 1967.

Rosemann, Philipp. "Heidegger's Transcendental History." *Journal of the History of Philosophy* 40 (2002): 501–23.

Russell, Bertrand. *A Critical Exposition of the Philosophy of Leibniz*, 2d ed. London: Bradford & Dickens, 1937.

Sallis, John. "Imagination, Metaphysics, Wonder." In *American Continental Philosophy: A Reader*, ed. Walter Brogan and James Risser, 15–43. Bloomington: Indiana University Press, 2000.

Schalow, Frank. *Departures: At the Crossroads between Heidegger and Kant*. Berlin: Walter de Gruyter, 2013.

———. *The Renewal of the Heidegger-Kant Dialogue*. Albany, NY: The State University of New York Press, 1992.

Schmitz, Kenneth L. *The Recovery of Wonder: The New Freedom and the Asceticism of Power*. Montreal: McGill-Queen's University Press, 2005.

Schoenbohm, Susan. "Heidegger's Interpretation of *Phusis*." In *A Companion to Heidegger's 'Introduction to Metaphysics*, ed. Richard Polt and Gregory Fried, 143–60. New Haven: Yale University Press, 2001.

Seidel, George. "Heidegger's Last God and the Schelling Connection." *Laval Théologique et Philosophique* 55 (1999): 95–6.

Selcer, Daniel. "Heidegger's Leibniz and Abyssal Identity." *Continental Philosophy Review* 36 (2003): 303–24.

Sheehan, Thomas. "Astonishing! Things Make Sense." *Gatherings: The Heidegger Circle Annual* 1 (2011):1–25.

———. "Dasein." In *A Companion to Heidegger*, ed. Hubert L. Dreyfus and Mark A. Wrathall, 193–213. Malden, MA: Blackwell Publishing, 2005.

———. "*Hermeneia* and *Apophansis*: The Early Heidegger on Aristotle." In *Heidegger et l'idée de la phénoménologie*, ed. Franco Volpi, Jean-François Mattéi, Thomas Sheehan, Jean-François Courtine, Jacques Taminiaux, John Sallis, Dominique Janicaud, Arion L. Kelkel, Rudolf Bernet, Robert Brisart, Klaus Held, Michel Haar, and Samuel Ijsseling, 67–80. Dordrecht: Kluwer, 1988.

———. "*Kehre* and *Ereignis*: A Prolegomenon to *Introduction to Metaphysics*." In *A Companion to Heidegger's "Introduction to Metaphysics"*, ed. Richard Polt and Gregory Fried, 3–16. New Haven: Yale University Press, 2001.

———. *Making Sense of Heidegger: A Paradigm Shift*. London: Rowman & Littlefield International, 2015.

———. "A Paradigm Shift in Heidegger Research." *Continental Philosophy Review* 34 (2001): 183–202.

Sherover, Charles. *Heidegger, Kant, and Time*. Bloomington: Indiana University Press, 1971.

———. "Heidegger's Use of Kant in *Being and Time*." In *Kant and Phenomenology*, ed. Thomas Seebohm and Joseph Kockelmans, 185–201. Washington, DC: The Center for Advanced Research in Phenomenology, 1984.

Sokolowski, Robert. *The God of Faith and Reason: Foundations of Christian Theology*. Notre Dame: University of Notre Dame Press, 1982.

———. *Husserlian Meditations: How Words Present Things*. Evanston, IL: Northwestern University Press, 1974.

———. *Introduction to Phenomenology*. Cambridge: Cambridge University Press, 2000.

———. *Presence and Absence: A Philosophical Investigation of Language and Being*. Bloomington, IN: Indiana University Press, 1978.

Sullivan, Peter and Joel Smit, ed. *Transcendental Philosophy and Naturalism*. Oxford: Oxford University Press, 2011.

Tugendhat, Ernst. *Der Wahrheitsbegriff bei Husserl und Heidegger*, 2d ed. Berlin: de Gruyter, 1970.

———. "Heidegger's Idea of Truth." In *Martin Heidegger: Critical Assessments*, ed. Christopher Macann. Vol. 3, *Language*, 79–92. London: Routledge, 1992.

Vallega-Neu, Daniela. *Heidegger's 'Contributions to Philosophy': An Introduction*. Bloomington, IN: Indiana University Press, 2003.

Van Buren, John. *The Young Heidegger: Rumor of the Hidden King*. Bloomington: Indiana University Press, 1994.

Velkley, Richard. *Being after Rousseau: Philosophy and Culture in Question*. Chicago: The University of Chicago Press, 2002.

———. *Heidegger, Strauss, and the Premises of Philosophy: On Original Forgetting*. Chicago: Chicago University Press, 2011.

Weatherspoon, Martin. *Heidegger's Interpretation of Kant: Categories, Imagination and Temporality*. New York: Palgrave Macmillan, 2003.

Wolfe, Judith. *Heidegger's Eschatology: Theological Horizons in Martin Heidegger's Early Work*. Oxford: Oxford University Press, 2013.

Wolff, Christian. *Logica, Opera* I. Verona: Apud Haeredes Marci Moroni, 1779.

———. *Ontologia, Opera* V. Verona: Apud Haeredes Marci Moroni, 1779.

Wood, Robert E. *The Beautiful, the True, and the Good: Studies in the History of Thought*. Washington, DC: The Catholic University of America Press, 2015.

———. "The Fugal lines of Heidegger's *Beiträge*." *Existentia* 9 (2001): 253–66.

Zahavi, Dan. *Husserl's Phenomenology*. Stanford, CA: Stanford University Press, 2003.

———. *Husserl and Transcendental Intersubjectivity: A Response to the Linguistic-Pragmatic Critique*. Translated by Elizabeth A. Behnke. Athens, OH: Ohio University Press, 2001.

Index